LOOK WHO'S LAUGHING

TI

Studies in Humor and Gender

A series edited by Regina Barreca, *University of Connecticut, Storrs,* and Nancy Walker, *Vanderbilt University, Nashville, Tennessee.*

Volume 1
Look Who's Laughing: Gender and Comedy
Edited by Gail Finney

This book is part of a series. The publisher will accept continuation orders which may be cancelled at any time and which provide for automatic billing and shipping of each title in the series upon publication. Please write for details.

Look Who's Laughing
Gender and Comedy

Edited by

Gail Finney

University of California, Davis

Taylor & Francis
Taylor & Francis Group
LONDON AND NEW YORK

First printed 1994 by
Gorden and Breach.
Reprinted 2004 by
Taylor & Francis,
2 Park Square, Milton Park,
Abingdon, Oxon, OX14 4RN

Transferred to Digital Printing 2004

Library of Congress Cataloging-in-Publication Data

Look who's laughing : gender and comedy / edited by Gail Finney.
     p.   cm. -- (Studies in humor and gender ; v. 1)
    Includes bibliographical references and index.
    ISBN 2-88124-644-3. -- ISBN 2-88124-645-1 (pbk.)
    1. Comedy.   2. European drama (Comedy)--History and criticism.
3. Women and literature.   4. Women in literature.   5. Comic, The.
I. Finney, Gail.   II. Series
PN1922.L66 1994
809'.93352042--dc20   93-44165
                                                     CIP
                                                     REV.

CONTENTS

Introduction to the Series   vii

Contributors   ix

Introduction: Unity in Difference?
   Gail Finney   1

I. DRAMA

"That's How It Is": Comic Travesties of Sex and
Gender in Early Sixteenth-Century Venice
   Eric A. Nicholson   17

Imagining Consummation: Women's Erotic Language
in Comedies of Dekker and Shakespeare
   Mary Bly   35

Dwindling into Wifehood: the Romantic Power of the Witty
Heroine in Shakespeare, Dryden, Congreve, and Austen
   Donald A. Bloom   53

Confinement Sharpens the Invention: Aphra Behn's
The Rover and Susanna Centlivre's The Busie Body
   Suz-Anne Kinney   81

Masquerade, Modesty, and Comedy in Hannah
Cowley's The Belle's Strategem
   Erin Isikoff   99

The Sphinx Goes Wild(e): Ada Leverson, Oscar Wilde, and the
Gender Equipollence of Parody
   Corinna Sundararajan Rohse   119

II. FICTION

When Women Laugh Wildly and (Gentle)Men Roar: Victorian
Embodiments of Laughter
   Karen C. Gindele   139

The Feminine Laughter of No Return: James Joyce
and Dorothy Richardson
Kristin Bluemel 161

Courtship, Comedy, and African-American Expressive Culture
in Zora Neale Hurston's Fiction
Barbara Monroe 173

Feminism/Gender/Comedy: Meredith, Woolf, and
the Reconfiguration of Comic Distance
David McWhirter 189

"Between the Gaps": Sex, Class and Anarchy in
the British Comic Novel of World War II
Phyllis Lassner 205

Alice Childress's *Like One of the Family*: Domestic
and Undomesticated Domestic Humor
Zita Z. Dresner 221

Funny, Isn't It?: Testing the Boundaries of Gender
and Genre in Women's Detective Fiction
Gloria A. Biamonte 231

III. FILM, STAND-UP COMEDY, AND CARTOON ART

Hollywood, 1934: "Inventing" Romantic Comedy
Kay Young 257

Mae West Was Not a Man: Sexual Parody and Genre
in the Plays and Films of Mae West
Andrea J. Ivanov 275

Women on the Verge of a Nervous Breakdown:
Sexism or Emancipation from Machismo?
Florence Redding Jessup 299

Between the Laughter: Bridging Feminist Studies
through Women's Stand-Up Comedy
Allison Fraiberg 315

Comic Strip-Tease: A Revealing Look at Women
Cartoon Artists
Jaye Berman Montresor 335

Index 349

INTRODUCTION TO THE SERIES

Humor as a human activity crosses — and double-crosses — many lines and boundaries, including those of gender. *Studies in Humor and Gender* will explore these boundaries and the territories encompassed by them. The monographs and collections published in this series will provide useful and original perspectives on the interaction of gender and humor in many of their possible combinations. An interdisciplinary field by its very nature, the study of humor, comedy, joking, and play draws together the interests and expertise of those working in literature, anthropology, sociology, linguistics, communication, film studies, folklore, medicine, and, increasingly, gender studies. The works published under the aegis of *Studies in Humor and Gender* will offer scholars, writers, and general readers alike a forum for examining and discussing insights into a vital field of study.

By making available the best discoveries and theories about humor and comedy in books framed by issues of gender, we believe that this series will inevitably also shed light on the larger questions of culture, power, sexuality, and the imagination. Its texts will feature sound scholarship, integrative approaches to the study of humor and gender, and clear, lively prose. We have no doubt that the volumes published in *Studies in Humor and Gender* will generate interest, debate, dissent, recognition, and attention. Destined for personal bookshelves as well as libraries, these volumes will be widely read, consulted, quoted, and discussed both inside and outside classroom walls.

CONTRIBUTORS

GLORIA A. BIAMONTE is a visiting assistant professor of American studies/women's studies at Hampshire College, where she teaches classes on nineteenth- and twentieth-century American literature, women's literature, African-American literature, and popular culture. Her essays and book reviews on nineteenth-century women writers, Charlotte Perkins Gilman, and women detective novelists have appeared in *Legacy: A Journal of American Women Writers* and *Consumable Goods II*. She is currently at work on a book-length study of three of the earliest American women authors of detective fiction.

DONALD A. BLOOM received his PhD in English from the University of Washington and has taught at Wabash College, Davis & Elkins College, and Wilkes University. He is currently on the faculty of The Alabama School of Mathematics and Science. He has written on a variety of topics that trace the use of literary ideas over time, including the depiction of hope and despair and the relationship of fiction, film, and modernism.

KRISTIN BLUEMEL is a doctoral candidate in the English department at Rutgers University, New Brunswick. Now dissertating on Dorothy Richardson, modernist aesthetics, and gender politics, she keeps herself amused by participating in a weekly *Finnegans Wake* reading group, reciting poetry by Stevie Smith, and hiking in the Adirondacks.

MARY BLY received an MPhil in Renaissance drama from Oxford University and is currently completing her doctoral dissertation for the Renaissance studies department at Yale University. Her dissertation examines the influence of Ovidian and Petrarchan imitation on English drama and should be completed by May 1994.

ZITA Z. DRESNER, professor of English at the University of the District of Columbia, is coeditor of *Redressing the Balance*, an anthology of American women's humor, and has contributed articles on women's humor to a number of journals and books.

GAIL FINNEY came to the University of California, Davis, as professor of German and comparative literature in 1988, following eight years on the faculty of the German department at Harvard. She has published *The Counterfeit Idyll: The Garden Ideal and Social Reality in Nineteenth-Century Fiction* (1984), *Women in Modern Drama: Freud, Feminism, and*

European Theater at the Turn of the Century (1989), and articles on a number of aspects of nineteenth- and twentieth-century German and comparative literature. Her current focus is gender and European comedy.

ALLISON FRAIBERG teaches courses in women's studies and contemporary literature at the University of Washington. She has just completed a book on the practices of agency in contemporary women's comedic writings and performance.

KAREN C. GINDELE completed her doctorate in Victorian fiction and feminist theory at Brown University in 1992. Revising her dissertation, "Means to an End: Narrative Middles in the Victorian Novel," she is currently working in Cambridge, MA, where she is at an early stage in trying to establish an alternative college.

ERIN ISIKOFF is a doctoral candidate in the department of English at Columbia University. She received her BA in literature at Harvard University in 1989 and her MA and MPhil degrees at Columbia University in 1990 and 1993, respectively. She has taught at Columbia University and at the New School for Social Research.

ANDREA J. IVANOV is currently completing her dissertation, "Sexual Parody in American Comedic Film and Literature, 1925–1945," in the department of English at the University of Southern California. "Sexual Parody" examines gender construction and sexual parody in the filmic and literary comedy of Mae West, Preston Sturges, Dorothy Parker, and James Thurber. In addition to related work on her dissertation topic, she has also published and presented papers on nineteenth-century sensation fiction, feminist film and literary theory, the Marx Brothers, Lewis Carroll, and the short fiction of Grace Paley and Andre Dubus.

FLORENCE REDDING JESSUP is professor of Spanish at Butler University, where she has served as head of the department of modern foreign languages and acting associate dean of the College of Liberal Arts and Sciences. Her research interests include contemporary Spanish literature and gender in Spanish society. She is currently working on a book about women and Spanish laws during Franco's military regime and in the democracy established in Spain after the general's dictatorship ended in 1975.

SUZ-ANNE KINNEY is a doctoral candidate at the University of North Carolina at Greensboro. She received her MA at Ohio University and is currently teaching at Queens College in Charlotte, North Carolina.

PHYLLIS LASSNER teaches at Northwestern University. She is the author of two books on Elizabeth Bowen and essays on British women writers of

World War II and on feminist theory and composition studies. She also rediscovered and wrote a new introduction to *The Dangerous Age*, a feminist novel of women's mid-life, by the Danish writer Karin Michaelis.

DAVID McWHIRTER is associate professor of English at Texas A&M University, where he teaches modern British and American literature. He is the author of *Desire and Love in Henry James: A Study of the Late Novels* and the editor of a forthcoming collection of essays on James's New York Edition. He is currently working on a book-length study of tragicomic modes in literary modernism.

BARBARA MONROE received her PhD from the University of Texas and is currently teaching composition at the University of Michigan. Besides the American comic novel, her other area of interest is computer software development for the writing classroom. This article was inspired by the Clarence Thomas confirmation hearings, specifically when Orrin Hatch asked if it were believable that any man would court a woman in the manner that Anita Hill had described.

JAYE BERMAN MONTRESOR is assistant professor of English and women's studies at Villanova University, where she specializes in contemporary American fiction. She is the editor of *The Critical Response to Ann Beattie* (Greenwood Press), and her essays have appeared in numerous books and periodicals. She is currently working on the interplay between photography and literature.

ERIC A. NICHOLSON is an assistant professor of literature and drama studies at the State University of New York at Purchase. He teaches Shakespeare, Renaissance drama, and theatre history, and also directs and produces plays: for example, Shakespeare's *A Midsummer Night's Dream* (Purchase, 1992) and Machiavelli's *Mandragola* (Purchase, 1993). His publications include a chapter on the theatre for *A History of Women, Volume III: Renaissance and Enlightenment Paradoxes* (edited by Natalie Zemon Davis and Arlette Farge), and the translation of Jean Delumeau's *Le Péché et la peur*, titled *Sin and Fear: The Emergence of a Western Guilt Culture* (St. Martin's Press, 1990).

CORINNA SUNDARARAJAN ROHSE is a Mellon Fellow and graduate of the University of British Columbia and Harvard University. An assistant professor in the English department of the University of Western Ontario, she writes on Victorian literature and aesthetics, and is currently completing *Manufactured Maidens: Metaphor and the Feminine in Nineteenth-Century Literature*.

KAY YOUNG is the Bradley Assistant Professor of Literature at the honors program of the University of Wisconsin-Milwaukee. A Mellon Fellow, she received her PhD from Harvard University in 1992, where she was awarded the Howard Mumford Jones Prize for her doctoral dissertation. Currently, she is at work on two books, one on the narrative design of mutuality in conversation and comedy, and the other on the construction of privacy in architecture, epistolary fiction, and melodrama.

1

Unity in Difference?: An Introduction

GAIL FINNEY

The title of this collection is no joke. While the first half — "Look Who's Laughing" — self-consciously plays on a common expression of social one-upmanship, on a less jocular level the title alludes to some facts which have only recently been systematically acknowledged and documented: that not only men but also women can laugh; that what's more, not only men but also women can make others laugh; and that the gender of the creator of comedy can make a difference in the kind of comedy produced.

These observations are the fruit of a decade of research. Judy Little's *Comedy and the Woman Writer: Woolf, Spark, and Feminism*, published in 1983, was the first book-length study in a succession of recent investigations devoted to the subject of women and comedy.[1] Little's work, together with that of Judith Wilt, Nancy Walker, Susan Carlson, Zita Dresner, Regina Barreca, June Sochen, and others, has effectively exploded the myth that women have no sense of humor.

This myth, which might more accurately be called a misperception, has a long and firmly entrenched history. In relatively modern times, thinkers as earnest as Schopenhauer, Bergson, and Freud have disqualified women from the comic arena; when they and other men have written about humor, laughter, and jokes, they have meant male humor, laughter, and jokes. In a more popular vein, as late as 1962 a writer for *Mademoiselle* claims that "a

1

woman who really makes one laugh is about as easy to find as a pauper taking his Sunday brunch in the Edwardian Room [of the Plaza Hotel]" (quoted Martin and Segrave 17). The statement by critic Reginald Blyth that women are "the unlaughing at which men laugh" (15) intimates a major reason for women's putative humorlessness: precisely they have been the objects of a good deal of male humor, and most people are disinclined to laugh at jokes of which they are the butt. The pejorative character of many of the female stereotypes in humorous works by men — the nag, the gossip, the randy widow, the henpecking housewife, the shrew, etc. — doubtless contributed to the dissociation of women with humor.

A further factor is the ideology of the "lady," which gained a firm foothold in early nineteenth-century American genteel society. As Walker observes, the passivity and desire for male approval associated with ladylikeness are antithetical to the creation of humor: a lady does not tell jokes ("Toward Solidarity" 59). Barreca notes that these qualities are still important in the 1960s distinctions between the "Good Girl," who is not supposed to "get" the hidden sexual meaning often present in male humor, and the "Bad Girl," who not only understands but might dare to make a joke herself (*Snow White* 1–69). Traditionally, women are supposed to be nice, and comedy necessitates aggressiveness, satire, and ridicule, not niceness (Martin and Segrave 20). Along similar lines, because of the inherently social nature of humor, which moves us to laugh more readily with others than alone, comedy is often best enjoyed in a performance setting, a sphere from which respectable women were long excluded. As Sochen comments, "Women's place was decidedly in the home, not the lecture hall, the burlesque stage, or the saloon" (12).

But while humor in women was discouraged in public, it flourished in private. Taking the United States as an example, the valuable detective work of Nancy Walker and Zita Dresner has made available in one collection humorous texts by dozens of American women writers, many of which were previously unpublished or out of print. Ranging from seventeenth-century poet Anne Bradstreet through nineteenth-century writers such as Frances Whitcher, Emily Dickinson, Harriet Beecher Stowe, Marietta Holley, and Louisa May Alcott to modernists like Gertrude Stein and Charlotte Perkins Gilman through Dorothy Parker to such domestic humorists as Betty Mac-Donald, Alice Childress, Jean Kerr, and Erma Bombeck to twentieth-century feminists like Erica Jong, Rita Mae Brown, and Gloria Steinem, *Redressing the Balance* deals the death blow to the misperception that women have no sense of humor.

The failure of many of these works to achieve widespread recognition in their day stemmed in large part from their highly domestic quality. It stands to reason that people talk and write about what they know, and until well into the nineteenth century in Europe and the United States, what women knew was limited for the most part to their homes, their children, their husbands, and — if they were lucky — each other. Tongue-in-cheek discourses on matrimony, witty accounts of sewing societies, satirical recountings of local gossip, and exaggeratedly despairing portrayals of a housewife's day — humorous though they might be — could not compete with works by men satirizing *their* world: matters of politics, business, law, and international relations. Concomitantly, given that in the past women were financially dependent on men, on whom much of their humor inevitably focused, it comes as no surprise that they obeyed the law that one does not bite the hand that feeds her. As Walker puts it, paraphrasing Mahadev Apte's anthropological study of humor, "whenever men control women's political, economic, and personal lives, humor that makes men the target must be shared in secret" ("Toward Solidarity" 66).

To an extent this disparity between published and unpublished applied to men's and women's experience as documented in all types of literature, a disparity given one of its most eloquent formulations by Virginia Woolf: "It has been common knowledge for ages that women exist, bear children, have no beards and seldom go bald; but save in these respects, and in others where they are said to be identical with men, we know little of them and have little sound evidence upon which to base our conclusions" (quoted Barreca, *Snow White* 152). In the case of humor, the differences were exacerbated by the commonly held view, mentioned above, that it was improper for a lady to be funny.

We are brought to a rather ironic conclusion: for women to be humorous in a way that achieved large-scale recognition, they had to become involved with serious things. Hence it is not surprising that a good deal of the most significant comedy by American and European women has been created in the wake of the two major women's movements. Not only did the campaign for suffrage that fueled the nineteenth-century women's movement engage women in matters of political substance; the achievement of the right to vote and the attendant drive for equal rights in other areas gave women a measure of power unprecedented in their history. And a sense of power is central to the creation of humor, which is in turn empowering. In the words of Erica Jong, "the ability to joke about something implies an underlying security of belief" (quoted Walker, "Toward Solidarity" 77). As women acquired increased power, confidence, and autonomy, they dared to become funnier — in print and in public. Emblematic of this development in the American tradition is Dorothy Parker, whose outspoken, sardonically witty writings of the 1920s and 30s are still appreciated today. Similarly, as the careers of performers like Sophie Tucker, Fanny Brice, and Gracie Allen in vaudeville demonstrate, by the turn of the century funny ladies had gained access to the stage and were enjoying considerable success there.[2]

After the vote had been won and the early feminist movement was gradually superseded by the cult of the housewife, women's domestic humor

proliferated with renewed energy. Walker summarizes the basic elements of
the domestic saga in the period just after World War II: "a female *persona* or
first-person narrator recounts, with some degree of self-deprecation, her
chaotic attempts to achieve a level of ideality as a homemaker that is dictated
by the culture in the form of older women, men (usually husbands), advertising, and women's magazines" (*A Very Serious Thing* 52). Judith Wilt's
description of the comic matriarch created in a 1980 column by Erma Bombeck shows that the humorous housewife has undergone some changes in the
intervening years:

> [K]nowing, sly, packed full of ripe experience, aware of the price being
> paid by all, capable of giving shocks. And yet she has certainly ac-
> cepted the saga itself as is; she is proud of her survival, committed to
> small revelations and large reconciliations. She speaks, with her consid-
> erable intelligence, from within the myth. She speaks, in less rich tones,
> in all the most popular and acceptable female comics — Phyllis Diller,
> Joan Rivers, Jean Kerr — and in that most ubiquitous female comic of
> all, the multiple woman who mocks and tyrannizes, and accepts in the
> television commercials, who squeezes the Charmin and stocks only
> Maxwell House and chooses the Jif and knows the difference between
> an air conditioner and an air *conditioner*, Herb. (176)

A housewife who is knowing and sly, "capable of giving shocks," and whose
experience informs the routines of female comics — while far from radical,
such details betray the influence of the women's movement of the 1960s and
70s, which had a profound effect not only on domestic humor but on comedy
by women in general. Helping to create a common female consciousness, the
twentieth-century feminist movement both induced women to discover the
comic tradition which they had long possessed and encouraged them to
become the subjects of comedy, its creators, rather than merely the objects of
humor. Nowhere is the autonomous female subject of humor more evident
than in the stand-up comic, alluded to in Wilt's passage. Performing, public,
and powerful, the modern female stand-up comic epitomizes the strides made
in the evolution of women's humor in recent decades. In the wake of the
1960s/70s women's movement and the sexual revolution, women have finally
arrived at a point where, in the words of Barreca, "both Good Girls and Bad
Girls can laugh out loud" (*Snow White* 37).

   Concomitant with the increasing volume of comedy by women and the
corresponding growth of critical literature on it, during the last ten years a
consensus of characteristics associated with women's humor has developed.
Unearthing female-authored work which had either never been published or
had lapsed into obscurity, or presenting known material by women from a
new perspective, critics such as Walker, Barreca, Little, and Carlson have
understandably focused on difference. They claim, for example, that women

tend to tell comic stories whereas men prefer telling jokes; that the primary aim of women's humor is communication and the sharing of experience in contrast to men's use of humor as self-presentation and the demonstration of cleverness; that comedy by women is less hostile than that by men: female comics are more prone to self-directed put-downs than to putting down others, the object of women's humor is the powerful rather than the pitiful, and women are less likely than men to laugh at those hurt or embarrassed; that women's stories are often nonlinear; and that in women's comic literature there is frequently more emphasis on recognition than resolution and on process than conclusion, leading to a lack of happy endings or closure altogether.

As *Look Who's Laughing* demonstrates, however, many of these differences belie underlying similarities. It is in this connection that the second part of the book's title is significant: examining not women and comedy but gender and comedy, this volume of eighteen essays explores gender issues in both female and male humor. Whereas critical literature on women's comedy has concentrated either on one genre in one national tradition (usually American or British) or on work by women only, the following collection, while building on this earlier work, is heterogeneous in terms of gender, genre, period, race, and national tradition treated: it deals with comic theory, drama, fiction, stand-up comedy, and comic strips by both male and female artists, both white and of color, working in the United States, Britain, and Europe from the sixteenth century to the present. As these essays show, differences between men's and women's comedy such as those cited above vary according to the time and national tradition of a work's composition. Through viewing comedy by women and men in juxtaposition rather than in isolation, *Look Who's Laughing* seeks to establish a dialogic context which will illuminate both and bring into sharper relief the similarities as well as the differences between them.

This cross-illumination is most evident in the four articles which treat both male and female authors. Bringing Jungian thought to bear on Shakespeare's *As You Like It*, Dryden's *Secret Love* and *Marriage a la Mode*, Congreve's *The Way of the World*, and Austen's *Pride and Prejudice*, Donald Bloom compares male and female depictions of the witty, independent-minded heroine whose behavior resists stereotypes for women, in particular for wives. Drawing on Freud's writings on jokes as well as on theories of comedy and the body formulated by Bergson, Meredith, Gagnier, Irigaray, Fuss, and others, Karen Gindele investigates scenes of laughter in selected novels by Thackeray, Meredith, and Margaret Oliphant to show how the laughing body is defined in relation to desire. She argues that the representation of laughter defines not only a mind but also a body coded by gender and class. Kristin Bluemel compares the relationship between experimental narrative forms, humor, parody, and feminism in Dorothy Richardson's novel *Pilgrimage* and the "Penelope" chapter of Joyce's *Ulysses* in order to shed light on the respective positions of the two authors within the canon. And Phyllis Lassner examines comic fiction of World War II by Evelyn Waugh, Marghanita Laski, and Beryl Bainbridge to compare the ways in which male and female writers use satire, parody, and mockery to unsettle well-established ideologies of class and gender in a society that was able to sustain its fundamental infrastructure despite the global cataclysm of war. Direct juxtaposition of comic portrayals by men and women yields some provocative results.

But the other essays in the volume, along with the theoretical writings they employ, also disclose a number of affinities between male and female humor. Jaye Berman Montresor studies the work of Lynda Barry, Barbara Brandon, Cathy Guisewhite, and Nicole Hollander to demonstrate that, in contrast to the aesthetically perfect and hence estranging female figures previously drawn by male comic strip artists, the women cartoonists who have emerged since the 1970s have tended to employ a "grotesque realism" and "carnival humor" in the depiction of female characters, modes with which female readers can more readily identify. Yet these concepts are based on the male humor of Rabelais, as described by Bakhtin in *Rabelais and His World*. This conjunction offers a paradigmatic example of the importance of period and national tradition in talking about differences and similarities between male and female comedy, or between the work of any two artists or groups of artists, for that matter. Bakhtin's notion of the "carnivalesque" aspect of humor finds its direct or indirect echo in numerous other recent discussions of comedy by women as well, such as in Little's analysis of the unresolved imagery of "festive license" in the work of Virginia Woolf and Muriel Spark (*Comedy and the Woman Writer* 1).

Another concept which is common to both male and female humor is its particular combination of sociability and subjectivity. This two-sidedness is well summed up by Bergson in his essay on laughter of 1900:

> How often it has been said that the fuller the theatre, the more uncontrolled the laughter of the audience! On the other hand, how often has the remark been made that many comic effects are incapable of translation from one language to another, because they refer to the customs and ideas of a particular social group! ... To understand laughter, we must put it back into its natural environment, which is society, and above all must we determine the utility of its function, which is a social one. (64–65)

Nearly a century later, Barreca writes, "Comedy, out of all the textual territorities explored, is the least universal. It is rigidly mapped and marked by subjectivity" (*New Perspectives*, 2). Bergson and Barreca, theorists of male and female comedy, respectively, concur: comedy is social, but the given "society" is rigidly circumscribed. Comedy is based on shared experience, attitudes, and values; creates in-groups and out-groups by mocking aberrations from the norm or the norm itself; acts as a form of social control. In other words, men poke fun at women, women poke fun at men, and everyone pokes fun at blondes.

The mocking of norms and stereotypes which is so central to all comedy has been discussed in terms of the double-voiced or "palimpsestic" discourse which Gilbert and Gubar have shown to characterize much women's writing in general, "works whose surface designs conceal or obscure deeper, less accessible (and less socially acceptable) levels of meaning," both conforming to and subverting patriarchal literary standards at the same time (73). As Little notes in her 1991 essay "Humoring the Sentence," the woman writer's bifurcated discourse described in Gilbert and Gubar's model is analogous to the concept of double-voiced discourse which Bakhtin elaborates in *The Dialogic Imagination*: in the novels of Cervantes, Pushkin, Dostoevsky and others, Bakhtin writes, different and competing voices are internally dialogized, existing in a state of tension with each other, so that the author's intentions emerge only in refracted form. Offering another example of congruence between women's comedy and male-authored texts, Little finds double-voiced discourse to be especially prevalent in comic writing by women, which often interweaves elements of a subversive discourse into the language of the status quo — the discourse of power and control — using the former to ridicule, subvert, or deconstruct the latter:

> When these writers humor the sentence, they make it unsay, or partly unsay, what it seems to say. In so doing, these women expose the ambivalent structures of language and its implied worldview. Power is revealed as a linguistic posture (and a bodily posture in the case of drama), while gender categories unravel in the linguistic stripping. ("Humoring the Sentence" 31)

The present collection offers further examples, in both male and female comic artists, of the kind of dialogic discourse which Bakhtin identifies in male authors and Little adapts in talking about women's comedy. One of the main vehicles for dialogic tension is parody, which can "expose to destroy" the language of another (Bakhtin, *The Dialogic Imagination* 364). In addition to the above-mentioned treatments of parody in the essays by Bluemel and Lassner, Eric Nicholson's analysis demonstrates the ways in which several early sixteenth-century Venetian comic plays by men parody gender norms and sexual laws through their dramatization of cross-dressing and through the comic theater's association with illicit sexual practices such as prostitution and sodomy. Focusing on a subject quite different in time, place, genre, and style but linked by its aim to the plays Nicholson discusses, Andrea Ivanov's contribution examines the creation of Mae West's self-authored persona through her camp or parodic manipulation of gender roles and sexualities —

her female female impersonations, status as "phallic" woman, and the recurring comic constellation of her multiple lovers — as well as the degree to which West's persona was also constructed through hybrid genres like the comic melodrama and Western. In their studies of variations on the grotesque in comedy, Nicholson and Ivanov reaffirm the gender-crossing implications of Catherine Clément and Hélène Cixous's assertion that "All laughter is allied with the monstrous" (33).

Raising parody to yet a higher power — in focusing on the parody of a parodist — Corinna S. Rohse employs the work of Linda Hutcheon, Michele Hannoosh, and Margaret Rose in examining Ada Leverson's parodic sketches of Oscar Wilde's writings. Rohse explores the complex play of authority and priority between authorship and parody, between the original and the imitative work, and between the male (homosexual) and the female (heterosexual) voice. Studying double-voiced discourse of quite a different kind, Gloria Biamonte's essay on humor in women's detective fiction calls attention to the dialogues between the "speaking selves" of parody, such as the dialogue between the traditionally perceived hard-boiled detective and the evolving countertradition of the female investigator, or the dialogue between the feminist sensitivity of the female investigator and the authority of the rigid and often amoral institutions she must confront. By using the one voice to subvert the other, such parodic dialogizing functions as an emancipatory strategy.

One of the most effective means of mocking gender stereotypes in comedy by both men and women is role reversal. Mary Bly's contribution takes a close look at the rhetoric of Renaissance comedies by Dekker and Shakespeare in which female characters explicity refer to erotic consummation, thereby assuming the male role and thwarting audience expectations for comedic personae; whereas in tragedy the expression of sexual desire by a female character invites the audience to condemn her morally, Bly shows that in comedy a woman's wish for consummation goes unpunished and hence serves to destabilize conventional gender roles. In a similar vein though different mode, Kay Young's article discusses the emergence in the 1930s of a cinematic genre which presents a model of marriage with new parameters: reflecting the widespread unemployment of the Depression era, the Hollywood romantic screwball comedy typically celebrates a newly empowered female character, often an heiress, teamed up with an out-of-work househusband.

The collection that follows treats the comic questioning not only of gender stereotypes but of racial preconceptions as well. Zita Dresner's essay compares the black writer Alice Childress's *Like One of the The Family: Conversations from a Domestic's Life* with the white domestic or housewife humor popularized by Erma Bombeck, Shirley Jackson, and Jean Kerr to determine commonalities in structure and style. But Dresner also points out the distinct features of black women's humor, showing for example how Childress further deconstructs the myth of the happy housewife by challenging white stereotypes of blacks. Barbara Monroe discusses the ways in which Zora Neale Hurston's *Mules and Men* and *Their Eyes Were Watching God* burst stereotypes of race, genre, and class. Focusing on the verbal duels or joking rituals that characterize the mock-courtship and post-courtship routines between men and women in Hurston's novels, Dresner places these routines in the historical context of African-American expressive culture by linking them with elements of antebellum minstrelsy, man-and-wife acts in vaudeville, blues, and stand-up comedy. Comparisons with mainstream romantic comedy, moreover, illuminate important class and racial differences in women's humor, above all concerning domestic violence. Finally, although Jaye Berman Montresor's article is devoted primarily to white female comic strip artists, she also treats Barbara Brandon, the first black woman cartoonist in national syndication, who uses humor to address issues of race and class as well as gender.

Closely related to the issue of comedy's mockery of stereotypes and norms is the vexed question of whether it is ultimately conservative or subversive with regard to the status quo. It has frequently been argued by theorists of women's comedy that men, as those traditionally in power, use humor to vent dissatisfaction but ultimately to preserve things as they are, whereas women use humor to shake things up; in support of this view, Cixous's well-known statement about women's writing in general is often cited: "A feminine text cannot fail to be more than subversive... [The woman writer's task is] to break up the 'truth' with laughter" (258). Yet in this connection as in others, it should be kept in mind that differences in male and female humor exist not in a vacuum but within a specific sociohistoric context. Depending on the period and milieu producing a text, differences can shade into similarities and vice versa, and the lines of demarcation are not always sharply drawn, as this collection shows. For example, Florence Redding Jessup's close analysis of female roles in the 1988 Spanish film *Women on the Verge of a Nervous Breakdown* concludes that director Pedro Almodóvar uses humor to create not sympathy for but rather distance on the film's machismo gender schemes; that he wishes to preserve the status quo is far from a given.

As would be expected, the claim that women's comedy is subversive is especially applicable to the late twentieth century. Allison Fraiberg's essay explores the ways in which contemporary American women stand-up comics Paula Poundstone, Ellen DeGeneres, and Margaret Cho, attempting to mediate the gaps between the theoretical positions of academic feminism and the experiences of women who attend their performances, employ humor to call critical attention to status quo mechanisms of power and subordination. For female stand-up comics like these, entertainment is the sugar that coats pills often otherwise difficult for audiences to swallow. But in the world of

Restoration and eighteenth-century British drama, the subversive status of the female creator of comedy is more ambiguous. Suz-Anne Kinney's study of Aphra Behn's *The Rover* and Susanna Centlivre's *The Busie Body* shows that despite the presence of nontraditional elements such as women-centered scenes, strong female characters, and the critique of women's oppression in the "narrative middle" of the texts, both plays close with the conventional comic ending in marriage. Hence the statement Susan Carlson makes about the British (male) comic tradition in general applies to these comedies by women as well: "Women are allowed their brilliance, freedom, and power in comedy only because the genre has built-in safeguards against such behavior" (17). Similarly, Erin Isikoff uses Hannah Cowley's play *The Belle's Strategem* to elucidate two eighteenth-century tropes of feminine behavior, modesty as a respectable, nonsexual uniform essential for women and masquerade as a degrading and dangerous sexual garb. Yet Isikoff points out that it is not clear to what degree the play's masks and veils empower or imprison the heroine in restrictive social norms, nor how the happy ending in marriage mediates between the two states.

A final point that should be mentioned in comparing comedy by women and men is the element of aggression, which plays a role in numerous theories of humor. Bergson makes the following observation in his essay on laughter: "Always rather humiliating for the one against whom it is directed, laughter is really and truly a kind of social 'ragging'" (148). Freud's *Jokes and Their Relation to the Unconscious* theorizes that jokes, originating like dreams in the unconscious and undergoing similar processes of condensation, displacement, and indirect representation, express repressed or unconscious wishes, most often of an aggressive or sexual nature. Where a joke is not an aim in itself, in other words, not an innocent joke, Freud believes that "[i]t is either a *hostile* joke (serving the purpose of aggressiveness, satire, or defence) or an *obscene* joke (serving the purpose of exposure)" (97). Recent feminist theory has begun to associate aggression with women's comedy as well. Arguing that women often inject an element of "incipient rage" into their humor, Barreca claims that "comedy and anger are two fundamental mainstays of women's writing" (*Last Laughs* 7). What is often different is the reception of anger in comedy. Barreca's distinction is illuminating:

> when a man demonstrates his anger through humor, he is [seen as] showing self-control, because he could be acting destructively instead of just speaking destructively. When a woman demonstrates her anger through humor, however, she is seen as losing self-control, because she isn't meant to have any angry feelings in the first place. (*Snow White* 94)

Speaking not of reception but of substance, however, my brief survey suggests that as many features link comedy by male and female writers as distinguish it: elements of celebration, festive license, in short, the carnivalesque; sociability combined with subjectivity; the mocking of stereotypes and norms, often through role reversal or through a double-voiced or dialogized discourse, such as parody, in which transgressive elements are woven into the dominant language; subversion of the status quo, either temporarily, in the narrative middle of a text, or ultimately; and aggression or anger.

Is women's comedy, then, anything more than comedy by women? A more precise way of differentiating from the traditional canon of male humor might be to talk of "feminist comedy." Little's book on comedy and the woman writer characterizes the fiction of Virginia Woolf, Muriel Spark, and other twentieth-century writers such as Jean Ryhs, Penelope Mortimer, Beryl Bainbridge, and Margaret Drabble as "feminist comedy" — comedy which depicts, using distinctly female or organic imagery, threshold or "liminal" experiences which are marked by celebration or ordeal, revolt, and inversion; insofar as liminality is not resolved, Little argues, these novels advocate a radical "politics of holiday" which reorders conventional social structures. Similarly, Walker includes a chapter entitled "Feminist Humor" in her book on women's humor and American culture, in which she concludes that feminist humor "both elucidates and challenges women's subordination and oppression" and that "the impulse for all feminist humor is the fundamental absurdity of one gender oppressing the other" (*A Very Serious Thing* 152, 163). In general, however, theorists of women's humor have tended to talk of women and comedy, women's comic visions, women's use of humor, etc. and to avoid the adjective "feminist." The reason may be that, while some grant *women* a sense of humor, "feminist humor" strikes many as an oxymoron.

One advantage of the concept of "feminist comedy" is that it is not gender-specific; it can be created by men as well as women. The same is of course true of criticism and theory of feminist comedy, as the collection at hand demonstrates: David McWhirter contrasts Bakhtin's writings on distance as an aesthetic category with reconceptualizations of objectivity and distance by George Meredith, as well as by feminist thinkers such as Chodorow and Keller, in order to postulate a new comic distance that can accommodate a feminist political vision. McWhirter discusses Virginia Woolf's novel *Between the Acts* as an illustration of this refiguration of comic distance.

The procedure of McWhirter's essay, in which a male critic discerns a feminist comic vision in a woman writer with the aid of male and female feminist theorists, can be seen to epitomize process the of cross-gender illumination in which this volume is engaged. If the juxtaposition of comedy by women and men offered by this collection can help bring about a heightened awareness of the affinities linking them and hence a regard for women's comedy as existing on an equal footing with men's rather than in a subcategory, then perhaps something of the classic spirit of comedy can be achieved. To describe this spirit, one need add only the word "gender" to Judy Little's characterization of a common feature of comedy: "a festive sense of community which celebrates a shared humanity rather than respecting the distinctions of class, prestige, and role" (*Comedy and the Woman Writer* 2).

NOTES

1. This time span embraces only critical studies pertinent to the essays included in this volume. For references to older anthologies of humor by women (in America), see Walker and Dresner xvi–xvii. I omit Linda Bamber's *Comic Women, Tragic Men: A Study of Gender and Genre in Shakespeare* (Stanford: Stanford University Press, 1982) from consideration here because it focuses on Shakespeare per se rather than on the issue of women and comedy in more general terms.

2. See Martin and Segrave for profiles of successful female comic performers in the United States from 1860 to the 1980s.

WORKS CITED

Bakhtin, Mikhail. *The Dialogic Imagination: Four Essays*. Trans. Caryl Emerson and Michael Holquist. Austin: University of Texas Press, 1981.

──────────. *Rabelais and His World*. Trans. Hélène Iswolsky (1968). Bloomington: Indiana University Press, 1984.

Barreca, Regina, ed. *Last Laughs: Perspectives on Women and Comedy*. New York: Gordon and Breach, 1988.

──────────, ed. *New Perspectives on Women and Comedy*. Philadelphia: Gordon and Breach, 1992.

──────────. *They Used to Call Me Snow White ... But I Drifted: Women's Strategic Use of Humor*. New York: Viking, 1991.

Bergson, Henri. "Laughter," in: *Comedy*, ed. Wylie Sypher (1956). Baltimore: Johns Hopkins University Press, 1980, 61–190.

Blyth, Reginald. *Humour in English Literature: A Chronological Anthology* (1959). Folcroft, Pa.: Folcroft Press, 1970.

Carlson, Susan. *Women and Comedy: Rewriting the British Theatrical Tradition*. Ann Arbor: University of Michigan Press, 1991.

Cixous, Hélène. "The Laugh of the Medusa." Trans. Keith and Paula Cohen. *New French Feminisms*. Eds. Elaine Marks and Isabelle de Courtivron (1980). New York: Schocken, 1981, 245–64.

Cixous, Hélène. and Catherine Clément. *The Newly Born Woman*. Trans. Betsy Wing. Minneapolis: University of Minnesota Press, 1986.

Freud, Sigmund. *Jokes and Their Relation to the Unconscious*. Trans. and ed. James Strachey. New York: Norton, 1960.

Gilbert, Sandra M., and Susan Gubar. *The Madwoman in the Attic: The Woman Writer and the Nineteenth-Century Literary Imagination*. New Haven: Yale University Press, 1979.

Little, Judy. *Comedy and the Woman Writer: Woolf, Spark, and Feminism*. Lincoln: University of Nebraska Press, 1983.

_____. "Humoring the Sentence: Women's Dialogic Comedy," in: *Women's Comic Visions*, ed. June Sochen. Detroit: Wayne State University Press, 1991, 19–32.

Martin, Linda, and Kerry Segrave, eds. *Women in Comedy*. Secaucus, NJ: Citadel Press, 1986.

Sochen, June, ed. "Introduction." *Women's Comic Visions*. Detroit: Wayne State University Press, 1991, 9–16.

Walker, Nancy. "Toward Solidarity: Women's Humor and Group Identity," in: *Women's Comic Visions*, ed. June Sochen. Detroit: Wayne State University Press, 1991, 57–81.

_____. *A Very Serious Thing: Women's Humor and American Culture*. Minneapolis: University of Minnesota Press, 1988.

Walker, Nancy, and Zita Dresner, eds. *Redressing the Balance: American Women's Literary Humor from Colonial Times to the 1980s*. Jackson: University Press of Mississippi, 1988.

Wilt, Judith. "The Laughter of Maidens, the Cackle of Matriarchs: Notes on the Collision between Comedy and Feminism," in: *Gender and Literary Voice*, ed. Janet Todd. New York: Holmes & Meier, 1980, 173–96.

I.
DRAMA

2

"That's How It Is": Comic Travesties of Sex and Gender in Early Sixteenth-Century Venice

ERIC A. NICHOLSON

I.

If comedy knows that rules are made to be broken, it also knows that rules for gender are among the most fun — and funniest — to break. This pattern of comic sexual and theatrical misrule played its own prominent role in early modern European crises of gender construction and sexual litigation (Laqueur, Jones and Stallybrass, Garber). Witness the following two documents from Northern Italy: "The proclamation was renewed on 18 April [1518], that no one should dress in transvestite fashion": this from the diary of Marin Sanudo, the unofficial chronicler, à la Samuel Pepys, of early sixteenth-century Venice. The following, by contrast, comes from *La Calandria*, the hit comedy by Bernardo Dovizi da Bibbiena first performed in Urbino in 1513: the servant Fessenio tells his master Lidio that

> Calandro, marito di Fulvia tua amorosa e padrone mio posticcio, che
> castrone è e tu becco fai, mentre che tu, li di passati, da donna vestito,
> Santilla chiamatoti, andato da Fulvia e tornato sei, credendo che tu

17

donna sia, si è forte di te invaghito e pregatomi che io faccia si che egli
ottenga questa sua amorosa: la qual sei tu.

[Calandro, your lover Fulvia's husband and my so-called master, that
old fool whom you make a cuckold, well, just the other day — when
you were dressed as a woman, and had just finished your visit with
Fulvia — well, thinking you actually were a woman, he falls madly in
love with you, and so he asks me to do all I can to get him this lovely
young lady — meaning you!]. (I.iii; 20)[1]

Appropriately, Lidio responds by exclaiming, "that is definitely something to
laugh about. Ha ha ha ha!"

This passage thus identifies some of the supposed effects of transvestism
that the Venetian authorities sought to curb: illicit sex, adultery, sodomy,
counterfeit identity, in short, sexual and social disorder, and perhaps even the
laughter provoked by such disorder. Indeed, as I hope to show in regard to
the comic theatre of this period, laughter itself could function as a form of
disorder. If, however, cross-dressing is officially denounced as a dangerous
crime, in *La Calandria* its disruptive effects receive ironic vindication. The
adulterous wife Fulvia is allowed to assert her equal right to dress as a man
and pursue the young Lidio, the male cross-dresser who sparks unchaste
passion in Fulvia's imbecilic husband. In a soliloquy, she asks, "perché non
mi è lecito da omo vestirmi una sol volta e trovar lui, come esso, da donna
vestito, spesso è venuto a trovar me? Ragionevol è" (III.v; 50) ["why should
it be unlawful for me to dress up as a man, just this once, and visit him, since
he, dressed up as a woman, has so often come to visit me? It's perfectly
reasonable"] Since the play depends on the comic discomfiture of Calandro,
it thus also endorses the transvestite means by which he is cuckolded and
ridiculed. In doing so, the play develops a critique of the sexual double
standard, as it applies to both adultery and personal attire. Along with Lidio's
twin sister Santilla, who dresses as her brother, Fulvia successfully usurps
male privileges by dressing as a man; having just cause for her action, the
target for derisive laughter becomes not only mistaken identity but also the
very attempt to define gender and control sexuality through codes of dress.

In this regard, *La Calandria* and the Renaissance comedies which followed its lead accomplish a potentially radical form of parody, providing
comic pleasure for both performer and audience through the experience of
acting out and witnessing travesties of rigid sexual laws and gender categories
(Butler, 135–6, Garber, 16–17). I here use "travesty" in both its literal and
figurative senses. As shown by so much of the comic tradition from Aristophanes to the present, to travesty someone or something often means
achieving parody and ridicule precisely through the action of wearing clothing usually worn by the opposite sex. Put simply, the woman who wears
man's clothing, or vice versa, creates opportunities for parody and laughter.
For travesty exposes the ludicrous artificiality of supposedly "natural"

relationships, institutions, and hierarchies in western society. Although my focus in this essay will on the one hand extend beyond the topic of cross-dressing, and on the other be mainly limited to the Veneto region, I thus cite *La Calandria* as a revealing case study: like several others which would follow its lead, this play uses travesty and sexual role reversals to raise provocative questions of sexual transgression and ambiguity. As one of the first, most popular, and most influential examples of the so-called *commedia erudita* or "learned comedy," Bibbiena's play also attests to its contemporary audience's own preoccupation with images and problems of illicit sexuality.

Moreover, this phenomenon points to disputes and contradictions involving sexual practices outside the world of the stage. For example, the prominence and ambivalent treatment of prostitute characters in these comedies had a more than coincidental link with paradoxes of the early modern sex trade. After a century or more of relative protection and even support, prostitutes in various Italian cities — Florence and Venice included — were undergoing increased restrictions from the civic authorities. Such factors as the outbreak of syphilis in the 1490s, a return of urban populations to more stable levels than in the decades following the Black Death, and the concern of both merchants and families to occupy separate zones away from ill-reputed women, contributed to more severe measures against prostitution.[2] At the same time, the social and economic upheavals caused by a succession of wars, combined with a vogue for refined and glamorous courtesans, increased the numbers, notoriety, and allure of prostitutes at both the lower and upper echelons of the profession.[3] In particular, Venice was a focal point for these trends, and its comic theatrical productions both derisively and compassionately dramatized practices and practitioners of sexual commerce, transgression, and experimentation. As with *La Calandria*, the dramaturgy of these plays incites audiences to laugh, and in their laughing to criticize stereotypes of gender and codes of sexuality.

Moreover, at a time when female roles were almost always played by male actors, the Venetian comic theatre itself indulged the ambiguities of cross-dressing. In other words, such performances not only represented but *enacted* the disordering practice of transvestism. Moreover, this enactment again coincided with the transgressive activities of at least some of the audience. In this context of presentational theatre, comic performance could itself become an act of transgression. The above-cited renewal of the Venetian proclamation against transvestism was a response to the public wearing of women's clothing by the gentlemen Zuan Bembo and Antonio Arimondo, who were apprehended during an outdoor wedding dance given by the Ortolani, one of the city's most prominent Compagnie della Calza ("stocking-companies"). These mainly patrician organizations, whose youthful constituency and often unruly activities can be instructively compared with French "abbeys of misrule," adopted their own pseudo-heroic or festive

names and insignia (such as the Eterni and Zardinieri), drew up official
statutes, and sponsored banquets, receptions, and theatrical productions (Venturi, Davis, Muraro; Muir, 167–73). For their part, the Ortolani or "market-
gardeners" frequently organized wedding festivities, at which comedies were
a main feature: for instance, in February 1518, two months before the
Bembo/Arimondo arrest, the Ortolani had performed a comèdy for the wedding of Gasparo Brexalù, a lavish affair which lasted over eight hours. As in
the modern Venetian carnival, cross-dressing, erotic dancing, and provocative
comic performances were main features of such occasions.

     Given a relative lack of separation between stage and audience, the latter
became all the more implicated as transgressors of sumptuary laws and
statutes against sexual licence. A major feature of these decrees is their casting
of licentious dress and behavior as sacrilegious, and thus a cause of divine
retribution (Bistort, Lorenzi). Whether or not they were consistently enforced,
these laws reveal an authoritarian mentality that viewed masking, gender
confusion, personal ostentation, and theatrical performance as links in a chain
of immorality and potential disorder. Such legislation thus targets both the
concealment of individual identity and the confusion of gender distinctions
as threats to the well-being of the state. As Diane Owen Hughes observes,
the fifteenth-century civic officials who drafted sumptuary laws perceived
fluctuations and extravagance of fashion, and especially such deviances as
cross-dressing, as "the sign of a profoundly disordered society." (91) For a
man to dress as a woman was not only to confuse binary gender oppositions,
but to reverse the model of a single biological male sex, and thus to promote
the more generally disordering effeminization of society. Thus in 1505, at the
moment when Venetian anxieties regarding unorthodox sexual customs and
costumes were reaching a crescendo, the Senate aimed at "youths" (zoveni)
who were tempting "divine wrath" with their ornate, expensive, and open-
collared doublets, since these were "feminine rather than masculine clothes."[4]
This particular decree also connects to the world of theatrical production, as
it goes on to prohibit the wearing of decorated stockings by these same
youths: such stockings, embroidered with the insignia of the Compagnia della
Calza, were the group's identifying trademark.

     A deadlier factor, however, in both the framing and execution of laws
concerning dress and illicit sex, was the Venetian government's — and particularly the Council of Ten's — preoccupation with the crime of sodomy.
Unlike other sexual malefactors, who usually received lenient sentences,
individuals convicted of sodomy were frequently pilloried and burned, either
alive or after decapitation, between the two columns of the Piazzetta San
Marco. While the majority of these victims had been found guilty of
homosexual relations with other men, some were executed for heterosexual
anal intercourse, even with their own wives (Ruggiero, 109–45).[5] An ambiguous entry by Sanudo (dated 28 August, 1500) mentions the burning of a

"woman named Rada with two prostitutes," for her being a bawd or "*rufiana* of women with whom the art of sodomy was used": it is unclear whether Sanudo means the sale of these women to male sodomites (whose passive female partners were almost never sentenced to death), or women who committed sodomy or "unnatural" acts with one another.[6] In any case, prostitutes were associated with gender confusion and sodomy in the context of cross-dressing. In 1480, the Council of Ten had published an edict against Venetian women who in men's clothing "dissimulate their sex, and in the guise of men strive to please men, which is a kind of sodomy" (Lorenzi, 233). Moreover, Venetian magistrates sometimes viewed both sodomy and prostituion as adjuncts to theatrical production. In a letter of 1462, the Patriarch of Venice requests the Council of Ten to permit the construction of a stage only if the boards will be dismantled immediately after the performance. The reason? As many witnesses could supposedly attest, the dark space beneath a stage afforded a locale for sodomitic assignations (Pavan, 271). Like later opponents of the Elizabethan English stage, Venice's social legislators thus conflated the spaces of theatre and of sodomy.

As for the association between stage and bordello, a more visible pattern prevailed. First, in the 1490s, when theatrical activities in Venice were on the rise, the prostitutes of the city were evicted from the Rialto, which had been their zoned area of operation since 1360 (Pavan, 244–54; and Casagrande, 24–30). The consequence was for these women, whether common *puttane* or high-priced *cortigiane*, to transfer their places of business to domestic spaces scattered throughout the city. Thus another contiguity developed, between the private space of Venetian prostitution and the often indoor stages of the period. Upon these stages, prostitutes sometimes appeared as dancers and comic entertainers.[7] For example, at one *festa* held by the Compagnia degli Zardinieri in 1514, a comedy was performed, "and there were some prostitutes, nor did they wish any other people to attend" (Sanuto, xviii, 265). This note of exclusiveness again conveys the perceived link between comedies and private erotic delectation.

For the Council of Ten, such theatrical and sexually suspect gatherings posed a special dilemma. On the one hand, they served as pseudo-rites of passage, giving young and still disenfranchised patricians a chance to release unruly energies within the context of organized and sometimes diplomatically useful social events (Chojnacki, 792–6; Muir, 168–71; Cozzi, "Authority and the Law"). Nevertheless, particular strains — such as the supposedly related phenomena of rampant sodomy and military setbacks — conspired against easy tolerance of these young Venetian nobles' patronage of lavish feasts, sexually provocative dances, and ribald comedies. In December 1508, the Council of Ten published a decree citing "evil and lascivious things" as a direct consequence of the playing of comedies "in which disguised actors say and perform many unseemly, lascivious, and most immodest words and deeds" (Padoan, 39). The decree then prescribes penalties of one-year's imprisonment and five-years' banishment for anyone who might try to stage comedies. As their own words confirm, the Council of Ten — and presumably a sizable portion of the Venetian elite — perceived the bawdy, cross-dressing comic theatrics sponsored by the Compagnie della Calza as a threat to the moral and political well-being of the Republic.

A few months after this ban, Venice's worst political fears were indeed realized when the Venetian army was convincingly defeated at the battle of Agnadello (May 1509). Divine retribution, it was argued, had been visited on the city for its moral laxity and wasteful, frivolous expenditures, especially on the part of the formerly sober patriciate (Gilbert). The banker Girolamo Priuli, for one, blamed the influx of French, in other words enemy, fashions for Venice's downfall: one of the most notorious of these was the "balla di capello," an energetic dance which called for leaps, erotic gestures, and the choice of partners by masked women. The Venetian Senate went so far as to pass laws against this dance, which was seen to "offend our Lord and give a bad example to our modest virgins" (Bistort, 222). Even if these measures were only rarely enforced, their very proposal and acceptance suggest that male Venetian lawmakers seriously feared the disreputable and disordering implications of letting their wives, sisters, and daughters participate in sexually bold entertainments.

Since comedies in particular indulged sexual role reversal, as well as opulent display in both men and women, their production could be seen as an added defiance of sumptuary laws, and a vehicle for illicit sexuality. In Februrary, 1515, the Zardinieri, Ortolani, and Immortali entertained their guests with the "most sumptuous feasts," despite the "great expense and taxation" that they caused the city. At their spectacular dinners, the *compagni* and their friends performed comedies, encouraged masquerading, and dressed themselves in prohibited stockings, doublets, and dresses of gold cloth and jewelled embroidery. According to Sanudo, this "was the greatest shame, nevertheless they [the women] came wearing wooden platform shoes" (xix, 418), the notorious *zoccoli* used by Venetian prostitutes to increase their height and masculine appearance.[8] During the next two weeks of this notably licentious Carnival season, the Zardinieri and Ortolani staged several other comedies, almost all of them "new," at least one of them "lascivious," and with audiences in which the "ladies were very ornately dressed, even though the Collegio had re-proclaimed the law against ostentation" (Sanudo, xix, 434 and 424).

Having established this context of sumptuary legislation, anxieties over sodomy and cross-dressing, and youth group patronage of both prostitutes and theatre, I now want to examine more closely the evidence from the plays themselves, in order to clarify how certain comedies confronted their audiences with unorthodox images of women and explicit, provocative, and even scandalous portrayals of illicit sexuality. Focusing on selected plays by anonymous Venetian authors, Pietro Aretino, and the playwright/actor Angelo Beolco ("Il Ruzante," ca. 1492–1542), I will argue that like the legislators and social commentators, these works put special emphasis on problems of identity, desire, and reproduction. Unlike their censorious contemporaries, however, they stage these problems in ways that offer a comic critique, indeed a travesty, of sexual stereotypes and relationships.

II.

Laughable contradictions surrounding the construction of gender and relations between the sexes could and did become all the more manifest during times of crisis: when the patriarchal order and its governing assumptions were put under pressure and sometimes deflated, the expression of alternative social and sexual options appears to have increased. Although by no means uncontested, there developed a certain privileging of women, low-status figures, and reformist viewpoints over and against prevailing models of male oligarchy or despotism. In Venice, a preexisting vogue for sensual images of femininity — as made most visible by Giorgone, Bellini, and Titian — gained even more impetus following 1490s losses to the Turks and the ensuing disgrace of Agnadello, which did so much to discredit the Republic's expansionism and pretenses of military supremacy (Gilbert). As the authority of the ruling patriciate came into question, so too did distinctions between its members and individuals of lower rank: in Mansueti's and Carpaccio's paintings of Venetian processions, gondoliers and members of the Compagnie delle Calze wear nearly identical costume (Carroll, "Who's on Top?"). The masquerades of these same young noblemen as peasants and shepherds also reflect this levelling tendency. Finally, the apparent increase in cross-dressing shows how a spirit of experimentation informed the definition (or indefinition) of gender in early sixteenth century Venice.

As part of this same trend, ridicule of male sexual and military bravado assumed a prominent place in the Venetian comic repertoire. On more than one occasion, the Compagnie delle Calze staged Plautus' *Miles Gloriosus*, the prototypical satire on pugnacious blustering.[9] In the fall of 1514, a play with a similar theme met with similar success. In this case, the Zardinieri performed "an amusing comedy" of "the *sbrichi veneziani*, a fine piece of work, and many went there to see it" (Sanuto, xix, 122). Although the exact name of the play is not mentioned, most scholars agree that it can be identified as the "Comedia de alcuni bravi, vulgar, bellissima," preserved in a single manuscript and now known as *La Bulesca*.[10] This title derives from the character Bule, a braggart soldier ("bravo" or "sbricho") enamoured of the prostitute Marcolina. In the course of the one-act play, Bule and his companion Bio attempt to gain entry to Marcolina's house, where she and her cousin Zuana rebuff them, and watch while a noisy fight transpires between the two men and their rival, the pimp Fracao. Bule's cowardice, combined with the intervention of an aristocratic "Misier," averts bloodshed, but Marcolina has seen enough to convince her to repudiate her suitors, and so the play ends.

It starts, appropriately, with a "proemio" spoken by none other than Mars, and just as appropriately, he promises the audience grand deeds of valor and fearful combat which the ensuing comedy does not come close to delivering (compare Shakespeare's later use of this device in *Troilus and Cressida*). Even in his words, however, Mars belies the "sbricaria" that he claims strikes fear into any listener's heart: after giving a more or less accurate summary of the unheroic plot, he concedes that the play's main lesson is in the superior wit, vigor, and deceptive trickery of prostitutes.

The "putana fina" Marcolina is indeed at the center of the play. Her house is the magnet of the action, and her character dominates all the men who try to accost and seduce her. In short, this brief comedy develops into a celebration of Marcolina's ability to maintain her sexual independence. Paradoxically, she can achieve the latter by rejecting all customers and devoting herself to a rich gentleman, and thus entertain only whom she pleases, when she pleases. Now defined as "fina," Marcolina has recently ascended to a higher, wealthier position, and her attitude bespeaks a consciousness of social rank and privileges. As she explains in her long opening monologue, "l'è pur belo,/ esser so dona, esser in casa soa/ e no scovar e questo e quel bordelo" ["Ah how lovely it is/ To be my own woman, in my own house/ Not having to fuck my way from this to that bordello"] (ll. 170–2). She is thus cast as a self-made prostitute, whose own independent rise in status travesties the social and financial inadequacies of her male counterparts. In spatial terms, the scene subordinates the braggart suitor to the woman on top: appearing at the window above, Marcolina twice asks Bule "Chi estu?," then after admitting that she does recognize him, refuses him entry. Reduced to begging for her favors, Bule demands why she should reject him, and she simply explains, "Perchè cusi" ["because that's how it is"] (l.353). In other words, Marcolina insists on her right to do as she wills, and not as she is cajoled or forced to do. The would-be conquering hero Bule comes across as impotent, as does his sidekick Bio, who has to resort to the usually feminine tactic of merely talking and not acting: again, though there is no literal cross-dressing, the male character plays the woman's role, and is made to look ridiculous in the process. Bio's cliché taunts, however, are not only ineffectual but absurd, since they bear no relation to Marcolina's restraint or eloquence. "Ah mamola deserta, ah zangolera,/ ah grota senza fondi, ah refudà!" ["O unwanted harlot, o shitcan,/ Bottomless pit, garbage!"] (ll.361–2), Bio hollers, but with absolutely no effect on the self-possessed Marcolina, who merely calls her assailants crazy, and asserts that she has no fear of them. Thus the probable staging of this sequence, with Marcolina elevated above her "suitors," would have physically reinforced the verbal expression of male inadequacy and sexual role reversal.

The preposterousness of male sexual bravado increases in the following sequence, when the sbrico or tough-guy Fracao appears with Marcolina, and descends to fight over her with Bule. When Marcolina's patron the "Misier" stops the brawl, and proposes a drinking party, Fracao persists in his desire for noisy abuse, and makes the counter-proposal to "far le matinata." This overt reference to the Italian version of the charivari clarifies and extends the attitude of sexual mockery established in the preceding scene by Bio's "putana rota" serenade of Marcolina.[11] The men's attempted mattinata, however, receives an ironic reversal, not only from their own mutual reconciliation, but from Marcolina's final rejection of Fracao's invitation to join him. "Perchè?" he asks, and she answers yet again, "Perchè cusi." The exact echo of her rebuttal of Bule doubles the humiliation of "Marcolina's unsuccessful clients," who become even more the object of the audience's laughter. Since the play's original audience of Compagnia members would themselves have been primarily aristocratic, they might have enjoyed seeing a higher-ranking figure and his paid mistress mock and repudiate would-be competitors. Moreover, Marcolina traces their public sexual discomfiture to their own efforts to exploit her for self-interested pleasure. Why should she comply, she asks, "with you who have so disgraced me?" (l. 678) The shame thus rebounds on the Venetian bravi, who succeed only in displaying their impotence in the service of both Mars and Venus.

Sometime in the early 1520s, or a few years after the production of *La Bulesca*, Angelo Beolco wrote and performed his "Primo Dialogo," or *Parlamento de Ruzante che iera vegnù de campo*.[12] Even more than its anonymous Venetian antecedent, this play in Pavan dialect develops a topical and scathing satire on war, its fighters, and its brutal effect on sexual relations. The scene is Venice, where the protagonist arrives after his three-day flight from the front line at Cremona, begrimed, lice-ridden, exhausted, and cursing: "Cancaro ai campi e ala guera e ai soldè, e ai soldè e ala guera!" ["to hell with the fields, the war, and the soldiers, and to hell with the soldiers and the war!"] (I.2). Encountering his old friend Menato, Ruzante describes the battlefields as nothing but mounds of bones and complains of other Italians and Frenchmen who insult him as a "cuckolded peasant." This association of military with sexual repudiation becomes the central issue of the play: Ruzante has come to Venice not merely to escape the fighting, but to reclaim his wife Gnua, who has deserted him for a Venetian *bravo*. Blind to his own utter destitution and bedraggled appearance, and deaf to Menato's warning that Gnua has become a *bravaccia* ("braosa") protected by *bravacci* ("brausi"), Ruzante plays the *miles gloriosus*, exclaiming "chi è pi braoso de

mi?" ["who's more macho than I?"] (II.75); seeing Gnua enter, he boasts to
Menato, "veri se la me farà carezze" ["now you'll see how she'll caress me!"]
(II.82). Like his dream-like account of his exploits as a soldier, Ruzante
fantasizes that he is someone else, in this case a dominant lover and not a
cuckolded husband.

For when Gnua beholds Ruzante, she instantly deflates his masculine
pretensions, and when Ruzante tries to assert that Gnua has no other man in
the world but him, his attempted claim of ownership becomes his downfall:
her lover enters, and proceeds to beat Ruzante soundly, while Menato and the
audience look on. Moreover, this humiliation comes across as a parodic
reenactment of Ruzante's battlefield experiences: he is convinced that one
hundred men attacked him, and thus forced him to play dead and refrain from
using his "lanzoto" or lance (the unused prop/weapon doubles as a sexual
metaphor). As Falstaff would propound over seventy years later, Ruzante
defends his "discrizion" or discretion in avoiding such an imbalanced fight.
When he finally does admit that there was only one assailant, he turns to
demonizing his own wife as a "strigona" or witch, who used some spell or
incantation to delude his senses. Again, soldierly cowardice and weakness
become equated with an inability to maintain control over women. Gnua
resembles Marcolina in freeing herself from an unwanted relationship, and
determining her own sexual future; Ruzante, meanwhile, ends the play in a
state of pointless fantasy, laughing at what he might have done had he been
able to catch his wife and her lover, and throw them into a canal.

The last laugh for the audience, however, is provided by a self-reflexive
gesture from Ruzante the author and actor. In response to Ruzante's pretense
of laughing off his humiliation, Menato observes that the whole affair
resembles the kind of ridiculous comedies that are performed at weddings
(V.150). With this comment, the space and time of the comic performance
collapse into the space and time of Ruzante's absurd, pathetic story, and the
audience members, quite possibly guests at a wedding reception, are invited
to laugh, *mattinata*-style, at a cuckolded peasant, and yet at the same time at
the theory and practice of marriage itself. In other words, the metatheatrical
comedy of adultery demands that its audience re-evaluate the categories of
"wife" and "husband," "whore" and "cuckold."

Before the Counter-Reformation started its general suppression of unorthodox viewpoints, one of the last plays to test its audience's attitudes toward
sexual exploitation and prostitution was Aretino's *La Talanta*,[13] staged in
1542 by the Compagnia dei Sempiterni, with sets by Vasari (Venturi 230).
Even more thoroughly than *La Bulesca*, Aretino's comedy dramatizes a
prostitute's comic mockery of the sexual double standard. Like Marcolina,
its protagonist operates at its center, young, attractive, and astute enough to
keep her many suitors romantically enthralled. She herself, however, has no

desire to play the mute Petrarchan love-object, nor any illusions about what men seek in her. As she aptly remarks about one of her admirers,

> Orfinio ama non me, ma il suo trastullo, e spende non in mio pro, ma in suo piacere: ecco un ghiotto compra una starna, non per amor che gli porti, ma per la voglia che egli ha di mangiarsela, come esso mangia me nel piacer che trae di quel ch'io sono. [Orfinio does not love me, but his plaything, and does not spend his money for my sake, but for his own pleasure: just as a glutton buys a partridge, not because he loves it, but because he wants to eat it; and so this man eats me in taking pleasure from what I am] (I.i.;346).

Talanta's perceptive analysis of her lover's self-interested desire gains corroboration in his frantic swings from abuse to self-pity. Likewise, her eventual if ironic part in reuniting two young married couples belies the diatribe against her profession made by Orfinio's friend Pizio. While on the one hand her captivity of an innocent (and cross-dressed) young man and woman sustains the negative prostitute image, on the other her shrewd insights combine with the folly and corruption of a male-dominated milieu to exonerate if not vindicate her.

At some point in the previous decade, however (most likely 1535–6), an even more exceptional play evoked many of the transgressive interests of the early sixteenth-century Venetian youth culture. The anonymous *La Veniexiana*, self-described as a true story, dramatizes the obsessive desire of two Venetian gentlewomen, the widowed Anzola and the married Valeria, for the visiting Milanese youth Iulio.[14] In doing so, it not only stresses the power of love but that of women, bespeaking the social independence and uninhibited sexual advances that Venetian women were sometimes allowed during this period (Chojnacki, "La posizione della donna"). Choosing her lover, an out-of-town youth named Iulio, stripping him of his clothes and weapons, and making him her "prisoner," Anzola takes the erotic implications of the wildly popular and female-dominated *balla di capello* to their full conclusion. Moreover, while this scene (III.iii.) is figured as taking place in a paradisiac *locus amoenus*, it is simultaneously shown to transpire in a contemporary Venetian mansion: the identification of this "Venetian comedy" with Venetian reality thus becomes emphatic (Padoan; Valeri).

This same sense of documentary truth therefore distinguishes the play's homoerotic elements, as well as its depiction of unrepentant transgression. The Prologue calls attention to the former material by beseeching the audience to look upon the "women" of the play not only as love objects but as fellow male lovers: the jest here is on the sexual ambiguity of the actors playing the female characters, who deserve to be placed in the same erotic category with men. During the ensuing action, the active lovers Anzola and Valeria, each in turn arranging and consummating a tryst with the passive

Iulio, fulfill the Prologue's injunction. The inversion of gender pervades the play: Iulio is described as "una bela puta" (II.vii.357) who has "quel'aria da fomnèla" ("that little-girl look"; II.v.351), Valeria behaves as if she and not her husband were the lord and master of her house, and in Anzola's first appearance on stage, she asks her servant Nena to play Iulio, to speak like a man, and say "Quele sporcarie che se dise in bordelo" ["those dirty words they say in the bordello"] (I.iv.341). In her passion, Anzola caresses, embraces, and kisses Nena to the orgasmic point where she exclaims, "Sun morta, mi. Sudo, in aqua, tuta" ["I'm dying, I am. I'm sweating, drowning, swooning"] (I.iv.339). This explicit scene would thus have played on the double inversion of two boy actors performing a sexual encounter between two women, one of whom is yearning for a man; it also epitomizes the double and triple entendres of sexual identity brought about by cross-dressing and reversed gender roles. Furthermore, while the script makes this only a brief, apparently accidental, and even deluded encounter, the performance demonstrates that audiences of this period did witness frank depictions of female homoeroticism, without being asked to think such passion "unnatural" or "sodomitic." On the contrary, the often provocative conditions of theatrical production and reception — not the least of which were the practice of cross-dressing and interaction with prostitutes — encouraged at least a recognition if not also an endorsement of transgressive sexual behavior. In performance, then, these comedies thematized the multiple possibilities for both male and female homoeroticism occasioned by transvestism and/or the reversal of gender roles.

In sum, the women in this play take the dominant position, the man becomes the love object, and a plot that begins with Iulio's professed aim to seduce Valeria and "take her for wife" ends with his submitting to her adulterous command. In short, *La Veniexiana* insists on the pleasure of erotic adventure, and refuses to observe the propriety of either wedded chastity or a final comic wedding. Iulio speaks for a realistic mode of comic dramaturgy, as well as for a philosophy of sexual behavior, when he declares that "Lo experimentar è cosa bellissima, per aver avvantaggio in conoscer" ["direct experience is a most wonderful thing, for getting the upper hand in knowledge"] (IV.iv.383). The indecisive ending of *La Veniexiana* indeed confirms and extends this emphasis on gaining knowledge — of all kinds — through experience or even experimentation (both senses of "experimentar" may have applied at this time). This spirit of experimentation, moreover, affirms this comedy's topical defiance of the rules, precisely those rules which claim to define gender, and organize the identities of men and women.

The unconventional comedies produced in and around Venice during the first half of the sixteenth century thus bespeak the activity of groups and individuals who were willing to take sexual and artistic risks. Despite the efforts of the ruling authorities to curb licentious behavior on and off the stage, the sponsors of such playwrights as Beolco, Aretino, and the anonymous authors of *La Bulesca* and *La Veniexiana* dared to present unorthodox comedies which questioned the sexual standards of their audiences. As cross-dressing, homoerotic innuendo, and the presence and sometimes valorization of prostitutes contributed to the dramaturgy of these plays, they were even more explicitly and self-consciously scandalous in their transgression of civic statutes against both sodomy and the theatre. While I do not presume to locate the exact causes and effects of this comic theatrical trend, I would suggest that these sexually provocative works were responses to a time of cultural upheaval and, to some degree, social protest: this particular historical moment, also known as the High Renaissance, was one of urgent crisis and debate, which saw the expression of alternative images and innovative viewpoints.

This expression, moreover, pertained especially to the field of sexuality, and appeared most forcefully and scandalously upon the comic stages of the period. A useful analogy can be drawn between the daring sexual and theatrical culture of early sixteenth century Venice and that of Berlin during the 1920s and early 1930s. Like the Venice of four hundred years earlier, Germany was suffering the effects of political defeat, economic hardship, and moral uncertainty. One symptom of this experience was an outburst of criticism, experimentation, nonconformity, and exceptional richness and complexity in both art and society: the "cabaret culture," for example, echoed Venice's challenging theatrical diversity and eroticism. Also like Venice and Italy's experience of the repression of Imperial takeover and the Counter-Reformation after the 1540s, Berlin's outstanding artistic and cultural innovations would be even more abruptly and thoroughly crushed by the totalitarian Nazi regime. What had been bold, groundbreaking, and provocative was now labelled as "degenerate," amidst a silencing of the thought and laughter stimulated by both political satire and gender parody.

NOTES

I would like to thank a number of people, including Gail Finney, Thomas M. Greene, Giuseppe Mazzotta, Natalie Zemon Davis, Laurie Nussdorfer, Guido Ruggiero, Wendy Steadman Sheard, Gary Spear, John Paoletti and the members of the Wesleyan University early modern studies seminar for invaluable suggestions and revisions to my paper. Any faults remain entirely my own. I would also like to cite two relevant recent publications which were published too late to be incorporated into my preparation of this text: Guido Ruggiero, *Binding Passions: Tales of Magic, Marriage,* and *Power at the End of the Renaissance* (Oxford: Oxford UP, 1993), and Margaret T. Rosenthal, *The Honest Courtesan:*

Veronica Franco, Citizen and Writer in Sixteenth Century Venice (Chicago: University of Chicago Press, 1993).

1. The Sanudo [sometimes spelled "*Sanuto*"] reference appears in vol. xxv, p. 350, of Marin Sanuto, *I Diarii*, edited by Rinaldo Fulin et al. (Venice, 58 vols., 1879–1903). Page references to *La Calandria*, by Bernardo Dovizi da Bibbiena are from the Davico Bonino edition.

2. Prostitutes and their trade figure prominently among a number of sixteenth century Italian comedies, including Aretino's *La Cortigiana* (1534), *Lo Ipocrito* (1542), and *La Talanta* (1542), and Ariosto's *La Lena* (1528) [all these plays appear in the De Sanctis collection]: these last two plays feature prostitutes as their protagonists. Aretino's major works on the subject, however, are the *Ragionamento* (1536) and *Dialogo* (1556), sometimes known as the Sei Giornate, in which the bawd or "ruffiana" Nanna explains the ups and downs of prostitution to her daughter and younger colleagues. See Aretino, *Ragionamento-Dialogo*. On the first day of the *Dialogo*, for example, Nanna reveals that men are sexually excited by female transvestism (244). On official measures against prostitution in the early sixteenth century, see Casagrande di Villaviera, Trexler, Pavan, and Ferrante. On the spread and ideological uses of syphilis, see Foa, and for informative essays on demographic patterns in this same period, see Herlihy, Scarabello, and Tucci.

3. On this topic, see Casagrande da Villaviera, 31–63, Larivaille, 65–123, Barzaghi, and Lawner.

4. See Bistort, 128. The same decree (Archivio di Stato di Venezia, *Senato Terra* R. 15, c. 86) includes a measure which may have taken direct aim at the Compagnie della Calza: "che le calze siano foderate di tela o lana, e non d'altro, e siano tutte semplici, senza striche, liste, cordele, franze, nè panni sfiladi, nè ornato de alcuna sorte" ("stockings are to be lined with coarse-cloth or wool, and not otherwise, and of simple design, without stripes, bands, cords, fringes, nor with unstitched cloth, nor decorated in any way").

5. Ruggiero cites the revealing case of the fisherman Giovanni Furlan, who in 1481 "had his head cut off and his remains burned for his 'frequent sodomy with his own wife'" (119). On this subject, see also Pavan, 266–83, and Scarabello, 81–2.

6. Sanudo, iii, 272, entry for August 28, 1500: "Item eri dapoi disnar fo menato per canal una femena nominata Rada con do meretrice da le bande sopra uno soler fino a Santa Croce dove dismonto e venuta per terra a San Marco fo brusata iuxta la parte dil Conseio di X e le do bandizate. Et questo per sodomia; questa era rufiana di femene con quelli vi andava a usar l'arte di sodomia." ["Item: yesterday afternoon a loose woman named Rada with two banished prostitutes was rowed through the canals, standing in the boat on a raised platform, unto Santa Croce, where they disembarked, and then went to San Marco where she was burned by order of the Council of Ten, and the two others officially banished. And this for sodomy; this woman was a procuress of loose women with whom the art of sodomy would be used"]. If this punishment was indeed enacted for sodomy between women, it would add to the cases cited and discussed by Brown, 3–28. Brown's illuminating study, which concentrates on the case of Benedetta Crivelli in the Tuscan town of Pescia, 1618–23, underrates

and to a certain extent neglects the evidence of literary and theatrical sources, especially those which exploit the motif of cross-dressing. See my discussion below of the anonymous Venetian play *La Veniexiana* (ca. 1535–6).

7. On the relocation of Venetian prostitutes and courtesans, see Pavan, 244–54, Casagrande da Villaviera, 24–30, and Barzaghi, 155–66, who reproduces a 1566 catalog of "all the principal and most honored courtesans of Venice." Sanudo's entries for these performances by prostitutes provide early evidence of an association between prostitutes and actresses which if not always direct or factual was widely perceived as such by many early modern Europeans. See the studies of seventeenth and nineteenth century English theatre by, respectively, Jacqueline Pearson and Tracy Davis: *The Prostituted Muse: Images of Women and Women Dramatists, 1642–1737* (New York: St. Martin's Press, 1988), and *Actresses as Working Women: Their Social Identity in Victorian Culture* (London and New York: Routledge, 1991). Although far less commercial and consumerist that the Victorian public theatre, production and performance in sixteenth century Venice did transpire amidst an increasingly capitalist, commodity-oriented economy. Furthermore, as the sumptuary laws, moral critiques, and visual records attest, Venetian prostitutes put themselves on conspicuous display, and the more ornate and glamorous the image they could project, the higher price for their services they could command.

8. The Venetian Senate had outlawed such shoes just three years before this date, on May 8, 1512: "vieta gli zoccoli, le pantofole, le scarpe, che fossero fatti di stoffe d'oro, d'argento o di seta, ed ingiunge ad uomini ed a donne, di non calzare che scarpe di cuoio o di panno, senza ornato alcuno." ["we prohibit zoccoli, slippers, and other shoes that are made with gold, silver, or silk cloth, and enjoin all men and women to wear only leather or linen shoes, without any ornamentation"] On zoccoli as part of the prostitute's costume, see Barzaghi, 74, with a reproduction of an engraving from P. Bertelli's *Diversarum Nationum habitus* (Padua, 1594), labelled "Cortigiana Veneta." The engraving of the woman's skirt is printed on a separate flap of paper, which lifts to reveal her men's breeches and ten-inch high zoccoli underneath. Since Bertelli's engraving dates from the 1590s, it shows that the sumptuary laws had little long-term effect, at least on the dress of courtesans. Sanudo's objection, and the scandal that he may indicate, would have resulted from the fact that the zoccoli-wearers in question were married gentlewomen.

9. For example, during the Carnival of 1515, the Immortali Compagnia gave a performance of the play, with interludes featuring the professional improvisation artist Zuan Polo. This famous *buffone* at one point turned himself into the God of Love, "and was carried into hell, where he encountered Domenego Taiacalze [a recently-deceased comic performer] pursuing castrati": again, homoerotic overtones accompany the comic routine.

10. This play survives in manuscript at the Biblioteca Marciana in Venice (Marciano it. IX 288 (6072, cc.52r–69v). I have used the thoroughly annotated version of the play by Bianca Maria da Rif, in her anthology *La letteratura alla bulesca: testi rinascimenti veneti* (Padua: Antenore, 1984), pp. 1–84; line references are to this edition (I am grateful to Guido Ruggiero for this reference). For a historical study which closely documents and explains the distinctions between

"meretrize" and "cortegiane" (the latter, more privileged class being the one Marcolina aspires to), see Cathy Santore, "Julia Lombardo, 'Sumtuosa Meretrize': A Portrait by Property," *Renaissance Quarterly* 42 (1989), pp. 44–83.

11. The most complete study of the mattinata is by Klapisch-Zuber, in Le Goff and Schmitt, pp. 149–63. For additional citations, see Pola Falletti-Villafalletto, 214–8.

12. References to this and other Ruzante texts are from the edition by Ludovico Zorzi. For my analysis of Ruzante's work, I am indebted to Zorzi's notes and introductions, and to the studies by Baratto, Borsellino, Padoan, and Carroll.

13. References to *La Talanta* are from the De Sanctis edition.

14. References to *La Venexiana* are from the Davico Bonino edition of the play.

WORKS CITED

Arnaldi, G., and M.P. Stocchi, eds. *Storia della Cultura Veneta III/3*. Vicenza: Neri Pozza, 1981.

Baratto, Mario. *Tre studi sul teatro*. Vicenza: Neri Pozza, 1964.

Barzaghi, Antonio. *Donne o Cortigiane?: La prostituzione a Venezia: documenti di costume dal XVI al XVIII secolo*. Verona: Bertani, 1980.

Bistort, Giulio. *Il Magistrato alle Pompe della Repubblica di Venezia*. Venice, 1912.

Borsellino, Nino. *Rozzi e Intronati: Esperienze e Forme di Teatro dal Decameron al Candelaio*. Rome: Bulzoni, 1976.

Brown, Judith. *Immodest Acts: The Life of a Lesbian Nun in Renaissance Italy*. Oxford: Oxford University Press, 1986.

Butler, Judith. *Gender Trouble: Feminism and the Subversion of Identity*. New York: Routledge, 1990.

Carroll, Linda. *Angelo Beolco (Il Ruzante)*. Boston: Twayne, 1990.

_____. "Who's on Top?: Gender as Societal Power Configuration in Italian Renaissance Drama." *Sixteenth-Century Journal* 20/4 (1989): 531–58.

Casagrande da Villaviera, Rita. *Le cortigiane veneziane nel cinquecento*. Milan: Longanesi, 1968.

Chojnacki, Stanley. "La posizione della donna a Venezia nel cinquecento," pp. 65–70, in: *Tiziano e Venezia: Convegno internazionale di studi, Venezia 1976*. Vicenza: Neri Pozza, 1980.

_____. "Political Adulthood in Fifteenth-Century Venice." *American Historical Review* 91 (1986): 791–810.

Cozzi, Gaetano. "Authority and the Law in Renaissance Venice," pp. 293–345, in: *Renaissance Venice*, ed. J.R. Hale. London: Faber and Faber, 1973.

_____. "La Donna, l'amore, e Tiziano," pp. 47–63, in: *Tiziano e Venezia: Convegno internazionale di studi*. Venezia 1976. Vicenza: Neri Pozza, 1980.

Davico Bonino, Guido, ed. *Il Teatro Italiano*, vol. 2: *La commedia del cinquecento*. Turin: Einaudi, 1977.

Davis, Natalie Zemon. "The Reasons of Misrule," pp. 97–123, in: *Society and Culture in Early Modern France*. Stanford: Stanford University Press, 1975

Dersofi, Nancy. *Arcadia and the Stage: A Study of the Theater of Angelo Beolco*. Madrid: Porrua, 1978.

De Sanctis, G.B., ed. *Pietro Aretino: Tutte le commedie*. Milan: Mursia, 1973.

Ferrante, Lucia. "L'Onore ritrovato: Donne nella casa del soccorso di S. Paolo a Bologna (sec. XVI–XVII)." *Quaderni Storici* 53 (1983): 499–527.

Finlay, Robert. *Politics in Renaissance Venice*. London: Benn, 1980.

Foa, Anna. "The New and the Old: The Spread of Syphilis (1494–1530)," pp. 26–45, in: *Sex and Gender in Historical Perspective*, eds. Edward Muir and Guido Ruggiero. Baltimore and London: The Johns Hopkins University Press, 1990.

Garber, Marjorie. *Vested Interests: Cross-dressing and Cultural Anxiety*. New York: Routledge, 1992.

Gilbert, Felix. "Venice in the Crisis of the League of Cambrai," pp. 274–292, in: *Renaissance Venice*, ed. J.R. Hale, London: Faber and Faber, 1973.

Ginzburg, Carlo. "Tiziano, Ovidio e i codici della figurazione erotica nel '500," pp. 125–35, in: *Tiziano e Venezia: Convegno internazionale di studi*. Venezia 1976. Vicenza: Neri Pozza, 1980.

Hale, J.R., ed. *Renaissance Venice*. London: Faber and Faber, 1973.

Haskell, "Titian: A New Approach?," pp. 41–45, in: *Tiziano e Venezia: Convegno internazionale di studi*. Venezia 1976. Vicenza: Neri Pozza, 1980.

Herlihy, David. "Popolazione e strutture sociali dal XV al XVI secolo," pp. 71–74, in: *Tiziano e Venezia: Convegno internazionale di studi 1976*. Vicenza: Neri Pozza, 1980.

Hughes, Diane Owen. "Sumptuary Law and Social Relations in Renaissance Italy," pp. 60–99, in: *Disputes and Settlements: Law and Human Relations in the West*, ed. John Bossy, Cambridge: Cambridge University Press, 1983.

Jones, Ann Rosalind, and Peter Stallybrass. "Fetishizing Gender: Constructing the Hermaphrodite in Renaissance Europe," pp. 80–111, in: *Body Guards: The Cultural Politics of Gender Ambiguity*, eds. Julia Epstein and Kristina Straub. London and New York: Routledge, 1991.

Klapisch-Zuber, Christine. *Women, Family and Ritual in Renaissance Italy*. Trans. Lydia Cochrane. Chicago: University of Chicago Press, 1985.

Laqueur, Thomas. *Making Sex: Body and Gender from the Greeks to Freud*. Cambridge: Harvard University Press, 1990.

Larivaille, Paul. *La vie quotidienne des courtisanes en Italie au temps de la renaissance*. Paris: Hachette, 1975.

Lawner, Lynne. *Lives of the Courtesans*. New York: Rizzoli, 1987.

Le Goff, Jacques, and Jean-Claude Schmitt, eds. *Le Charivari*. Paris: EHESS, 1981.

Lorenzi, Giovanni Battista, ed. *Leggi e memorie veneta sulla prostituzione fino alla caduta della republica*. Venice, 1870–72.

Lovarini, Emilio. *Studi sul Ruzzante e la letteratura pavana*. Padua: Antenore, 1965.

Molmenti, Pompeo. *La Storia di Venezia nella vita privata*, 3 vols. Second ed. Bergamo, 1919–12.

Muir, Edward. *Civic Ritual in Renaissance Venice*. Princeton: Princeton University Press, 1981.

Muraro, Maria Teresa. "La Festa a Venezia e le sue manifestazioni rappresentative: Le Compagnie della Calza e le sue momarie," pp. 315–41, in: *Storia della cultura veneta 3/III*. Vicenza: Neri Pozza, 1981.

Padoan, Giorgio. *La commedia rinascimentale veneta*. Vicenza: Neri Pozza, 1982.

Pavan, Elisabeth. "Police des moeurs, société et politique à Venise à la fin du Moyen Age." *Revue Historique* 264/2 (1980): 241–88.

Pola Falletti-Villafalletto, C. *Associazioni giovanili e feste antichi: loro origini*. Milan, 1939.

Priuli, Girolamo. *I Diarii*. 5 vols. Eds. G. Carducci et al. Bologna, 1912–33.

Rif, Maria da, ed. *La letteratura alla bulesca: testi rinascimentali veneti*. Padua: Antenore, 1984.

Ruggiero, Guido. *The Boundaries of Eros: Sex Crime and Sexuality in Renaissance Venice*. Oxford: Oxford University Press, 1985.

Santore, Cathy. "Julia Lombardo, 'Sumtuosa Meretrize': A Portrait by Property." *Renaissance Quarterly* 42 (1989): 44–83.

Sanuto, Marin. *I Diarii*. 56 vols. Eds. Rinaldo Fulin et al. Venice, 1879–1903.

Scarabello, Giovanni. "Devianza sessuale ed interventi di giustizia a Venezia nella prima metà del XVI secolo," pp. 75–84, in: *Tiziano e Venezia: convegno internazionale di studi: Venezia 1976*. Vicenza: Neri Pozza, 1980.

Trexler, Richard. "La Prostitution florentine au xve siècle: patronages et clientèles." *Annales* ESC 36, 6 (1981): 983–1015.

Tucci, Ugo. "The Psychology of the Venetian Merchant in the Sixteenth Century," pp. 346–78, in: *Renaissance Venice*, ed. J.R. Hale. London: Faber and Faber, 1973.

Valeri, Diego. "Caratteri e valori del teatro comico," pp. 221–232, in: *Storia della civiltà veneziana*, Vol. 2, ed. Vittore Branca. Florence: Sansoni, 1979.

Venturi, Lionello. "Le compagnie della calza (sec. XV–XVI)." *Nuovo Archivio Veneto* ser. 3, 16 (1908): 161–221, and 17 (1909): 140–233.

Zorzi, Ludovico. *Ruzante: Teatro*. Turin: Einaudi, 1967.

——————. *Il teatro e la città*. Turin: Einaudi, 1977.

3

Imagining Consummation: Women's Erotic Language in Comedies of Dekker and Shakespeare

MARY BLY

Renaissance comedies of love are inherently both erotic and chaste. They must begin with desire in order to lead to marriage; they must end with love in order to qualify as comedy. The whole can be reduced to an echoing formula: "[they] no sooner met but they looked; no sooner looked but they loved … and in these degrees have they made a pair of steps to marriage."[1] The disturbing potential of turning this simple progression into a play has never been ignored. Sixteenth-century critics warned of wanton speeches and lascivious delights; twentieth-century critics delineate the crucial erotic investment that seduces a willing audience. Thus despite the fact that many comedies of the English Renaissance retrace a pattern beginning with love and ending in marriage, very few lovers express physical desire at the same time as love. Although comic plots often revolve around thwarted love, consummation — and explicit reference to it — is generally delayed until the play's conclusion. By endowing lovers with felicitous, wrought descriptions of pure love, an author avoids condemning his characters with the shadow of lust, particularly at issue if a woman is speaking. When it occurs, desiring rhetoric spoken by a woman provides a focus for public anxiety and condemnation.[2] It is exceptional for there to be a sexual encounter within the five acts of a comedy, but it is even rarer for there to be a revelation of desire spoken by a woman.[3] In contrast to comedy, however, Renaissance tragedy manipulates these anxieties, often using a woman's invitation and the ensuing sexual act as the prelude to death. When, in Dekker's *Lust's Dominion* [1600], his lascivious Queen calls to her black lover Eleazar "Come let's kisse ... In my all-naked arms, thy self shalt lie" [I.i.14,60], the audience knows that the Queen's lust will be punished. Dekker's Queen compounds the sexual guilt of Shakespeare's Desdemona: the love affair is both interracial and adulterous. The play is able to dramatize the Queen's cajolery precisely because of its subtitle: "A Tragedie." A comedy cannot allow such a fall from rectitude into lust; it is difficult to refashion a lecherous woman into the chaste model demanded by patriarchy. Playwrights often address this problem by effecting a rapid repentance at the end of a play. In *Lust's Dominion* the Queen's son is able to announce that he will "with Comick joy ... end a Tragedie," due to the Queen's recantation in Act V, Scene 6. Such a capricious turn to remorse transforms a tragedy into a tragicomedy, essentially by allowing piety to redeem a condemned woman.[4]

But there are several comedies, written around 1600, that experiment with a female expression of desire not answered either by death or repentence. Shakespeare's Helena in *All's Well that Ends Well* [1604] is a master of Petrarchan idiom, yet her initial sonnet-like revelation of love for a "bright particular star" is immediately followed by a jest regarding her virginity: "How might one do, sir, to lose it to her own liking?" a question far from lyrical chastity [I.i.147]. Helena's blunt demand for "what law doth vouch mine own" expresses a desire literally unspeakable in Petrarchan simile. For the most part, lovers in comedies clothe desire in extravagant phrases distilled from Petrarch. The use of Petrarchan code turns the lover's rhetoric to a mannered display of idealization, sustained by reiterations of female beauty.[5] So Fontinelle in Dekker's *Blurt, Master Constable* [1602] sees Violetta and cries: "her glorious eyes / Can make as lightsome as the fairest chamber / In Paris Louvre: come, captivitie, / And chaine me to her lookes" [I.i.165–8].[6] At the same time, the code's limited stock of conceits — physical in that they refer to body parts (such as eyes), but wholly uncorporal in that they eschew erotic desire — prohibits any sexual coloring. Yet like Helena, Imperia in *Blurt, Master Constable* does not use the distancing language of Petrarchan verse when she invites Fontinelle: "come, come, come; will you condemne the mute rushes to be prest to death, by your sweet body? downe, downe, downe, heere, heere, heere" [V.ii.21–3].[7] Imperia's words deliberately evoke action; the audience is directed to imagine consummation.

In Shakespeare's and Dekker's two comedies, the heroines insistently pursue a sexual encounter to the point of trickery. Both comedies follow similar lines: a maiden obstinately marries the man she chooses, her young husband importunes another woman, a bed-trick is enacted by the deserted wife, and the husband turns abruptly from the woman he desired to the wife now confronting him. Both plays deliberately juxtapose Petrarchan rhetoric, bawdy jokes and a recusant female stubbornness in matters of sexuality; both are laden with sexual language, foregrounding women whose desiring voices are not quelled by repentance. Unlike the transformative ending of *Lust's Dominion*, at the close of *Blurt, Master Constable* Imperia refuses a proffered marriage and remains brazenly unrepentant. Violetta and Helena, on the other hand, manage secretly to consummate the marriages they demanded. Since their desire is not subdued, the plays are marked by that experiment with female erotic rhetoric: they may also be destroyed by it.

All's Well that Ends Well and *Blurt, Master Constable* represent the height of a localized experiment in English comedy: that of presenting "lascivious Scenes" as explicitly as possible, while at the same time guarding the desiring woman from wholesale condemnation.[8] The result does not produce an oasis of feminist heroines. Dekker and Shakespeare experiment not with female rebellion *per se* but with sexual daring in general. Both plays probably date between 1602 and 1604; by 1606, the Prologue to *The Woman Hater* warns "If there be any amongst you, that come to heare lascivious Scenes, let them depart: for I doe pronounce this ... you shall have no bawdrie in it."[9] The experiment centers on attempts to manipulate the audience by dramatizing desire as clearly as love. Petrarchan rhetoric dispenses information at the same time as adoration; the lover tells us (the audience) as much as he tells his beloved (who often is not within earshot of his or her protestations). The potentially seductive effect on the audience of watching a less informative, but more sexually explicit scene was not lost to playwrights and theater critics.[10] Dramatists circumscribed seductive potential by marking the relation as an example of wickedness. That explicit condemnation allows relationships condemned as incestuous, adulterous or interracial to be more sensual; by punishing a lascivious woman, the playwright is able to portray her behavior. Thus the most provocative and sensual scenes on the Renaissance stage are nearly all found within tragic relationships — Ford's Giovanni crying "Kiss me, so; thus hung Jove on Leda's neck" or Marston's Isabella, "Thus will I clip thy waist, embrace thee thus: / Thus dally with thy hair, and kiss thee thus."[11] Within a tragic provenance, explicit references to sexual dalliance (especially as in these examples, obviously directing the actors' movements) are judged to lose their transgressive qualities through social condemnation. So Isabella's "diseased lust" is fiercely reconstructed as an example: "Their pleasure like a sea groundless and wide, / A woman's lust was never satisfied" [IV.ii.82–3]. After her repeated, explicit seductions, Marston's tale of Isabella ends primly: "She died deservedly, and may like fate / Attend all women so insatiate" [V.ii.230–1].

Thus the experimental quality of the two comedies I am discussing, *Blurt,
Master Constable* and *All's Well that Ends Well*, lies less in their free-speaking
heroines (neither of whom approaches the explicitness of Marston's Isabella),
but in the fact that these women occur in a comic framework. Neither play
condemns the woman who expresses desire; neither follows the pattern of
containment of lust through condemnation. I would argue that the experiment
of the early 1600s with erotic rhetoric is brief due to this nonconformity; by
1610 desiring heroines appear in tragicomedies and tragedies, but not in
comedies. Shakespeare's plays after this period grow notoriously chaste:
Perdita and Miranda exhibit none of Helena's — or even Juliet's — spoken
desire. In comedy, sexual desire may not be contemptible, as in tragedy, but
it is disrespectable. The line between "diseased lust" and untarnished chastity
is a clearly demarcated part of most Renaissance plots; the effort to breach
that line — to allow a female character an improper thought and plan — was
an extremely difficult one. Possibly as a result, *All's Well that Ends Well*
suffers from the opprobium of being a "problem play," and *Blurt, Master
Constable* has seemingly been read only as a cynical denunciation of the
possibility of true love.[12] I suggest that the problem lies in the characterization
of Dekker's and Shakespeare's women, particularly in the conjunction of
Petrarchan verse and openly expressed sexual intention.

Blurt, Master Constable begins in a placidly Petrarchan vein. Fontinelle,
a French prisoner, is ceremoniously delivered to Violetta by her admirer
Camillo. Fontinelle immediately falls in love with Violetta and she responds
as impetuously. Later he is imprisoned by Violetta's brother and in Act IV
the lovers are secretly married by a Friar. The first act, I would argue, is
deliberately hackneyed in its portrayal of young love: Violetta and Fontinelle
are enemies by nation, meet at a banquet and dance, fall in love to the tune
of Petrarchan idiom. Camillo yields Fontinelle to be "beauties worthy
prisoner," a cliché redoubled by Fontinelle's courtly rejoicing at being
"beauties thrall." Commonplaces give way to bombast: Violetta declares
herself slave to Fontinelle and he cries "Oh what a heaven is love! oh what
a hell!" closing the first scene [I.i.214]. Essentially the dance is a Petrarchan
fest, underscored by overstatements and worn-out oxymorons: "Such beautie
be my Jaylor? a heavenly hell!" [I.i.163].

The parallels with Romeo and Juliet are unmistakable, even to the extent
of explicit paraphrase.[13] Camillo at the banquet steals from Romeo at the
dance:

> And of Beautie what tongue would not speake the best, since it is the
> Jewell that hangs upon the brow of heaven, the best cullor that can be
> laide upon the cheeke of earth? [I.i.90–93]

and Romeo:

It seems she hangs upon the cheek of the night
As a rich jewel in an Ethiop's ear —
Beauty too rich for use. [I.v.44–6]

Shakespeare's play juxtaposes rhapsody and sexual puns; the moonlit balcony is balanced by Mercutio's wish that "she were / An open-arse and thou a poperin pear!" [II.ii.37–8]. But in *Romeo and Juliet* bawdy witticisms are confined for the most part to secondary characters — the Nurse teases Juliet, but Juliet herself cloaks anticipation in simile:

Come night, come Romeo, come thou day in night,
For thou wilt lie upon the wings of night
Whiter than new snow upon a raven's back. [III.ii.17–9]

She remains, even in her directness, untouched by ribald vulgarity or lustful punning. Although she clearly longs for Romeo "to leap to these arms," her thoughts are not physically explicit: "O, I have bought the mansion of a love / But not possess'd it, and though I am sold, / Not yet enjoy'd" [III.ii.26–8].[14]

In *Blurt, Master Constable*, on the other hand, Mercutian ribaldry overtakes every character, including the heroine. The Petrarchan lyricism of the first act is upstaged by eroticized rhetoric. The play opens with Violetta's brother saying "I Mary Sir, the onely rising up in Armes, is in the armes of a woman... I have seene more mens heades spurn'd up and downe like foote-balles ... than are Maiden-heads in Venice" [I.i.1–2,21–2,24].[15] Violetta responds in kind: "I doe not thinke for all this, that my brother stood to it so lustilie as he makes his brags for" [I.i.30–1]. Unlike Juliet, she has not the sheltered innocence of adolescence, and rather than engaging in a sonnet with Fontinelle, she breaks off their dance: "I have, on the sodaine a foolish desire to be out of the measure." "What breeds that desire?" asks Camillo. "Nay I hope it is no breeding matter: tush, tush, by my maiden-head I will not" [I.i.171–5]. Violetta is explicitly neither maidenly nor sexually delicate. On falling in love she is ruthlessly possessive: "no, no, my French prisoner; I will use thee Cupid knowes how, and teach thee to fall into the hands of a woman: if I doe not feede thee with faire lookes, nere let me live: if thou getst out of my fingers til I have thy verie heart, nere let me love" [I.i.194–8].[16] Whereas Juliet mislikes a contract so rashly entered into, Violetta announces she will lock Fontinelle's "wanton eye" into a small room until he succumbs. Her language is gloriously rough. After Fontinelle is imprisoned by Camillo, she shouts at her brother, "Harke, tosse-pot in your eare, the French-man's mine, / And by these hands Ile have him" [III.i.157–8]. She combines disrespect with risqué insinuation: "I love a life to heare a man speake French / Of his complection: I would under-goe / The instruction of that language rather far, / Than be two weekes unmaried"[III.i.165–8]. Hippolytus's language to her has the pruriently vicious tone of Ferdinand's to the Dutchess of Malfi: "You scurvey Tyt ... doe you heare Susanna: you puncke, if I geld not your Muske-Cat" [III.i.152–4]. Her brother's language incorporates lurid imagination and anger. He harangues the boy who has been arranging meetings between the lovers: "Ist you Sir Pandarus, the broking Knight of Troy? are your two legs the paire of tressels, for the French-man to get up upon my Sister?" [II.i.118–20]. We have, then, a heroine given the boldness — and addressed with the sexual explicitness — elsewhere reserved for widows.[17] Even more remarkably, Violetta, the Petrarchan focus of the play, is deliberately provided with a double: the courtesan Imperia. The two women are linked by context, similar language, Fontinelle's love for both, and most damningly, parallel desire.

Imperia, like Violetta, falls in love with Fontinelle at first sight (although she sees only his picture). Just as Violetta mused on Fontinelle's physical attributes ("a very pretty French man; the carriage of his bodie likes me well" [I.i.188–9]), Imperia anatomizes his features:

> A little face, but a lovely face; fye, fye, fye, no matter what face he make, so the other parts be Legittimate, and goe upright ... as I live I must love thee, and sucke kisses from thy lips. [II.ii.131–3,137–8]

She too decides to marry him, resolving if he should refuse her, he must become her Ganymede. Violetta, as we have seen, swears by her maidenhood and is surrounded by talk of lost maidenheads. Imperia, on the other hand, characteristically swears by her virginity. Hippolito addresses both women as "puncke." Fontinelle is torn between the two. Seeing Violetta, he loves her; confronted by Imperia, he again falls violently in love. In the minute before he is fetched by Violetta to his marriage, Fontinelle is informed by Imperia's page that his mistress waits for him to "play a game at noddy." When Fontinelle promises on his honor to attend her, Frisco remarks that "she does not greatlie care whether you fall to her upon your honour, or no" [III.ii.8–9]. Thus minutes before his marriage Fontinelle finds himself contemplating a liaison with Imperia:

> shall I prophane
> This Temple [the monastery] with an Idole of strange love?
> When I doe so, let me dissolve in fire;
> Yet one day will I see this Dame. [III.ii.15–8]

No matter which woman Fontinelle addresses, he does so in Petrarchan verse. So he responds to Imperia in his customary vein: "Shoote home (faire Mistris) and as that kisse flyes, / From lip to lip, wound me with your sharpe eyes" [V.ii.29–30]. In the last act he defends his (supposed) night with the courtesan: "who dyes / For so bright beauty, is a bright Sacrifice," and returns to language virtually identical to that which he applied to Violetta in scene 1: "She is my heaven; she from me, I am in hell" [V.iii.77–8,83].

As in many Renaissance plays, the passage of time in *Blurt, Master Constable* is highly confused. How much time lapses between the banquet and Fontinelle's imprisonment, between the scene of his marriage (III.ii) and the beginning of Act V? Camillo opens the last act vowing revenge:

> he hath dar'd to adde the sweet theft of Ignoble marriage; shee's now, nones but his, and hee (treacherous villaine) any ones, but hers; hee dotes (my honor'd friends) on a painted Curtizan, and in scorne of our Italian lawes, our familie, our revenge, loathes Violettaes bed for a harlots bosome. [V.i.7–12]

Camillo's anger, directed at one who loaths Violetta's bed, implies that their marriage sanctioned entrance into that bed, as does the Duke's rebuke in the last scene: "The beautie you adore so is prophane, / The breach of wedlocke (by our law) is death" [V.iii.79–80]. Yet it is not clear whether the marriage was ever consummated. The scene between Imperia and Fontinelle (V.ii) does not explicate this confusion. Fontinelle waxes rhapsodic about his newest beloved:

> Deare Ladie, o life of love, what sweetnes dwels
> In loves varietie? the soule that plods
> In one harsh booke of beautie but repeates
> The stale and tedious learning that hath oft
> Faded the sences: when (in reading more)
> We glide in new sweets, and are starv'd with store. [V.ii.8–13]

He calls his wife a foul weed, a black negro by comparison with Imperia: "O most accurst! / That I have given her leave to challenge me" (a reference to his marriage) [V.ii.17–18]. A.H. Bullen argues that the play might be missing a scene in which the lovers agree to use Imperia's bed to consummate their marriage, but the evidence against this interpretation is weighty [Bullen: xxii–xxiii]. Not only does Fontinelle contemplate a visit to the courtesan before his marriage to Violetta, but his wife expresses jealousy of Imperia by the third act. Fontinelle's speech above, praising diversity, gives no indication of such a rental agreement; neither do the kisses they exchange. Even more indicative is Violetta's attitude when she arrives at Imperia's house looking for her husband: "good faith I doe not blame him, for your beautie glides over his error" [V.ii.104–5]. Violetta then persuades Imperia to allow her to join Fontinelle in the courtesan's bed where "(in supposed follie) he may end / Determin'd sinne" [V.ii.128–9].[18] This persuasion — and the Courtesan's agreement — would of course be unnecessary if a rental agreement had been negotiated. Pulled out of bed by an enraged Camillo and Hippolytus, Fontinelle declares his willingness to die for Imperia, a statement with no logic if he knew the woman in his bed was in fact his wife. Violetta then unmasks and announces that she and Fontinelle hired the house together. The untruth of her ploy is patently revealed by Fontinelle's reaction:

> O sweetest Violet; I blush —
>
> Vio: Good signe,
> Weare still that maiden blush, but still be mine.
> Fon: I seale my selfe thine owne, with both my hands. [V.iii.119–121]

Had the lovers planned the liaison together, the play would be missing the bed-trick we see revealed above. Fontinelle blushes because he did not know until that moment that the woman with whom he lodged in the back room was not Imperia, but Violetta.

At the heart, both *All's Well that Ends Well* and *Blurt, Master Constable* speak to the magic of the bed-trick — the substitution of one body for the expected lover. Violetta, requesting that she, rather than Imperia, join Fontinelle in the back room: "lodge me in thy private bed, / Where (in supposed follie) he may end / Determin'd sinne" [V.ii.127–9], is sister to Helena, who anticipates "wicked meaning in a lawful deed, / And lawful meaning in a lawful act" [III.vii.45–6]. Bed-tricks generally fall into the provenance of fairy stories and Italian novelle. They are contrived with a clear objective, often impregnation as in Boccaccio's story of Giletta of Narbonne, Shakespeare's source for *All's Well that Ends Well*.[19] Yet fairy tales retain a romantic sweetness which Shakespeare and Dekker discard. Such tales have a self-contained timelessness and evade the explicit:

> The next evening the [disguised] wife ... told the prince that she would send him a beautiful female slave. Retiring to her tent, she then assumed that disguise and came back to her husband. He was inflamed with love for the supposed slave and lay that night with her. [Qtd. in Lawrence: 68]

In fairy tales, intercourse is a spare factual occurrence; the motivation, the exchange and the event itself can be told in the same sentence. Essentially, they rely on an evasion of explicit reference similar to that employed by Petrarchan rhetoric. The conclusion of Boccaccio's tale provides a particularly good example of the assumptions of genre: the final paragraph is fable shorthand, an expected, rounded ending coming after the individuality of the clever tale itself. In William Painter's translation [1575], the husband "abjected his obstinate rigour, causing her to rise up, and embraced and kissed her ... and from that time hee loved and honoured her as his dere spouse and wyfe" [Bullough: 396]. In endings such as this, the body of creativity is assumed by the crafty plot, and the end reverts to generic expectation. Problematic aspects of the substitution and the miraculous declaration of love by an erring husband are dismissed. The audience assumes that love will appear and thus it does not need to be believable. Consummation guarantees that the husband will express love; the sexual act itself takes on a magical efficacity, a control over the man's emotions.

Both Dekker's and Shakespeare's transformations of the simple clarity of a fairy tale depend on emphasizing the suggestiveness behind the bed-trick, keeping basic events untouched, but adding a leavening catalyst of sexual detail. Whereas Dekker makes Violetta both bold and further emboldened by her doubled position with Imperia, Shakespeare continuously forces Helena to express a physical awareness of Bertram. Helena is the lynchpin on which Shakespeare's interpretation of the fairy tale depends, and she is both singularly talkative about sex and brilliantly Petrarchan in her language.[20] As noted above, in the first scene Helena's lyrical ability — "he is so above me. / In his bright radiance and collateral light / Must I be comforted" — is coldly juxtaposed with her intention to lose her virginity to her own liking [I.i.85-7]. The language of this first scene is very sexual: "'Tis pity—" says Helena, "That wishing well had not a body in't / Which might be felt" [I.i.175-8]. The scene between Parolles and Helena is one which debunks a traditional heroine's behavior; her buoyant responses to Parolles wittily defend her virginal status, but not in a coldly chaste and unawakened fashion.[21] Her wish is "To join like likes, and kiss like native things" [I.i.219]. Shakespeare has created a heroine with a demanding and explicit relation to the man she chooses to marry, very similar to Violetta's. As in Dekker's play, an accompaniment of minor characters — the Clown, Parolles, Lafew, the Dumain brothers — contribute to an ongoing sexual commentary. Incidental details are bawdy in themselves: Parolles's declaration that one Lord was a "botcher's prentice in Paris, from whence he was whipp'd for getting the shrieve's fool with child, a dumb innocent that could not say him nay," and the Clown's quibbles with "old lings" and Isbells of the country and court [IV.iii.180-3]. Similarly, subplots bolster the sexual current of *Blurt, Master Constable*, most remarkably in Lazarillo's importuning of Imperia: "Venus, give me sucke, from thine owne most white and tender dugs, that I may batten in love" [II.ii.308-9]. And, as Dekker's play focuses in the end not on the illicit marriage but on the scorning of the marital bed, so *All's Well* constantly returns its focus to consummation as the cornerstone of marriage. Virtually every character in *All's Well that Ends Well*, from Helena and Parolles to the Countess and King, is drawn into an erotic commentary on the story. Boccaccio's tale has multiplied from a fable-like singularity to a wealth of suggestive characterizations, from a King made "Lustick" by a virgin's magic, to a hero who is "a whale to virginity" and a heroine who marvels at the "sweet use" men make "of what they hate."

Bertram's verdict after his marriage is immediate sexual refusal: "I will not bed her ... I'll to the Tuscan wars and never bed her" [II.iii.266; 269]. Parolles answers in proper vein: "He wears his honour in a box unseen / That hugs his kicky-wicky here at home / Spending his manly marrow in her arms" [II.iii.275-7]. Parolles, leaving the scene in which Bertram has determined never to bed Helena, says "A young man married is a man that's marr'd. /

Therefore away, and leave her bravely; go" [II.iii.294–5]. Yet Parolles in fact becomes the mouthpiece acknowledging the conjugal bliss which should belong to Helena: "The great prerogative and rite of love, / Which as your due time claims, he does acknowledge, / But puts it off to a compell'd restraint" [II.iv.39–41]. Bertram tells Helena herself not to marvel that he does not fulfil his "ministration and required office" [II.v.60]. Helena's response is to ask for a kiss, again a demand for sexual demonstration: "most fain would steal, / What law does vouch mine own" [II.v.81–2]. The complex relations entwined around Helena's legal right to consummation make love seem a literary commonplace, celebrated by Helena's vaunting and lucid verse, yet even in her most poetic revelation, tainted by a covetous note: "Th'ambition in my love thus plagues itself: / The hind that would be mated by the lion / Must die for love" [I.i.88–90].

What emerges is a powerful erotic undercurrent — the question of who will "[flesh] his will" in the spoil of another's honour. Will Bertram, that "dangerous and lascivious boy," cure his "sick desires" with Diana or will Helena, as Bertram sees it, trick him into bed? The reasoning behind sexual acts comes up over and over again: "Loss of virginity is rational increase," Parolles tells Helena [I.i.125] and Bertram rebukes Diana: "now you should be as your mother was / When your sweet self was got." But Diana points out, "My mother did but duty" [Iv.ii.9–10,12]. When Bertram rejects his (supposed) sexual relations with Diana as nothing more than an encounter with "a common gamester to the camp," he abolishes the assumption that a consummated relationship must be a loving one:

> Certain it is I lik'd her,
> And boarded her i' th' wanton way of youth ...
>   she got the ring,
> And I had that which any inferior might
> At market-price have bought. [V.iii.209–10;216–8]

The fact that Bertram, in the last scene, declares that he earlier had "stuck [his] choice" on Lafew's daughter, and when requested hands over the ring Diana gave him, as a favour "to sparkle in the spirits" of that daughter, remorselessly undermines the expected fairy tale closure, so weakly resolved by his couplet: "If she, my liege, can make me know this clearly / I'll love her dearly, ever, ever dearly" [V.iii.309–10].

The simple plot-line of a love story, then, has been embroidered with conscious carnal knowledge, a duality clear in the text itself. We can see it in Helena's plea to the Countess:

> My dearest madam ... if yourself,
> Whose aged honour cites a virtuous youth,
> Did ever, in so true a flame of liking,

> Wish chastely and love dearly, that your Dian
> Was both herself and love — O then, give pity [I.iii.202,204–8]

Helena's "flame of liking," in other words, is both that of Diana, goddess of virginity, and of Eros, god of erotic love.[22] She makes this even clearer when she chooses her husband: "Now, Dian, from thy altar do I fly, / And to imperial Love, that god most high / Do my sighs stream" [II.iii.74–6]. Significantly, Diana the maiden guards her virginity; Helena, substituted for that maiden, does not. For Helena, intercourse seems to be the primary reason for marriage, whether accompanied on both sides by romantic love or not. She "would be mated by the lion"; without consummation, she is "but the shadow of a wife ... The name and not the thing" [I.i.89; V.iii.301–2].

Violetta's bed-trick, like Helena's, is explicitly linked to the heroine's physical desire for her husband. Her exchange has even less rationale behind it than Helena's: she has no direct need for impregnation or a ring. The bed-trick is enacted due to her desire. When Violetta pleads with Imperia to allow the exchange to take place, she has no object beyond consummation: "give me leave to love him, and Ile give him a kinde of leave to love thee" [V.ii.115–6]. There is no implication in her words that consummation will magically result in a faithful husband, nor that his love will be bound to the woman he slept with. She swears, in fact, not to scold or "my pennaunce shall bee to see him kisse thee, yet to holde my peace" [V.ii.120–2]. Imperia responds directly to Violetta's ambition: "thou shalt injoy my bed, and thine owne pleasure this night" [V.ii.138–9]. The transgressive element of these two bed-tricks, I would argue, lies precisely in the expression of sexual desire by the women.[23] Helena's determined pursuit of "what law doth vouch mine own," and Violetta's plea to "love him," cast the bed-trick not in the light of a mechanism undertaken to achieve a further object but in the light of one enacted for the pleasure of intercourse itself.

How are we to characterize these comedies? Can they be termed a radical experiment — a bold effort to place on the comic stage women who show sexual desire, pursue consummation, have intercourse during the five acts, and are celebrated at the end? Essentially, are we still in the realm of romantic comedy, a genre insistent on the division between "true love" and disreputable desire? The fact that both husbands, so easily false, rely on Petrarchan verse to seduce various women suggests that the plays may debase that rhetoric in order to devalue the idea of true love. Bertram importunes Diana in Petrarchan terms — "A heaven on earth I have won by wooing thee" [IV.ii.66]. His easy use of Petrarchan idiom parallels Fontinelle's adroit flexibility in the same situation. The purity of Petrarchan idealism is debased by context; Petrarchan rhetoric has become a tool contaminated by proximity to sexual desire. Here the bed-trick is brilliantly self-damning. Pulled from Imperia's bed, Fontinelle breaks into rhapsodic verse. He will die for the woman he thinks to be Imperia, for she has "immortal joyes" in her eyes. Yet the eyes he indicates are the eyes of a different woman. The irony of such empty language may preclude the truth of any emotion other than lust, reducing "love" to a linguistic construct used to manipulate situations governed by sexual desire. The genre slides, then, from romantic comedy into burlesque. Both dramatists' insistence on Helena's and Violetta's physical desire would seem to bolster this generic distinction. In fact, were the two women purely lascivious, the result would certainly be burlesque. The disjunction between professed (Petrarchan) love and lustful desire — between language and emotion — would rule our interpretation of every character. The effect would ensure the audience's scorn, but we are not led to scorn Helena or Violetta. If Fontinelle and Bertram issue compliments in a particularly serial manner, Helena's and Violetta's language is sternly referential. Helena's odd mix of Petrarchan charm, deliberate manipulation, and extraordinary self-knowledge does not lend itself to a judgment of caricature. As G.K. Hunter points out, to fit Helena into the play is a central interpretative problem; neither she nor her love for Bertram can be dismissed: "I am undone; there is no living, none, / If Bertram be away" [I.i.82–3] [Hunter: l]. Similarly, Violetta's response to Imperia's scorn gives weight to her claim to love truly: "What loosenes may terme dotage (*truelie read*) / Is love ripe gather'd, not soone withered" [V.ii.130–1: my emphasis]. Clearly the plays skirt on the edge of burlesque, but neither dramatist allows his heroine to overbalance into pure lust; both are endowed with an earnest, interpretative gift of their own. Because the women claim the ability to "truelie read" the difference between love and lust, they force us to take their claims of love seriously, thereby disqualifying the view that the plays deride the whole idea of romantic love. I would argue that these plays, which are so intently similar in their focus on the bed-trick, script the women's manipulation of that consummation (as opposed to *Measure for Measure*, for example, where the Duke organizes the trick) through an emphasis on the heroines' interpretative stance towards the conventions of romantic love. Violetta insists on her ability to truly read the signs of love; Helena dismantles the conventions of the bed-trick itself:

> strange men!
> That can such sweet use make of what they hate,
> When saucy trusting of the cozen'd thoughts
> Defiles the pitchy night; so lust doth play
> With what it loathes for that which is away. [IV.iv.21–25]

Helena acknowledges in five lines not only her enjoyment of Bertram's "sweet use," but his continued hatred and loathing for her person. She knows, then, that "sweet use" and lust have no magical effect on love; in the last scene she tells Bertram that, disguised as Diana, she found him "wondrous kind." Her frankness is remarkable. When Renaissance heroines discuss their loss of virginity, it is in terms of honor lost, rarely in terms that encompass their enjoyment of that event. Shakespeare has imposed a contemplative gift on his heroine that is incompatible with the generic commitment of fairy tales to the silent marriage-to-sex-to-love progression. Yet both women must be so expressive in order to explain their manipulation of a sexual encounter while remaining romantic heroines. Even as their husbands deflate Petrarchan oaths, Violetta's and Helena's interpretative stance allows them to claim that their own oaths, truly read, fall outside convention and are thus genuine.

Thus these plays on the one hand avoid characterizing their heroines as lustful, and on the other, portray those women as more desiring than is normal in romantic comedy. I would argue that they are able to achieve this due to the dramatic role of the bed-trick. The bed-trick presents a sexual act undertaken by the woman for just, chaste motives. The act of intercourse is cleansed of wanton impact; consummation is allowed on the stage — and in the play — without the threat of an over-seductive effect on the audience. Dekker's and Shakespeare's experiment in comic eroticism is fundamentally reliant on the presence of the bed-trick, which navigates between the extremes of chastity and lust. Because this convention carries with it certain assumptions, namely the purity of the woman's intentions and the ensuing love of the man, the dramatists were able to allow Helena and Violetta an explicitly desiring presence on the stage. Yet I would also suggest that the very mechanism which allowed that frankness is defeated by it. Because these plays focus so acutely on the expression of sexual desire, the bed-trick is no longer reducible to a prank, praiseworthy for its cunning trickery. Instead, it takes on a shadowy sexuality, an erotic weight of its own. The bed-trick alters its tone with its context; when decorum is lost, our delight in the trick is lost. The audience's imagination turns to "sweet use" in the "pitchy night," to Imperia's promise of "thine owne pleasure." A play pervaded by desire, and denied the rapid magic of instantaneous Petrarchan love, sits uneasily in the genre of romantic comedy. When the simplicity of the bed-trick is dispelled, so too is dispelled the efficacy of its finish — the ready promise of true love by the deceived husband.

NOTES

1. William Shakespeare, *As You Like It*, V.ii.31–32;35–36.
2. A point that has been thoroughly addressed. See Valerie Traub, who addresses the erotic component of male anxiety; Coppelia Kahn, who traces problems of desire to changing conceptions of Eve; and Clifford Davidson, who discusses the fear of emasculation bred by sexually demanding females.

3. Carol Neely's argument that convention in romantic comedies acts to "contain sexuality and ... mitigate its threatening aspects" is very interesting in this regard. Neely: 61. Paula S. Berggren points out that Shakespeare rarely writes a scene delineating female sexual longing. It should be noted, however, that there were in fact few love comedies written before 1590 (see Jensen).

4. By tragicomedies, I refer to plays in which a plot leading to death is almost magically coerced into a comic ending. I think, for example, of *The Laws of Candy*, in which Erota passionately importunes Antonius, but ends by disclaiming her "too passionate thoughts." Characters such as Erota are transformed rather than reformed, a standard practice in Fletcherian tragicomedies. For "sexualized" tragicomedy, see McLuskie.

5. My truncated summary of "Petrarchan" refers to its use as an idiom within a larger discourse, a fragment of Petrarchan verse as used in a play, rather than in a Petrarchan sonnet. See Evans; Jones and Stallybrass; Vickers. See Leonard Foster for a discussion of the Petrarchan rejection of sexual implication (as opposed, for example, to the explicit sexuality of troubadour genres).

6. Critical opinion now gives this play to Dekker, not Middleton. See Lake: 66–90.

7. Imperia's "downe, downe, downe" is reiterated by another courtesan two years later. Bellafronte in *The Honest Whore* I, a play on which Dekker and Middleton collaborated, sings "Downe, downe, downe, downe, I fall downe, and arise I neuer shall" [II.i.27].

8. Catherine Belsey argues that *Edward II* [1592] attempts much the same experiment, except that the desire is not female but, even more problematically, homosexual. Zimmerman: 84–102.

9. 1602–04 is a tentative range; I employ the the dates suggested in G.K. Hunter's introduction to *All's Well that Ends Well* and Thomas Leland Burger's introduction to *Blurt, Master Constable*. Francis Beaumont and John Fletcher, *The Woman-Hater*. ll.3–6.

10. See Boose; Belsey; and Howard, "Sex and Social Conflict," for discussions of plays which attempt to breach dramatic conventions regarding the staging of erotic scenes.

11. John Ford, *'Tis Pity She's a Whore* [II.i.16]; John Marston, *The Insatiate Countess* [IV.iii.240–1]. The rhetoric of Alice in *Arden of Feversham* [1592] and Tamara in *Titus Andronicus* [1592] further exemplify the seductiveness allowable in a doomed relationship.

12. Bains: 41–57; Berger's introduction to *Blurt, Master Constable*: 37–42.

13. For example, Fontinelle refuses to dance: "bid him whose heart no sorrow feeles / Tickle the rushes with his wanton heeles" [I.i.181–2], whereas Romeo lets "wantons light of heart / Tickle the senseless rushes with their heels" [I.iv.35–36]. The links between Fontinelle and Romeo are especially interesting: both men, dazzled by Petrarchan hyperbole, apply similar rhetoric to successive women. On Romeo's use of Petrarch, see Gayle Whittier's excellent study of *Romeo and Juliet*.

14. For Juliet's mannered speech, see Mertner; Snow; Estrin.

15. This is a pun Dekker also uses in the masque *The Sun's Darling*. II.i.208–9 reads "Com then, let thou and I rise up in arms / The field embraces, kisses our alarms." Qtd. in Lake: 76–77.

16. In an article otherwise flawed by misreadings, Yashdip Bains points out that "feeds" has a bawdy connotation. He cites Shakespeare's Venus: "Feed where thou wilt, on mountain or in dale: / Graze on my lips, and if these hills be dry, / Stray lower, where the pleasant fountains lie." Qtd. in Bains: 55.

17. Widows are regularly characterized as more subject to impropriety than virgins. An obvious example is the Dutchess of Malfi; I would also point to the characterization of Isabella in *The Insatiate Countess* and that of Gertrude in *Hamlet*. Comedies are also replete with widows accused of lustful dealings: Lady Hartwell in Fletcher's *Wit Without Money*, and Cynthia in Chapman's *The Widow's Tears* are good examples.

18. In A.H. Bullen's defense, the text is clearly corrupt. At one point Violetta says "I know he heer's me," but in the next breath she begs to enter the bed secretly, thereby ending Fontinelle's "sinne."

19. See Simonds and Honigman for discussions of bed-tricks occuring in a variety of genres. Robert S. Forsythe lists 21 bed-tricks in extant English plays; it is interesting to note that only *one* bed-trick is earlier than 1602 (Grim's *The Collier*, 1576); all 20 follow *All's Well that Ends Well*. He does not mention *Blurt, Master Constable*. 330–331.

20. See Brooke: 12–13 who argues that Shakespeare allows the "natural" to govern the romance plot, and Hunter: xlix–l who analyzes Helena as a fairy tale heroine incompatible with a realistic setting. Richard Levin attempts to settle the argument about Helena's character by portraying her as a cruel and effective schemer.

21. Lisa Jardine writes of this scene that Helena betrays herself as too "knowing" for the innocent virgin she professes to be, linking sexual unruliness to Helena's position as a learned woman. Susan Snyder approaches Helena's indecorous speech by suggesting that her "peculiar situation" as a locus of active desire may be complicated by implicit reference to Helen of Troy.

22. David McCandless discusses the "simultaneous heightening of Helena's sexuality and chastity," arguing that the two are not in opposition, but complementary.

23. Janet Adelman sees the bed-trick as the center of the *All's Well* problem, arguing that it reveals a deep ambivalence towards female sexuality. Adelman: 78–86.

WORKS CITED

Adelman, Janet. *Suffocating Mothers*. London: Rouledge, 1992.

Bains, Yashdip. "Thomas Middleton's *Blurt, Master Constable* as a Burlesque on Love." *Essays Presented to Amy G. Stock*, ed. R.K. Kaul. Jaipur: Rajasthan University Press, 1965, 41–57.

Beaumont, Francis, and John Fletcher. *The Woman-Hater*, ed. George Walton Williams. *The Dramatic Works in the Beaumont and Fletcher Canon*, I, ed. Fredson Bowers. Cambridge University Press, 1966.

Belsey, Catherine. "Desire's Excess and the English Renaissance Theatre: *Edward II, Troilus & Cressida, Othello*." Zimmerman: 84–102.

Berggren, Paula S. "The Woman's Part: Female Sexuality as Power in Shakespeare's Plays." *The Woman's Part: Feminist Criticism of Shakespeare*, eds. Carolyn Lenz et al. University of Illinois Press, 1980, 17–34.

Boose, Lynda. "Let it be hid: Renaissance Pornography, Iago, and Audience Response." *Autour d'Othello*, eds. Richard Marienstras and Dominique Goy-Blanquet. Université Picardie, 1987, 135–143.

Brooke, Nicholas. "*All's Well That Ends Well*," *Aspects of Shakespeare's Problem Plays*, eds. Kenneth Muir and Stanley Wells. Cambridge University Press, 1982.

Bullen, A.H. Introduction to *Blurt, Master Constable. The Works of Thomas Middleton*, I. New York: AMS Press, 1964, xi–xciii.

Bullough, Geoffrey, ed. *Narrative and Dramatic Sources of Shakespeare*, III. London: Routledge & Kegan Paul, 1968.

Davidson, Clifford. "*Antony and Cleopatra*: Circe, Venus, and the Whore of Babylon." *Shakespeare: Contemporary Critical Approaches*, ed. Harry R. Garvin. Lewisburg: Bucknell University Press, 1980, 31–55.

Dekker, Thomas. *A Critical Old-Spelling Edition of Thomas Dekker's Blurt, Master Constable (1602)*, ed. Thomas Leland Berger. Austria: Salzburg Institute, 1979.

_____. *Lust's Dominion or, the Lascivious Queen. Dramatic Works of Thomas Dekker*, IV, ed. Fredson Bowers. Cambridge University Press, 1961.

Dekker, Thomas, and Thomas Middleton. *The Honest Whore*, Pt. I. *Dramatic Works of Thomas Dekker*, II, ed. Fredson Bowers. Cambridge University Press, 1961.

Estrin, Barbara. "Romeo, Juliet and the Art of Naming Love." *Ariel* 12 (1981): 31–49.

Evans, Malcolm. "'In Love with Curious Words': Signification and Sexuality in English Petrarchism." *Jacobean Poetry and Prose*, ed. Clive Bloom. London: Macmillan, 1988, 119–150.

Ford, John. *'Tis Pity She's a Whore*, ed. Derek Roper. Manchester University Press, 1975.

Forster, Leonard. *The Icy Fire*. Cambridge University Press, 1969.

Forsythe, Robert S. *The Relations of Shirley's Plays to the Elizabethan Drama*. Columbia University Press, 1914.

Honigmann, E.A.J. "Shakespeare's Mingled Yarn and 'Measure for Measure.'" *Proceedings of the British Academy* 67 (1981): 101–121.

Howard, Jean E. "The Difficulties of Closure: An Approach to the Problematic in Shakespearean Comedy." *Comedy from Shakespeare to Sheridan*, eds. A.R. Braunmuller and J.C. Bulman. University of Delaware Press, 1986, 113–130.

_____. "Sex and Social Conflict: the Erotics of *The Roaring Girl*." Zimmerman: 170–190.

Hunter, G.K. Introduction to *All's Well that Ends Well*. London: Methuen, 1959, xi–lix.

Jardine, Lisa. "Cultural Confusion and Shakespeare's Learned Heroines: 'These are old paradoxes.'" *Shakespeare Quarterly* 38 (1987): 1–18.

Jensen, Ejner J. "The Changing Faces of Love in English Renaissance Comedy." *Comparative Drama* 6 (1972): 294–309.

Jones, Ann Rosalind, and Peter Stallybrass. "The Politics of *Astrophil and Stella*." *Studies in English Literature* 24 (1984): 53–68.

Kahn, Coppélia. "Whores and Wives in Jacobean Drama." *In Another Country: Feminist Perspectives on Renaissance Drama*, eds. Dorothea Kehlen and Susan Baker. New Jersey: Scarecrow Press, 1991, 246–260.

Lake, David. *The Canon of Thomas Middleton's Plays*. Cambridge University Press, 1965.

Lawrence, W.W. *Shakespeare's Problem Comedies*. London: Penguin, 1969.

Levin, Richard A. "*All's Well that Ends Well* and 'All Seems Well.'" *Shakespeare Studies* XIII (1980): 131–144.

Marston, John et al. *The Insatiate Countess*, ed. Giorgio Melchiori. Manchester University Press, 1984.

McCandless, David. "'That Your Dian / Was Both Herself and Love': Helena's Redemptive Chastity." *Essays in Literature* 17 (1990): 160–178.

McLuskie, Kathleen. *Renaissance Dramatists*. Herfordshire, Eng: Harvester Wheatsheaf, 1989.

Mertner, Edgar. "'Conceit Brags of His Substance, Not of Ornament': Some Notes on Style in *Romeo and Juliet*." *Shakespeare: Text, Language, Criticism*, eds. Bernhard Fabian and Kurt Tetzeli von Rosador. New York: Olms-Weidmann, 1987, 180–192.

Neely, Carol Thomas. *Broken Nuptials in Shakespeare's Plays*. Yale University Press, 1985.

Shakespeare, William. *All's Well That Ends Well*, ed. G.K. Hunter. London: Methuen. 1959.

——————. *As You Like It*, ed. Agnes Latham. London: Methuen, 1975.

——————. *Romeo & Juliet*, ed. Brian Gibbons. London: Methuen, 1980.

Simonds, Peggy Munoz. "Overlooked Sources of the Bed Trick." *Shakespeare Quarterly* 34 (1983): 433–434.

Snow, Edward. "Language and Sexual Difference in *Romeo and Juliet*." *Shakespeare's 'Rough Magic': Essays in Honor of C.L. Barber*, eds. Peter Erickson and Coppélia Kahn. University of Delaware Press, 1985, 168–92.

Snyder, Susan. "*All's Well that Ends Well* and Shakespeare's Helens: Text and Subtext, Subject and Object." *English Literary Renaissance* 18 (1988): 66–77.

Traub, Valerie. *Desire and Anxiety: Circulations of Sexuality in Shakespearean Drama*. New York: Routledge, 1992.

Vickers, Nancy. "Diana Described: Scattered Woman and Scattered Rhyme." *Critical Inquiry* 8 (1981): 265–279.

Whittier, Gayle. "The Sonnet's Body and the Body Sonnetized in *Romeo and Juliet*."
  Shakespeare Quarterly 40 (1989): 27–41.
Zimmerman, Susan, ed. *Erotic Politics: Desire on the Renaissance Stage*. New York:
  Routledge, 1992.

4

Dwindling into Wifehood: The Romantic Power of the Witty Heroine in Shakespeare, Dryden, Congreve, and Austen

DONALD A. BLOOM

The relationship of wit, power, gender, romance, and comedy may seem hopelessly obscure, a mere piling up of complex terms until they become conflicting. But actually I have a rather simple point to make: a witty heroine can give added pleasure and depth to a comedy through expanding our sense of the romance, the added depth and pleasure deriving from the sense of power that wit brings to a character, and particularly to a heroine. To illustrate this, I propose to look at the witty dialogue of five comic heroines: Rosalind from *As You Like It*, Florimell from Dryden's *Secret Love* and Doralice from his *Marriage a la Mode*, Millamant from *The Way of the World*, and Elizabeth Bennet from *Pride and Prejudice* (which is not, of course, a drama but includes many scenes that are superb comic drama, and is written by a woman). In each case, the witty heroine plays a dual part, both fulfilling an archetypal role necessary to romance, and establishing her independence through the use of wit in her power games with the romantic hero. It is the union of these two factors that makes these heroines so memorable.

Before going into specific characters, I must clarifiy some terms. By wit, first, I mean statements that in general or in context show significant insight, and are phrased in a particularly apt and vivid way, generally involving either the surprise of humor or the irony of satire, or both. The witty heroine, then, displays a talent for these well-turned and amusing insights, and in doing so, shows both her wisdom and the power of her personality. By power I mean not dominance or authority over another, but freedom from such dominance over oneself — that is, independence — remembering that established legal and customary authority does not necessarily reflect the practical and psychological dominance of a given relationship. We find this especially in the case of women, who have, in most times and places, found themselves subordinated to the men of the same rank to whom they are legally attached, such as their husbands, fathers, or brothers. Thus, the gender (both her chromosomal sex and the mythology attached to it) of the witty heroine plays a central part not only in the romance, but in the comedy, for the wit and independence of such a heroine tends to undermine or overturn the expected hierarchical order. Yet, as we shall see, she fulfills the romantic myth more completely than other heroines.

Most complicated is the idea of romance. By this I mean either or both of two related literary phenomena: a story that depicts the search for and discovery of the inner or true or total Self, what Jung calls the process of Individuation; or a story that deals with falling in love. These I take to be almost, but not completely, overlapping, for I assume that what we call "falling in love" occurs when we find someone who exactly matches the matrix we have built up in our unconscious, which Jung associates with the archetypal figure of the Animus / Anima, and which is the ultimate goal of the search. In a pure romance the search for self (the quest) may sprawl over many hundreds of pages and involve the ego figure in dozens of adventures with a variety of archetypal figures (including the Shadow, the dark Self, often a rival for the Animus/Anima). In a romantic comedy, however, this quest is commonly compressed into a very small number of adventures, but all pointing toward the culminating event of romance and comedy — the marriage of hero and heroine. For, as Northrop Frye as shown, the comic resolution of a restored society centering on the youthful hero and his bride blends naturally with the romantic resolution of a hero culminating his (or her) archetypal quest of self-discovery with marriage.

In this sense, romance is not only a literary form but an aspect of human development, a process of self-exploration and self-realization that all undergo, including finding the archetypal matrix of the Other in our deep unconscious. In order to do this we project the archetype onto some real human being who closely matches it — that is, we fall in love. This kind of love (which I will subsequently refer to as Love) bears a certain kinship to other kinds of affectionate attachment (love) that we may feel towards our parents, siblings, children, friends, and pets, not to mention religions, countries, causes and so forth, because they all bring together affection, a sense of belonging, and a desire to help and even to sacrifice ourselves for them. Likewise, Love shares with erotic desire a need for closeness and touching of a sexually stimulating sort, yet the two are easier to tell apart than is commonly credited. One of the strongest stimulants to desire, unfortunately, is the desire to dominate the other, which can become an urge to harm. Not only is harm to the Other incompatible with any kind of love, but domination absolutely negates Love.

This point has great relevance to a discussion of the witty, independent heroine of romantic comedy. In the first place, just as you cannot dominate your unconscious, so you cannot dominate its archetypal figure, the object of your Love, for Love simply does not exist where it is not freely given. In this sense, Love cannot be seized, forced, bought or attained by any process except wooing, the process by which you offer yourself as an archetypal pattern to the Other, dressing yourself attractively, speaking whatever you think is loving, bringing presents, performing deeds, hoping to generate in the Other what already exists in the Self. But the Other's choice remains unconstrained — *truly* unconstrained because the choice ultimately lies outside the control of the Other's consciousness.

Wooing, however, has a great deal in common with seducing, an aspect of erotic dominance, and they cannot easily be told apart even by the wooer or seducer, because the wooer, being a sexual animal stirred by the passion of Love, desires much that the seducer also wants. The wooer differs because sexual congress is not an end in itself but merely physical expression of the total spiritual union of the two Lovers. Although neither wooing nor seducing would appear to have anything innately gender-specific about them, these activities have been commonly associated with men. At the same time, because throughout history females have generally faced much greater risks, socially and biologically, from seduction, they have needed to tell the difference and avoid a disastrous mistake. But marriage customs, especially arranged marriages enforced by law or custom, may take any choice in that matter out of the hands of either or both parties of the courting couple. Where choice exists, however, or is imagined to exist, an Other (whichever gender) must decide whether the suitor is a wooer, a seducer, or merely some irrelevancy. To Elizabeth Bennet, for example, Darcy is a wooer, Wickham a seducer and Collins an irrelevancy. Mirabell, a notorious seducer, has to persuade Millamant of his seriousness as a wooer, while Witwoud, Petulant and Sir Wilful all belong to the irrelevant group. Orlando is no seducer, but he could be an irrelevance to Rosalind if his love should prove inadequate — and marrying an irrelevance could generate as much misery as succumbing to a seducer. Doralice and and Florimell face still more complex situations, living in a time when ambiguous attitudes toward marriage make the difference between wooer and seducer almost disappear.

In every case, however, the witty heroine provides an amazing complex of literary attractions: from a masculine standpoint, her intelligence and insight allow her to establish her autonomy, thereby making her that much more attractive, if sometimes more threatening to vulnerable male egos; from a feminine standpoint, she provides a powerful ego identification figure for a feminine romance; at the same time she supplies a solid partner for the comic resolution in marriage, a satirist of the masculine power structure, and a commentator on the realities of woman's existence. Not every man will be attracted to such a woman, but a man who appreciates her insight and humor will be naturally drawn to such a woman, and find immense satisfaction in being loved by her, since her wittiness derives from her intelligence and her independence of mind. If she, who can see so much and judge so acutely, loves you, then there must be something *to* you. From her own standpoint, the witty female will often find that her wit frightens away many suitors, so that she has to hide it, or else, if she is not left alone, be faced with the fact that it is only her looks (or worse, her fortune) that are gaining attention. A man, however, who loved her *for* her wit, that is, for the person she truly is, would be a man after her own heart, a man likely to fit the archetypal matrix of her own unconscious. The potential of such heroines in a romantic comedy, though immense, is infrequently realized, so that when we do find them, we find not only wonderfully rewarding literature, but some very interesting insights into the possibilities of human relationships.

2

Of the witty heroines of Shakespeare's three comic masterpieces — Beatrice, Viola, and Rosalind — the last best serves my purposes, for the first has little serious problem with Benedick once their love for each other is discovered, and the second has no fulfilling love relationship until the very end of the play. Although Rosalind, like Viola, changes her garb in order to change her sex role, she uses her changed role to explore the possibilities of Love and marriage with Orlando. Like much of Shakespeare — like much of *literature* — this play can be confused by excessively subtle readings, which, fascinating though they may be, lose track of its fundamental simplicity. In it, a young man, victimized by his older brother, and a young woman, victimized by her uncle, meet briefly and fall in love. Escaping separately from danger, they fetch up in the same forest where the young woman, disguised as a boy, agrees to instruct him in what Love, courtship, and women are like. In doing so, she exercises her wit at the expense of both sexes and leads him through a maze of possibilities, which, I feel, lay the groundwork for a lasting relationship. Rosalind's effervescent wit explores the meaning of Love, not just as an ideal or fantasy but as a practical possibility.

Love, we should note here, has only obliquely to do with any feminist issues. Male chauvinism or patriarchalism can interfere with its personal realization, as can any other imposition of tyranny or injustice, but it can do nothing about its existence or its etiology. Thus, responses to the play like Clara Claiborne Park's "As We Like It: How a Girl Can be Smart and Still Popular" and Peter Erickson's (in his *Patriarchal Structures in Shakespeare's Drama*), though useful for many insights, strike me as mostly beside the point. If she is in Love, Rosalind would have no desire to dominate or humiliate Orlando in any substantive way, as that negates Love no matter which gender is doing the dominating. On the contrary, what is most important about Rosalind is that, as C. L. Barber put it, "[r]omantic participation in love and humorous detachment from it ... meet and are reconciled in Rosalind's personality" (233). Most especially, "Shakespeare keeps that part of the romantic tradition which makes love an experience of the whole personality" (238). Ruth Nevo has also noted the importance of wholeness of personality and self-exploration in her remarks on the play. I agree with her that the role of "Ganymede releases in Rosalind her best powers of improvisation, intuition, and witty intelligence" (190), and that, as a result, she "can discover not only what he is like, but what she is like; test his feelings, test her own" (191). Alexander Leggatt also points out how liberating the Ganymede role is for her (202), but that she must balance it with a return to her "self" (203), and he compares her to Millamant (206). Robert Ornstein emphasizes her "schooling" of Orlando that is also "playfully extracurricular" (147), and demonstrates that "she can dissect the artificialities of the romantic convention at the same time that she ardently affirms the meaning of romantic commitment" (149). None of these, however, reaches quite the point about Rosalind that I am seeking to make.

We already see the greater depth of Rosalind in her first conversation with Celia, for although the latter offers a well-phrased but fairly stock idea (that they "sit and mock the good housewife Fortune from her wheel, that her gifts may henceforth be bestowed equally" (1.2.30–2)), the former makes us think ("I would we could do so; for her benefits are mightily misplaced, and the bountiful blind woman doth most mistake in her gifts to women" (33–5)). Not only do we sense her wistfulness about her own hapless state, but we glimpse how different, when we think about it, is Fortune for a man and a woman, for it frequently refers not to luck, but to the results of public actions — just the sort of actions which women were largely excluded from. We know she is thinking of her father, displaced by the machinations of his younger brother, a fall of Fortune having nothing to do with luck. Similarly, when Celia tries to top Rosalind, she only can only resort to a nice phrasing of a rather hackneyed — and anti-feminist — linking of beauty with unchastity: "'Tis true; for those that she makes fair she scarce makes honest, and those that she makes honest she makes very ill-favouredly" (36–8). Hamlet may have reason for such a remark, but Celia has none — as her cousin and herself stand in proof of. Rosalind, however, is wiser for she answers, "Nay, now thou goest from Fortune's office to Nature's: Fortune reigns in gifts of the world, not in the lineaments of Nature" (49–41). That is, beauty is a gift of Nature not Fortune, and while it might appear to be a great good fortune to its possessor, actual experience proves otherwise. Moreover, the religious undertone of the key phrase, "reigns in the gifts of the world," should remind us how little we should trust it.

If Rosalind has the superior wit, that wit is nonetheless grounded on a kind of sympathetic wisdom that has long been associated with the feminine. She immediately sympathizes with both the old man, grieving for his three sons, all terribly injured in wrestling against Charles, and with Orlando, who is to try his skill next. Yet she falls for Orlando not (it seems) for his strength, skill and looks, but for his courage, natural good manners, and pride in his father. She has already stated that she was thinking of love, and her match with Orlando has all the logic of both comic myth and human nature behind it. Orlando is courageous and heroic, yet also pitiable — and so is Rosalind. Orlando, sensing the burgeoning love of Rosalind, as she gives him the chain, in turn falls in love with her. They have, for the moment, matched: the romance is complete. Sort of.

Reality requires a bit more than a look, a few kind words, and a gift to make a marriage of true minds last, and for all its fantastic trappings, the play is very strongly rooted in the realities of human relationships. There remains, in fact, the rest of the process of self-exploration, for Rosalind possesses wit and independence, and the two must come to terms with the full range of their personalities. Though Rosalind says, "He calls us back: my pride fell with my fortunes" (1.2.225), the point is neatly ironic, both true and untrue. Yes, she must sacrifice some of the beautiful lady's tyrannous vanity when falling in love, and even some of her social independence, but she gains something far more valuable and liberating — her inmost self. She will experience the exact opposite of a fall of fortune, and nearly the opposite of a fallen pride — provided Orlando should love her as much as she loves him. And therein lies the tale: having intelligence and independence of mind, she will explore and test this Love thoroughly, using her talent for wit to make the exploration both funny and satiric, both delightful and instructive, as well as romantically satisfying.

When the two meet again, Rosalind is already disguised and now adopts her role of "saucy lackey" (3.2.292), putting Orlando through the catechism on Time to establish her own wit credentials and making up a story about being raised in the forest by an "old religious uncle," who not only taught her to speak correctly, but "read [her] many lectures against" love, courtship and women. As many commentators have said, she is clearly luring him into this discussion in order to test his love and her own, and to teach him about the conflicts of human relationships. Orlando, who knows nothing of women, takes the bait and asks about the "principal evils ... laid to [their] charge," but Rosalind refuses on the grounds that she "will not cast away [her] physic but on those that are sick," the logical patient being "that fancy-monger" who "haunts the forest ... abuses our young plants with carving Rosalind on their barks; hangs odes upon hawthorns and elegies upon brambles." Orlando claims to be the young man, but she assures him that he cannot truly be a lover for he lacks the "marks": "a lean cheek ... a blue eye and sunken ... an unquestionable spirit ... a beard neglected ... hose ... ungartered ... bonnet unbanded ... sleeve unbuttoned ... shoe untied ... and everything about [him] demonstrating a careless desolation" (350–9).

This catalogue of the lover's marks, though traditional and subject to a good deal of scoffing, has a logic of its own. As Rosalind says, at the end of that speech, Orlando's being well-groomed ("point-device") is suggestive of his "loving himself than seeming the lover of any other." The absurdity of the tradition aside, the point is well taken: the attention of the seducer (whether outright rake or not) is on himself and his own pleasures; the attention of the Lover is on the Other. The catalogue represents the extremist view, that all moderation is tepidity or even falseness, so that the more the Lover loses any sense of himself the more truly he is a Lover. If the Lover is to woo the Other by showing the intensity and thus authenticity of his Love, he must (in this view) show a complete loss of Self. Or, as Rosalind puts it a few lines later, "Love is merely madness, and, I tell you, deserves as well a dark house and a whip as madmen do" (391–3).

But this is one of Shakespeare's favorites jokes, even though — as the sonnets indicate — told on himself. In the world of wit, in which Rosalind is one of the reigning queens, you must have judgment, which requires not only the reason that madmen have lost, but a strong, though ironical, sense of self. Rosalind is as foolishly in love, as "fond," in the old sense, as Orlando, but she does not lose her wit as a result. Thus, she does not simply borrow a dress and make herself known to Orlando as "his Rosalind" immediately. Romance or no, two people do not stop being being two people just because they have fallen in love, and Rosalind, needing to find out just how true this Love is, embarks on the more dangerous ground of the list of women's "giddy offenses" and "principal evils" —

> I being but a mooning youth will grieve, be effeminate, changeable, longing and liking, proud, fantastical, apish, shallow, inconstant, full of tears, full of smiles; for every passion something and for no passion truly anything, as boys and women are for the most part cattle of this

colour; would now like him, now loathe him; then entertain him, then
spit at him. (379–86)

These constitute, of course, a traditional catalogue of such offenses and evils,
and can be looked at superficially as just another annoying example of
gender-prejudice. Looked at again, however, they take on a rather more
ambiguous cast. To call a woman effeminate, for example, is hardly insulting,
being essentially tautological. Other terms, taken out of context, reveal their
uncertainty: would any man want his Beloved to be unsmiling and ungriev-
ing, never "longing and liking" at all? Finally, the remainder (changeable,
proud, fantastical, apish, shallow, inconstant) have as much application to one
gender as the other, but may indeed be applicable to "his Rosalind." In the
long run, as Rosalind is a human being she will display all these foibles at
times. So will he. Once the initial infatuation wears off, the Lover must still
desire to *be with* the Other, despite her humanity. Will he?

Rosalind herself then brings up the question of his being "cured," although
Orlando (fortunately) does not want any such cure. She needs, however, to
explore and test Orlando's feelings for her still further, by regaling him with
more horrifying possibilities. Thus, at their next meeting, when Orlando fails
to arrive on time, we find her calling him a snail both for his tardiness and
the fact that, as a snail, "he brings his destiny [horns] with him" (4.1.49).
Orlando takes (or pretends to take) this possibility seriously, and asserts that
Rosalind, being virtuous, would not do such a thing. Satisfied with this, she
urges him to press his opportunity, as she is in a "holiday humour and like
enough to consent" (58–9). But when Orlando tries to play the role of courtly
lover, she constantly interrrupts him to correct or tease. When he puts forth
the standard idea that rejection will cause his death, she responds with her
most famous line, "Men have died from time to time, and worms have eaten
them, but not for love" (91–2). When he asks for her love, she assents, but
when he asks her to have him, she assents too much — "Ay, and twenty such"
— for if Orlando is good, "can one desire too much of a good thing?" (105)
Before he can respond to this possibility she shifts into the mock-wedding.
Once that is completed she asks him how long he will "have her after [he
has] possess'd her." Once more his response (the cliché, "forever and a day")
causes her to pounce: "Say 'a day' without the 'ever.' ... Men are April when
they woo, December when they wed. Maids are May when they are maids,
but the sky changes when they are wives" (125–8). She goes on to warn him
to expect Rosalind to be jealous, clamorous, newfangled, giddy, and prone to
inappropriate tears or laughter.

Near the end of this scene Celia remarks that Rosalind deserves to be
stripped and exposed for her abuse to her own sex, but Rosalind has more
going on than the intelligent but unimaginative Celia suspects. In the first
place, the accusation of change from courtship to post-marital tedium or

dismay is applied first to men. In the second place, he needs no warning against the moodiness of men since he does not propose marrying one. Third, all these are merely wifely versions of the "giddy offenses" iterated in the previous scene. Fourth, however much these may be slanders against the gender as a whole, they may be at any time true of any individual woman — some of them for very good reasons — which is what he proposes to marry, not the Anima archetype which she represents. He would thus be wise to determine what this *woman* is like, and whether he can enjoy or at least put up with her human foibles.

Orlando, we see, is still much too naive. When he is told that Rosalind will do as Ganymede is doing, he responds: "O, but she is wise!" He is correct that she is wise, or wiser than most young people, and probably wiser than he — wise enough, at any rate, to make as sure as she can of her husband, the way he ought to of his wife. Still, his point is correct: the key is wisdom, that is, good judgment. But where before he was counting on *her* virtue, so now he is counting on *her* wisdom — an unwise method that, in this case, will work for him, but might lead to disaster with another woman (as it does with Elizabeth Bennet's father). Still, he is learning. When she expatiates on the impossibility of stopping up a witty woman's wit, he responds with the pun, "Wit, whither wilt?" Once more she threatens cuckolding ("Nay, you might keep that check for it till you met your wife's wit going to your neighbour's bed"), and when he asks how that could be justified ("And what wit could wit have to excuse that?"), she responds with an answer worthy of the Wife of Bath ("Marry, to say she came to seek you there. You shall never take her without her answer unless you take her without her tongue."). But Rosalind is no Wife, nor is Orlando a Jankyn. These are tests, puzzles, challenges. Rosalind can use them to explore the kind of man Orlando really is. Clearly, he is no cynical seducer, and he does not seem to have the kind of arrogance that would make him an unpleasant partner to a woman of independence and spirit. But he might be little better than a fool. If he should prove such, Rosalind would face another kind of challenge.

Here, however, the author brings this game to an end. Rosalind is trapped. She would like to keep playing, but she cannot expect him to take Ganymede very seriously. Nor would she want him to. If Orlando is naive enough to need the instruction Ganymede can offer into the realities of human interaction at its most intimate (including its possible horrors), and witty enough to enjoy the word-play of a master-wit, he is wise enough to remember that his responsibility to the duke, his new master, outweighs any game-playing. The play concludes, therefore, with the ritualized game that Rosalind plays in sorting out the couples, winding up her role as the mediator between Orlando and his own Love, which he so poorly understood, as well as between herself and hers, which she explored along with his. By the end she is ready to *be* that Love, and he as ready to be hers, the archetypal conclusion we are surely supposed to derive from the appearance of Hymen to confirm all engagements. Rosalind's efforts have not been merely for fun, but to match the archetypal fulfillment of romance with the reality of human foibles.

3

If in Shakespeare's time the fulfillment of romance through marriage was only occasionally managed, and thus remained largely in the realm of the fantastic, by Dryden's time it had become much more common, though arranged and compelled marriage also remained common enough. In the meantime, however, the whole institution, as John Harrington Smith shows in *The Gay Couple in Restoration Comedy*, had taken on a rather bad odor. Although in an arranged marriage the couple had almost no hope of romantic fulfillment, marrying to please themselves left them stuck for life with someone they might as easily fall *out* of Love with as they did *in*. Thus, the cynicism about Love that characterizes Suckling's cavalier poetry also permeates the drama, or at least the comic side of it. The heroic and tragic drama still followed the idealized love-and-honor themes of the Caroline court, and can be seen in the companion plots of both plays: the hopeless love of the Queen for the courtier Philocles, himself in love with someone else, in *Secret Love*; the dilemma, in *Marriage*, of Leonidas and Palmyra, as first one and then the other is identified as the long-lost child of the usurper, Polydamas, and each is ordered to reject the True Love they feel for each other to marry someone else. But these idealized plots are as unreal as the characters who enact them. In the comic plots the characters represent more or less accurate versions of contemporary courtiers, who view love as primarily lust, and courtship as a self-serving game. Thus, in the one type, romantic fulfillment by Love and marriage turns out a lifeless charade, and in the other a self-deception fit only for fools. Nevertheless, like other playwrights of the time, Dryden had a strong romantic streak, which he could not suppress even in the sub-plots, and they reveal a longing after romantic fulfillment even as they are built on the countervailing cynicism. This internal contradiction, however, leaves us wondering just what these characters want, or hope to achieve.

Smith shows how, in *Secret Love*, Dryden reworked the witty heroines of earlier playwrights (especially Fletcher), changing them from widows to girls (Florimell), approximately the equivalent to the rakish hero (Celadon) in wit and wildness — approximately, because although she talks gaily enough about having many lovers or servants, she is also militantly virginal. Though they eventually marry after several wit-duels and comic "situations," through most of play Florimell finds herself in a tricky position — wanting something that perhaps cannot exist. She has no interest, she says, in "one of those solemn Fops; they are good for nothing but to make Cuckolds: Give me a servant who is an high Flier at all games, that is bounteous of himself to many women; and yet whenever I pleas'd to throw out the lure of Matrimony, should come down with a swing, and fly the better at his own quarry" (3.1.296–302). We may take it as a rule that at least some women are attracted to men who are great womanizers, because they are elusive, or because they make themselves interesting, or because they radiate a kind of sadism that attracts a corresponding masochism. But what Florimell wants may be impossible to *have*: wildness and yet reliability. Her use of the image from falconry is significant, but ambiguous. If successful, she would reach the seductively powerful position of dominating the Other as the human does the trained animal, doubly ego-gratifying where the animal has a powerful and fiercely independent personality. But this is not, of course, Love. If she does not care about Love, it doesn't matter, for if she is only interested in affection, passion or sexual pleasure, they can love or not, marry or not, have sex or not, and the question of "with whom" never means much.

The issue comes up only because Celadon holds to the standard contempt for marriage — "Marriage is poor folk's pleasure that cannot go the cost of variety" (1.1.29–30) — yet unexpectedly falls in love with Florimell. When she queries him about this ("But, without raillery, are you in Love?"), he responds frankly, "So horribly much, that contrary to my own Maxims, I think in my conscience I could marry you" (2.1.57–9). Florimell thus faces a dual dilemma: is he really in Love? and does she want to marry him, whether he is or not? The advantages, we remember, are all on his side; if they marry, but become estranged or even just bored, he can return to his old life with comparative ease, but she cannot. And, of course, he may not really be in Love with Florimell, but just subject to a transitory infatuation, for he doesn't stop being attracted to other women, in particular, the two sisters, Sabina and Olinda, whom he was courting before he met Florimell.

She tests him by proposing that he act the part of the True Lover, willing to kill himself out of despair, or at least developing the "pale, and lean, and melancholick" air, but he brushes these aside as unreasonable. She then proposes "a whole year of probation ... to grow reserv'd, discreet, sober and faithful, and to pay [her] all the services of a Lover" (2.1.89, 107–9). He accepts on the condition that if he does well the time will be reduced, and she allows the condition, though noting that if he "prove unfaithful" the time will be extended. Sure enough, when Florimell makes a wager with her friend Flavia as to Florimell's power over Celadon, he promptly fails. In the midst of excusing himself for recent attentions to Sabina and Olinda, he receives a bogus invitation from the sisters, actually from Flavia, and accepts. But Florimell finds herself more jealous than angry, and vows to win him over yet. Catching him in the midst of his attentions to the others, she jeers the other two out of countenance, and rails about taking a "Wencher's word," but he escapes again through appeal to the cynical standard of the day: "Why should you speak so contemptibly of the better half of Mankind. I'le stand up for the honour of my Vocation" (4.1.194–6).

Florimell has her greatest success in pretending to be a young fop, cutting the two sisters away from Celadon before her disguise is broken. He makes the best of his embarrassment, but she is now in the driver's seat. When he attempts to swear "by these Breeches," which we assume are hers, since it would be odd to swear by his own, she retorts, "Which if I marry you I am resolv'd to wear" (5.1.171). She succeeds not only in driving away the two girls he is dallying with, but in exposing, through parody, the whole shallow business. If she can seduce girls as well as he can, without the slightest real interest in them, how much point is there to it? If he wants sex, wouldn't a prostitute be more straightforward? If he wants merely the satisfaction to his vanity that these games afford, what kind of flimsy person is he? If he wants more, that is, the fulfillment of himself through Love, why can't he pay the necessary price in fidelity?

These questions are never fully answered. At the end of the play, after an early contest of wills, they resolve to wed if they can only, as Florimell says, "invent but any way to make it easie" (5.1.531–2). As Celadon sees it, the problem is that "[s]ome foolish people have made it uneasie by drawing the knot faster than they need" (533–4), to which she agrees and they make up a list of provisos so that the idea of marriage will be tolerable: giving up jealousy and pretense, not inquiring about gambling losses or excursions. Most important, they agree that "the names of Husband and Wife hold forth nothing, but clashing and cloying, and dulness and faintness in their signification," so that "they shall be abolish'd for ever betwixt" them, and instead they "will be married by the more agreeable names of Mistress and Gallant" (571–6). The goal clearly is still romance, and for the moment we might imagine we are back in the Middle Ages where it must be divorced from marriage. But this is no love out of the courtly love cycles, passionate but eternal. They have no faith in the continued need for that particular Other, but rather assume that this Love will wear out as all loves do, only lasting some months longer.

The play thus ends as *Marriage a la Mode* begins: it is impossible for Love to last through the eternity of marriage. Doralice's song, "Why should a foolish marriage vow," which begins *Marriage*, reiterates how love wears out, making the married state a waste. A few lines later, Rhodophil describes to his friend, soon to be rival, Palamede, what has happened to his relationship with Doralice. Though once he "lov'd her passionately," now "those golden days are gone" and all he knows of "her perfections ... is only by memory." Again we find the mixture of cynicism and regret. He claims to have "lov'd her a whole half year, double the natural term of any Mistress," and admits that he "could have held out another quarter; but then the World began to laugh at" him, and he was shamed by fashion into giving up so soon. Love did not last, he says, because there was "nothing left in us to make us new to one another," now they pace like "lions in a room" and lying as far apart as their fashionable "great Bed" will allow (1.1.162–77).

Both say much the same thing: love is something vitally important but transitory; if marriage must be permanent, then everyone must accept the fact that people will continue to pursue love outside it. The song, indeed, is much more sinister, for mariage is associated with an array of negative terms (foolish, decay'd, dead, madness and pain), and set in opposition to passion, pleasure and joy, defining the anti-marital, anti-romantic code of the time. But it is only a song, and not necessarily to be regarded as the opinion of the singer. Indeed, when Doralice is approached by Palamede, she keeps him at some distance, agreeing only to listen to his suit, and then only for the three days before his marriage. Moreover, Rhodophil's statement includes two mitigations: one, the admission that he was partly motivated by a sense of being out of fashion; the second, the observation that their passion for each other lasted twice as long as the normal affair — or more, since they were first in love two years ago and it is only now that he is seriously pursuing an affair.

As he says, however, they are now as friendly as caged cats. For example, once pretence is unnecessary, they begin to bicker like a sitcom couple, with Doralice generally winning the duels. When Rhodophil wonders about his sins that led him into this marriage, Doralice asserts, "Whatever your sins, mine's the punishment" (3.1.57); when he contemplates his "Holy-day" at her death, she agrees that he has surely made her a martyr; when he says he will swear over her corpse never to marry again, she resolves "to marry the very same day" he dies, "if it be but to show how little" she is concerned for him (70–2). Having lost these rounds, he asks what she would suggest to end their "heathenish life," offering any "reasonable atonement" before they sleep. But she demolishes him: "What should you talk of peace abed, when you can give no security for performance of Articles?" (80–1).

At first this appears to be merely a cutting, even slightly cruel joke, with a double entendre attached — a sure-fire laugh line in the long tradition of the bickering couple, provided the audience is sufficiently sophisticated. But Rhodophil's subsequent defensiveness indicates that it is true. He complains that it is too "easy" to have her, and insufficiently "unlawful" (84). He has, in fact, exercised his erotic imagination to "enjoy" her, "fancied [her] all the fine women in the town to help [himself] out," but failed. Thus, he says, "Thou art a wife, and thou wilt be a wife," as harsh a condemnation as imaginable under the circumstances. In some ways, we feel sorry for Rhodophil, since it is easy enough to imagine the falling off of his performance as a sexual athlete, and his subsequent attempt to protect his self-esteem by blaming his wife. But he does not seem to understand or care about how his coldness undercuts *her* self-esteem. Moreover, the immediate advantages lie with him: he can return to his earlier womanizing, gain prestige and risk nothing except a tongue-lashing from his wife. She cannot follow his lead without gaining the brand of whore and facing the possibility of a major scandal, even a duel (as nearly happens in the play).

Justice, in fact, lies with her, since she is approximately as vulnerable as he in the area of self-esteem, and at a serious disadvantage in the game of sexual self-indulgence. After her husband's departure, Doralice reiterates the wife's lament: "'Tis a pretty time we Women have on't, to be made Widows, while we are marry'd." Their husbands complain that they are the same, when they "have more reason to complain, that [the husbands] are not the same." And she concludes with a surprisingly raunchy conceit on marital sex as a kind of *table d'hote* meal ("'Tis enough that they have a sufficient Ordinary, and a Table ready spread for 'em: if they cannot fall to and eat heartily, the fault is theirs"). But her most telling remark comes at the beginning of her complaint, when she turns his insulting term back on him: "Well, since thou art a Husband, and wilt be a Husband, I'll try if I can find out another!" But *husband* means not only dull drudge as *wife* does; it means cuckold. There lies her greatest power and the key to restoring their relationship, though she does not realize it yet.

In the first of her efforts to gain revenge, the grotto scene, she goes to keep a rendezvous with her suitor, Palamede, only to run into her husband trying to keep an assignation with Melantha, his prospective mistress and Palamede's wife-to-be. Each must lie barefacedly in order to avoid the difficult truth. Later, with both Melantha and herself disguised as boys, they again all meet and she has the opportunity to flirt openly with her lover in front of her husband, though he does the same to her. At the end, though, Doralice reluctantly disconnects herself from Palamede because she knows that his father has arrived to stand upon terms in the arrangement with Melantha's father and she has no interest in a married servant. Their only hope is to outlive their spouses, to which they dedicate themselves. Discovered by her husband, Doralice persuades him out of forcing Palamede into a duel, but also realizes her opportunity: "Then have I found my account in raising your jealousie: O! 'tis the most delicate sharp sawce to a cloy'd stomach; it will give you a new edge" (5.1.348–50). Moreover, when Rhodophil tries to make it conditional on his being sure she was "honest," she shrewdly refuses, "If you are wise, believe me for your own sake: Love and Religion have but one thing to trust to; that's a good sound faith" (353–55). Perpetual jealousy does not constitute much of a solution, but it is the best, perhaps, that a cynical and materialistic age has to offer. Doralice, at at any rate, seems to have the skill to make the best of it.

4

By the end of the century, the cruder sort of cynicism about marriage had ebbed away again. Though we find it in the backbiting of the Fainalls in *The Way of the World*, this hardly constitutes an attack on marriage as romantic fulfillment, since the Fainalls were never in love in the first place. More telling are Millamant's remarks during the proviso scene, where she says she won't be called names after marriage:

> Aye, as wife, spouse, my dear, joy, jewel, love, sweetheart and the rest of that nauseous cant, in which men and their wives are so fulsomely familiar... Let us never visit together, nor go to a play together. But lets us be very strange and well-bred; let us be as strange as if we had been married a great while, and as well bred as if we were not married at all (4.1.175–87).

Mirabell accepts this condition as well as the others without demur, so we can assume he feels much the same, and for a moment we might be back in the world of Doralice and Florimell. But there is more going on in Millamant's provisos than some leftover Restoration clichés on the contemptible state of marriage.

We must remember that her first demand was that she be allowed to loll in bed as late as she likes in the morning ((163–9), and her third a whole series of fundamental rights guaranteeing her privacy in visits, letters, and meals, and her freedom of choice in friends, acquaintance, garb, and conversation. "These articles subscribed ... [she] may by degrees dwindle into a wife" (202–3). The effect is cumulative. If in the first condition she merely demands the right to go on being a coquette, and in the second to avoid the cloying sentimentality of some couples, in the third she puts forward a feminist Bill of Rights. Even the very adaptable Mirabell finds these "something advanced," but accepts on the simple conditions that she avoid behavior that would make him a fool or damage the health of his unborn children. But if the third set of conditions is a clear statement of personal freedom, the other two have their points as well. In the class to which she belongs, this apparent laziness — her enjoyment of solitude, contemplation, morning thoughts, *douceurs, sommeils du matin* (164–7) — defines her. She will not become a busy housewife for any husband. The point, I think, is not that she will not at times be housewifely, but that she will not be forced into such a role.

Likewise, the "nauseous cant" that she refers to is not merely sentimental but frequently hypocritical, as the example of Sir Francis and Lady Fadler (178–9) makes evident. It has, moreover, an undertone of possessiveness, which, even if the terms themselves are used by both genders, almost invariably works to the disadvantage of the female. Finally, the last part takes us once more into that fascinating world of Millamant's imagination, for it suggests they act at once as if they no longer cared for each other and as if they were having an adulterous affair. I suggest that this is a tentative, if slightly fantastical solution to the dilemma posed by the Restoration critique of marriage — that it must inevitably spoil romance. Congreve uses "never" to make it a joke — surely they must sometimes visit together — but if they remain at once new and well-mannered to each other, they may avoid the over-familiarity, the bickering, the humdrum conversations that doom so many marriages. Millamant sees the danger, and this demand leads naturally into her demand for large-scale personal liberty, for as a woman she has much more to lose if the marriage should go flat. When Mirabell recognizes the rightness of her conditions, and proposes nothing that she objects to in return, then she can rest as secure in her marriage as she could ever hope to be.

Reaching this point requires a significant change in the character of Mirabell, however, and this change has not been well understood. A number of critics (Van Voris, Roberts, Foakes, Donaldson, for instance) have exercised themselves on the general unworthiness of Mirabell, though he has been admirably defended by others (the Mueschkes, Williams). Likewise, Millamant, though appreciated for her wit, has often been thought affected and illogical, while even Virginia Birdsall, who correctly identifies her creativity, also remarks on her self-admiration — which to me is nothing more than a gambit in the game she is playing. More to the point, from my view, are several recent studies that have gone back to the question of marriage and society. Alvin Snider, for example, has shown how Congreve rejects the popular neo-Epicureanism with its antagonism to a romantic ideal of marriage, while Richard Kroll makes a strong point about the struggle of all the characters, but Millamant especially, to achieve a "contingent but real social liberty" (749). Most significant, Richard W. F. Braverman emphasizes the emerging companionate marriage, and demonstrates the way that Millamant can gain both social and political power through a "productive marriage which [combines] sentimental love and sexual satisfaction" while still legitmating the ancient dynastic function (155).

Frankly, I also find a great deal more to Millamant than whimsy, fancy and vanity, and I think Kroll and Braverman, in their different ways, are quite right to point out the tricky sociopolitical situation all the characters, especially Millamant, find themselves in. Her position as queen of coquettes, so apparently easy, has many pitfalls. Though it gives her great power for the moment, that power lasts only as long as her beauty. Like an athlete, she must win her gold medal while she can, for she cannot hope to compete in another Olympics — but what is a victory? She may have her pick of men, but after the ceremony she is stuck for life with that husband, and has little recourse if he turns out a boor or a cad. Moreover, her very beauty puts her in greater peril of an unwise choice, for many of the men flocking around her will be stimulated by a desire to possess her beauty not love her self. With more

choices, she has perhaps a better chance of finding her own romantic fulfillment in one of those paying court, but she must also sift those suitors to find
one that will truly Love her. Thus, she must make sure of Mirabell's intentions: a mere offer of marriage is not enough, for it may be simply a more
honorable way to possess her. Toward deciding this question most of her
dialogue runs.

When, on her first appearance, Witwoud remarks that she did not inquire
of Mr. Fainall about the location of his wife and Mirabell, she responds, "By
your leave, Mr. Witwoud, that were like asking after an old fashion, to ask a
husband for his wife" (2, 1, 317–8), showing she has no delusions about the
importance of many wives to their husbands: about as much as out of fashion
gowns to wealthy ladies. When she sails off into the wondrous and delight-
fully goofy fantasy about the use of love-letters as curling papers, and the
disastrous effect of prose on her hair-do, she affirms her social power as belle
of belles and her intellectual power as a wit of wits — and shows in the
process why Mirabell is crazy about her. When Mirabell attempts to deflect
her annoyance at his jealous behavior of the previous night by suggesting that
her cruelty is affected and not natural, while her "true vanity is in the power
of pleasing," she retorts, "Oh, I ask your pardon for that. One's cruelty is
one's power and when one parts with one's cruelty, one parts with one's
power; and when one has parted with that, I fancy one's old and ugly"
(347–51). Never mind the medieval tradition of the Lady's cruelty, Millamant
has neatly synopsized the coquette's dilemma. While it would be handy to
Mirabell, as to any other importunate male, if Millamant were to opt for the
power to be had from "pleasing" her suitor by giving up her power, Millamant
is too wise for any such thing, not when she holds the high trumps, and not
until married to a man she can trust to Love her. To Muir the key word is
"respect" (237); to Birdsall "love of freedom" (243); in either case Millamant
has no desire to lose what she sometimes calls "power" and "liberty" but is,
at bottom, selfhood.

When Mirabell, faced with the "challenge that Millamant flings at him"
(Birdsall, 241), loses his confidence and resorts to whining that it is only in
the eyes, and thus the praises, of the lover that a woman is beautiful, Millamant rightly accuses him of "vanity," and demolishes his image by reversing it. Far from the lover creating the lady's beauty, it is the beautiful lady
who creates the lover "as fast as [she] pleases" (365–7). To Witwoud's
complaint that this reduces the lover to a kind of home-made kitchen match,
she retorts: "One no more owes one's beauty to a lover than one's wit to an
echo" (370–1). The world is full of men who desire to possess the lovely
Millamant — rakes, fops, humorists, bumpkins — but how many are truly
interested in the person inhabiting the exquisite body and residing behind the
beautiful face? Such echo-lovers do play up to one's vanity, but no more, and

until she finds one who isn't, she is safer and happier treating them all as such.

As soon as they are alone, Mirabell begins crabbing at her, ostensibly giving her advice on the folly of spending time conversing with fools like Witwoud and Petulant, but actually giving vent to his own wounded vanity. Millamant dismisses this complaint first by saying simply, "I please myself" (and why shouldn't she?), before going into another of her fantasies: fools as a kind of antibiotic for the "vapors," that all-purpose term for boredom masquerading as melancholia. But when Mirabell takes her literally ("You are not in a course of fools?"), the crude suggestiveness of this offends her and she presses her advantage, offering the possibility of rejecting him absolutely. The problem, she correctly foresees, is that they "shall be sick of one another." Most especially, "I shan't endure to be reprimanded nor instructed; 'tis so dull to act always by advice, and so tedious to be told of one's faults — I can't bear it" (408–10). We must not overlook the absolute forthrightness of these remarks. Who *does* like to be reprimanded or instructed? Certainly not Mirabell. Moreover, it doesn't matter whether Mirabell is mainly a male chauvinist trying to exert control or mainly a jealous lover trying to sequester and enjoy alone the beloved, for both roles are innately egocentric and oppressive, denying the independent human subjectivity of the love object. As long as he continues in this frame of mind, Millamant has good reason for keeping him at a distance.

As Mirabell loses points in the wit duel, he becomes more self-pitying and she becomes wittier. When he grumbles about the impossibility of "win[ning] a woman with plain dealing and sincerity," she annihilates him: "Sententious Mirabell! Prithee, don't look with that violent and inflexible wise face, like Solomon at the dividing of the child in an old tapestry hanging" (420–2). She is correct: Mirabell has begun taking himself seriously, congratulating himself on his honesty, while whining to Millamant about how little she praises him for it. But a stuffed shirt can be regarded as little improvement on a rake as a bad bet for a husband. If Mirabell has reformed from rakishness, as the lines suggest, he must also be reformed from pomposity. Ignoring his plea for her "for one moment to be serious," she says, "What, with that face? No, if you keep your countenance, 'tis impossible I should hold mine. Well, after all, there is something very moving in a love-sick face. Ha! ha! ha! — Well, I won't laugh, don't be peevish — Heighho! Now I'll be melancholy, as melancholy as a watch-light. Well, Mirabell, if ever you will win me, woo me now. — Nay, if you are so tedious, fare you well" (425–431). And, leaving him sputtering, she departs.

Vanity? Affectation? Perhaps. But also great good sense to go along with her flights of wit. Mirabell, having fallen in love, still wants everything his own way. He wants Millamant to be serious, when her most lovable trait is her *joie de vivre*. And he wants her to be schooled by him when she is at least as wise as he. Thus he grumbles about women that "[t]here is no point of the compass to which they cannot turn, and by which they are not turned" (446–7). Yet there is nothing whimsical about Millamant below the surface. She needs to get along with her guardian aunt, and she does so. She wishes to have a good time in her inevitably temporary position as chief coquette: ditto. She will not allow Mirabell to spoil either of these, but cares for him enough to keep him encouraged. However flighty or foolish other women may have been, Millamant moves in a straight and predictable line: she will not jeopardize her present happiness, but she will not interfere with Mirabell's efforts to free her from Lady Wishfort's control.

This utter defeat seemingly wakes Mirabell up, for in their next encounter he is more like himself, and the easiness that marks his relationships with others now manifests itself in his dialogue with her. Yet he cannot top her. When he asks slyly if his finding her locked in a room is "a pretty artifice contrived, to signify that here the chase must end and my pursuit be crowned for you can fly no further" (4, 1, 136–8), she dismisses the idea as vanity: "No, I'll fly and be followed to the last moment. Though I am upon the very verge of matrimony, I expect you should solicit me as much as if I were wavering at the grate of a monastery, with one foot over the threshold. I'll be solicited to the very last, nay and afterwards" (139–43). This idea naturally startles Mirabell, since solicitation has a decidedly sexual undertone, and he, the ex-rake, imagining himself honorably wedded to the girl of his dreams, naturally also imagines himself exempt from the necessity of "solicitation." Not Millamant, or so she claims: "Oh, I should think I was poor and had nothing to bestow, if I were *reduced to inglorious ease and freed from the agreeable fatigues of solicitations*" (145–7, emphasis mine). The phrasing of this passage is wonderfully ironic. The idea of ease being inglorious, as if she were of that hardworking, Puritanical sort that would find loafing shameful, and of solicitation being fatiguing (a dirty job, listening to handsome men plead for your favors, but someone has to do it), throws us once more into that slightly surreal world of Millamant's imagery, but the satire is directed as much at herself as Mirabell.

When Mirabell tries to reason her out of the position, she rejects the premises of his logic ("[i]t may be in things of common application, but never sure in love"), and she also isolates the real issue: "There is not so impudent a thing in nature as the saucy look of an assured man, confident of success. The pedantic arrogance of a very husband has not so pragmatical an air" (155–7). These last two sentences need little comment. They are witty, yet very true and very much to the point. Mirabell's attitude will determine the outcome. The romantic impetus requires independence of both, and the reduction of either destroys the validity of the experience — they could have sex, of course, and even some degree of love, but they could not have Love. Thus she concludes, "Ah, I'll never marry, unless I am first made sure of my will and pleasure" (158–9).

Mirabell pretends to misunderstand, taking "pleasure" with a sexual undertone, and making it into a rather off-color joke, but she is not distracted any more than she is offended, and dismisses his remark as impertinence. There follows her disquisition on liberty, and the proviso scene considered earlier. Even with the provisos accepted on both sides, she finds herself still reluctant to take the final step until urged to by her cousin Mrs. Fainall. Even then she won't be kissed, except on the hand, until there is public recognition of all in the final scene: she will be no one's toy, not even Mirabell's, whom, she now admits, she loves violently. While it has been accurately said that the play, especially the proviso scene, brings her "from girlhood to maturity" (Holland 185), I think the phrase applies more strongly to Mirabell, for it is the rake's life that is the most thoroughly adolescent — with its antagonism to established morals, its slangy and obscene barracks wit, its preoccupation with girls as sexual objects, its endless drinking parties, brawls, and scrapes. Millamant, however, displays no girlish traits except her enjoyment of what is enjoyable in her youth, though that she enjoys to the fullest. What Millamant must make sure of is that Mirabell does not regard her as simply a new acquisition, a mistress more difficult to obtain than others. Once she's sure that *he* is grown up, then she knows that she can put away her own coquetry. This romance is complete.

5

What makes *Pride and Prejudice* perhaps the most profound of all the works we have been reviewing is the way that Austen shows the relationship of romantic love to archetypal need, accomplishing this without overburdening the manners comedy or spoiling our enjoyment of Elizabeth's (and her own) satiric wit. If we look back to *AYLI*, we see that although Shakespeare gives us many reasons to enjoy the play, he does not give us a very clear reason why Orlando and Rosalind should love each other and not someone else. Congreve goes farther: making use of the wit duels from Restoration comedy, he gives us at least an idea of Mirabell's and Millamant's need for each. To graduate from casual affairs into something profound, Mirabell has had to find a woman who can match his wit and social graces, who is romantically sensual yet not a slut. Millamant's need for him specifically is less pressing (giving her the advantage), but she too must find an archetypal mate to gain archetypal fulfillment, and only Mirabell — the changing Mirabell — fills that bill. Similarly, but even more intensely, Darcy needs Elizabeth to achieve personal wholeness: she has, or is, what he lacks most. She, more like Millamant, has not such an obvious need, but only Darcy, who also must change even as he forces her to a self-examination and change, can do for her what she most needs.

For a long time, however, criticism generally ignored this matter of mutual needs, tending to focus on the title faults, their application to the central couple, and blame — finally resolved, I believe, by Howard Babb's landmark book (see also Heilman, Craik, and Kroeber). Beginning with Gilbert and Gubar's *The Madwoman in the Attic*, though, attention shifted to feminist issues, especially power, and Austen's alleged sell-out to patriarchal ideology, es evidenced by her romantic endings. Several feminist critics (Newton, Newman) have modified this initial harsh judgment by suggesting that Austen was instead subverting or parodying this ideology. And now at least one (Shaffer) has gone so far as to accept *Pride and Prejudice* at face value, and claim that Elizabeth is able to assert herself both before and after marriage (as the text of the book clearly suggests). Moreover, some useful new comments have been offered on the characters, including Darcy's shyness (Ewin) and Elizabeth's Spenseresque quest through the cardinal virtues (Wiesenfarth). Nevertheless, none of these quite gets at the point I am trying to make.

As we all know, the faults of Elizabeth and Darcy can be found in the title of their story. Both have both faults, but they are not so confirmed in their sinfulness as some of the more rigorous critics would suggest. On the contrary, both are decent, moral individuals whose judgments are more often right than wrong. Darcy, for example, is correct in his condemnation of Elizabeth's mother and two youngest sisters, but he is not the snob that Bingley's sisters are. He misjudges, perhaps partly because it is handy to do so, the fervor of Jane's love for his friend, and he forgets that his own connections (most obviously Lady Catherine, but also Miss Bingley) are less than perfect. But his apparent coldness we discover to be shyness, and his arrogance, though real, is not so strong as some have claimed. He has more self-confidence, and less humility, than is good for him, so that he takes himself and his judgment a bit too seriously. Which of us does not?

Elizabeth likewise rushes headlong into judgments about others, allows her prejudice to cause serious misreadings of the facts, and thus acts on her misreadings with unfortunate consequences. Although we see more intimately Elizabeth's failures in this regard, and especially her humiliating trust in the despicable Wickham, her sins are less serious than his. In fact, Elizabeth would not have been so likely to fall into her basic misjudgment of Wickham had not Darcy already antagonized her with his rude comment during his first appearance. Though it was given in a private conversation and inadvertently overheard by Elizabeth, the insult can only be regarded as the result of insufferable arrogance. Of course, it turns out to be something else, the defensive reaction of a shy man, who can be sociable only in circumstances where he feels very secure. Elizabeth, her vanity nettled, and her prejudice against him invoked first by his general coldness and then later by Wickham's crafty slanders, conceives a decided antagonism toward him. Moreover, Darcy is a very imposing figure, not only rich and well-born, tall and good-looking, but highly intelligent and well-educated. Even if he is no seducer of the Lovelace sort, nor even a Rochester, she must regard him as a dangerous and intimidating figure. She herself notes his "satirical eye," and tells Charlotte Lucas, "[I]f I do not begin by being impertinent myself, I shall soon grow afraid of him" (15).

Thus, the contest between Elizabeth and Darcy, unlike the usual battle of the sexes plot, begins with her genuine dislike of him. At their second encounter, when Sir William Lucas tries to promote a partnership between them in the dance, Elizabeth refuses, and responds to Darcy's effort to recover the situation from Sir William's ineptitude by saying, "Mr. Darcy is all politeness" (17), a piece of acidulated irony that unfortunately none but Elizabeth and the reader can enjoy. Typically, however, as Elizabeth fails to realize how Darcy's opinion of her is changing, Darcy also fails to understand how Elizabeth's ironic independence is motivated partly by antipathy.

When they are thrown together at Bingley's house by Jane's illness, we find that they are not bickering like Benedick and Beatrice, but simply working and thinking at cross-purposes, like a comic Lovelace and Clarissa. Darcy has no idea how suspicious Elizabeth is of his arrogant aloofness, while she has no idea how intrigued he is becoming by her "fine eyes." Elizabeth first enters the skirmishing to defend Bingley from the criticisms of his friend. Moreover, when Bingley remarks that she has only changed what Darcy had said about his weakness of will "into a compliment on the sweetness of [his] temper," she responds, "Would Mr. Darcy then consider the rashness of your original intention as atoned for by your obstinacy in adhering to it?" (33) Bingley himself is befuddled, and leaves it up to Darcy, who, of course, is much too intelligent to be taken in by Elizabeth's rhetorical trick of casting the argument in heavily loaded terms like "rashness" and "obstinacy." But he can only answer in a rather ponderous fashion about "propriety" and "understanding," which allows Elizabeth to point out that he has overlooked the claims of "friendship and affection." Both are right in their different ways. Bingley is both impressionable and flighty, as Darcy claims, and Darcy likewise sees through Bingley's effort to make his slovenly letter-writing into a virtue. On the other hand, as Elizabeth sees, Darcy has momentarily forgotten that there is virtue in complying with the wishes of a friend. Brought up short by her, he doubtless could, if Bingley had not interrupted, have worked out his precise claims of "friendship and affection." But even that would miss the real point, his humorless and overbearing preachiness. If Darcy has seen through Bingley, Elizabeth has at least partly seen through Darcy.

A short time later, Elizabeth notices "how frequently Mr. Darcy's eyes were fixed on her," but concludes only that he considered her somehow "reprehensible." She is thus startled (though the reader is not) when he suggests they dance a reel while Miss Bingley plays "a lively Scotch air." She refuses in terms that make clear her suspicion of his motives — "You wanted me, I know, to say 'Yes,' that you might have the pleasure of despising me" (35) — but fails to affront him because the "mixture of sweetness and archness in her manner ... made it difficult for her to affront anybody" (35). For his part, "Darcy had never been so bewitched by any woman as he was by her" (35). Though sounding enough like an ordinary romantic love story, so that the reader can now look forward to the ultimate resolution in marriage, the story really explores their mistaken judgments. Elizabeth, blinded by prejudice, misses the possibility that Darcy could have changed his mind. Fortunately, her "mixture of sweetness and archness," both facial expression and general body language, mitigate any rudeness in her response. She is, after all, neither arrogant nor vain, but rather a nice, warm-hearted, intelligent young woman, who wants to be loved and appreciated the same as any other human being — on the right terms. But she is really as lost as Darcy, or more so. He knows, or is coming to know, what he wants. Still far from such knowledge, Elizabeth pushes ahead, daring him to try and get the better of her in a battle of wits, and thereby following by accident the design most likely to win his heart.

Their next verbal encounter illustrates this unknowing and accidental strategy even more vividly. Darcy has suggested that Miss Bingley and Elizabeth are walking about the room mainly to show off their figures, but when Elizabeth suggests they tease him back and Miss Bingley refuses, she protests that being exempt from teasing is an "uncommon advantage" which she hopes remains uncommon. Darcy responds, from the height of his superiority, that "the wisest and best of men ... may be rendered ridiculous by a person whose first object in life is a joke." Elizabeth is not awed by this sentence: "I hope I never ridicule what is wise or good. Follies and nonsense, whims and inconsistencies *do* divert me, I own, and I laugh at them whenever I can. — But these, I suppose, are precisely what you are without" (50-1).

Darcy has tried to do back to her what she has done to him, put the opponents on the defensive, make them explain, backtrack, bluster, excuse themselves. But she is too fast for him. When he tries to recast the argument in terms of the frivolous and the wise, she readily explains the seriousness, and thus wisdom, of being satirical at the expense of folly and nonsense, and then once more puts him on the defensive by assuming that he has thus characterized himself as altogether wise and good. His response is significant for what it reveals about him and his need for Elizabeth: "Perhaps that is not possible for any one. But it has been the study of my life to avoid those weaknesses which often expose a strong understanding to ridicule" (51). While wishing not to go overboard — that is, into Darcyism — one can see the problem of the man very clearly. No one would dispute the worthiness of a program of avoiding blamable weaknesses, but Darcy has adopted a rather skewed value system in pursuit of it. Rather than avoiding doing harm to others or to his own moral standing, he merely wishes to avoid ridicule for looking foolish. That is manifestly impossible. We are all fools, and wise only to the degree that we recognize our folly. But Darcy is so full of his self-conceit as a man of stature and wisdom that he has forgotten it.

Elizabeth, who has the same problem, overconfidence in her judgments, immediately seizes on the key point: Darcy's self-satisfaction about avoiding weaknesses. She responds, "Such as vanity and pride." Once more he is forced to justify himself, and the justification he offers is still more telling: "Yes, vanity is a weakness of mind indeed. But pride — where there is real superiority of mind, pride will always be under good regulation." To this Elizabeth responds by hiding a smile. If her mind is not superior to Darcy's, her insight certainly is. Thus, when Miss Bingley re-enters the conversation to ask the result of Elizabeth's "examination of Mr. Darcy," she can offer one of the perfect touches in all of literature: "I am perfectly convinced by it that Mr. Darcy has no defect. He owns it himself without disguise" (51).

Darcy, of course, has not said exactly that, but has come close enough to it to make the exaggeration very just. If you do not want to be accused of thinking yourself faultless, you must go much farther than Darcy has into the depressing swamp of self-inspection, where no gentleman wishes to go. Half of Elizabeth's success, however, lies in the way she phrases her insight. If she only pounced on his remarks and accused him of conceit, he could ignore her as merely rude, and dispose of her remarks with the self-assured logic he generally displays. By agreeing with his "claim" of faultlessness she attributes the insight to him — yet with an irony that is expertly phrased. To a humorless arguer of Darcy's sort, this attack can scarcely be met, for the second sentence is an irony worthy of Swift, pretending to praise him for courage and forthrightness when it actually refers to his smugness and vanity.

As Darcy tries to reassert his mastery of the situation, he reveals more of his patronizing attitude toward mere mortals, and falls into another trap by concluding: "My good opinion once lost is lost for ever." Elizabeth promptly seizes this point, identifies it as "implacable resentment," and admits that she cannot possibility laugh at such a failing (51). Elizabeth's responses, generated partly by self-defense and partly by antipathy, constitute precisely the right strategy to win his heart. Caroline Bingley has no clue as to how to deal with him, and her efforts to be ingratiating annoy him, while those to be fashionable and witty merely expose her limitations. Attacked for his smug vanity, Darcy is left astonished. A man in Darcy's position can hardly be too careful: short of murder or abject flight, he has few options in regard to a woman like Elizabeth except marriage. He cannot hope to shut her up, of course, but at least he could make her his ally.

And this he eventually does, though not before he offers his condescending proposal, is bitterly refused, and justifies himself by revealing the humiliating (to her) truth about Wickham. Over the variety of episodes that follow we see Elizabeth blaming herself for her pride and prejudice, but late discover that Darcy has also reevaluated his own attitudes and behavior, and now can perform an appropriately heroic deed in finding and buying off Wickham. As a result, when they do at last achieve that "understanding" for which the reader becomes so impatient, Elizabeth's joy causes the normal bubbliness of her temper to turn almost into giddiness. She begins an inquisition on how he came to love her, and supplies most of the answers herself, correcting his "liveliness of ... mind" to "impertinence" (319). Nevertheless, her view is typically accurate: "The fact is you were sick of civility, of deference, of officious attention. You were disgusted with the women who were always speaking and looking and thinking for *your* approbation alone. I roused, and interested you, because I was so unlike *them*" (319–20). Darcy is wise enough to realize that he needs Elizabeth to make him what he wishes to be, that she represents the other half of himself — demonstrably affectionate where he is cool and distant, effervescent where he is serious, yet his match in intelligence — his Anima, but the key to his completion as a human being. But she can only do this by being as complete, and intellectually powerful, a person as himself. She must find her own completion in him, a little more judgment and restraint, and, more than anything, a sober and intelligent appreciation for the woman she can be.

With the marriage of Elizabeth and Darcy we reach the end of our investigation of the witty heroine in romantic comedy. No author has, I believe, ever explored the psychological and literary potential of this figure as profoundly as Austen. Even Millamant, even Rosalind, wonderful as they are, pale in comparison. Moreover, we can also see why the character is not attempted more often — not, I believe, because of antagonism to her on the part of some male power structure, but simply because she is very difficult to bring off well. For the romance to work she must have a powerful character, an inner self that is worth exploring, that we can view in heroic terms, and that can make the idea of Love profound instead pedestrian. For the comedy to work, she must be lighthearted yet true, able to provide a point of stability in the conflict of societies or ideals that interferes with the marriages that will form the new society. But at the same time, she must be a wit, an intelligent, insightful, and verbally skillful person who can express truths vividly. It is a rare author (male or female) who can bring off such a character (male or female). But when we find one, we should enjoy her to the fullest, just as the authors clearly did.

WORKS CITED

Auburn, Mark S. "Introduction" to John Dryden, *Marriage a la Mode*. Regents Restoration Drama Series. Lincoln: University of Nebraska Press, 1981.

Austen, Jane. *Pride and Prejudice*. New York: New American Library, 1961.

Babb, Howard S. *Jane Austen's Novels: The Fabric of Their Dialogue*. Columbus: Ohio State University Press, 1962; reptd. New York: Archon, 1967.

Barber, C. L. *Shakespeare's Festive Comedy*. Princeton: Princeton University Press, 1959.

Beaurline, L. A. "General Introduction" and "Introductions" to *Secret Love* and *Marriage a la Mode*, in John Dryden, *Four Comedies*, eds. L. A. Beaurline and Fredson Bowers, Curtain Playwrights Series. Chicago: University of Chicago Press, 1967.

Birdsall, Virginia Ogden. *Wild Civility: The English Comic Spirit on the Restoration Stage*. Bloomington: Indiana University Press, 1970.

Braverman. Richard. "Capital Relations and *The Way of the World*." *ELH* 52 (Spring 1985) 133–158.

Bruce, Donald. *Topics of Restoration Comedy*. New York: St. Martin's, 1974.

Congreve, William. *The Way of the World*, ed. Kathleen M. Lynch. Regents Restoration Drama Series. Lincoln: University of Nebraska Press, 1965.

Craik, W. A. *Jane Austen: the Six Novels*. London: Methuen, 1965.

Donaldson, Ian. *The World Upside Down*. Oxford: Clarendon, 1970.

Dryden. John. *Four Comedies*, eds. L. A. Beaurline and Fredson Bowers. Curtain Playwrights Series. Chicago: University of Chicago Press, 1967.

Erickson, Peter. *Patriarchal Structures in Shakespeare's Drama*. Berkeley: University of California Press, 1985.

Ewin, R. E. "Pride, Prejudice and Shyness." *Philosophy*. 65 (April 90): 137–54.

Foakes. R. A. "Wit and Convention in Congreve" in Bernard Morris, ed., *William Congreve*. Totowa, NJ: Rowan & Littlefield, 1974.

Frye, Northrop. *Anatomy of Criticism*. Princeton: Princeton University Press, 1957.

Gilbert, Sandra M., and Susan Gubar, eds. *The Madwoman in the Attic*. New Haven: Yale University Press, 1979.

Heilman, Robert B. "Parts and Whole in *Pride and Prejudice*," in *Jane Austen: Bicentenary Essays*, ed. John Halperin. Cambridge: Cambridge University Press, 1975, 123–43.

Holland, Norman N. *The First Modern Comedies*. Cambridge: Harvard University Press, 1959.

Jung, C. G., and M.-L. von Franz, eds. *Man and His Symbols*. New York: Dell, 1964.

Kroeber, Karl. "*Pride and Prejudice*: Fiction's Lasting Novelty," in *Jane Austen: Bicentenary Essays*, ed. John Halperin. Cambridge: Cambridge University Press, 1975, 144–55

Kroll, Richard W. F. "Discourse and Power in *The Way of the World*." *ELH* 53 (Winter 1986) 727–58.

Leggatt, Alexander. *Shakespeare's Comedy of Love*. London: Methuen, 1973.

MacCary, W. Thomas. *Friends and Lovers: The Phenomenology of Desire in Shakespearean Comedy*. New York: Columbia University Press, 1985

Muir, Kenneth. *The Comedy of Manners*. London: Hutchinson, 1970.

_____. "The Comedies of William Congreve," in *Restoration Theatre*, eds. John Russell Brown and Bernard Harris. New York: Capricorn, 1967, 221–237.

Mueschke, Paul, and Miriam. *A New View of Congreve*. Ann Arbor: University of Michigan Press, 1958.

Nevo, Ruth. *Comic Transformations in Shakespeare*. London: Methuen, 1980.

Newman, Karen. "Can This Marriage be Saved: Jane Austen Makes Sense of an Ending." *ELH* 50 (Winter 1983): 693–70.

Newton, Judith Lowder. *Women, Power and Subversion*. Athens: University of Georgia Press, 1985.

Ornstein, Robert. *Shakespeare's Comedies*. Newark: University of Delaware Press, 1986.

Park, Clara Claiborne. "As We Like It: How a Girl Can be Smart and Still Popular." *The American Scholar* 42 (Spring 1973): 262–78; rev. and rptd. in Carolyn Ruth Swift Lenz, Gayle Green, and Carol Thomas Neely, eds., *The Woman's Part: A Feminist Criticism of Shakespeare*. Urbana: University of Illinois Press, 1980, 100–116.

Roberts, Phillip. "Mirabell and Restoration Comedy," in *William Congreve*, ed. Bernard Morris. Totowa, NJ: Rowan & Littlefield, 1974.

Shaffer, Julie. "Not Subordinate: Empowering Women in the Marriage Plot — the Novels of Frances Burney, Maria Edgeworth, and Jane Austen." *Criticism* 34 (Winter 1992): 51–73.

Shakespeare, William. *As You Like It*, rev. ed., eds. Irving Ribner and George Lyman Kittredge. Waltham, MA: Ginn, 1941, 1971.

Smith, John Harrington. *The Gay Couple in Restoration Comedy*. Cambridge: Harvard University Press, 1948; rptd. New York: Octagon, 1971.

Snider, Alvin. "Professing a Libertine in *The Way of the World*." *Papers on Language and Literature* 25 (Fall 1989): 376–97.

Van Voris, W. H. *The Cultivated Stance*. Dublin: Dolmen, 1970.

Williams, Aubrey L. *An Approach to Congreve*. New Haven: Yale University Press, 1979.

Wiesenfarth, Joseph. "The Case of Pride and Prejudice." *Studies in the Novel*, 16 (Fall 1984): 261–73.

5

Confinement Sharpens the Invention: Aphra Behn's The Rover and Susanna Centlivre's The Busie Body

SUZ-ANNE KINNEY

Aphra Behn's contribution to the history of literature is, by now, well known. In 1929, in her study of women and literature *A Room of One's Own*, Virginia Woolf marks Aphra Behn's career as a "very important corner on the road," a turning point. With Behn, Woolf argues

> We leave behind, shut up in their parks among their folios, those solitary great ladies who wrote without audience or criticism, for their own delight alone. We come to town and rub shoulders with ordinary people in the streets. Mrs. Behn was ... forced ... to make her living by her wits... She made, by working very hard, enough to live on. The importance of that fact outweighs anything that she actually wrote, ... for here begins the freedom of the mind, or rather the possibility that in the course of time the mind will be free to write what it likes. For now that Aphra Behn had done it, girls could go to their parents and say, You need not give me an allowance; I can make money by my pen. (66–67)

While we have no way of knowing for certain the number of women who actually decided to make their livings as writers as a direct result of Behn's pioneering career, the connection between Susanna Carroll Centlivre's career and Behn's is perhaps the most direct. In 1700, eleven years after Behn's death, Susanna Centlivre wrote her first play, *A Perjur'd Husband*. From the mid-1680s to 1722 — the years that Centlivre worked in the theatre as both playwright and player — Aphra Behn's works were performed on a regular basis. *The Rover*, for instance, was produced 70 times between 1700 and 1725. While we can only assume that Centlivre saw — perhaps even acted in — a number of Behn's plays, her general opinion of Behn was a matter of public record in 1701. In one of the letters included in *Familiar and Courtly Letters* (1700), Centlivre praises Behn's "genius" and wishes an equivalent talent for herself. In letters that she contributed to *Letters of Wit, Politicks and Morality* (1701), Centlivre's use of the *nom de plume* Astraea — the name that Behn was known by a generation earlier — is a defining gesture, not only a conscious act of homage, but a conscious act of appropriation as well.

For Centlivre, the act of appropriating Behn's poetic name implies her own desire to be like Behn, to share in the nominal and monetary rewards associated with being a successful woman playwright. Certainly, a need to identify with someone who had lived through similar experiences would not have been out of the question for Centlivre, for many of her experiences in the theatre were remarkably similar to Behn's. Chief among these similarities is the fact that the plays of Behn and Centlivre were attacked because they were written by women. Not surprisingly, they responded to this criticism in much the same way. In the Preface to *The Dutch Lover*, which was first produced in 1673, Behn writes:

> I printed this Play with all the impatient haste one ought to do, who would be vindicated from the most unjust and silly aspersion, Woman could invent to cast on Woman; and which only my being a Woman has procured me: *That it was Baudy*, the least and most Excusable fault in the Men writers, to whose Plays they all crowd, as if they came to no other end than to hear what they condemn in this: *But from a Woman it was unnaturall*.

Centlivre, in her dedication to *The Platonick Lady* (1707), expands upon this analysis when she chastises

> the Carping Malice of the Vulgar World; who think it a proof of their Sense, to dislike every thing that is writ by Women.
>
> A Play secretly introduc'd to the House, whilst the Author remains unknown, is approv'd by every Body: The Actors cry it up, and are in expectation of a great Run; the Bookseller of a Second Edition, and the Scribler of a Sixth Night: But if by chance the Plot's discover'd, and the Brat found Fatherless, immediately it flags in the Opinion of those that

extoll'd it before, and the Bookseller falls in his Price, with this Reason, *It's a Woman's*. Thus they alter their judgment, by the Esteem they have for the Author, tho' the Play is still the same. They ne'er reflect, that we have had some Male Productions of this Kind, void of Plot and Wit, and full as insipid as ever a Woman's of us all.

While these frontispieces show that Behn and Centlivre were capable of recognizing and exposing the absurd ideology of the dramatic criticism that was practiced upon their plays, the very criticisms they were protesting became the basis for much of what has been said about them in the last 250 years. In 1754, for instance, John Duncombe was expressing a popular attitude when he wrote *The Feminiad*:

The modest Muse a veil with pity throws
O'er Vice's friends and Virtue's foes;
Abash'd she views the bold unblushing mien
Of modern Manley, Centlivre, and Behn;
And grieves to see One nobly born disgrace
Her modest sex, and her illustrious race.
Tho' harmony thro' all their numbers flow'd,
And genuine wit its ev'ry grace bestow'd,
Nor genuine wit nor harmony excuse
The dang'rous sallies of a wanton Muse

This belief that the plays of Behn and Centlivre were dangerous lasted until well after the end of the Victorian era; in a 1905 edition of Behn's novels, for instance, Ernest Baker charged that Behn's plays were "false, lurid and depraved." As a result of this type of criticism, Behn was seen as a "colosal and enduring embarrassment to the generations of women who followed her into the literary marketplace" (Gallagher 23). It was not until 1929, when Woolf wrote *A Room of One's Own*, that the process of reclamation began.

As Susanna Centlivre understood when she took the name Astraea, the similarites between her career and Behn's were many. Perhaps the most ironic similarity given the criticisms they endured for being women is that both wrote immensely popular plays. Behn's *The Rover* (1677) was performed 158 times from 1700 to 1760 (Link xiii). Centlivre's *The Busie Body* (1709) was performed in London 475 times between 1709 and 1800 (Frushell 16). They were both accused of plagiarism, for although it was very common for dramatists to borrow from and rewrite the works of other playwrights, both Behn and Centlivre turned other playwrights' ideas to their own purposes and suffered virulent criticism as a result. Knowing that publication of their names could result in serious personal consequences, both — without success — tried to publish plays anonymously. Perhaps most interesting though is the fact that both were forced, due to the circumstances of their lives, to support themselves through the money they received from writing plays. In mid-1663,

Aphra Behn's father was appointed Lieutenant General of Surinam, a commission which promised to make his fortune. On the voyage to South America, however, he became ill and died. Though Behn completed the journey and spent a short time in Surinam (a period in which she enjoyed unusual autonomy and had the experiences that would later contribute to her novel, *Oroonoko*), she had neither income nor prospect of income when she returned to London in 1664 (Goreau 71). Pressed by circumstance, she became a spy for Charles II during the second Anglo-Dutch War. But this occupation, far from making her self-sufficient, led to a substantial debt, and she may have spent time — from late 1668 to the middle of 1669 — in a debtor's prison. It was only after these extraordinary experiences that Behn decided to become a writer. If Susanna Centlivre's life was less adventurous, it was no more secure financially. While the details of her early life are sketchy and difficult to substantiate, several accounts suggest that Centlivre left home before she was fifteen with little money and no connections (Bowyer 7; Lock 15–16). To support herself, she joined a company of strolling players. She was married twice before 1700, but neither marriage lasted much longer than a year and neither provided her with any financial security. In 1700, *The Perjur'd Husband* was produced, and she became a professional. Despite her early successes, however, she was forced to supplement her income by acting. While her marriage to Joseph Centlivre, one of the Queen's cooks, in 1707 provided Centlivre with a degree of financial security, she continued to write plays until 1722, a year before she died.

Other similarities emerge from a study of their writings. In "Aphra Behn and Sexual Politics: A Dramatist's Discourse with her Audience," for instance, Cheri Davis Langdell focuses on the addendum to the plays — the prologues, epilogues, and dedications. Because these writings were not governed by the conventions that the plays themselves were, Langdell argues, they were a place where Behn's views about her own role in the theatre could find fuller, more honest expression. As a result, Langdell concludes that Behn's "writing and her attitude toward it are acts of sexual politics": they exemplify "woman's resourceful exertion of whatever power she may have — sexual, social, economic, or political — so as to redress the social and psychosexual balance ever so slightly in her favour" (113). Langdell also points to the Centlivre's prologue to *The Platonick Lady* (the one which I have excerpted above) as a continuation of Behn's sexual politics, an illustration of the extent of Behn's legacy and her influence on Centlivre in both content and attitude.

I would like to suggest a reading of Aphra Behn's *The Rover* and Susanna Centlivre's *The Busie Body* in which these concerns — the sexual politics of both writers — are not marginalized, are not extrinsic to the plays. Within the texts of the plays, female experience, including the experience of female authorship, is dramatized. Because of this unique perspective, Behn and

Centlivre began to establish what Susan Carlson, in *Women and Comedy*, calls a "countertradition" to what was (and still is in many respects) a male-dominated theatre. Their plays, like all others, are governed by social and literary conventions, conventions that conform to established attitudes about appropriate behavior for women. And, as in all drama of these periods, these conventions erupt most forcefully into the plays' endings. As Rachel Blau DuPlessis says in *Writing Beyond the Ending*, "social convention is like a 'script,' which suggests sequences of action and response, the meaning we give these, and ways of organizing experience by choices, emphases, priorities" (2). These social scripts control the whole of narrative or plot, but the endings are the place where plot meets ideology most forcefully. Not surprisingly, the priorities of the seventeenth- and early eighteenth-century scripts demanded that the ending of the plots either deemphasized or completely silenced any potential for women characters beyond those conventions. For these reasons, my objective here will be to recover the narrative middle from these plays — to reclaim any possible revolutionary characterizations, attitudes, or structures — before they are sacrificed for the common good known as communal values. At the same time, I would like to recover from the endings any trace of ambiguity over the scripted resolution, for as DuPlessis says, "Any resolution can have traces of the conflicting materials that have been processed within it. It is where subtexts and repressed discourses can throw up one last flare of meaning; it is where the author may sidestep and displace attention from the materials that a work has made available" (3).

Early in her career, Behn saw herself and her work as outside the tradition of male playwriting. In the epilogue to *Sir Patient Fancy* (1678), for instance, Behn criticizes the traditionalists who are more concerned about unities than audience:

> Your way of Writing's out of fashion grown.
> Method, and Rule — you only understand;
> Pursue your way of fooling, and be damn'd.
> Your learned Cant of Action, Time and Place,
> Must all give way to the unlabour'd Farce.

In the prologue to her first play, *The Forc'd Marriage; or, the Jealous Bridegroom* (1671), Behn describes a different approach to drama. She outlines the differences she sees between female writers and their male counterparts:

> Women those charming Victors, in whose Eyes
> Lie all their Arts, and their Artilleries,
> Not being contented with the Wounds they made,
> Would by new Strategems our Lives invade.

> Beauty alone goes now at too cheap rates;
> And therefore they, like wise and Politick States,
> Court a new Power that may the old supply,
> To keep as well as gain the Victory.
> They'll join the force of Wit to Beauty now,
> And so maintain the Right they have in you.

Uttered by a male actor, this prologue warns the audience that playwriting, which requires the writer join a new weapon (her wit) to her old weapon (her beauty), has become a means of extending and exerting female power. As Catherine Gallagher says in "Who Was That Masked Woman? The Prostitute and the Playwright in the Comedies of Aphra Behn," Behn "creates the possibility of a woman's version of sexual conquest [in this prologue]. She will not be immediately conquered and discarded because she will maintain her right through her writing" (25).

Certainly, these prologues and epilogues are statements of intention, the place where Behn articulates her dramatic theory most directly. They point to the fact that her purpose in writing these plays was to carve out a countertradition in the theatre, one that would not only defy the classical unities, but would value both female writers and female experience as well. This feminist countertradition is one that still exists. Susan Carlson, for instance, sees the connection between Behn and contemporary feminist comedy in the following way:

> despite the qualified nature of her comic rebellion, in her controversial women and their unorthodox behavior Behn still manages to sketch the outlines of what I would like to call a "countertradition" of comedy. In her shaping of women characters and especially in her frank portrayal of women's sexuality, she prefigures contemporary British comedy by women, a comedy that still more clearly asserts a tradition of its own. (128)

If Aphra Behn first envisioned this countertradition, Susanna Centlivre certainly benefited from her vision. In her prologues, epilogues, and dedications, she too carried on the struggle to win legitimacy for the female voice and female experience in the early eighteenth-century theatre. In her preface to *Love's Contrivance*, Centlivre outlined her own method of writing plays, a method that she contrasts with traditional ones:

> The Criticks cavil most about Decorums, and cry up Aristotle's Rules as the most essential part of the Play. I own they are in the right of it; yet I dare venture a wager they'll never persuade the Town to be of their Opinion, which relishes nothing so well as Humour lightly tost up with Wit, and drest with Modesty and Air... I do not say this by way of condemning the Unity of Time, Place, and Action; quite contrary, for I think them the greatest Beauties of a Dramatick Poem; but since the

other way of writing pleases full as well, and gives the Poet a larger Scope of Fancy, ... why should a Man torture, and wrack his Brain for what will be no Advantage to him.

This statement of dramatic theory is similar to Behn's: Centlivre criticizes what Behn called "Cant of Action, Time and Place." Her "other way of writing," which gives the Poet "a scope of fancy" beyond the conventional, can be seen as the equivalent to Behn's "new Strategems": her "Humour tost up with Wit." Because too many rules confine the poet, they not only inhibit the playwright's creativity, but fail to produce entertaining drama as well. This final point is important, for throughout part of her career, Centlivre felt compelled (perhaps because she had learned from Behn's experience) to please her audience. The popularity of her plays proves this other way of writing was successful.

So, while both of these playwrights were inevitably constrained by the tradition of comedic drama that they inherited, they also both envisioned their work as being somehow distinct from this tradition. How successfully their feminist visions were translated into the texts of their plays, however, is a controversial issue. Many contemporary readers and critics have perceived a gap between the intentions that they articulated in their prologues, epilogues, and dedications and their ability to accomplish these intentions. In *Feminism in Eighteenth-Century England*, for instance, Katharine M. Rogers says that "[n]either Behn nor Centlivre ... wrote plays distinguishable from men's. They might protest vigorously against sexual discrimination in their prefaces, but they followed literary forms that provided no scope for feminine perceptions or feminine experience" (100). While the plays of Behn and Centlivre certainly seem conservative to a modern reader, we must also acknowledge, as Moira Ferguson does in *First Feminists*, that the definition of feminism changes with time and place — what seems extreme or revolutionary in one age often becomes part of the mainstream culture in another (xi). For their respective historical periods, these plays were clearly viewed by audiences as nontraditional, as "dang'rous sallies of a Wanton Muse," a fact that becomes clear through a comparison of their early plays and their later plays. Over the course of their careers, due (we can only assume) to the increasing virulence of the criticism they received, both Behn and Centlivre began to conform to audience tastes for tradition in two ways: overall, fewer women appeared in their later plays, and the women who were in these later plays spoke fewer lines than their sisters in the earlier plays (Pearson 146, 209).

Aphra Behn's *The Rover* and Susanna Centlivre's *The Busie Body* are amazingly similar comedies. They both operate within the Spanish intrigue comedy tradition, and both focus primarily on two couples — the witty couple and the romantic couple — who are attempting to thwart the wishes of the father or male guardian of the woman. Both end in multiple weddings. They were also, as I noted above, extremely popular plays, so popular in fact that their writers subsequently penned sequels to them: *The Rover, Part II* (1681) and *Mar-Plot* (1710). Their most remarkable similarities, however, can be found in the ways they diverge from tradition. In both *The Rover* and *The Busie Body*, a critique of the way women are treated is an essential element of the plot. At the same time, both Behn and Centlivre attempt to create a positive space outide of that critique, a place where their women characters can have supportive friendships with one another, a place where strong women characters can make their own decisions and act on them, a place where their characters' actions do not have to be driven along a linear and unified path to a predetermined end such as marriage. Finally, in the characters of Angellica and Miranda, Behn and Centlivre inscribed images of the woman playwright into their plays. Because they wrote plays in a period that undervalued their abilities and their contributions, both of these dramatists attempted to create a positive space wherein the woman playwright could exist.

The Rover and *The Busie Body* begin — in keeping with traditional dramatic structure — by establishing a status quo. In *The Rover*, the "virtuous" women — Florinda and Hellena — are under the control of their father, who has planned their futures in advance: Hellena will take vows and enter a nunnery, and Florinda will make an advantageous marriage to an unattractive aristocrat. A critique of this position of authority is facilitated by the fact that the patriarch himself does not appear in the play. Instead, Don Pedro, the brother of Florinda and Hellena, is the patriarch's spokesperson in the scheme of the play; as a member of the younger generation, however, Pedro's ability to protect and sustain the status quo is ineffectual. Because there is no vocal, embodied representation of the view that women should submit to the law of their fathers, then, Behn's critique of patriarchal authority is achieved rather easily. Florinda, for instance, makes the following comment about her forced marriage to Pedro: "I hate Vicentio, sir, and I would not have a man so dear to me as my brother follow the ill customs of our country and make a slave of his sister" (I.i). Hellena sides with Florinda, of course; she comments on her father's choice of a husband for Florinda and — indirectly — on her own probable future as a nun: "Marry Don Vincentio! Hang me, such a wedlock would be worse than adultery with another man. I had rather see her in the *Hostel de Dieu*, to waste her youth there in vows, and be a handmaid to lazars and cripples, than to lose it in such a marriage" (I.i). In the course of the play, when both Florinda and Hellena extricate themselves from the control of their father and assert their love and sexual attractions to their respective prospective husbands, the audience approves their triumph.

This approval, of course, was not socially acceptable during the period. As Rogers points out, "Marriage was more or less forced on women, as their only way to a recognized position in society... [It] ranged from mild subjection to virtual slavery" (7); "[w]omen who married contrary to their parents' wishes were apt to find themselves without portion or inheritance and with reputations damaged by such evidence of uncontrolled passion and willfulness" (11). In the play, the concept of forced marriage is often seen in terms of slavery (as Florinda points out). Often in Behn's play, relationships are viewed in terms of power struggles. In forced marriages — like the one Florinda is destined for at the beginning of the play — women usually lose this struggle. But in marriages of choice — like the Hellena/Willmore match — women often win the struggle. Because of this differential in sexual politics, Behn takes on the institution of forced marriage in her plays in order to criticize its unjust control over women. As Jacqueline Pearson says in *The Prostituted Muse*, Behn often "attacks the control exerted on the young and unmoneyed, both male and female, by patriarchal authorities, fathers and guardians and husbands, but the emphasis most often falls on the suffering of women" (160).

Pearson's observations could just as easily apply to Susanna Centlivre, for a similar resistance to the status quo is represented in *The Busie Body*. Sir Francis Gripe and Sir Jealous Traffick, as the ruling patriarchs in the scheme of the play, have ultimate control over virtually all the characters. Whether it is for consent to marry (as is the case with Miranda and Isabinda), or for payment of an inheritance (as is the case with Marplot, Miranda, Isabinda, and Charles) most of the characters in this play must rely upon the protection and support of these two domestic tyrants. Because they appear in the play as actual characters, though, Centlivre can critique them in both their characterizations and the speeches of other characters. Both Sir Francis and Sir Jealous are depicted as insidious money-grubbers and foolish old lechers. Sir Francis' lack of good faith pervades the administration of all of his duties. Once he has convinced his brother patriarchs to place their estates in his control, he abuses his power. In one of his most insidious acts, he becomes Miranda's pimp; he sells her time — one hour for 100 pounds — to Sir George as if she were a prostitute. Not satisfied with a mere 100 pounds, however, Sir Francis sets his goal at nothing less than Miranda's money and body: "Some Guardians wou'd be glad to compound for part of the Estate, at dispatching an Heiress, but I engross the whole [by marrying her myself]" (III). Sir Jealous is only slightly better than Sir Francis. His obsession with Spanish customs makes him appear only foolish at first. But in his desire to make Isabinda live according to Spanish customs — "No Galloping abroad, no receiving Visits at home; for in our loose Country [England], the Women are as dangerous as the Men" (II) — Sir Jealous' actions are as motivated by monetary considerations as Sir Francis'. Deeply suspicious, he attempts to control all of Isabinda's actions: from her walks on the balcony to the choice of her husband. He is consistently locking her in her rooms in order to prevent "some sauntering coxcomb" from thinking that "by leaping into her arms, [he can] leap into my estate" (II).

The women in *The Busie Body* — Miranda and Isabinda — actively (though sometimes covertly) rail against these treacherous oppressors and their ultimate weapon, marriage. Both women resist the marriages which Sir Francis and Sir Jealous have contrived for them, and both women succeed in achieving the marriages they desire, an ending that is — like the ending of *The Rover* — approved in the scheme of the play. At the same time, however, Miranda resists the confines of marriage itself, first to Sir George in act I: "Matrimony! Ha, ha, ha; what Crimes have you comitted against the God of Love, that he should revenge 'em so severely to stamp Husband upon your forehead" (I). Later, Miranda tells Sir George during their scaled-down version of the proviso scene that marriage is a "terrible Bugbear" (IV); she knows that she is trading her dependence upon a *certain* tyrant for dependence upon a *possible* tyrant. Even though Sir George is a "man of sense" and not as unreasonable and disagreeable as Sir Francis, Miranda knows that "If he should despise, slight or use me ill, there's no Remedy from a Husband, but the Grave" (V). This attitude toward marriage — the ultimate patriarchal institution — is supported by the end of the play. There, Whisper and Scentwell (two people who because of their class would seem to have less control over their lives than their employers) are given the choice to marry or not. Given this choice by Charles, both Whisper and Scentwell claim an equal distaste for the "terrible Bugbear." They both opt for the benevolence and loyalty they have found in service over the forced servitude of marriage.

In both of these plays, many of the social conventions that solidify the oppression of women are critiqued by Behn and Centlivre. Yet, as dramatists, they do not settle for mere critique of social and dramatic conventions. One of the counter-strategies that they offer to these limited views and treatments of women characters is the possibility of female friendship. Unlike their counterparts in plays like *The Way of the World*, *The Man of Mode*, *The Tragedy of Jane Shore*, and *The Beggar's Opera*, where women only pretend friendship and later turn out to be rivals and enemies, the women in these two comedies create a space where women can not only cease to be rivals, but actually understand, sympathize with, and respect each other. One of the most remarkable aspects of *The Rover*, for instance, is its opening scene; this play is one of the few in Restoration drama that opens with a woman-only scene. This fact is significant, for it allows the audience to view the rest of the play — particularly the actions of men — through the perspective of the women who appear in the scene. A similar woman-only segment occurs in the beginning of act III, scene i as well, before the men enter the scene. Pearson has surveyed all of Behn's plays and concludes that she is unusual "in allowing women to speak first in plays so often, and in including so many scenes in which only women appear, scenes which are often particularly vivid and convincing" (146). What is even more unusual in *The Rover*, though, is how women characters who are set up into rival positions react to one another. In act IV, scene ii, Angellica and Hellena (dressed in man's clothing) find themselves in the same room with Willmore. Instead of fighting each other, they both question Willmore's intentions and character. Hellena, who knows that Willmore is involved with Angellica, does not attack her rival, but warns her of Willmore's "inconstancy" (IV.ii). When Hellena tells her story, Angellica — while she does not know Hellena's true identity — immediately reacts by questioning Willmore — "Is't thus you pay my generous passion back?" (IV.ii) — and promises revenge not on Hellena but on Willmore — "I am resolved to think on a revenge/On him that soothed me thus to my undoing" (IV.ii).

While Susanna Centlivre does not use as many women-centered scenes as Behn does in *The Rover*, the friendship that is established between Miranda, Isabinda, and Patch is a much more thorough one. Miranda and Isabinda are genuinely friends in this play. Miranda works as hard to extricate her friend from the clutches of a controlling father and an unknown mate as she does to free herself from Sir Francis' grip. She arranges for Patch to act as Isabinda's servant, a sacrifice that helps Isabinda gain intermittent freedom to see Sir Charles. Patch, in effect, becomes the conduit of their friendship. Both Miranda and Isabinda receive news of each others' circumstances from the servant that they both love and trust. And the only woman-only segments that occur in the play are between Miranda and Patch, and later Isabinda and Patch. Ironically, Isabinda and Miranda, who appear in the same scene only at the end of the play, never speak to each other. At the same time, their sisterhood is an integral part of the play.

Another counter-strategy used by these two playwrights involves their characterizations of women. Consistently, Behn and Centlivre imagine strong, witty, and active women, women who are capable of setting goals and making them a reality. *The Rover*'s most effective character in fact is not the title character, who is represented as either passive, ineffectual, or drunk, but Hellena. From early in the play, Hellena knows that she does not want to take her vows and join the convent. She wants marriage, and not just any marriage: "I don't intend every he that likes me shall have me, but he that I like" (III.i). She pursues her desired mate, effectively using disguises both at the carnival and in the confrontation scene with Angellica and Willmore. Throughout the play, she is active and effective in a way that the the Rover himself is not. As Pearson says, "Willmore is a passive centre of the intrigues of the women rather than, as they are, an active mover" (153). (Pearson's "they" is important here, for even the most passive woman character in the play — Florinda — acts with the purpose of escaping a forced marriage.)

Two other female characters in Behn's play help round out this pattern of behavior. The two prostitutes, Lucetta and Angellica, represent what Pearson calls the "most extreme examples of female power" and male powerlessness in the play. Both of these themes are demonstrated in the Lucetta/Blunt subplot. After luring Blunt to her home, she does not sleep with him, but instead robs him and has him dumped in the sewer. The most surprising aspect of this subplot is that it has no — realized — consequences. Lucetta is never punished for her treatment of Blunt, and Blunt's revenge — the attempted rape of Florinda — is thwarted as well. Angellica also provides an example of these themes when, in act V, she draws a pistol and threatens Willmore's life. This, according to Pearson, is the kind of sexual reversal that often occurs in Behn's plays. "Male sexuality in Behn is often an instrument of power, and she allows women to compete for this by allowing them to share the phallic power of swords, daggers, and pistols" (158). And while Angellica's revenge — like Blunt's — is never accomplished, this equality in representation is itself a mark of progress.

Representations of female power can also be found in *The Busie Body*, but they are representations of a kind of power that, like Hellena's, is often wielded indirectly — through disguise and manipulation — instead of directly as in the case of Lucetta and Angellica. Like Hellena, Miranda resists any attempt at masculine control. She is talking about Sir Jealous, for instance, when she tells Patch, "Suppose he could introduce his rigid Rules — does he think we cou'd not match them in contrivance? No, no; Let the Tyrant Man make the laws he will, if there's a Woman under the Government, I warrant she finds a way to break 'im " (I). Miranda's strategem to free both herself and Isabinda from their respective dictators reflects a more comprehensive power than Hellena's, for while Hellena can only affect her own fate, Miranda's actions affect every character in the play. Through her actions — her providing Isabinda a loyal servant in Patch, her manipulation of Sir Francis, and her ability to procure the "authentick papers" at the end of the play — the two couples achieve the economic independence they need to marry. Her greatest achievement is her manipulation of Sir Francis. In spite of the fact that he has technical control of both her body and her money, Miranda manages to outwit his scheme to become her husband and permanent master. Her strategem begins to take shape at the beginning of act 2, when she says to her guardian, "I am not to possess my Estate, without your Consent, till I'm Five and Twenty; you shall only abate the odd Seven Years, and make me Mistress of my Estate to Day, and I'll make you Master of my Person to Morrow." In act 3, scene 4, Miranda's plan has been revised, her argument substantiated:

> Sir Franc: [W]hen shall we marry, ha?
> Miran: There's nothing wanting but your Consent, Sir Francis.
> Sir Fran: My Consent! what do's my Charmer mean?

> Miran: Nay, 'tis only a Whim: But I'll have every thing acording to form — Therefore when you sign an Authentick Paper, drawn up by an able Lawyer, that I have your Leave to marry, the next Day makes me yours, Gardee.
>
> Sir Fran: Ha, ha, ha, a Whim indeed! why is it not Demonstration I give my Leave when I marry thee.
>
> Miran: Not for your Reputation, Gardee; the malicious World will be apt to say, you trick'd me into Marriage, and so take the Merit from my Choice. Now I will have the act my own, to let the idle Fops see how much I prefer a Man loaded with years and Wisdom.

Ultimately, this strategem works, for Miranda escapes the confines of a marriage to that "delicate bedfellow" Sir Francis by manipulating him with language. She is not, however, above using the disguise of silence when it suits her purposes. In the dumb scene in act 2, Miranda uses silence to resist a similar type of control by Sir George Airy. After he purchases the right to speak with her, Miranda, in Pearson's words, "punishes him for treating her as a commodity by refusing to speak": "It is only when he gives up his attempt to control her that she uses her powers over language to win him" (221).

Because of their depictions of women, both as individuals and friends, *The Rover* and *The Busie Body* become dialogues about sexual politics. What Aphra Behn originated with Hellena and Angellica, Susanna Centlivre continued with her portrayal of Miranda. Yet, despite these considerable successes in creating a tradition of their own in comedy, there are, as I pointed out in the beginning of this essay, considerable problems as well. Despite their ground-breaking depictions of women in their courtship and marriage plots, the endings of these two plays are extremely conventional. Both follow linear plots constructed on the desire of two young couples to marry and focus on the ways that their desires are acheived. Behn's *The Rover* ends shortly after the marriage of Florinda and Belvile, shortly before the marriage of Hellena and Willmore. Centlivre's *The Busie Body* ends with the marriage of both couples — Miranda and Sir George Airy and Isabinda and Charles. Because of their conventional closings, many of the revolutionary aspects of these plays that I have outlined above — the critique of marriage and the strong, independent women — seem to be undercut by the total immersion into the patriarchal institution of marriage. They are as Elin Diamond says in "*Gestus* and Signature in Aphra Behn's *The Rover*," "recuperated back into the economy they rebel against" (540). In effect, these endings trap the women they are about (and by) in the ideology of the times during which they were written. Carlson summarizes these concerns when she writes, "while a comic ending restores men to their power in the social heirarchy, it restores women to powerlessness" (22).

There are, in these two plays, however, traces of ambiguity over their endings, traces of ambiguity that highlight the concerns that I have outlined

above. Much of this ambiguity can be found in the characterizations of
Angellica and Marplot. Angellica and Marplot have been described by many
critics as the most striking characters to take the stage in their respective
plays. Both have also been the center of critical controversies because they
seem to rattle around in their respective plays' marriage plots like loose cogs.
Angellica disappears from the play half way through the final act. And
Marplot, while he is forgiven by the other characters and receives control of
his own estate at the end of the play, is the only character in the younger
generation who does not get married. This failure to include these two powerful characters in their resolutions has often been seen as a sign of weakness.
As Regina Barreca says in her introduction to Last Laughs, "The refusal to
supply closure has been misread as an inability to do so, as a failure of
imagination and talent on the part of the writer" (17). Instead of reading these
two characters as failures as so many critics have in the past, I suggest we
read them as examples of what Elin Diamond calls a feminist version of
Brechtian *Gestus*: a moment in a feminist text where the contradictory meaning of both theatrical and social conventions "for female fictions and historical women" become apparent to the spectator or reader (524).

In this context, the character of Angellica can be seen as a symbol for the
commodification of women. Because she is a prostitute, Angellica's body is,
in Marx's terminology, a commodity. But, unlike the other more virtuous
women in the play, Angellica has no owner, no father, husband, or brother to
act as her trader. She sets her own price, and the market is then regulated only
by whether or not a would-be purchaser can afford her price. Angellica, unlike
the other women in these plays, is in control of her only commodity — her
body. In a conversation at the end of act II, scene II, Angellica and Willmore
exchange the following words about her value:

Willmore:	Take heed, fair creature, how you raise my hopes,
	Which once assumed pretends to all dominion:
	There's not a joy thou hast in store
	I shall not then command.
	For which I'll pay you back my soul, my life!
	Come, let's begin th'account this happy minute!
Angellica:	And will you pay me then the price I ask?
Willmore:	Oh, why dost thou draw me from an awful worship,
	By showing thou art no divinity.
	Conceal the fiend, and show me all the angel!
	Keep me but ignorant, and I'll be devout
	And pay my vows forever at this shrine.
Angellica:	The pay I mean is but thy love for mine.
	Can you give that?
Willmore:	Entirely.

As Diamond says, "By eliminating her value-form [the fetishized, market form of the commodity which alienates the producer from the product], Angellica attempts to return her body to a state of nature, to take herself out of circulation" (533). But thematically, here, Angellica is more than just a symbol of Marxist political philosophy. Her character is, as Diamond points out, an example of Brechtian gestus, a place where the play itself (Angellica's characterization), the theatre apparatus (the actress and the female playwright), and the social struggle (an analysis of the commodification of women) intersect. Accommodating Angellica in the ending of the play, into the marriage plot, would have diminished her gestic significance. Angellica's function in the play is to reveal the contradictions inherent in a society which treats human beings as material objects and, as Laura Brown says in *English Dramatic Form*, reduces "human relationships to economic exchange" (62).

Marplot's character undergoes a similar symbolic transformation in *The Busie Body*. Like Angellica, his significance as a character can be seen as a result of his role in the sexual economy of the play. On one hand, Marplot is desexed in the play; he is a "curiously unmale figure, in some ways an embodiment and parody of stereotypical views of women" (Pearson 210). One the other hand, Marplot is like Willmore, the rake. He moves through this play in much the same way that Willmore moves through *The Rover*. Like Willmore, Marplot's chief pleasure is in knowing everybody's "business," a common pun for sex in Restoration drama. One of his primary functions is to "subvert male sexuality" (Pearson 210): he, like Willmore, continually interferes with the sexual intrigues of his friends. Furthering this ambiguity about Marplot's sexuality is his function in the plot. Marplot, more than any other character in *The Busie Body*, occupies the position of "Other" in this play. Throughout the play, he wants to be part of the action, part of the courtship plot; continually, however, he is marginalized by the other characters. Like Angellica, then, Marplot's characterization as Other becomes a gestic moment in the text. His ambiguous sexuality functions as comic relief in the play itself. Through his characterization, however, the theatre conventions of the rake and the Spanish intrigue comedy are parodied. Marplot is the rake who is actually desexed, no longer a potent force in the drama itself. Through his ineffectualness, he also parodies the male-originated form of the intrigue comedy, a form of drama that depends upon intelligence. Because he is not accommodated into the resolution of the play, Marplot also becomes a symbol of the contemporary social struggle over gender roles and exclusion, a subject that is very real to Centlivre as a woman writer in the eighteenth century.

In these two characters — Angellica and Marplot — Behn and Centlivre add gestic characters whose significance cannot be integrated into the conventional endings of the plays. But that fact does not undercut, I think, the importance of these characters within the schemes of the plays. In fact, this refusal to "supply closure" in these instances is one of the projects of feminist drama today. As Barreca points out, feminist drama depends "on the process, not on the endings" (17):

> Resolution of tensions, like unity or integration, should not be considered viable definitions of comedy for women writers because they are too reductive to deal with the non-closed nature of women's writings. As [Mary Ellmann in *Thinking About Women*] asserts, the woman writer cares less for what is resolved than for what is recognized in all its conceivable diversions into related or, for that matter, unrelated issues. Once rules are suspended, admirable and remarkable "exceptions are released," recognised, and embraced. (17)

Being confined by the dramatic conventions that limited the power of women in the theatre led Behn and Centlivre to create other possibilities in their plays. Because conventional comedy generally ended with marriage, and because Behn and Centlivre were writing for an audience that expected this type of ending, both of these writers gave their publics what they wanted. At the same time, this confinement, as Isabinda says in *The Busie Body*, can "sharpen the invention." This sense of confinement that Behn and Centlivre inevitably felt writing in a male centered tradition accounts for the final innovation that can be found in these two plays. In *The Rover* and *The Busie Body*, Behn and Centlivre inscribe a space where women writers can exist, and in doing so, they release another exception to tradition. As Diamond says about *The Rover*, "As a woman writer in need of money, Behn was vulnerable to accusations of immodesty; to write meant to expose herself, to put herself into circulation; like Angellica, to sell her wares. Is it merely a coincidence that Angellica Bianca shares Aphra Behn's initials, that hers is the only name from *Thomaso* that Behn leaves unchanged?" (536). Similarly, in *The Busie Body*, Miranda — because of the way she orchestrates the action of the play through language — can be read as a stand-in for the writer.

There is a significant difference, though, between these two characterizations, an ambiguity that their conflicted endings highlights. Angellica, as I have noted above, does not participate in the ending of the play; at great personal cost, she succeeds in remaining outside the control of the communal values that try to define her. As a result, her creator achieves a similar degree of literary freedom. Miranda, on the other hand, has a place in the resolution of the plot, a *telos* which reasserts the status quo. Similarly, Centlivre as a playwright — because of the changes that had occurred between Behn's time and her own, in the theatre and its audience's expectations — had less control than the previous Astraea. In the early eighteenth century, the British theatre was more conservative than it was during the Restoration. When Behn began writing, a relaxation of moral strictures was occurring in both society in general and the theatre in particular, a laxity that provided an opening for a freer, more innovative, drama. By the beginning of the eighteenth century, though, an increased sentimentalism led to a demand for a more moral drama. As J. H. Smith says in *The Gay Couple* in *Restoration Comedy*, "In the first half of the eighteenth century it becomes the principal business of comedy (if this term may still be used to describe the plays) to empty ... standard patterns, to repress rakishness and coquetry, and to recommend contrary ideals" (199).

This diminution in the acceptance of women in the theatre from Behn's time to Centlivre's was a precursor to what would happen to theatre in general — and specifically feminist theatre — in 1737 when the Licensing Act was passed. At this time, women writers in the theatre became even more rare. As Pearson says,

> The intention of this legislation was to bring the theatre under very firm government control and to 'limit the production of legitimate drama to two patent houses and place the licensing of plays under the Lord Chamberlain.' The Act was particularly troublesome to women like Charlotte Charke who were working in 'alternative' theatres and dramatising anti-establishment views; but by increasing the legal control over drama, it may have offered a more general deterrent to women, who were already nervous about appearing in public as writers. The Act also discouraged risk-taking by theatre managers, which may also have hit women disproportionately. (20)

Whatever the intention of the Licensing Act, its repercussions for women were long-felt: women playwrights were scarce between the periods when Behn and Centlivre wrote and the beginning of the twentieth century. And the prohibitions were not only institutional. Virginia Woolf was correct in pointing out that after girls began telling their parents they could make money by their pens, "the [parent's] answer for many years to come was, Yes, by living the life of Aphra Behn! Death would be better! and the door was slammed faster than ever" (67). By the beginning of the twentieth century, however, the lives of Behn and Centlivre — and their nascent visions of a dramatic countertradition — no longer seemed so dangerous. Between 1900 and 1920, some four hundred British women wrote plays (Carlson 164).

WORKS CITED

Baker, Ernest. "Introduction." *The Novels of Aphra Behn*. London, 1905.

Barreca, Regina. "Introduction," in: *Last Laughs*, ed. Regina Barreca. New York: Gordon and Breach, 1988, 3–22.

Behn, Aphra. *The Rover*, ed. Frederick M. Link. Lincoln: University of Nebraska Press, 1967.

Bowyer, John Wilson. *The Celebrated Mrs*. Centlivre. Durham: Duke University Press, 1952.

Brown, Laura. *English Dramatic Form, 1660 to 1760*. New Haven: Yale University Press, 1981.

Carlson, Susan. *Women and Comedy*. Ann Arbor: University of Michigan Press, 1991.

Centlivre, Susanna. *The Busie Body* (1709). Augustan Reprint Society 19. Los Angeles: University of California Press, 1949.

Diamond, Elin. "*Gestus* and Signature in Aphra Behn's *The Rover*." *English Literary History* 56 (1989): 519–41.

DuPlessis, Rachel Blau. *Writing Beyond the Ending*. Bloomington: Indiana University Press, 1982.

Familiar and Courtly Letters Written by Voiture. London, 1700.

Ferguson, Moira. *First Feminists*. Bloomington: Indiana University Press, 1985.

Frushell, Richard C. "Marriage and Marrying in Susanna Centlivre's Plays." *Papers on Language and Literature* 22 (1986): 16–38.

Gallagher, Catherine. "Who Was That Masked Woman? The Prostitute and the Playwright in the Comedies of Aphra Behn." *Women's Studies* 15 (1988): 23–42.

Goreau, Angeline. *Reconstructing Aphra*. New York: Dial, 1980.

Hume, Robert D. *The Development of English Drama in the Late Seventeenth Century*. Oxford: Clarendon, 1976.

Langdell, Cheri Davis. "Aphra Behn and Sexual Politics: A Dramatist's Discourse with her Audience." *Drama, Sex and Politics*. Cambridge: Cambridge University Press, 1985. 109–128.

Letters of Wit, Politicks and Morality. London, 1701.

Link, Frederick M. "Introduction." *The Rover*, by Aphra Behn. Lincoln: University of Nebraska Press, 1967, ix–xvi.

Lock, F.P. *Susanna Centlivre*. Twayne's English Authors Series, ed. Bertram H. Davis. Boston: Twayne–Hall, 1979.

Pearson, Jacqueline. *The Prostituted Muse*. New York: St. Martins, 1988.

Rogers, Katharine M. *Feminism in Eighteenth-Century England*. Urbana: University of Illinois Press, 1982.

Root, Robert L. "Aphra Behn, Arranged Marriage, and Restoration Comedy." *Women and Literature* 5 (1977): 3–14.

Smith, J.H. *The Gay Couple in Restoration Comedy*. Cambridge: Harvard University Press, 1948.

Woolf, Virginia. *A Room of One's Own*. New York: Harvest-Harcourt, 1929.

6

Masquerade, Modesty, and Comedy in Hannah Cowley's The Belle's Strategem

ERIN ISIKOFF

Hannah Cowley's comedy, *The Belle's Strategem* (1780), recounts Letitia Hardy's successful attempt to win the affections of her fiancé, Doricourt, with a strategy of varied personas. Letitia orchestrates her own romance by acting out alternate female identities and thereby tricking Doricourt into his role of the faithful hero. Hidden behind different female facades, Letitia experiments with the possible allures inherent in vulgarity, wit, and propriety. Thus, the play calls for a critical examination of its constructions of female identity and a careful evaluation of the ideals of behavior and self that are sanctioned for the heroine as either proper or powerful. Indeed, an analysis of Letitia's encounters with her intended constructs a dichotomy between the eighteenth-century tropes of modesty and of masquerade, the two sorts of veils that obscure our heroine and engender her successes and failures.

Modesty and masquerade can be understood as two versions of the same practise, two methods that disguise the nature of a woman's true identity and feelings. However, eighteenth-century commentators viewed the matter differently, considering the former as a respectable (unsexual) and essential female uniform and the latter as a degrading (sexual) and dangerous garb. *The Belle's Strategem*[1] suggests that both a modest demeanor and a masquerade costume are types of trappings to be put on and off as the occasion suits, but it leaves open the question of which is the better strategy for Letitia and for any woman intent on charming. It is not immediately clear which type of mask empowers Letitia and which veil cages her within delimiting social norms. Nor is it obvious how the ending of the comedy, as usual a happy marriage, mediates between the two. As modesty is both a sort of masquerade and its counteragent, its joyous triumph at the finale needs clarification.

Cowley's play reads as a comic meditation on not only the pleasures but also the limitations of disguise for a heroine intent on her own plot, intent on plotting. Letitia's stratagems easily triumph over the selfish fop who is its object until the two are joined in marriage and the fool becomes the husband. Indeed, *BS* figures the female discourse of desire as a masked discourse, both in the sense that Letitia reveals her love for Doricourt only when her identity is hidden and also as the play effectively veils its advocacy of female empowerment with a reestablishment at its closure of patriarchal proscriptions against female activity. This masked discourse signals an author reliant herself on strategies of indirection, strategies that are masked. The true nature of Cowley's positions is hidden; the play evaluates virtue and vice inconsistently and obscures its morality. Cowley, like Letitia, plots and, like Letitia, she plots in disguise.

The text of the play insists on the link between Cowley and Letitia. Significantly, Letitia's various identities rely not only on facial disguise, but also on the mask of language. It is precisely Letitia's varied conversational personas (like Cowley's comic talent) that earn our notice and our interest. Through vulgar, witty, and proper language, Letitia also writes a comedy for herself. In addition, the prologue and the epilogue to *BS* address the issue of masquerade and by so doing construct parallels between author and heroine. Cowley presents herself anonymously, veils herself, and her mask too is a sort of emancipation from the perils of public performance. The resumption of patriarchal values that concludes the work comments not only on Letitia's presumption, but on Cowley's own masquerade and her plot of female empowerment in and through disguise.

The prologue to *BS* invokes the image of the masquerade as theater. Behind the curtain, "train-bearers to tragic queens" mingle with "Harlequin, and Punch, and Banquo's ghost," so that "all this night perform a grand review" (284). However, this description of assorted costumes effectively unmasks the male players who will perform Cowley's work; Cowley's first maneuver of *BS* is to deny the theater's power of masquerade in a play that presents a heroine's attempts to conceal identity. Does this demystification of the theater foreshadow the necessary failure of Letitia's masquerade plot? The prologue then levies a curse on Hannah Cowley, "To *damn* this author — but oh! save her play" (286). To counteract, perhaps, her insistence on unmasking, the prologue speaks in favor of a plot of mystery and drama, in favor of masquerade, in favor of the belle's (Letitia's) stategem of disguise. Thus Cowley institutes in the prologue a dialogue about the possibilities of masquerade, so that the drama begins with its moral debate already underway. This debate is established as both contentious and firmly undecided. At the moment when the prologue most vehemently declaims against Cowley it also conceals her identity so that the defamation of demystification enacts another transformative mask, that of anonymity. "Tis thus we're serv'd, when saucy women write — ... When lady writers crowd our Covent stage!" (285).

The prologue raises the issue of masquerade in order both to thematize it and to denote Cowley, along with Letitia, as a masquerading subject. Both author and heroine are engaged in the debate about the propriety of false or anonymous identities. Both are also potentially guilty of the impropriety, the "sauciness," of plotting ("writing"). Cowley implicates Letitia and herself in these unresolved debates, thus enmeshing them both in strategems necessarily accommodating, necessarily indirect.[2] By writing a self-damning prologue, Cowley promises her audience a performance that contradicts its own mastery and a heroine both damned and saved. Letitia and Cowley both may be accused of indelicacy, but from their unseemly disguises emerge comic, delightful plots.

It seems likely that Cowley took the issue of masquerade, its propriety and impropriety, seriously. An important dramatist of the late eighteenth century,[3] Cowley put on plays with David Garrick, R. B. Sheridan, George Coleman, and Thomas Harris, London's most prominent contemporary producers. *BS* itself, her fourth piece, had a twenty-eight-night run in 1780 and earned Cowley over 500 pounds (Link xix). However, Cowley published many of her poems under a pseudonym, "Anna Matilda." Authorship and decorum are sometimes at odds, but through the agency of a mask, of a false identity, Cowley reconciles respectability and accomplishment. Masks, then, not only mediate identity but also manage to protect it, so that a woman in disguise can plot with gentility.

Letitia's masquerade plot and the various identities it engenders register this debate between disguise and propriety. Cowley allows the adventures of a young girl to attest to the arguments for and against masquerade and modesty. It is Letitia who concocts the plot of the *BS*, telling her father Mr. Hardy, "a plan has struck me, if you will not oppose it, which flatters me with brilliant success" (296). The rather intellectual plan, which is opposed by Mrs. Rackett as "good philosophy," but "a bad maxim" (296), is even in Letitia's own estimation, "a little paradoxical" (296). It centers on its own "brilliancy," for it exploits Lady Brilliant's masquerade, which all the play's characters plan to attend. Letitia, determined to reverse Doricourt's unfavorable reception of her charms at their first meeting, contends that "as he does not like me enough, I want him to like me still less, and will at our next interview endeavor to heighten his indifference into dislike" (296). She further explains, "'tis much easier to convert a sentiment into its opposite, than to transform indifference into tender passion" (296). Specifically, Letitia, perceiving that her modest demeanor has veiled her talents and left her loved one uninterested, imagines alternate personalities in which to appear to more or less advantage. By this method, Doricourt will be tricked out of his indifference, an indifference he might never take the trouble to evaluate of his own accord. Because "Men are all dissemblers, flatterers, deceivers!" (294), Letitia schemes to seduce with lies.

Letitia's intentions shape the comedy, which only ends with the success of her plot and its revelation to Doricourt. And Cowley reserves for Letitia all the energy and activity of the play. When Letitia remarks of her plot, "I have the strongest confidence in it. I am inspired with unusual spirits, and on this hazard willingly stake my chance for happiness. I am impatient to begin my measures" (296), it is apparent that the issues at stake for the heroine yoke the comic to the dramatic. Letitia responds to romantic crisis with vigor and invention, with high seriousness, because it seems that her guardians are no guarantors of her happiness. Mrs. Rackett, her chaperone, answers Letitia's fears and schemes with nonchalance: "I can't stay now to consider it. I am going to call on the Ogles, and then to lady Frances Touchwood's, and then to an action, and then — I don't know where" (296). Her father, Mr. Hardy, is both too ignorant and too indolent to bother about his daughter's welfare: "Well 'tis an odd thing — I can't understand it, — but I foresee Letty will have her way, and so I shan't give myself the trouble to dispute it" (297). Thus Letitia monopolizes our attention with good reason. When Letitia recruits all the "spirit or invention in woman" (296), she claims a lion's share of Cowley's dramatic power as well.

Mr. Hardy, patriarchy's representative, brings his assumptions about proper venues for female invention to bear on Letitia's dilemma, encouraging her to win Doricourt's affection by resorting to all the powers of her toilette (296). But Doricourt has no objection to Letitia's physical attractions, no criticism of her "complexion, shape, and features" (289). He judges her "a fine girl, as far as mere flesh and blood goes" (289). Mr. Hardy seems unaware of the issues truly at stake in the match, and hence unable to ensure its completion. Significantly, Letitia's command of language, her art, empowers her in the very transaction about which the play concerns itself and yet in which she is otherwise disempowered, her marriage. The agreement made years ago between Mr. Hardy and Doricourt's father renders Letitia passive in this most important occasion; Letitia's witty transformation ensures her own active participation in the disposal of her body and her property. By masquerading Letitia enters the patriarchal discourses of economics and law.

Ironically, patriarchy's contractual negotiations could not come off sucessfully without her help.

For Doricourt, Letitia lacks "spirit! fire! l'air enjoue! that something, that nothing, which every body feels, and which nobody can describe, in the resistless charmers of Italy and France" (289). Thus her masquerade plot is particlarly well suited to win over a man enamored of nameless effects and mysterious charms. Doricourt, bored already with his fiancée now that the "hour of expectation is past" (289), is ripe for a trap which entices with variety and paradox. Indeed, the more usual strategies of increasing romantic interest are shown not to work in Doricourt's case; when Letitia absents herself from dinner in order, perhaps, to peak his interest by thwarting his expectations of her company, Mrs. Rackett reports the failure of such an attempt. Letitia asks if her absence was "a severe mortification to him" (306), but her chaperone reponds in the negative: "I can't absolutely swear it spoiled his appetite; he ate as if he was hungry, and drank his wine as though he liked it" (306). Letitia learns from this mistaken strategem and plans something more "rash" and complex, her first transformation into that which he cannot but despise, a vulgar coquette.

Letitia's first mask relies primarily on language to evoke the indelicacy and insipidity of the false persona. Here, Letitia does not literally cover her face, but rather changes her speech (and mimics unseemly behavior) to establish an alternate identity. Ironically, Letitia's artificial vulgarity suggests Doricourt's feminine ideal, in whom, "A mind, a soul, a polished art is seen" (307). Although Letitia uses linguistic wiles to pervert that ideal, already the play privileges Letitia's masquerade plot for its ingenuous approximation of Doricourt's desires and its consequent devaluation of them.

Letitia's first masquerade, as a "vulgar soul" (307), illustrates exactly the qualities that Doricourt despises, and thus relies on reversal in its triumph over him. First Letitia exaggerates and mocks the modesty which for Doricourt "wants ... zest, it wants poignancy" (290), by hiding behind Mrs. Rackett and peeping at Doricourt through her fingers (308). Then she begins a recitation whose pettiness, rudeness, and coquetry are enough to turn his heart to "marble" (307). Doricourt responds to Letitia's image of low breeding just as she might wish him to; his indifference "'tis advanced thirty-two degrees towards hatred" (320). It may be, of course, that Letitia's linguistic vision of indecorum is only a "literary" depiction — but even if this is so, her representation is immediately readable to Doricourt because he too is removed enough from the actuality of immodest behavior to be aware only of his own upper-class assumptions surrounding it, the same assumptions upon which Letitia has constructed her pastiche.

In the eighteenth century, the age of the dictionary and of the stabilization of spelling and grammar, polite and proper conversation marked gentility.[4] The mechanics of cultured speech identified the educated upper class and the lack thereof pointed to a more humble social position. Letitia chooses her vulgar words carefully so that they break a number of the neoclassical rules of language usage. Her mask relies on colloquialism, solecism, and archaism — categories of lower-class linguistic error which Carey McIntosh has identified (12–33). Letitia relishes her colloquialisms, substituting adjectives for adverbs ["I can talk as fast as any body" (309)], attaching prefixes to verbs ["When papa was a hunting, he used to come a suitoring" (308)], making unclear pronoun references ["I was daunted before my father, and the lawyer, and all them" (309)], relying on clichés ["I wasn't born in a wood to be scared by an owl" (308)], continually asserting authority for her statements ["Sure I may say" (308)], and signaling the direction and intention of her discourse with repetitions and verbal commas ["laws," "why," "you know," "I used to say" (308–09)]. And she does not neglect to pepper her discourse with solecisms, disorderly and imprecise usages of grammar and diction which create ambiguities and inaccuracies. Letitia constructs sentences notably unparallel ["he's as slow in speech as aunt Margery when she's reading Thomas Aquinas — and stands gaping like mumchance" (308)], for example, and is often vague ["I have read it in a book" (308)]. Lastly, she is guilty of archaism, of speaking in an old-fashioned (seventeenth-century) style, when she heavily labels her antitheses ["Sure I may say what I please before I am married, if I can't afterwards" (308)] and when she uses the relative pronoun "that" incorrectly ["Laws, don't snub me before my husband — that is to be" (309)]. McIntosh's categories aside, Letitia's colorful expressions ["Oh, lud," "flim-flams," "ifags" (308–309)], her blatant references to courtship ["D'ye think a body does not know how to talk to a sweetheart?" (308)], her unbridled laughter ["He, he, he!" (308)], and her shameless boasts ["cousin, you may tell the gentleman what a genus {sic} I have" (309)] pointedly identify her as vulgar and ill-bred. This first persona, by inverting the normal relationship between language and identity, allows Letitia to use social assumptions to her own purposes.

Although Letitia schemes for the hand of a man of whom patriarchy approves, her strategies of deception and inversion blatantly contradict notions of morality and seemliness. Letitia's first masquerade links her with all of the ignorance and ugliness that she portrays. Letitia's new personality temporarily endangers her social position; although her disingenuous masquerade plot does not threaten her sense of self-worth, in Doricourt's eyes it strips her of her dignity and value. Letitia's first bold maneuver, taken alone, might deprive her of her lover's respect and, ultimately, his hand. As Doricourt tells Mrs. Rackett: "Doricourt's wife must be incapable of improvement — but it must be, because she's got beyond it" (310). However, Letitia's plot calls for both the subversion of her own honor, and for a reversal of Doricourt's own expectations and opinions. Now that he despises Letitia

Hardy, he must be forced into a passion, and his object can only be Letitia if her face is masked instead of her wisdom.

In the second installment of her masquerade romance, Letitia adopts not only an alternate persona, that of the witty charmer, but also an alternate physical identity, that of masked grace. This transformation takes place at Lady Brilliant's masquerade ball where Letitia takes advantage of the opportunity for disguise. However, the success of Letitia's first mask, her cleverly imitated vulgar speech, points to the ease with which the heroine adopts another persona and to the suspicion that every character trait, both undesirable and desirable, that she evinces may be only a disguise. Now Letitia tries to be witty or modest enough to change Doricourt's hatred into passion; to some extent Cowley must also intend these more seemly behaviors to appear as those of convenience.

The inappropriate immodesty of Letitia's first persona pales in comparison with the assertiveness and daring with which Letitia enacts her second identity at a masquerade proper. The masquerade, in eighteenth-century England, was tainted by associations of at least exoticism, and often sexual, intellectual, and even moral chaos.[5] The masquerade allowed all its participants to disguise themselves with other identities; its enjoyment stemmed from the liberation that accompanied such a loss of position in the social hierarchy. Masked, a man might insult his neighbor, or even his superior. A woman in disguise might boldly flirt with a man to whom she had never been introduced. Such a spectacle of collective disorder necessarily evoked powerful responses. Some participants delighted in impersonation and the colorful mix of characters that lent a surreal air to the event. Others bemoaned the contortion of reality and absence of decorum therein. Critics repeatedly inveighed against the licentious antics which a masked ball occasioned, from jostling to dancing to embracing. The masquerade facilitated "improper" assignations of all sorts; adultery, prostitution, and homosexuality all profited from its particular freedoms.

As always, the repercussions of masquerade libertinage were felt mostly by the women who succumbed to the temptations of its emancipations. The *Weekly Journal* of April 18, 1724 warned: "Fishes are caught with Hooks, Birds are ensnar'd with Nets, but Virgins with Masquerades" (qtd. in Castle 43). How significant then that *BS* dramatizes the tale of a virgin who masquerades to ensnare a suitor and not the more usual narrative of a virgin seduced by a masked villain! Indeed, Cowley's comedy does formulate the latter story, but only as a counterpoint to Letitia's plot. The Touchwood subplot describes Courtall's evil scheme against female virtue, in the person of Lady Frances Touchwood, but his intentions are frustrated by the Wise (Savvy) Man of the Town (Ville), Saville.

The masquerade, with all its pleasures and dangers, permits the impermissible, and thus is essentially an imaginative moment par excellence. As Terry

Castle has noted, it is throughout eighteenth-century literature a powerful plot catalyst,[6] facilitating flirtations, liasons, abductions, heroics and the like. Cowley's play is no exception in its reliance on the masquerade's dramatic power. The prologue introduces the theme and in Act I, scene ii Doricourt tells Saville, his confidante, that he intends to accompany the Hardy's to Lady Brilliant's (290). No other event vies for the theatrical interest that is concentrated in Act IV, scene i, the masquerade scene. All Cowley's characters share in its energies; in fact, they all attend! Lady Frances Touchwood's idealized view of the spectacle indicates its enticements: "Delightful. The days of enchantment are restor'd; the columns glow with saphires and rubies, emperors and fairies, beauties and dwarfs, meet me at every step" (318). But Saville cautions her about its concomitant evils: "lady! there are dangers abroad — Beware!" (322). As it did in the prologue, *BS* continues to engage in a debate about the masquerade, and in this debate it invests the majority of its intensity.

Cowley heightens the importance of Lady Brilliant's masked ball by hinting that the whole society of the comedy operates, on a larger level, as just such a festival of disguise. Cowley suggests that Act IV, scene i is no aberration — but rather the most obvious manifestation of evil inclinations that are permanently sustained, albeit hidden. Instead of painting the masquerade as society's designated receptacle for the improper desires which it cannot expunge, Cowley compares everyday polite behavior with disguise, deceit, and vulgarity. Courtall lies to his "unpresentable" country cousins, so that he will not have to introduce them into society as his relations (287). Doricourt's foreign manner of dress excites the whole *ton* into a fervor of fashionable affectation (287). Sir George Touchwood, having sworn himself an enemy to British women of fashion, marries one and earns Doricourt's scorn, "Why, thou art a downright, matrimonial Quixote" (297). Flutter, in his own flighty way the consummate man about town, identifies the system of values that underpin the social world. Flutter says: "A fair tug, by Jupiter — between duty and pleasure! — Pleasure beats and off we go. lo triumphe!" (305). It is Sir George who most clearly denominates what Cowley means us to see: "And what is the society of which you boast? — a mere chaos, in which all distinction of rank is lost in a ridiculous affectation of ease. In the same select party, you will often find the wife of a bishop and a sharper, of an earl and a fiddler. In short, 'tis one universal masquerade, all disguised in the same habits and manners" (303). Sir George blames the masquerade society on the wives, on the women, whose pernicious desires inculcate the destruction of the social hierarchy and the salubrious order which stemmed from it. As Cowley masks herself in anonymity to protect herself from the particular audacity of female authorship, and creates a heroine who plots a masquerade romance, the connection between women and masks seems to be sustained as a truth in *BS*; to what extent the masquerade and women are to be castigated for society's evils, however, is less clear.

Only at the masquerade proper can Letitia hone her "polished art"; while the vulgar speech patterns of her first charade successfully alienated Doricourt's already weak sense of attachment to his fiancée ["Though she has not inspir'd me with violent passion, my honour secures her felicity" (290).], it is the masking of the face which permits the enactment of the more difficult proposition of producing a passion. Terry Castle notes that costume in general was thought to prompt sexual transgression (38), but that "it was the mask in particular, that indispensable element of masquerade disguise, that was thought most powerfully aphrodisiacal — for wearer and beholder alike... Anonymity, actual or stylized, relaxed the safeguards of virtue [and] ... masked individuals were seen as fetishistically exciting" (39). The masquerade as a whole was a spectacle of disorderly sensuality, the perfect setting for Letitia's flirtation; her disguise in particular ensured that any of Doricourt's attentions to her would be erotically charged. Indeed, throughout Act IV, scene i Letitia refuses Doricourt's insistent pleas that she remove her mask, urging: "Beware of imprudent curiosity; it lost Paradise" (321). To appease Doricourt's desire for knowlege would be to satiate his desire for anything else. The mystery of her countenance stimulates his interest and aids in the incitement of ardor.

The masquerade licensed both of Letitia's required devices, mystery and wit. The *Weekly Journal* of February 15, 1718, in a glowing description of one of the first masked assemblies to take place in Haymarket, noted: "There is an absolute Freedom of Speech, without the least Offence given thereby" (quoted in Castle 25).[7] Not all observers agreed that the unbounded raillery left the rules of decorum unviolated. Critics anxiously denounced the indulgence of rude, familiar, or loud speech and the prevalence of unabashed and promiscuous flirtation. Ironically, this unregulated intercourse facilitated Letitia's carefully disciplined witty discourse with Doricourt. Letitia's control over her speech is as absolute in her public guise of the charming incognita as it is in her private portrayal of a foolish coquette. There reigns in her masquerades a method to her madness, a regulation of her bold disguises.

Indeed, the masquerade itself was an organized inversion, founded on the principles of reversal and paradox. As Castle expresses it, "the controlling figure was the antithesis" (5). Letitia's strategy of inversion (turning indifference to hatred to passion) and varied disguises is a distillation of the properties of the masquerade and a concise manifestation of it. As a vulgar miss in the drawing room, she introduced low, ill manners where only high breeding should be; as a precise wit at the orgiastic masked ball, she introduces high-society decorum where only indecent liberties are taken. And, to find paradoxes within paradoxes, just as Letitia personifies the rebellious perversions of the masquerade, with all the improper emancipations that it

promised women, she also thereby personifies the mystery and diversity of
the woman who Doricourt imagines as ideal, the woman of "spirit! fire! l'air
enjoue! that something, that nothing, which every body feels, and which
nobody can describe" (289). Doricourt follows Letitia's masked figure
throughout the rooms of the assembly, entranced by her "spirit" (320), her
"air bewitching" (322), her "Delightful wildness!" (324), and, of course, the
continual frustration of his desire to unmask her. Doricourt finally exclaims
his intensely felt passion: "Fate has ordained you mine ... I never met with
a woman so perfectly to my taste; and I won't believe it formed you so, on
purpose to tantalize me" (324). Just when Letitia's self-creations liberate her
from anyone's preconceptions of female identity and womanly methods of
charming, her second mask tallies exactly with Doricourt's vision of female
perfection. Thus, her revolutionary strategem, while it steals from Doricourt
the energy of their courtship, does not challenge its existence. Letitia wears
masks only to guarantee that someday she might appear before an adoring
husband without one. Still, she revels in her success, "This moment is worth
a whole existence!" (324).

It seems that only at the masquerade, the site of especially female im-
prudence, can Letitia win the man patriarchy has chosen for her as a prudent
choice. So Letitia's plot is ironically premised both upon female desire and
female complacence, both upon rebellion and dutifulness. Letitia, the
"enchantress who can go to masquerades, and sing, and dance, and talk a man
out of his wits!" (328), puts her second successful charade in the service of
patriarchal ideology. Letitia's excursion to Lady Brilliant's renders her both
the ideal (redeemer) and fallen (redeemed) woman of the text; Letitia's
masquerade plot seduces Doricourt's false prejudices and yet ensures Letitia's
own transformation from independent heroine to good wife. It is the specific
discourse of the second mask which records Letitia's disempowerment. The
wit with which she entices Doricourt subtly yet efficiently displaces her
control over the masquerade scene and over her suitor.

The language she chooses to engage his interest is as consciously part of
high culture as the vulgar discourse of her first persona was consciously part
of the low. It is best denoted as the "courtly-genteel" (McIntosh 69),[8] a
discourse passed down from the *amour courtois* tradition founded in
Provençe in the late eleventh century (Boone 34).[9] Courtly-genteel language
retained, in the eighteenth century, its links to privilege and culture and was
used by the upper classes to add grace and refinement to their speech.
Specifically, its themes of "dependency, courtship, petition, dedication,
honor, unsalaried service, friendship, and prayer" (McIntosh 69) denoted
polish and discrimination. Its archetypes, the knight errant and the lady love
for whom he lives and dies, represented the union of desire and purity, passion
and honor (Boone 34), and thus suggested ideal models of romantic behavior.
How unusual and determined, then, must Letitia's courtly-genteel romance

be at a masquerade where speech otherwise floundered in its own emancipated coarseness.

Letitia wins Doricourt's admiration at the masquerade by exploiting the concerns of the courtly-genteel and by choosing words which signaled courtly taste. "Your mistress will be angry" (321), she teases Doricourt when he flirts with her, invoking the medieval language of courtship. Later, Letitia insists on her personal honor: "At present be content to know that I am a woman of family and fortune" (324). Letitia's genteel strategy impresses her lover as "most charming" (321), as full of "vivacity — wit — elegance" (323), so that he believes her "a woman of brilliant understanding!" (327). After the masked ball, Doricourt admits that he "loved her, died for her — without knowing her" (330). Letitia's second mask of language also triumphs; Letitia's linguistic disguise successfully plots another manipulation of Doricourt, the metamorphosis of his hatred into passion.

Certainly, Letitia's genteel wit constructs romantic relationships between women and men that emphasize the ascendancy of the female. She tells an anonymous masker, vying for her attention: "Charity! If you mean my prayers, heaven grant thee wit, pilgrim" (319). To toy with him further, she asks him (!) for a dance, "*Dare* you dance?" (320; italics mine). To Doricourt, she is aloof and superior, in marked contrast to her vulgar coquetting. At Lady Brilliant's, Letitia even evinces a distrust of love talk, chastising Doricourt, "You grow too free" (322). In her second charade, through the courtly-genteel discourse, Letitia attempts to establish a barrier between Doricourt and his desires and to challenge, in order to tame, his passion with her own repulse. "My name has a spell in it" (323), she rebuffs him. "As you value knowing me, stir not a step. If I am followed, you never see me more. Adieu" (324), she commands, orchestrating their relationship according to her own plot. At their first meeting, she felt, with mortification: "at the same moment his slave, and an object of perfect indifference to him!" (294). Now she can reverse the rhetoric, configuring Doricourt's slavery with equanimity. For Letitia, courtly-genteel conversation offers a ready-made language (female superiority, centrality, purity) with which to assert her own power over her lover so that his expressions of devotion cannot deviate from the prescribed path of her intentions.

However, Letitia's use of the courtly-genteel discourse, her second mask, hinders the straightforward success of her masquerade plot because her understanding of the nature of courtliness, with its veneration of women, does not encompass its underlying hierarchy, the subservience of the feminine ideal to the knight of action who is nominally her defender.[10] In other words, Letitia's invocation of genteel speech exposes her not only to Doricourt's passionate submission but also to his threatening passion. Indeed, Letitia errs in employing a genteel discourse in a setting expressly un-genteel; her insistence upon polished conduct where all rules of behavior are thwarted is

decidedly inopportune. Paradoxically, the strength of Letitia's masquerade
plot diminishes at the point of its conceptual origination. Letitia's power relies
upon masks, upon false identities, and upon the freedom from feminine
propriety which they bring, but her ability, while masked, to control Doricourt
decreases when he too perceives himself emancipated from the constrictions
of decorum.

Indeed, in the masquerade scene, the most fervent practitioners of the
courtly-genteel conversation turn out to be men with suspect designs. The
anonymous masker repeatedly petitions Letitia for her attentions: "Charity,
fair lady! Charity for a poor pilgrim" (319); "Will you grant me no favour?"
(319); "I dare do anything you command" (320). And Doricourt swamps her
with avowals of courtship and dedication: "you, the most charming being in
the world, awaken me to admiration. Did you come from the stars?" (321);
"By heavens! I never was charmed till now" (323); "Married! the chains of
matrimony are too heavy and vulgar for such a spirit as yours. The flowery
wreaths of Cupid are the only bands you should wear" (323); "An angel!"
(323). But these declarations soon exhibit their nature. The confessions of
passion and service mask (and only lightly) other intentions, less focused on
Letitia's power over men and more on their power over her.

Letitia's second mask of wit betrays her plot of independent assertion by
encouraging a response which would again entrap her in situations not of her
own making. Doricourt endeavors to kiss her against her will. "[Y]our chin
would tempt me to kiss it, if I did not see a pouting, red lip above it, that
demands — (Going to kiss)" (322), he exclaims. He twice grabs her indeli-
cately, once crying "oh, to catch thee, and hold thee for ever in this little cage!
[Attempting to clasp her]" (324). This prompts Letitia's cool response, "Hold,
sir," but Doricourt, unwilling to be deferred, insists, "Tis in vain to assume
airs of coldness — Fate has ordained you mine" (324). And rudely clutching
her another time, he implies that her own flirtation, her own use of the
courtly-genteel discourse, encourages his coarse actions: "What! you will
have a little gentle force?" (322). Clearly, men and women refer to the courtly
tradition with differing expectations. Men expect that it licenses a bodily
passion and women imagine that it encourages a passionate dedication that
transcends the physical. But the conjunction between the genteel sallies and
the location of conversation, the masquerade, privileges the knight over the
lady; even Doricourt, ironically named "the knight of the woful [sic] countenance" (335) by Sir George Touchwood, intimidates Letitia, the play's
heroine, at her own game.

The masquerade, then, is a problematic festival of freedom for women and
the masquerade plot an encumbered method of comedy. Letitia's romance
dares Doricourt's rude freedoms, dares lesser indignities such as sexual favors
in a quest for greater dignities such as a husband's love and a happy marriage
finale. But only to the extent that Letitia ultimately succeeds in winning

Doricourt's love will the risk she takes, throwing away an indifferent respect in exchange for hatred and disrespect, be justified. Letitia might have been expected to inculcate his conversion by placing "trust to the good old maxim, — Marry first, and love will follow" (307). But because Letitia insists that "never to be his wife will afflict me less than to be his wife, and not be beloved" (307), she plots an unseemly romance which embraces freedoms of behavior and speech and threatens to self-destruct into tragedy. Yet, her experience at Lady Brilliant's must have functioned as some sort of rude awakening; immediately afterwards, Letitia's plot undergoes a striking change.

When Letitia returns from her second encounter with Doricourt, she seems to have realized that her plot has endangered her self-sufficiency, has threatened her independence. Forced to endure insults, while without patriarchal protection, she now turns over her strategy to those of her father's household who would oversee it. Her father, good naturedly inept, admits his lack of influence over Doricourt: "when I went up to him, ... out of downright good nature, to explain things — my gentleman whips round upon his heel, and snapp'd one as short if I had been a beggar woman with six children, and he overseer of the parish" (327). Still, he cannot stand idly by as Letitia manages her own future and after "thinking of plots to plague Doricourt ... they drove one another out of my head so quick, that I was as giddy as a goose, and could make nothing of them" (328), he thoughtlessly offers a rather casual acquaintance control over Letitia's destiny. This man, one Mr. Villers, the Man of the Town (Ville), has played only a minor comedic role in the play thus far, and his usurpation of Letitia's plot and her enthusiastic acceptance of his presumption reveal just how jarring and unpleasant the masquerade must have been to a heroine capable of delicate feelings.

By turning over her strategy to a man of the *ton*, Letitia ensures her own recuperation as a worthy wife, and a modest woman. At their first meeting, this modesty prompted Doricourt's indifference, and Letitia's bold impersonations of characters with which to actively engage his interest, both unfavorable and favorable. But after a sexually charged encounter that left her discomfited, Letitia wants to resume the persona of a proper lady so that she might transform Doricourt's indelicate passion into respectful love. Letitia encourages patriarchal regulation so that her plot can no longer detour outside the boundaries of propriety and threaten to leave her a social outcast. Letitia resorts to proper, modest femininity in the service of the happy ending; we might say she turns her plot over to patriarchy in the service of comedy.

Mr. Villers, acting as patriarchy's representative in the absence of any ability in Mr. Hardy, jumps at the chance to organize a young woman's romance merely for his own aggrandizement. He directs Mr. Hardy to feign mortal illness in order to force Doricourt to marry the vulgar Miss Hardy however much he may pine for the incognita with whom he has had an improper liason. The levity with which he treats his scheme contrasts sharply with the high seriousness that Letitia evinced as she plotted to secure her own happiness. "Nothing so easy" (328), he promises, "I have it all here; [*Pointing to his Forehead*]" (328). And though he claims, "I'll answer for the plot" (329), he then heads for Parliament, inviting Mr. Hardy who, if the new plot is to work, cannot be seen in public. This contradiction is noted by the least insightful character of the comedy, Mr. Hardy himself, but Mr. Villers laughs off his mistake.

But Letitia, however Villers discounts the importance of their maneuvers, continues to view events with gravity. Viller's plot, an odd concoction of events usually held as sacred, death and marriage, impresses Letitia with its finality. Usually concise and determined, she wavers, "Oh, heavens! — I — 'Tis so exceeding sudden, that really" (329). Already, Letitia has ceased to be the heroine of the play, and the center of its action and energy. Cowley begins to write Letitia as indecisive and fearful, patriarchy's heroine, not *BS*'s. Viller's strategy of inversion, for Letitia and Doricourt to be "married in jest" (329), now appears to Letitia as an "odd idea" (329), and although she agrees to "venture it" (329), she clearly is suspicious of the central trope of masquerade which has been the basis of her own plots against Doricourt. It is Villers who enables her continued participation in the charade, walking her through the necessary steps, "You go and put off your conquering dress, and get all your awkward airs ready" (329).

Doricourt, like Letitia, also registers dissatisfaction with the masquerade and the blatant sexuality of his encounter with the masked charmer. Indeed, Act V, scene ii, with its insistence on the suffering Letitia's scheme causes Doricourt, and on the power she now wields over him through the absolute success of her first two machinations, reads as rather disjunctive with Letitia's abdication that has gone before. However, because her masked strategy permits Doricourt both to love her with respect and to desire her without it, it seems to him "Oh, insufferable!" (330). Doricourt, like Letitia, cannot bear that the purity of their relationship, a relationship for which they have the highest hopes, be tainted with improper sexuality. He too wants to erase the indelicate associations that surround his mystery lover: "The sentiment I have conceived for the witch is so unaccountable, that, in that line [a possible assignation], I cannot bear her idea" (330). Doricourt, like Letitia, no longer believes in the trope of masquerade, in his principles of spirit, fire, and playfulness. He disparages the "mystery in her manner" (330), as illicit, and goes so far as to speak in favor of a "woman of honour" (330) as a wife worthy of adoration. Now Doricourt also begins to hope for a comic resolution to his difficulties.

And although this comedy now discredits masquerade as Letitia constructed it, it does not discount the possibility of a patriarchal orchestration of the same. All the peripheral male characters somehow emerge as central to the final comic charade. Villers plots a false death and a marriage founded on deceit, and in a parallel subplot Saville disguises himself in order to protect Lady Frances Touchwood from the perverse desires of Courtall. Doricourt himself pretends to be mad. Indeed, once Villers' scheme gets underway it enlists Saville's aid in entrapping Doricourt. It is really Saville who manages Doricourt, who pushes and pulls him about with language, so that he agrees to "act the lunatic in the dying man's chamber" (334). And, importantly, Saville manages Letitia's last masked appearance: "*Enter* LETITIA, *masked, led by* SAVILLE" (338). Under Saville's aegis, her final disguise renders her a victim, no longer able to use mystery and language to put herself at an advantage over Doricourt, and to make herself master of the situation. Viller's plot demands that Letitia despairingly cry out her powerlessness: "I believed him, gave him up my virgin heart — and now! — Ungrateful sex!" (338). In addition, Letitia's last charade again subjects her to pernicious speculation about her honor and to consequent disrespect, forcing her to explicitly, "in this company" (338), defend herself by asserting that "my heart, my honour, my name unspotted as hers you have marrried; my birth equal to your own, my fortune large" (339). Viller's strategy thereby reminds her of the dangers for women inherent in the masquerade and the necessity of giving up control of her own romance. *BS* devolves into the comic tale of men (Villers, Saville, Doricourt, Hardy) deceiving one another during contractual negotiations surrounding a society marriage.

What differentiates Letitia's masquerade from that of Villers and Saville, that of polite society (Ville)? Letitia's own strategems, for all that they empowered her, did not challenge the intentions of Mr. Hardy and the properly patriarchal negotiations to dispose of her future. Letitia's schemed only to convert Doricourt to a willing and passionate husband, not to thwart her father's plans for her match. Since the patriarchal plot shares its end with Letitia's, and even appropriates most of her means, it must really be a strategy to repress female desire and the plot of its self-fulfilment. The target of the patriarchal scheme enacted in Act V is not Doricourt's self-determination in marriage, but Letitia's. Her masquerades have to be contained so that heroines do not learn to invoke principles of inversion and paradox. Her false identities, vulgar and witty, have to be recuperated as devices of polite society, approved and disciplined. Villers' masquerade plot allows Letitia to appear in both her disguises once more, but these representations of her inventions prove her a pawn of plot not its master. Letitia's final evocation of other female personas, under the auspices of patriarchy, stifles the rebellion of her masquerade plot, annulling its emancipatory quality.

Masquerade and modesty are now indistinct tropes for the heroine whose reintegration into patriarchy requires a well-harnessed charade. Letitia's re-adoption of a modest demeanor at the end of the comedy suggests the interchangeable nature of modesty and other more subversive female per-

sonas such as vulgarity and witty forwardness. At Lady Brilliant's, Letitia
hinted at the ease with which one changes one's identity for the love and
acceptance of a man: "I'd be anything — and all! — grave, gay, capricious
— the soul of whim, the spirit of variety — live with him in the eye of fashion,
or in the shade of retirement — change my country, my sex" (324). Letitia,
pointing to the ease with which she might transform herself into the most
proper or the most perverse of women, is not highlighting the invention and
poetry of the female mind, but rather proposing her own insignificance;
without a man she represents a blank, a cipher. In the final scene of the play,
she attempts to explain: "The timidity of the English character threw a veil
over me you could not penetrate. You have forced me to emerge in some
measure from my natural reserve, and to throw off the veil that hid me... You
see I can be any thing: choose then my character — you shall fix it" (340).
Letitia claims that modesty, "timidity," is itself a screen over a woman's true
self; thus, she leaves to Doricourt's discretion the choice among wifely
possibilities, between modesty and something else again.

As *BS* is a comedy, Doricourt does not complain that his "charming,
charming creature!" (340) cannot lay claim to her "natural reserve" without
our suspicion that she embraces it out of convenience; in fact, he closes the
play by remarking that her "innate modesty" is a "sacred veil" (340), without
noticing the paradox, the contradiction between an inherent quality and a
chosen one. Thus, although Letitia dreads the "awful moment" (339) when
"the slight action of taking off my mask stamps me the most blest, or
miserable of women" (339), Doricourt's blindness to the difference and to
the similarity between modesty and masquerade smooths over the crisis.
Doricourt's conversion from a "strange perversion of taste" (340) to "the
grace of modesty" (340) is weak and incomplete. The patriarchal plot to
discipline Letitia for her interchangeable adoption of good and evil personas
deconstructs at the end of the text when Letitia marries a man who cannot
fathom her infractions against propriety.

Doricourt's conversion to the ideal of the "sacred veil" challenges the
patriarchal prohibition against female self-creation and is in fact a conversion
to Letitia's masquerade plot. This feminization[11] of the anti-hero resuscitates
Cowley's feminist subtext and reinscribes subversive value upon the marriage
of Letitia and her beloved. Without Doricourt's positive evaluation of Letitia's
strategem, it would be much more problematic that Cowley privileges the
patriarchal masquerade plot and permits it to oversee the marriage of
Doricourt and Letitia. Perhaps in order for Cowley to safely dramatize (to
mask) the story of a woman who writes her own romantic comedy, she needed
to discipline the heroine in several ways, wresting from her the controls of
her strategems, marrying her off under duress, and reinscribing her within the
confines of modesty and propriety. Cowley mediates the plot of female desire

so as to mask its arrangement of a woman's life history and the liberating possibilities it promises to those intent on directing their own life stories.

By focusing instead on the Good Husband and the promise of a companionate marriage, Cowley disguises the preeminence she attaches to rebellious masquerading.[12] She subsumes her representation of Letitia's triumphant desire by yoking it to a proper marriage; *BS* functions as another text which "legitimize[s] romantic passion *within* approved social bonds" (Boone 59), another eighteenth-century text which reintegrates antisocial passion into comic ending. At the masquerade Letitia seduced Doricourt with visions of a "Persian pavilion," and a "mogul's seraglio" (324), but this indelicate speech, unsuitable to a virgin and thereby punishable, portrayed sensuality as a wife's domain (323). The conclusion of the play (Doricourt's equation between feminine seemliness and masquerade liberties) suggests that Letitia will have the opportunity to experience sexual adventure with a husband who appreciates her eroticism. Hence Cowley's own masquerade demanded the comic form. In order to represent alternate, rebellious femininities, and some of them empowering, Cowley needed to write within a form which promised social reintegration and rehabilitation.

The ideal compensation which Cowley permits her heroine presumably points to the author's own evaluation of modesty as itself a fiction, no better than other fictions, especially those one might choose to write. Modesty, itself a performance,[13] cannot damn other performances of female possibility, especially those that celebrate their illusory nature, in other words, masquerades. Perhaps, then, Cowley entrusts the epilogue of the text (a defense of masks) to Letitia in order to reassign the trope of masquerade to women, to ultimately return it to its most legitimate employers. Letitia's epilogue wrests the "arts" (341) of disguise away from patriarchy: "And you, my gentle sirs, wear vizors too, But I'll unmask you, and expose to view Your hidden features" (341). In the place of the theatrical players (also male) of the prologue, she unmasks the "Tyrant," and the other "monstrous features" (341), of the men in the audience, men who hypocritically conceal their true natures from each other. Letitia reserves for women the positive qualities of concealment — and defends the "mask of softness ... at once applied, And gentlest manners decorate the bride!" (341). She speaks in favor of masked strategies of lovemaking like her own. Thus when Letitia closes the comedy by appearing to speak for all the players, it seems clear that she speaks for a woman's right to orchestrate her own fate, her own way of achieving shared ends: "Our wish to please cannot be mere disguise!" (341). And she speaks for Cowley's desire to write a comedy of female participation in the significant events that make up a woman's life. Cowley glosses over the possibility that a heroine or a woman writer might not desire "to please" the patriarchy, but to do something totally different, something that might be untenable within an ideal pattern of compensations, untenable within comedy. Patriarchy subsists on disguise,

Letitia's epilogue reports: "'Tis plain, in real life, from youth to age, All wear their masks" (341). But *BS* suggests that if a daughter of patriarchy were to exploit these normative means to a radical end, the means itself would become radicalized and the comedic license permitted to Letitia and Cowley herself would be revoked.

NOTES

1. Hereafter *BS*.
2. See Poovey for a discussion of eighteenth-century women and their necessary and typical strategies of indirection and accommodation (28–9).
3. See Link.
4. See McIntosh (1–9).
5. See Castle. I owe my description of the eighteenth-century masquerade to her much fuller depiction of it.
6. Castle describes the masquerade as "the mysterious scene out of which the essential drama of the fiction emerged" (viii). See Castle (119–120).
7. See Castle (34) for a description of the linguistic freedoms of the masquerade.
8. See McIntosh (69–78).
9. See Boone (32–40)
10. See McIntosh (78–79) and Boone (42)
11. The patriarchal plot against Doricourt feminizes him in many ways. It forces him to act according to the feminine values of "honour" and "compassion" (338), and to make the ultimate "sacrifice" (338) and marry against his inclination.
12. Schofield makes a similar point about eighteenth-century female novelists who employ the masquerade trope; she points to "the masks the novelists themselves adopt by disguising their serious statements under the cloak of the romance" (10).
13. See Yeazell (10–11) and Poovey (21–23).

WORKS CITED

Barthes, Roland. *A Lover's Discourse: Fragments*, trans. Richard Howard. New York: Farrar, Straus and Giroux, 1978.

Boone, Joseph Allen. *Tradition Counter Tradition: Love and the Form of Fiction.* Chicago: University of Chicago Press, 1987.

Castle, Terry. *Masquerade and Civilization: The Carnivalesque in Eighteenth-Century English Culture and Fiction*. Stanford: Stanford University Press, 1986.

Cowley, Hannah. *The Belle's Stratagem*, in: *The Other Eighteenth Century: English Women of Letters 1660–1800*, eds. Robert W. Uphaus and Gretchen M. Foster. East Lansing: Colleagues Press, 1991, 284–341.

Gauthier, Xaviére. "Is There Such a Thing As Women's Writing?" in: *New French Feminisms*, eds. Elaine Marks and Isabelle de Courtivron. New York: Schocken Books, 1981, 161–4.

Hagstrum, Jean H. *Sex and Sensibility: Ideal and Erotic Love from Milton to Mozart*. Chicago: University of Chicago Press, 1980.

Jones, Vivien, ed. *Women in the Eighteenth Century: Constructions of Femininity*. London: Routledge, 1990.

Link, Frederick M., ed. *Introduction to The Plays of Hannah Cowley*. New York: Garland Publishing, 1979.

McIntosh, Carey. *Common and Courtly Language: The Stylistics of Social Class in 18th-Century English Literature*. Philadelphia: University of Pennsylvania Press, 1986.

McKenzie, Alan T. *Certain, Lively Episodes: The Articulation of Passion in Eighteenth-Century Prose*. Athens: University of Georgia Press, 1990.

Poovey, Mary. *The Proper Lady and the Woman Writer: Ideology as Style in the Works of Mary Wollstonecraft, Mary Shelley, and Jane Austen*. Chicago: University of Chicago Press, 1984.

Schofield, Mary Anne. *Masking and Unmasking the Female Mind: Disguising Romances in Feminine Fiction, 1713–1799*. Newark: University of Delaware Press, 1990.

Yaeger, Patricia. *Honey-Mad Women: Emancipatory Strategies in Women's Writing*. New York: Columbia University Press, 1988.

Yeazell, Ruth Bernard. *Fictions of Modesty: Women and Courtship in the English Novel*. Chicago: University of Chicago Press, 1991.

7

The Sphinx Goes Wild(e): Ada Leverson, Oscar Wilde, and the Gender Equipollence of Parody

CORINNA SUNDARARAJAN ROHSE

Is it possible to parody a parodist? What if the first parodist is always a self-parodist, like Oscar Wilde? Or if the second parodist is a self-parodist already? At what point in this vertiginous exchange of position and identity can it be said, except as part of the joke, that there is a first or a second writer, a first or a second work? In what sense is it possible for one author to parody another without detaching the style from the source, and in the act of imitating Oscar Wilde (the writer) become "Oscar Wilde" (the writing), and prove his outrageous claim that contingency rather than essence is the criterion of identity, or that the primary aim of a parodist — the critic as artist — is "to see the object as in itself it really is not"? (Wilde 1205, 1030). The more stages of reflexion through which this question passes, the more laughable the object under misrepresentation becomes. It is as if the comic energy of this metafictional genre — what Nabokov calls "a game" and Bakhtin a "gay deception" (Hutcheon 78; Morson *MB* 359) — spins serious conventions

119

about identity, priority and legitimacy into laughing truths interchangeable with laughing lies. It is as if the straight truth is not recognized or possessed until it becomes its gay double, and that to parody a work is simultaneously to author it — to define its natural identity by subverting that essence into pure contingency. Much like the structure of the liar's paradox, the circular chase for an original reference initiated by a parodic exchange short-circuits truth, transmitting claims with little or no resistance from a grounding context. It loops a semantic contradiction into a syntactic unity, and creates the perfect joke, posing a serious challenge to basic conventions of meaning that all of a sudden seem funny — so strange as well as so comical.

It is Aristotle who first looks and laughs at parody, giving it a double identity as a mimetic and a comic genre (*Poetics* 2.144.8a 12–13), and his Greek gift has since raised every instance of its creation or criticism to the second power — not only an original work, and its parody, but even the analysis of its secondary strategy, are caught up in this game of raising powers and changing positions. As one critic complains, even "definitions of parody tend to sound like parodies" (Danson 146), no more safe from reflection than other kinds of writing. By placing conventions of identity, priority and legitimacy at risk, albeit in a "joyful relativity" (Bakhtin *RW* 84), parody doubles the use of all codes from all genres, any act of writing, into an act of parody. This act of doubled writing, explains Linda Hutcheon, initiates "repetition with a critical distance" (Hutcheon 6), a play of similarity against difference already contained within the Greek term *parodia* or "counter-song," a para-ode licensed to rove *against, beside, beyond* — why not *before* the basis-ode? When Wilde discovered North America (excluding New-foundland), he quickly overtook the Gilbert and Sullivan opera *Patience*, a spoof on the aesthetic movement already delighting New York audiences who knew their Ruskin, Whistler, Rossetti and Swinburne. But D'Oyly Carte repeated his profits with a critical distance, hiring Wilde to cross from Halifax to San Francisco, often just days in advance of the musical travesty, and provide the general public with "a true and correct definition and explanation of this latest form of fashionable madness," or so his contract read (Ellmann 152). Lecturing on topics of beauty and truth, Wilde served as a moving target of parody, instructing audiences in codes always about to be exploded. He defended his originality against this overdetermining secondariness of a tour that overpaid and overpublicized his sacrificial substitution, announcing to the press with perfect ambiguity that "Imitation is the homage mediocrity pays to genius." But in this confession of complicity, who is the subject and who is the object? Who poses as the mediocre imitation and who claims to be the original genius? Reviewing the simultaneous successes of the real Oscar Wilde and the fictional Reginald Bunthorne ("Do you ever yearn?" Bunthorne asks the dairymaid Patience; "I earn my living!" she replies), the baffled journalists openly wondered: who now was parodying whom? Who is on first and who is on second?

Max Beerbohm later insisted that *Patience* prolonged the aesthetic movement it opposed (Ellmann 134, 136), and this fact of parody repeating what it cannot complete signals the inertia at work within its metafictional dynamic. Parody moves to totalize, even to synchronize, but never to finalize the conversion of essence into contingency. It drives that engine of self-expression, the first-person pronoun, past the scheduled stops but along the constructed tracks of its identity. The same convention of writing that legitimates the serious gift of authorship, generates the comic gift of parody — the sense of a self who writes *as* "Oscar Wilde" whether he is or not. "The whole man was not so much a personality as an attitude," remembers Arthur Symons. "Without being a sage, he maintained the attitude of a sage; without being a poet, he maintained the attitude of a poet; without being an artist, he maintained the attitude of an artist. And it was precisely in his attitudes that he was most sincere" (Symons 125). Put to trial, the pose and the person, the style and the man are found to be comically interchangeable and sensationally equivalent. This redefinition of identity as a default mode, a standard of secondariness and absence rather than primacy or presence, allows parody to acknowledge the uniqueness of an individual writer, then satisfy that condition of identity as contingency of style. Parody supplements without supplanting the original, since it refuses the finality of essence even to itself, and yields an endless generation of likenesses that repeat the author without his authority — or capture him "in cheerfully irreverent quotation marks" (Bakhtin *DI* 55). But what does this claim to equivalence and substitution now mean?

"That it can be parodied" argues David Bromwich, "most readers would admit, is one good test of an individual style" (Bromwich 328). But once a style has been parodied, in what sense can it still be admitted as individual? The typical Victorian parody asks its readers precisely to decode *this* style as evidence of *this* man (Caesar 25). We read Max Beerbohm writing *as* "Henry James" or Ada Leverson writing *as* "Oscar Wilde," not from an opaque interest in the parodists as authors themselves, but for their feat of transparency in making so clear to us the defining features of the original writer in the likeness of its imitation, *the writing*. We look through, not at, the effacements of parody — and then we laugh at its effrontery. For it dawns on us, all of a sudden, that what we now see is not up front, exactly, nor behind, neither the subject in the foreground nor the object in the background, but an oscillating perspective between priority and identity that creates a double vision. We get the joke, and like Jastrow's duck/rabbit puzzle that is first a "duck" and second a "rabbit," but finally both and neither, parody makes us look and laugh at the conceptual tease operating within a perfect representation that is and is not the original it imitates (Rose 89). That is why Henry James

complains to Max Beerbohm, "No one, now, can write without incurring the reproach of somewhat ineffectively imitating — *you!*" (Danson 144). It is the tease of reversing the original into an imitation of its own copy. The parodist switches places with the author, and like an outlaw turned hero, makes an honest living as a thief stealing from thieves. He seizes the conventions of style from private ownership and transfers any copyright on a "perfected voice" over to a free play of reproduction in the public domain. Once the inimitable proves imitatable, what becomes of this lyric ideal of original expression that limits claims of identity to a first-person utterance of self through style? It is the Romantic dream of a lyric pronoun, feeding on the honeydew of a mystical essence or feeling the gentle breeze of an autobiographical presence, that turns so catastrophically into its own double, a gothic nightmare in which contingency and absence break the spell or raise the storm that signals the creation not of the self, but of someone else, that *other* who meets the criterion of identity or sameness and so proves to be as much the author as the author himself. Any number of critics have traced the "double-voiced" strategy of parody to its logical conclusion in a doppelgänger crisis (Bromwich 341; Danson 156), an encounter between original and imitation who recognize one another as "secret sharers" of the same literary space, that shared resource of identity in style that proves to be a non-originary origin, or "archives which are always already transcriptions" (Derrida 211) — not because the parodist is *identical* to the author (a serious claim of essence), but because the author is *exactly similar* to the parodist (the comic revelation of contingency). This gothic double does not threaten the lyric self with its singular extinction, so much as haunt it by the fear of its infinite repetition, asking it frankly for the creation of more and more creatures as monstrous as itself — but which self? The creator or the creature? The man or the monster? Now that essence yields to contingency, who keeps the secret of identity?

Unlike the motive of nonsense verse that destroys meaning, or the structure of paradox that inverts it, parody repeats the same motive and structure of ordinary meaning, sharing the use of convention so transparent that it seems extraordinary only because encountered as its uncanny double. Like a Sphinx playing with her riddles, parody plays with open secrets, and the trial of answering the joke proves as fatal to the basis self as funny to its reflexive double. This is the laughing truth of parody, that the moment of self-possession is also the moment of self-succession, an acknowledgment that the sources of self come just before and follow soon after oneself. So, *is* it possible to parody a parodist? Or to pose the Sphinx's own riddles, which two sisters are born, the first to the second and the second to the first? What creature walks on four legs in the morning, two in the afternoon, and three in the evening? The answer to these riddles, on reflection, proves reflexive: myself as my other, my monster as myself. The creature is man (a masculine noun in Greek), the sisters are day and night (feminine nouns in Greek), and the parodists are Oscar Wilde and Ada Leverson (a homosexual man and a heterosexual woman) — masculine or feminine, male or female, man or woman: these riddles spin contrary definitions of identity into a circular construction of meaning, essence yielding to contingency, contingency deferring to essence, so that each begets the other in a reflexive exchange of position and priority, the first to the second and the second to the first. "Is your birthday really the 10th? Mine is the 16th!" exclaims Wilde to Leverson on discovering the coincidence of their October birthmonth — although she precedes him by six days and he precedes her by eight years, as the cycle of day following night. "How tragic" he concludes: "I fear that looks like brother and sister. Perhaps it is better so" (Hart-Davis 374). How better so? Better to *look like* than to be siblings? Or better to be *siblings* than to be something else, lovers or rivals perhaps? The original Theban cycle that sets man against monster, forcing a fatal confrontation between essence and nemesis, murderous rivals and transgressive lovers, allows only one of the two creatures to survive; but its comic repetition in the encounter between Oscar Wilde and Ada Leverson, the author of *The Sphinx* and his parodist of "The Minx," transforms the confusions of tragedy into an occasion for laughter — for he and she each generate the other out of an endless exchange of jokes, riddles and parodies in telegrams, letters, and publications: becoming intimate as friends, complicit as authors, and identical as styles.

It is one instance of their gay deceptions, a confusion of identity and priority, that biographers cannot fix the date or mode of their first encounter, whether it occured before or after the first parody, whether they first paired socially in conversation or textually in writing. Osbert Sitwell recounts the story as a parable of *différance*: that Wilde was so amused by an anonymous parody of his novel, he arranged to visit the author, "and when this took place Wilde had been amazed to find it was a woman who entered the room" (Sitwell 137–38 [in 1893]), a meeting both deferred and different from his original sense of the author. She thought him the wittiest man in the world, and he completed the chiasmus by calling her "the wittiest *woman* in the world" (Burkhart 21, my emphasis). Leverson, however, remembers befriending Wilde before parodying him (Hart-Davis 342–43 [in 1892]), and critics usually credit his friendship as the motive to her publishing, even though Wilde took to borrowing Leverson for his writing before lending himself to her own. As early as June 28, 1893, a month before her first parody and a year before her "Minx," Wilde was troping Leverson as his "Sphinx," telegramming ahead of his arrival that "The author of *The Sphinx* will on Wednesday at two eat pomegranates with the Sphinx of Modern Life" (Hart-Davis 342). She took of the fruit and ate, and promptly rebelled, parodying a succession of his works — *Salomé* and *The Picture of Dorian Gray* ("An Afternoon Party," *Punch*, 104, 15 July 1893: 13), *An Ideal Husband* ("Overheard Fragment of a Dialogue," *Punch*, 108, 13 January 1895: 24), *The Importance of Being Earnest* ("The Advisability of Not Being Brought Up in a Handbag," *Punch*, 108, 2 March 1895: 107); but most constitutive of their circle game, she parodied his poem *The Sphinx* ("The Minx — A Poem in Prose," *Punch*, 107, 21 July 1894: 33).

The sphinx figure invoked in Wilde's poem — "Come forth you exquisite grotesque! half woman / and half animal!" (Wilde 833) — claims her place in the decadent imagination's iconography of fatal women, a feminine enigma because doubly coded as a creature of beauty and terror, nature and artifice, immanence and transcendence (Pierrot 125). If at first she enchants the poet, whose command that she "sing me all your memories" generates the poem itself, he comes to fear this seductive control:

> Get hence, you loathsome mystery! Hideous
>   animal, get hence!
> You wake in me each bestial sense, you make me
>   what I would not be.

"Odd, after such a poem," puzzles Sally Beauman "to apply the term 'Sphinx' to a friend" (Beauman viii). A mystery indeed. Is it as Beauman suggests "a teasing salute to the feminine mystique"? What of her terrifying desires, or worse, her corrupting powers? The Sphinx rewrites the poet in her own monstrous image, degenerating him from man into beast, as does her Theban original whose riddle on mankind as a four-, two-, then three-legged creature confounds any normative reference to man. She is older than this poem, and has been written about many times, so that her memories not only constitute the stuff of the poem, but also determine the identity of the poet. She comes to control all his sources of meaning, first as his muse, sister and friend, but then as his lover, rival and enemy. Her power "to breed new wonders from your womb" embodies his worst fear, that the act of creation is a female power, and that a poet who imitates that power is doomed to a role of secondariness and overdetermination, even within his own poem. His fatal struggle with this secret sharer reminds us that the ancient motive of her command performance is a woman's revenge. For Hera, goddess and defender of heterosexual domesticity, sends the Sphinx to Thebes as punishment of its king, Laius: the father of Oedipus and in some accounts also the father of the Sphinx. In exile he had fallen in love with the youth Chrysippus, and abducting him, initiated the claims of homosexual love on Greek culture that so offend Hera. But the Sphinx is older even than her Greek sources, and in Egyptian mythology is a male creature, agent of the god Horus as depicted in the statue at Ghizeh, near the Great Pyramid. Hesiod treats her as this liminal, ambiguously coded figure, terrorizing the borderland of Thebes but bound to destroy herself once her riddle is solved, the fate Oedipus, her brother and her rival, completes.

But Wilde and Leverson, the poet and parodist taken together, repeat and resolve this riddle with a critical difference, not as a tragedy but as a comedy. In *his* poem, the Poet finally objects, "I weary of your steadfast gaze... False Sphinx! False Sphinx!" In *her* parody the Poet further corrects,

Poet:	In my opinion you are not a Sphinx at all.
Sphinx (*indignantly*):	What am I then?
Poet:	A Minx.

This parodic correction delighted Wilde as the equipollence he had long sought to brace his wearisome reputation as an author of repetition, derivation, even plagiarism — the charges *Punch* had made against his 1881 *Poems*, labelling them a tepid mixture of "Swinburne and water" (Ellmann 140, 144). Because Leverson stages a scene of recognition that uses the criterion of reflection rather than origin, she playfully grants Wilde his reputation as a poet. The parody never mentions his name nor even specifies his poem, simply taking *this* writer and *this* work as the basis of its own derivation, and so raises Wilde and *The Sphinx* to an uncanny power as its own double. The basis verification of an authentic original, the standard of an Arnoldian criticism of "high seriousness," yields to this parodic acceptance of an incorrigible fake. Poet and Sphinx change places, and turn rival claims into reciprocal interests. When he read the parody, aptly enough the day before its publication, he wrote to thank Leverson: "I am afraid she really was a minx after all. You are the only Sphinx" (Hart-Davis 357). There is now no mystery to this act of naming, since his Sphinx is not a monstrous amalgam of woman and beast, somehow predatory and prior to his authorial identity (we know this fatal creature to be the humorless "Minx"), but a playful pastiche of styles as secondary and contingent as his own authority. For if the etymology of parody expresses a double strategy of opposition and accord, working with and against its original in perfect counterbalance, so also the etymology of "sphinx" explains the secret of her duality: *sphínx* being equivalent to the base of the Greek verb *sphíngein*, meaning "to hold tight" in the double sense of a deathgrip or a lifehold, a grip that strangles and silences, or a hold that secures and saves. His Sphinx does not threaten Wilde with a denial of originality, the death of the author, but instead secures and raises his *writing position* to the higher power of parody in a laughing game of fin-de-siècle culture, where all authorship is parody, all parody is reflexive, and everyone ends up writing like "Oscar Wilde" (Wyndham 112).

The curious fact that the decadent imagination thrives as the secret sharer of fin-de-siècle parody creates an equipollence more like the eternal dynamism of Blake's contraries, the Prolific and the Devouring, than an historically curative stasis of "antibodies to the fevers of decadence" or "chastening astringency of comedy [to] overripeness" (Henkle 329; Burkhart 197). Parody keeps the secret of decadence, intensifying its morbid refine-

ments of style or unnatural cultivations of self into the pure repre-
sentationalism of pose, mask or fake. This complicity between the sublime
and the ridiçulous casts decadence and parody as performers of the same
aesthetic (Thornton 25), so much so that Leverson blithely stages "An Afternoon Teaparty" with characters drawn from Wilde and Ibsen, Pinero and
Carroll, all politely jostling for positions at the same verbal buffet:

> "Is that mayonnaise?" asked the Princess SALOMÉ. "I think it is
> mayonnaise. I am sure it is mayonnaise. It is mayonnaise of salmon,
> pink as a branch of coral which fishermen find in the twilight of the sea,
> and which they keep for the King. It is pinker than the pink roses that
> bloom in the Queen's garden. The pink roses that bloom in the garden
> of the Queen of Arabia are not so pink."

The self-parody secreting in the decadent style makes this extract from *Punch*
interchangeable with any passage from the original *Salomé*, and rescues such
lyricism from its own attenuation, not by cooling its fever or salving its decay
of expression, but by indulging this desire to reach the limits of its solipsistic
convention — and pause *there* with a wild surmise, staring into the demesne
of the dramatic, where the writing self ceases to be a sovereign territory,
something to be claimed and charted, and becomes instead a fluid position,
a space for spectacle and invention where identity is not fixed but performed
in writing.

Thus what John Barth terms "the literature of exhaustion" is paradoxically
the stylistics of energy, a sophisticated engagement in the "used-upness" of
codes and conventions (Barth 29) that results in a "recycling" (Hutcheon 15).
Wilde's admission that he had put his genius into life, and only his talent into
art, seems to allow his fame as a conversationalist priority over his value as
an author, but this remark rather confounds so facile an ordering of speech
and writing into competing sources of identity. For if Wilde is celebrated as
a unique personality (essence), but dismissed as a derivative author (contingency), what systemic catastrophe accounts for this difference between the
historical and textual self, the living man and the writing pronoun? Leverson
suggests that "Quicker in repartee and conversation than in his writing, he
constantly made use in his work, afterwards, of things he had improvised"
(Wyndham 108), as if a primary excess of speech fluxes and refluxes into
writing, depositing traces of itself in print, but only after a loss of heat and
speed. How then can Leverson parody what is absent or lost? Unless this
confession of *entrophy* signals his conversion *into trope*, a calculated looping
of the "man" back into the "manner" (Burkhart 193) through a continuous
circuit of speech into writing, writing into speech, so that nothing is lost,
reminding us of Symons' conclusion that Wilde is, in essence, a contingency.
"As far as I can ascertain," complains George Bernard Shaw, "I am the only
person in London who cannot sit down and write an Oscar Wilde play at will"

(Ellmann 429), although as it turns out neither could Ada Leverson. She revised the script of her comedy *The Triflers* over twenty years, unable finally to imitate Wilde despite her instant success at parodying him (Wyndham 40–42). What is the difference? Imitation is a monologue of sameness, and parody a dialogue of difference. Wilde did not seek more of the same — his true disciple, when he found her, he embraced not as his Echo but as a second Narcissus:

> Answered the Oreads, "Us did he ever pass by, but you he sought for, and would lie on your banks and look down at you, and in the mirror of your waters he would mirror his own beauty."
> And the pool answered, "But I loved Narcissus because, as he lay on my banks and looked down at me, in the mirror of his eyes I saw ever my own beauty mirrored." (Wilde 864)

He encounters her as an active source of acknowledgment, rather than a passive surface of reflection, so that unlike all his other friends and imitators whom Sitwell imagines as an endless chain of echoes (Sitwell 115), Leverson keeps in her possession the secret of true friendship and parody: opposition.

It is worth remembering that as the "Egeria of the whole Nineties movement," a title bestowed by her publisher Grant Richards (Wyndham 31), Leverson was a woman whose friendship and writing were much in demand, whether by Beardsley and his Nineties *The Yellow Book*, or by Eliot and his Twenties *The Criterion*. But then and now, Leverson is always known as "Oscar Wilde's 'Sphinx'" — a genitive coupling of identities already suspended between quotation marks, like corroborating fictions each unthinkable without the other. Any number of authors competed in her possessive naming, including George Moore, but only Wilde wooed and won, perhaps because he, like she, already possesses the identity of a pastiche — both are known as table talkers who plagiarize themselves in print, writing under a performative aesthetic that turns personality into style. Both demonstrate a strange passion for repetition (Ellmann 366; Sitwell 161) and a reckless aestheticism that tests the borders between life and art, as ready to write between the lines as erase the lines all together. "But I want to know what sort of dialogue you spoke between the acts," he demands of Leverson after a tedious play. "The critics say nothing about it. Why is this?" (Hart-Davis 381). She asks Wilde "to publish a book *all* margin; full of beautiful unwritten thoughts, and have this blank volume ... be a collector's piece, a numbered one of a limited 'first' (and last) edition: 'very rare'" (Wyndham 105). Many of these exchanges are conducted by telegram, an accelerated form of the letter so reponsive to the pace and precision of repartee that she praises him as "a master of the wire as a literary medium" and offers to edit and publish *The Collected Telegrams of Oscar Wilde*. He returns the compliment by suggesting, "Why don't you collect your wonderful, witty, delightful sketches

— so slight, so suggestive, so full of *esprit* and intellectual sympathy?" (Hart-Davis 343). Each teases the other with their shared peril of marginal authorship, both writing on the edge of identity, against the limits of invention, inscription, and attribution. Taking refuge in her home between trials, and wanting supplies to record his conversation, Wilde complains "You have all the equipment of a writer, my dear Sphinx, except pens, ink and paper" (Wyndham 117). In prison these supplies prove even scarcer, yet whereas his notoriety saves his telegrams for posterity, her respectability allows her sketches to "remain buried in the pages of *Punch*" despite bibliographical research by Burkhart and Speedie (Speedie 11).

Thus Wilde's ambition for Leverson's parodies is often ranked as hyperbole, and in an introduction to her memoir, his literary executor remarks that "if Prospero is dead we value all the more the little memories of Miranda" (Burkhart 88). But Wilde trusted her past the limits of his identity, once "suspecting" her of keeping his diary — "Everyone should keep someone else's diary" — and often "detecting" her sketches before she owned them (Hart-Davis 374). Sometimes he was wrong, and wronged her, apologizing for his misrecognition of Robert Hitchens' nasty satire *The Green Carnation* (1894) as a work from her pen, explaining that "treachery is inseparable from faith. I often betray myself with a kiss" (Hart-Davis 373). When the Old Bailey turned his libel action on "posing as a sodomite" into criminal trials against his homosexual practice, it used his works and many imitations as evidence against him, forcing Wilde to answer for writing not always his own, as if the law of parody ruled the court of law, and allowed free play between the style and the man, but only to the extent of anticipating its own transgression. First the pose "Oscar Wilde" was tried and convicted for gross indecency, then the man Oscar Wilde was convicted and sentenced to two years hard labor — and it is at this crisis in their literary friendship, when his imitators become his incriminators, that Leverson stops parodying Wilde, stops writing all together. The hiatus in her career coincides exactly with the period of his imprisonment, exile and death. Then in 1903 she begins writing again: narratives in her own voice, under her own name, substituting marriage-plot novels for the gay deceptions of parody. But a scene in the opening chapter of *Love's Shadow* (1908) quietly protests her dissatisfaction with this forced abandonment of reflexive games for a basis mode of writing:

> Edith took an extensive walk through the entire flat, going into each room, and looking at herself in every looking-glass. She appeared to like herself best in the dining-room mirror, for she returned, stared into it rather gravely for some little time, and then said to herself: "Yes, I'm beginning to look bored." (Leverson 4)

The loss of their table talk is reflected in the dining-room mirror, now dulled to a surface echoing back her condition of monologic isolation and lyric entrapment. The Sphinx of *Punch* becomes this bored housewife of *The Little Ottleys*, oppressed by the stasis of an identity secured apart from the risks and rewards of parody and its reciprocal dynamics. When Ada Leverson writes *as* "Ada Leverson," she separates herself from Wilde using an "original" style that establishes her reputation as "the mistress" of Edwardian novels equal to his status as "the master" of Edwardian plays (Burkhart 7); but this separate and equal ranking by gender or genre avoids the constitutive confusions between self and style as cautiously as parody rashly seeks them out. For who is this "Ada Leverson" if no longer the secret sharer of "Oscar Wilde"?

The "triumph of style," argues Virginia Woolf, is a clever masquerade: "never to be yourself and yet always" in the concerted effort "to write like oneself" and make an authentic presence out of a pronoun artifice, creating neither too serious nor too trivial a mask (Woolf 215–19). Whereas "Matthew Arnold was never to his readers Matt, nor Walter Pater affectionately abbreviated in a thousand homes to Wat," the styles of Wilde, Leverson and Beerbohm warmly introduce to us the personalities of Oscar, Ada and Max — making most intimate the most mediated pronouns, because the reward of recognition follows the risk of parody, and these *self-parodying* parodists trump the game. "When you are alone with him, Sphinx," Oscar asks Ada about Max, "does he take off his face and reveal his mask?" (Wyndham 119). Both Beerbohm and Leverson began writing by parodying Wilde and end up parodying the writing of themselves. "In order to know an essence," Wilde reminds another disciple "one must eliminate it" (Dollimore 25), hence his free borrowing and lending of styles between master and disciple, friend and rival. James Whistler disowned his creature as that "arch imposter and pest of the period — the all-pervading plagiarist!" (Whistler 236; Ellmann 133); but Beerbohm acknowledges his creator to be a plagiarist of invention and purpose:

> Speaking of plagiarism the other day, Oscar said: "Of course I plagiarise. It is the privilege of the appreciative man. I never read Flaubert's *Tentation de St. Antoine* without signing my name at the end of it. *Que voulez-vous*? All the Best Hundred Books bear my signature in this manner." (Ellmann 355)

Such deliberate "play-giarism" (Hutcheon 5) seems less a crime committed, than a committment to a crime, a new paradigm of authorship. If to read is to author and to author is to parody, then to parody is to come full circle into self-parody and reinvent the act of reading and writing by "treat[ing] the work of art simply as a starting-point for a new creation" (Wilde 1029). That is why Wilde does not hesitate to send autographed copies of *Intentions* (1891) to the very critics — Ruskin, Swinburne and Pater — from whom he plagiarizes his essays, since he signs his name as author or reader to all the books he absorbs and disseminates, endorsing a transgressive and transformative aesthetic of parody.

So like an Arnoldian critic run amok — more Pygmalion than Midas, animating touchstones of culture into versions of himself — Wilde unfixes hierarchies of style and categories of identity, liberating the self and its expressions into a performative mode that radicalizes itself as an act of self-parody, a floating construct somewhere between tragic aporia and comic redundancy. "It treats writing as a performance, rather than as a codification of significance" argues Richard Poirier, and so "makes fun of itself *as it goes along*" (Poirier 339). It is this instability of the self undergoing its own parody — a someone treating itself as something under construction — that prompts the denial, not of parody generating its endless repetitions, but of self-parody perfecting its balancing act: even if Jack and Algernon do take turns doubling as Ernest, in what sense is it possible for Bunbury always to be himself? This objection against the possibility of self-parody arises from a dissociation of the self into a primary, authorial subjectivity and a secondary, textual objectivity — *I* competing against *myself* — logically condemning the self-parodist "to eternal penultimacy" in a breathless relay race between pronoun cases, as in Tristram Shandy's lament "Write as I will — I shall never overtake myself" (Rose 79–88). But in fact, self-parody explodes this "realistic and rationalistic trap" (Poirier 340) that posits a false, lyric absolute outside the performance of a dramatic identity. Self-parody synchronizes *I* and *myself* into the balancing act of self-recognition, timing invention and possession to yield neither pure essence nor pure contingency but a coordinated performace of the two: *scribo ergo sum.* Despite the flux of photographs, interviews, memoirs, imitations and influences that make Wilde seem at times more a popular hoax than a cultural icon, a "precariously overdetermined signifier" (Craft 20), he never loses control over his limits of identity, because he never hesitates to abandon that control nor exceed those limits, trusting in other versions of himself — other readers, writers, parodists — to catch him in free-fall and deliver him safely to the starting point of his next transformative movement.

"Self-originating, it has no filial indebtedness" Camille Paglia observes about the Wildean androgyne (Paglia 91), although we now know this extrication from biological essence tells only half the story, since it then places its textual contingency in equipollence with sphinxes, bunburies and other marginal creatures — "peripheral figures that no authority can ever subjugate" explains Cixous, practicing what cannot yet be defined, a dynamic writing of a doubled self "working (in) the in-between, inspecting the process of the same and of the other ... not fixed in sequence of struggle and expulsion or some other form of death but infinitely dynamized by an incessant process of exchange from one subject to another" (Cixous 253–54). It is this reciprocal dynamic, an intersubjectivity working against hierarchical stasis, that averts the nightmare of a fatal, gothic double, and opens the sources of identity to parody's dream vision — perfect access to the self through free play with the other, each originating its other as a *self*, each possessing itself as the *other*. "Give me myself as myself" Cixous demands of a transgressive aesthetic between woman and woman, but it is the gift of parody to turn all "*marked* writing" into pure masquerade, crossing masculine and feminine, lyric and dramatic, primary and secondary, until the subversive transvalues the conventional and the straight corroborates the gay. In Jonathan Dollimore's witty phrase, "the outlaw turns up as inlaw" (Dollimore 32), so that the orphan androgyne of Wilde's writing never marries into a family nor settles into a home without first proving its criminal *alias* to have been its proper name all along (Wilde 383).

This reconstitution of blood family into *family likeness*, fulfilling parody's double criterion of sameness with a critical difference or treachery inseparable from faith, explains Wilde's sibling affection for Leverson, his interest and trust in her rival work. "You are more than all criticisms" he tells her. "Sphinxes are true" (Hart-Davis 380). Having survived the paternal wrath of Whistler (Ellmann 128) and the "parricidal impulse" of Beerbohm (Felstiner 156), he tires of competition and confrontation between men, the struggles and expulsions within a masculine economy that play identity as blood sport, a zero-sum game of essence that only the straight man survives. He turns instead to Leverson and a slant relationship that "*looks like* brother and sister," the funny version of Oedipus and his Sphinx, where the answers to her riddles give life rather than death, and the cypher of her existence stands for anything, not nothing. The radical politics of parody enfranchise this gender exchange, just as its reflexive aesthetic motivates it — for if identity is style, "a 'structure of iterability' that includes *both* identity and difference" (Taylor 48), then the sources of identity are not fixed sequentially as ground and abstraction, nor even reversed, but fed into a continuous loop like trapeze artists tumbling through the air, moving from position to position without any grounding except in one another's "brief, identificatory embraces" (Cixous 260). There is no marked position in this performance, only mutual precision, not even ground control. So when Wilde tropes Leverson as his Sphinx, and she returns the figure of a Minx, they play an authoring game more empowering — more faithful and more treacherous — than the fixed control of a Prospero over his little Miranda.

Gilbert and Gubar argue that women authors revise the power structure of patriarchy by writing about female experience in a female voice urging a feminist agenda "parodic, duplicitous, extraordinarily sophisticated" (Gilbert and Gubar 80), making parody an essentializing force that resists the troping of woman into a figuration of the male writer, his *feminine* other, repossessing her essence for herself as the ground to her own project of female authorship. Cixous demands more than this specular reversal, since the male hierarchy of binarisms too easily reasserts itself. She imagines an "I-woman, escapee" who uses parody "to dislocate this 'within,' to explode it, turn it around, and make it hers, containing it, taking it in her own mouth, biting that tongue with her very own teeth to invent for herself a language to get inside of" (Cixous 257), thus subverting female essence into *feminine* contingency, female authorship into the project of *l'écriture féminine* involving Colette or Genet, Duras or Artaud. One more step completes the *sexual* and *textual* pas de deux performed by Wilde and Leverson, the parody that Morson calls "boundary work" (Hutcheon 13) because it crosses the border in both directions: she as a woman writing among men, and he as a homosexual writing among heterosexuals. Both look and laugh at the confusion caused by their close work and double identity — *hypocrite reader, — my alias, — my twin*! Does the reader so addressed play along, and distinguish identical twins from sibling rivals, marking the critical difference within sameness that loops essence back into contingency and keeps the game going? If not, it is easy enough to mistake the fake for its original and close down the game. But if so, the game leaps to a higher power and the Sphinx goes Wild(e). At least three times in her career, once during his life and twice after his death, Leverson uses Wilde's *exact words* in her own works: an epistolary sketch "Letters of Silvia and Aurelia, XXII," *Black and White* 7 (13 January 1894): 36; a short story "The Blow," *English Review* 31 (December 1920): 515–20; and a dialogue "Gentlemen *v.* Players: A Critic Match," *English Review* 34 (April 1922): 331–34.

But is verbatim quotation parody? When Ada Leverson writes *as* Oscar Wilde writing *as* Ada Leverson ... she recycles the same words (even the same pronouns) two or three or more times, extracting choice phrases from his conversations, letters and works, inserting them back into her sketches, stories and dialogues with no alteration other than context (Wyndham 26–28, 105; Burkhart 66, 84–86; Speedie 14). In the 1894 sketch, Silvia and the celebrity Newman Haye, versions of Ada and Oscar, meet and become friends, exchanging jokes and gifts. He tells her "We can forgive a person for making a useful thing as long as he does not admire it. The only excuse for making a useless thing is that one admires it intensely." This epigram has no origin except in Wilde's table talk, a turn of thought or *epí-gramma*, meaning *at, near, before* and *after* something written — sound familiar? Wilde then publishes the phrase in his *Preface* to *The Picture of Dorian Gray* (1890), prompting Leverson to reuse it in her 1893 parody:

> "I say!" exclaimed Lord HENRY. "I say, you know, ILLINGWORTH — come — that's mine. I said it to DORIAN only the other evening. You are always saying my things."
> "Well, what then? It is only the obvious and the tedious who object to quotations. When a man says life has exhausted him —"
> "We know that he has exhausted life."

"Women are secrets, not sphinxes."

"Mine again," exclaimed Lord HENRY.

"It would be useful to carry a little notebook to note down your good things."

"Very useful. And I can forgive a man for making a useful thing as long as he does not admire it."

An epigram used three or more times between Wilde and Leverson proves a very useful thing, and admired intensely. But whereas the two men, Henry and Illingworth, contest its authorship, each struggling to speak phrases faster than his double notes them down, Silvia and Haye, the woman and the man, strike a balance between compliment and critique, teasing their rival ambitions into friendly laughter.

Neither Wilde nor Leverson, both avowed play-giarists, object to this verbatim quotation, although some critics do question its status as parody. On a scale of difference, quotation slides past plagiarism into pastiche before yeilding parody, so that Michele Hannoosh reasons, "The 'quotation' is clearly not *verbatim*, nor the imitation exact, due to the essential transformation involved in parody" (Hannoosh 13). Morson does allow a parody verbally identical to its original "if the parodist uses contextual, rather than textual, change to indicate the fact and grounds of double-voicing" (Morson *RB* 70), a condition that Wilde and Leverson challenge by their love of exact repetition, politic autonomy and artful inconsequence — making any mark of identity in text or context a nonfoundational tease between essence and contingency. These moments of verbatim doubling thus exemplify the secret of their parodic exchanges, a gay deception that achieves identity apart from the sequence and subordination enforcing straight values. In some sense, then, this homosexual man and heterosexual woman are the same *because* they are different (Dellamora 247), daring a solidarity between sexual and textual resources to construct a different kind of identity, not predicated but performed, an act of mutual recognition. "A person has no internal sovereign territory" speculates Bakhtin, "He is wholly and always on the boundary: looking inside himself, he looks *into the eyes of another* or *with the eyes of another*" (Bakhtin *PDP* 287). The difference between identity and identification is this reflexive criterion, the yielding of the self to the other and the return of the other to the self. It takes two to look and laugh — "You give me myself," he and she promise one another, "and I give you yourself." Wilde did not trust Alfred Douglas this way, nor did Leverson trust George Moore, but crossing the boundary both ways they meet as two self-parodists writing "the precursory movement of a transformation of social and cultural structures" (Cixous 249).

So look who's laughing: long after Wilde' death and the last plagiarisms, Osbert Sitwell finds her "quite alone, but shaking with quiet, irrepressible laughter" (Sitwell 136), and Harold Acton remembers her "chuckling to herself" in "sneezes of laughter" and remarks that, "It was comforting to know that she had died in a good humour" (Burkhart 28). This lasting image of Leverson as a laughing Sphinx, still delighting in friends and jokes, inspires Sitwell to take a final guess at her secret:

> Great loyalty, great wit:
>   (Each strives against the other)
> Both win: both lose; both benefit
> In laughter none can smother. (Wyndham 102)

But Wilde already knows her secret, having conspired to create and keep it. He recognizes his Sphinx to be "dear and rarely treacherous" (Hart-Davis 373), making her his partner in the equipollence of parody, for "to test Reality we must see it on the tight-rope. When the Verities become acrobats we can judge them" (Wilde 43). That is why Wilde reassures her, "You are the most wonderful Sphinx in the world," and on the vertiginous eve of his highest literary success and sudden social fall, he telegrams to remind her, "Rely on you to misrepresent me" (Hart-Davis 380, 383).

WORKS CITED

Bakhtin, Mikhail. *The Dialogic Imagination: Four Essays,* ed. Michael Holquist, trans. Caryl Emerson and Michael Holquist. Austin: University of Texas Press, 1981.

Bakhtin, Mikhail. *Problems of Dostoevsky's Poetics,* ed. and trans. Caryl Emerson, *Theory and History of Literature,* Vol. 8. Minneapolis: University of Minnesota Press, 1984.

Bakhtin, Mikhail. *Rabelais and His World,* trans. Helen Iswolsky. Cambridge: MIT Press, 1968.

Barth, John. "The Literature of Exhaustion." *The Atlantic* August 1967: 29–34.

Beauman, Sally. "New Introduction." *The Little Ottleys,* by Ada Leverson. New York: The Dial Press, 1982, vi–xvi.

Bromwich, David. "Parody, Pastiche and Allusion," in: *Lyric Poetry: Beyond New Criticism,* eds. Chaviva Hosek and Patricia Parker. Ithaca: Cornell University Press, 1985, 328–344.

Burkhart, Charles. *Ada Leverson.* New York: Twayne Publishers, 1973.

Caesar, Terry. "Betrayal and Theft: Beerbohm, Parody and Modernism." *Ariel* 17/3 (1986): 23–32.

Cixous, Hélène. "The Laugh of the Medusa," in: *New French Feminisms,* eds. Elaine Marks and Isabelle de Courtivron. New York: Schocken Books, 1981, 245–264.

Craft, Christopher. "Alias Bunbury: Desire and Termination in *The Importance of Being Earnest*," *Representations* 31 (1990): 19–46.

Danson, Lawrence. *Max Beerbohm and the Act of Writing*. Oxford: Clarendon Press, 1989.

Dellamora, Richard. "Traversing the Feminine in *Salomé*," in: *Victorian Sages and Cultural Discourse*, ed. Thaïs E. Morgan. New Brunswick: Rutgers University Press, 1990, 246–264.

Derrida, Jacques. *Writing and Difference*, trans. Alan Bass. Chicago: The University of Chicago Press, 1978.

Dollimore, Jonathan. "Different Desires: Subjectivity and Transgression in Wilde and Gide," *Genders* 2 (1988): 24–41.

Ellmann, Richard. *Oscar Wilde*. New York: Alfred A. Knopf, 1988.

Felstiner, John. *The Lies of Art: Max Beerbohm's Parody and Caricature*. New York: Knopf, 1972.

Gilbert, Sandra M., and Susan Gubar. *The Madwoman in the Attic*. New Haven: Yale University Press, 1979.

Hannoosh, Michele. *Parody and Decadence*. Columbus: Ohio State University Press, 1989.

Hart-Davis, Rupert, ed. *The Letters of Oscar Wilde*. London: Rupert Hart-Davis Limited, 1962.

Henkle, Roger B. *Comedy and Culture*. Princeton: Princeton University Press, 1980.

Hutcheon, Linda. *A Theory of Parody: The Teachings of Twentieth-Century Art Forms*. New York: Methuen, 1985.

Leverson, Ada. *The Little Ottleys*. New York: The Dial Press, 1982. [For a list of Leverson's periodical publications, please refer to text and bibliographies in Burkhart and Speedie.]

Morson, Gary Saul, and Caryl Emerson. *Mikhail Bakhtin: Creation of a Prosaics*. Stanford: Stanford University Press, 1990.

Morson, Gary Saul, and Caryl Emerson, eds. *Rethinking Bakhtin: Extensions and Challenges*. Evanston: Northwestern University Press, 1989.

Paglia, Camille A. "Oscar Wilde and the English Epicene," *Raritan* 4/3 (1985): 85–109.

Pierrot, Jean. *The Decadent Imagination: 1880–1900*, trans. Derek Coltman. Chicago: The University of Chicago Press, 1981.

Poirier, Richard. "The Politics of Self-Parody," *Partisan Review* 35/3 (1968): 339–53.

Rose, Margaret A. *Parody/Meta-Fiction: An Analysis of Parody as a Critical Mirror to the Writing and Reception of Fiction*. London: Croom Helm, 1979.

Said, Edward. *The World, the Text and the Critic*. Cambridge: Harvard University Press, 1983.

Sitwell, Osbert. *Noble Essences or Courteous Revelations: An Autobiography*. London: Macmillan and Company, 1950.

Speedie, Julie. "'Wonderful, Witty, Delightful Sketches': Ada Leverson's Periodical Contributions to 1900, A Checklist and an Introduction," *Turn-of-the-Century Women* 4/2 (1987): 11–22.

Symons, Arthur. *Studies in Prose and Verse*. London: J.M. Dent and Company, 1904.

Taylor, Mark C. *Erring: A Postmodern A/theology*. Chicago: University of Chicago Press, 1984.

Thornton, R. K. R. *The Decadent Dilemma*. London: Edward Arnold, 1983.

Whistler, James. *The Gentle Art of Making Enemies* (1892); rpt. New York: Dover Publications, 1967.

Wilde, Oscar. *The Complete Works of Oscar Wilde*. New York: Harper and Row, 1989.

Woolf, Virginia. *The Common Reader: First Series*, ed. Andrew McNeillie. New York: Harcourt Brace Jovanovich, 1984.

Wyndham, Violet. *The Sphinx and Her Circle*. New York: The Vanguard Press, 1963.

II.
FICTION

8

When Women Laugh Wildly and (Gentle)Men Roar: Victorian Embodiments Of Laughter

KAREN C. GINDELE

THEORETICAL LAUGHING BODIES

If we accept Henri Bergson's premise that "the comic comes into being just when society and the individual, freed from the worry of self-preservation, begin to regard themselves as works of art" (73), formal comedy would appear to be a luxury. It would seem to depend on the meeting of material needs, with the implication that desires, at least some desires, have been satisfied. As a luxury, comedy would therefore appear to be the privilege of wealthier classes, and in modern society, of the middle and upper classes, who have met material needs. Small wonder, then, that comedy is held to civilize people, if it is also in the possession of the "civilized." Small wonder, too, that a less formal comedy of wit and laughter flourishes at the dinner-table, in congenial company, and when bodies are satisfied in a sociable, civilized manner. But even laughter is a sign: it can signify pleasure, "detached" amusement, and anxiety. As a sign, with a tenuous relation to such referents, it can even be appropriated precisely in order to signify satisfaction and claim it as a luxury — a sign of assured, not threatened, position and power.

Accounts of comedy refer to its intellectual properties, the fabled absence of emotion, and the facility of verbal play which produces laughter. But Freud posits a physical ground for comedy in his argument that jokes are the sublimated outlets of the expression of both hostility and sexual desire (which is equally capable of assuming a hostile stance).[1] Ultimately, Freud, Bergson, and also George Meredith claim for comedy a civilizing role dependent on cultural sophistication, which would appear to minimize the ground of the body. I will examine representations of the laughing body in Thackeray's *Vanity Fair* (1848), Margaret Oliphant's *Miss Marjoribanks* (1866), and Meredith's *Diana of the Crossways* (1885) in order to theorize laughter in relation to desire. I will explore the gendered operation of the mind/body split in order to argue that the representation of laughter as expressive defines a gender- and class-coded body as much as a mind. Both laughing bodies and minds can threaten, even though laughter is also held to be cohesive and communal. But laughter simultaneously establishes and disrupts boundaries beyond the sense in which it organizes a group of people around an object at a given moment. I will investigate the ways in which laughter and narrative comedy both depend on and obscure their reliance on bodies. I will move freely among wit, laughter, and comedy, defining wit as a linguistic faculty, and, usually, comedy as the humor of material situations that necessarily involve bodies. Laughter needs both.

I propose that laughter disrupts desire and that comedy stages the collapse of desire. They do so in even if they reconfigure desire in another sphere. Whose desire and who desires its defeat are central questions. More precisely, individual desire, when constructed as opposed to the benefit of the group, is usually defeated so as to allow, in its place, social desire — desire for the group, which may be a marginalized group resisting the conventions of the status quo. Feminist comedy, aiming to liberate, stages the collapse of patriarchal desire to enable female individual *and* social desire. This dynamic underwrites Bergson's premise that comedy corrects the defect or abnormality by singling out the characteristic gesture for mimicry and ridicule (74–79) and requires conformity to a standard, old or new. The collapse of desire is effected by total frustration as a result of adverse circumstances, by the exposure of desire which humiliates it into nothing, and, paradoxically, by the satisfaction of desire: desire fulfilled in the marriage in a romantic comedy becomes no desire, kept within bounds hospitable to the society in which it occurs.

Comedy theory as drama theory addresses the staging of a spectacle that assumes the distanced viewer regards the scene as an object — especially as a work of art. Bergson is an obsessive gazer. When he begins looking at the comic body out of control because it appears like a machine unresponsive to the changing demands of specific situations in life, he very clearly speaks from a position that assumes scopic power, traditionally masculine. Luce Irigaray, in the context of a psychoanalytic critique of Freud and Jacques Lacan, has posited "touch" as an alternative domain and articulation of relationship. I will use this alternate register to amplify comedy theory, arguing for a progress in the novels I discuss. Their writers collapse a viewing distance between subject and object to establish a physically nearer relation that makes everybody both. Laughter enables increasingly direct connection among its subjects and objects, reconfiguring desire itself. This progress was neither steady nor irreversible, but traces the features of a Victorian transformation.

Freud argues, in the both funny and vexing analysis of *Jokes and Their Relation to the Unconscious,* that a joke and its ensuing laughter accomplish the satisfaction of a desire for the teller, in theory giving pleasure to the hearer, by substituting a verbal and symbolic form of obtaining the desire for a physical one, as in either a hostile joke, or a sexual joke. But Freud also argues for a real physical effect because of the (self-preserving) release of psychic tension. The pleasure of a joke comes in part from subverting authority — including the very rules by which we agree to live even if we are worried about self-preservation.

Recent critical work on feminist comedy makes a different claim: Regenia Gagnier argues that Victorian working-class and educated middle-class women, "however restricted they were in public, among themselves ... used humor neither for disparagement nor temporary release, but rather as a prolonged anarchic assault upon the codes restricting them. This is to say that their humor primarily lay within the category of incongruity but that their use of incongruity had socio-behavioral implications for exploring difference rather than merely disparaging it and for prolonged critical action rather than momentary release" (138). Gagnier locates the incongruities between "cultural and intertextual frames" that lead women to question the differing codes by which they live; notably women assault the system and not the individual, although any single person can certainly represent the interests of a system.

Gagnier's argument overtly refutes Freud's theory of "momentary release."[2] She also supports a theory of opposition to authority, and states, especially regarding working-class women, that women may laugh a lot, and produce a lot of jokes, when they are not necessarily free of worry about self-preservation. But it is not necessary to argue that one happens or the other, that there is an economy by which momentary release diminishes a prolonged assault. It may rather contribute renewed energy to such an assault. One might accomplish both.

All theories of comedy that I have seen take into account the idea of critique. Even in his discussion of nonsense jokes which are not tendentious, having no aim to ridicule an adversary, incite a sexual scene, or attack authority (possibly a variation on the first), Freud argues that pleasure in nonsense recovers an old pleasure in play with words, before we were required to be serious and logical. We take pleasure in and laugh at nonsense as an activity in which we do not have to exercise rational criticism (125–26). Moreover, we can follow whatever "irrational" association our minds produce, making links between things not "logically" associated, especially bringing together the "two circles of ideas," usually remote, that contribute to the incongruity theory.

In the scene of laughter there appears to be a sharp division of labor and even protocols attaching to positions: the joke-teller appears to have control; he or she appears to have the power of criticism of the object, of already grasping the joke itself, and commanding its linguistic and narrative presentation. The joker is supposed to remain in control of him or herself and should not laugh prematurely, if at all, keeping an air of polish and restraint. But against this apparent imbalance of power, some of the funniest witticisms are made by someone who assumes the position of ignorance, making her or himself the object (Freud's "naive" joke). The unaware speaker appears not to control either the situation or language itself. The multiplicity of figurative meanings escapes or falls abundantly on the agent/object, and we see his or her failure to grasp implications.

The hearer may have some expectation, but is best taken by surprise. The joke needs to happen suddenly. There is bewilderment and then sudden enlightenment, but no time for desire between the specific puzzle and its solution. Freud identifies the need for both "too few words" (13) and "multiple use of the same material" (36–42); that is, multiple meanings for one element. The gap in the first or the connection made in the second instance accounts for the necessary immediate apprehension (as of the angels) rather than the plodding piecemeal putting together of sense. Making the link produces the *effect* of an extra-linguistic faculty even if the joke occurs entirely in language. The teller and hearer both seem to have a special receptivity. The hearer in one sense completes the joke both by grasping that meaning that produces closure and by laughing to signify such closure. In another sense, laughter seems suddenly to open.

Laughter itself is plural. The single "ha!" occurs rarely. Even one person alone can laugh, although laughter loves company. Laughter produces plural sounds and tones with almost melodic lines, cadences, and "waves." The specific sounds are "material diversities," in Julia Kristeva's terms (132), those qualities which can only be inadequately represented by "ha ha ha" in the masculinist symbolic order of language that excludes so much from representation. Laughter's meaning comes from its sound; it carries no thesis. Its sounds might recover an "old pleasure" (Freud) related to the mother.

The surprise of the laugher, the being taken, is a seizure, a rapture, and places the hearer in the passive position: he or she not only receives but is acted on, responding from the body. Strange merit, that an articulated proposition should produce an inarticulate answer. Laughter cannot only *not* be controlled in some situations; it can control a subject who is pleased to be unsettled, even desiring such a passion. The "burst" of laughter — the *éclat* — conveys this sense of shattering into pieces that is a desired multiplicity both within the subject and by connection to other people. I posit a comic *jouissance* and apply Roland Barthes's ideas of textual pleasure to the pleasure of laughter, when he talks not about comedy or laughter but about the double-edgedness of "works of our modernity": "The subversive edge may seem privileged because it is the edge of violence; but it is not violence which affects pleasure, nor is it destruction which interests it; what pleasure wants is the site of a loss, the seam, the cut, the deflation, the *dissolve* which seizes the subject in the midst of bliss" (7; his italics). The double edge and the language of violence are not intrinsically violent: we can think of them as the two "circles of ideas" brought into sudden relation to each other — the "breaks" or "collisions" that "come into contact" (6); in other words, that are made to touch each other.

These circles of ideas (or in Gagnier's terms, frames of reference) that are brought into contact with each other can furthermore be fruitfully theorized as involving desire and the limitations imposed on desire by the material facts of the body. Such a construction forces the opposition of desire to the body and therefore locates desire as belonging to the mind, psyche, or spirit and at least partly within the domain of social constructions. The codes restricting the behavior of middle-class women, for example, or the working-class woman's joking at the middle-class woman's abstractions and failure to understand the material realities of her life — both illustrate this limitation by material circumstances, a body not so much of facts, but of actualities — of material existence. Even the smallest workings of comedy based on the discrepancy between the figurative and literal, or the expectation that results in nothing (Kant), are a setting in play of the idea or desire, and the material body that is, in fact, something, not nothing. The literal meaning functions as the body that limits and grounds flights of abstraction or expectations that are inseparable from desire, even if only the desire to produce meaning and knowledge. The most frequent direction of humor is to establish an expectation of the abstract and then deflate it, working from "large" to "small," which is usually constructed as not only material but feminine. The female body would appear to cause the collapse of masculine epistemological desire. Desire comes bolt up against the material fact; we also might laugh at the collapse of our own desire to produce large and important meanings.

At several points in "This Sex Which Is Not One," Luce Irigaray claims that a woman has plural erotic sites — more than the two of clitoris and vagina, the pleasure of the one subordinated to that of the other in order to sustain masculine sexuality around penetration by the penis. At one such point, she says that woman

> finds pleasure almost anywhere. Even if we refrain from invoking the hystericization of her entire body, the geography of her pleasure is far more diversified, more multiple in its differences, more complex, more subtle, than is commonly imagined — in an imaginary rather too narrowly focused on sameness.
>
> "She" is indefinitely other in herself. This is doubtless why she is said to be whimsical, incomprehensible, agitated, capricious ... not to mention her language, in which "she" sets off in all directions leaving "him" unable to discern the coherence of any meaning... What she says is never identical with anything, moreover; rather, it is contiguous. *It touches* (*upon*). And when it strays too far from that proximity, she breaks off and starts over at "zero": her body-sex... [28–29]. [Women's] desire is often interpreted, and feared, as a sort of insatiable hunger, a voracity that will swallow you whole. Whereas it really involves a different economy more than anything else, one that upsets the linearity of a project, undermines the goal-object of a desire, diffuses the polarization toward a single pleasure, disconcerts fidelity to a single discourse ... [29–30]. Woman always remains several, but she is kept from dispersion because the other is already within her and is autoerotically familiar to her. Which is not to say that she appropriates the other for herself, that she reduces it to her own property. Ownership and property are doubtless quite foreign to the feminine. At least sexually. But not *nearness*. [31]

Diana Fuss has identified Irigaray's concept of contiguity, proximity, touch, and nearness as the play of metonymy — specifically, the play of the feminine in the unconscious (62). Irigaray's conception of a metonymic relation of woman to woman, and woman to language, is a desiring, but not lacking, relation of nearness, of bordering and touching. It presents an alternative to the obsessively scopic regime of metaphor that demands visual likeness and conformity to models of sexual difference that maintain distance in order to ensure desire. Irigaray suggests that women constantly deflate masculine desiring expectations by considering near associations.

In previous work, I have argued that metonymy is the only poetic/rhetorical figure that accounts for motion, which is why it has so readily been used to characterize desire (motion towards an object). But this kind of desire has been formulated by Roman Jakobson and followers as forward-moving within prescribed ("logical") syntactic structures. Paul de Man formulates metonymy as chance (26) — what actually happens: the accidental, contingent link. I wish to articulate the associative capacity of metonymy — connections that actually happen — with Freud's notion of joking as linguistic play once available but later prohibited under the demands of rational critical thought — of "making sense" and being "coherent"; of curtailing the associative play of the mind that makes its own connections and follows its own desires (168). Play involves concepts of touch that Freud also notes has been forbidden for the substitution of looking, which he takes as the mark of civilized repression (98). But touch should not be taken lightly, even as the source of laughter in tickling.

This nearness and touch of mind and body, language and laughter, and the fluid exchange between activity and passivity, giving and receiving sudden pleasure, are exactly what is needed in a theory of feminist and materialist comedy. Both Oliphant and Meredith were working towards different conceptions of a metonymic theory of comedy. Oliphant develops the comedy of the accident, "falling towards," that brings people into relation with each other in the comedy of proximity, and therefore of bodies. Meredith proposes a relation of touch, motion, and wild laughter, that enables women to escape from the restrictions of and predations prompted by the masculine gaze. Thackeray is my ground for his early affiliations with an eighteenth-century sensibility, to which Oliphant and Meredith also felt connections, with differences. Perhaps Thackeray is also my straw man, though hardly my straight man.

FICTIVE LAUGHING BODIES

The violence that attaches to laughter in *Vanity Fair* is surprising even when one already knows it is there. The burst, explosion, volley, and roar without doubt reflect the volatile political climate of class conflict around 1848 with the eruptions of revolutions everywhere, even though most of the novel takes place around 1815. Nearly everybody at some point "bursts out" laughing in a sudden, uncontainable impulse. One character usually takes pleasure at the expense of another's humiliation, if not downright pain. This humiliation, involving the exposure of desire, works against both the strong and the weak — that is, "upward" against people empowered by the social order, and "downward" against those marginalized by it. Occasionally the underdog triumphs. Much of the novel's comedy results from the swift containment of "large" political desires to "small" domestic or personal desires and traces the defeat of imaginative desire by the limitations of real material circumstances. Bursting laughter establishes the expressiveness of the individual, often in defiance of social restrictions and decorum. It might at first seem to signal the desire of the individual against the social order rather than the neutralization of that desire. Laughter at least initially posits an interior self that *will* be heard and *will* take pleasure.

The full-bodied laughs of men in the novel most often mark the common man in the middle class or the outsider in the upper class — the isolated rogue or rebel, who does not wield power within the established system — mysteriously not the working man who in 1848 was threatening. Women, in contrast, when they reach a certain volume, are threatening because they represent either the revolt and violence of a mob or the superficial, artificial, inauthentic pleasure of the upper crust, who assume that wit is their luxury and the sign of their class position.

Amelia is defined in the wholly feminine, narrow limits "between her two customs of laughing and crying" (5). Her acceptable quiet laughter is not itself threatening to anybody but herself, for it seems to reflect good spirits and spontaneity without danger of critical, intellectual content, but her ease in crossing the border into tears bears out in the novel not merely sympathetic responsiveness but also an instability that verges on excess. Laughter and tears, reflecting opposed states of mind, are shown to be closely and hysterically linked by self-denial in the middle-class female body. (George, denying himself nothing but exploiting Amelia, epitomizes such self-interest and mean-spirited laughter, that he can only be shot.)

Dobbin presents the gentlemanly counterpart to Amelia. He is debonair *because* of (not despite) a gracelessness and awkwardness of body that show he does not usually wield or control its power. Yet he has desires that he enacts defending George or his country. He also shows himself a gentleman by *not* expressing his desire for Amelia, about which he laughs ruefully. He laughs *at* himself, transforming self-criticism into self-denial. He is not guilty of pretensions to a romantic, deluded "character" of himself that has no material reality. When left holding Amelia's shawl, excluded from the romantic pairings of Amelia and George, Becky and Jos, Dobbin tries to hum "a savage cantata against the Corsican upstart," but instead finds himself humming the tune Amelia had been singing when "her song flew into his heart." "He burst out laughing at himself; for the truth is, he could sing no better than an owl" (52). His self-criticism affirms his good ear and responsiveness to Amelia, but his laughter occurs at the sudden shift between political and domestic spheres. His political desire is contained in the also hopeless romantic realm, which, though involving desire, is "smaller."

Jos's large body — the large body of the bourgeoisie, about whom everything grows — is both the object and subject of much laughter. Amelia and Becky have a "fit of laughter" over Jos, who organizes homosocial pairs connected to each other. When he says, "I believe I'm very terrible, when I'm roused," which of course he is not, he makes "a grimace so dreary and ludicrous, that the captain's politeness could restrain him no longer, and he and Osborne fired off a ringing volley of laughter" (56). Jos is a map of desires, mostly appetites, both gratified and failed; for this reason Dobbin and George laugh so heartlessly. His hope and illusion that he is "terrible, when roused" and his claim to heroic military prowess, which increases from story to story, are deflated by his fear of both other men and women. The dimensions of his body suggest the acquisitiveness of the middle class, its narcissism, its "lower" physical desires met in excess of what is needed for self-preservation. He decorates his body in garish clothes that augment and exhibit rather than diminish his size. Jos's interest in food might be sublimated sexual desire, but he enjoys his small pleasures, refusing desire for the "small" sphere of romance in order to concentrate on the yet smaller and larger sphere of his own person.

His laughter is inspired by the slap-stick, the "practical" or physical joke: another body's loss of control. Becky dines with the Sedleys and unwittingly asks for very spicy curry in order to ingratiate herself. "'Try a chili with it, Miss Sharp,' said Joseph, really interested." "By Jove, how they made you cry out!" he later exclaims, "caught by the ridicule of the circumstance, ... exploding in a fit of laughter which ended quite suddenly, as usual" (25). Jos's abrupt halt suggests that his laughter is socially unacceptable and not quite in control; nor can he be satisfied if his laughter can't run a natural course.

Jos makes a comic and desiring spectacle of himself at the famous Vauxhall scene in which he drinks too much of "that bowl of rack punch" that is "the cause of all this history" (53–54). He mobilizes a social scene that becomes a class conflict. He responds with a "liveliness ... at first ... astonishing, and then ... almost painful; for he talked and laughed so loud as to bring scores of listeners round the box, much to the confusion of the innocent party within it." He sings a maudlin song, becomes "bold as a lion," and clasps Becky round the waist; the "laughter outside redouble[s]" and Jos challenges anyone to share his punch. Barbara Hardy imaginatively notes that this scene is a "small riot" (127); it indicates the disorganized beginnings of revolution. Interestingly, however, it is the middle class's uncontainable desire which leads to the failure of class divisions and boundaries. Jos himself becomes a grotesque body of carnival[3] before Dobbin arrives to disperse the crowd with his fierce warning, "Be off, you fools!" Becky's own pursuit and final containment of Jos encompass the large body of the novel, and Thackeray's comedy, too, depends on his body.

Becky is given multiplicity in her laughter: she can have a "comical and good-humoured air" (22); she can laugh "with a cordiality and perseverance" at Mr. Sedley's jokes (23–24); she can make "sweet little appeals, half tender, half jocular" to Jos (25); she lets out a scream and giggle at Rawdon's cigar (105); she can switch from laughter to fury in a trice and can also produce tears at will. Most often, with Rawdon, she, too, "bursts out laughing," but most frighteningly, most threateningly, she laughs the laugh of the Medusa.[4] She is continually constructed as a Medusa; the mermaid who "pickles" her victims (ch. 64) is kin. Small and blonde, with green eyes, she looks tame, but at the very start she laughs in Miss Pinkerton's face "with a horrid sarcastic demoniacal laughter."

Her insatiable desire is threatening[5] — a "voracity that will swallow you whole," to recall Irigaray, that accounts for the multiplicity of her roles, none of which provides a center except as void; most are masks. Becky's slipperiness derives from the separation of her projected surfaces — her production of affect — from her inner self. Thackeray constantly invokes not an expressive connection of interior and exterior, depth and surface, but a split between her "real" interior self and the many roles she assumes as social facades in order to climb the social ladder. Her surface multiplicities threaten the social order's own dispersion. Her laughter is sometimes her only authentic response, and even that is unsure. Upper-class English women "[writhe] with anguish at the success of the little upstart Becky, whose poisoned jokes quivered and rankled in their chaste breasts. But she had all the men on her side" (359). Finally, when Becky betrays Rawdon and he leaves her, "All her lies and her schemes, all her selfishness and her wiles, all her wit and genius had come to this bankruptcy" (556). No longer exposing the hollowness of the pleasure of the privileged — the fact that they desire much and are hardly happy or satisfied — Becky becomes a luxury herself. She is cut off from "legitimate" social power because, as a woman, she hasn't got a "legitimate" body to back such power. She can't be a man, and she can't be the right kind of woman. Thackeray keeps her in the unstable in-between of sexual difference and subversive sexual desire.

Except for occasional moments, at which he releases her from desire, letting her get tired of "that roving, restless life... [P]leased herself, she [tries] with all her might to please everybody" (711). The narrator forgets that Becky has used the fact that she gives pleasure, but has not done so *in order* to give pleasure; he keeps mostly separate, in an economy of exchange, her taking pleasure from her giving pleasure.

But when Becky is at her finest, she does both. These moments occur almost entirely in her marriage with Rawdon, when they are companions. Gender and sexual difference are eased; they laugh together, rogues and outsiders, exploiting the political system more than individual people within it. Becky masters Rawdon's "rude coarse nature" (299) and he adores her. His inherent goodness, given the chance now to flourish, shows in his laughter, a combination of simplicity, uncouthness, and relish in Becky's outsmarting the powerful. She proposes that he go into the Church: "The idea of this conversion set Rawdon into roars of laughter: you might have heard the explosion through the hotel at midnight, and the haw-haws of the great dragoon's voice" (299). Thackeray tries to represent the actual body of the sound of laughter in these "haw-haws." Rawdon's robustness grounds laughter in the solidity of the male body, reverberating outward, but delighting in the woman's resistance to patriarchal authority. Becky laughs at both Rawdon and herself when a joke, "too good," tells against their own desires (260). When, fleeing Napoleon's imminent arrival in Brussels, she unveils the money and jewels sewn into her dress, Rawdon "roared with delightful laughter, and swore that she was better than any play he ever saw, by Jove... [W]ith infinite fun, [she] carried up his delight to a pitch of quite insane enthusiasm. He believed in his wife as much as the French soldiers in Napoleon" (358).

Becky ends up attacking him; she turns her wit and satire against the man who is with and near her — not for his participation in the system of patriarchal privilege, but for his powerlessness, his "stupidity." She gives him pain while she appears to take pleasure. Freud argued that the symbol of the Medusa isolates the horrifying effects of the female genitals from the pleasure-giving ones. Thackeray likewise isolates the horrifying effects of Becky's wit and laughter from the pleasure of her comedy. She is most complex and most delightful when she disrupts that economy, that division of labor between giving and receiving pleasure, when she and Rawdon do both — when their laughter is intimate, yet breaks up the spectacle of desire.

In Margaret Oliphant's *Miss Marjoribanks*, nearly everyone laughs except the heroine Lucilla, and a good many people laugh at her. She has a desiring "programme" to center and organize the Carlingford community socially and aesthetically by means of her own activity. Her seriousness of purpose might but does not set her up as the object of ridicule at inevitable failures. She admits to having no sense of humor, for she does not often see what is ridiculous, but when people laugh at her, they usually laugh with admiration and attribute to her more wit, more ironic double vision and distance, than she in fact commands. Much of the comedy of the novel lies not in the accidents of failure, but in the astonishing serendipity of her successes.

Oliphant's coup in this narrative is to construct a version of female desire wholly antithetical to lack.[6] Lucilla encounters obstacles and has a few moments of loneliness when people doubt her, but she is neither self-divided nor thwarted. Laughter implies divisions, and she has few. She has confidence in herself, faith in her powers of management and organization without being a "managerial" woman, and her desires seem to develop from plenitude, self-sufficiency and energy which seek (but do not lack) a field in which to use them. The narrative embodies her intentions.

Lucilla has a large mind and a large body, which we see first. She has energy, mass, and radiance: "large in all particulars ... not at all pretty as yet, though ... somebody had said that such a face might ripen into beauty, and become 'grandiose,' for anything anybody could tell." She has a mass of hair which, "if it could have been cleared a little in its tint, would have been golden, though at present it was nothing more than tawny, and curly to exasperation ... ridiculously, unmanageably thick" (26–27). Her father wishes she were a son, or had been born to his sister, who would have known how to manage her (64), since his wife has died.[7]

Lucilla's large mind is mentioned in countless variations, all gently ironic, but so frequent as finally to be convincing. The most important occurrence follows one of the several failed marriage proposals which are themselves very funny, each of which Lucilla reads narratively as an approaching crisis and climax, only to become a "crisis *manqué*." Not only does one man fail to propose, but another, also beginning to be taken with her, sees her protegée, the woman he once passionately loved, and Lucilla is cheated again. She sees the unfitting irony in having helped the widow to be her rival, and feels the giddiness "from such a strange reversal of the position" (213). After a "temporary ebullition," however, her "great mind ... [recovers] its balance"; she "comes to herself" and her natural calm. "She regained bit by bit that serene self-consciousness which places spirit above the passing vexations of the world... Was not she still Lucilla Marjoribanks? and when one had said that, one had said all" (214–15).

Her first "programme," following her reading of novels, is to sacrifice herself totally "to be a comfort to poor Papa." But this plan is a self-disguised front for her revolutionization of Carlingford society. She wants to provide a center for the town, which has excellent families, "but then, without organisation, what good does it do to have a number of people together?" (42). Lucilla will aim at "knitting people together, and making a harmonious whole out of the scraps and fragments of society" (43).

Lucilla's method of direction is hands-on: "[S]he knew by instinct what sort of clay the people were made of by whom she had to work, and gave them their reward with that liberality and discrimination which is the glory of enlightened despotism" (57). Oliphant rewrites Enlightenment rationalism for women — not perfectly, perhaps, but nonetheless boldly. The language of eighteenth-century letters permeates the narrative, accounting for its mock-heroic tone.[8] However, appearing to grant the smallness of concerns because held by a young woman, Oliphant allows Lucilla's comparisons of herself to a general or a king actually to enlarge her sphere of action: "She felt like a young king entering in secret a capital which awaits him with acclamations" and she has plans "for the embellishment of this inner court and centre of her kingdom," her drawing-room, at present "a waste and howling wilderness" (48). Instead of confining her to the domestic realm, as Patricia Stubbs argues (40–43), the narrator shows Lucilla's power must start somewhere. Lucilla does not maintain a division but enacts an approach of spheres, ultimately an influence of the feminine on the masculine realm, radiating out from a center. The narrator's relation to Lucilla is close: laughing at her, the narrator never quite generates comedy at Lucilla's expense, even while she constantly plays off Lucilla as the desiring half of the dialectic of humor without deflating — instead satisfying — her aspirations. The narrator is not divided from her heroine; she is near her.

As Lucilla seems like a center of gravity, causing people and events to arrange themselves by and large harmoniously around her, she first asserts herself within the home controlled by her father. In the "wilderness" of the dark drawing-room, she lights all the candles. "She was standing in this flood of light, regarding everything around her with the eye of an enlightened critic and reformer, when Dr Marjoribanks came in." He is startled at the "amount of *éclairage*" that seems unnecessary.[9] But he kisses her with "real pleasure, and [owns] to himself that, if she was not a fool, and could keep to her own department, it might be rather agreeable on the whole to have a woman in the house" (49). This is one event in the comedy of positions that reverses power between father and daughter. Positions here are the property of bodies and are guaranteed by bodies. The daughter civilizes the father and even eclipses him. In this contestation of power, Oliphant overturns a masculinist Enlightenment policy and does so on the ground of Lucilla's mind, her "genius."

In this transferral, the Doctor's laughter is crucial. He often chuckles to himself, he laughs softly, he sometimes laughs and sighs; he most often laughs when he is beaten by Lucilla — partly at himself, partly in admiration of her. He also provides an internal perspective of pleasure in her, contributing to our own. Their struggle for position is organized around the dinner table. On her return from school, "He found her, to his intense amazement, seated at the foot of the table, in the place which he usually occupied himself." He is shocked by her "unparalleled audacity" but defers and finally says "Humph!" as he half realizes he has "abdicated" (50). Lucilla has also won the cook's acquiescence, assuring the safety of that woman's position as "prime minister." The doctor again "laughs out" at Lucilla's disarming sweetness, his fancy caught by "a keen perception of the ridiculous." "Very well, Lucilla," he concedes, "you shall try what you can do" (51). Such scenes occur often: he is angry at her boldness but "amused and pleased ... to have so clever a daughter" (68). He is one of many who credit her with wit when she is earnest, not seeing the incongruous larger picture that he does.

Nominally of her father's class, Lucilla is subordinate by gender, generational position, and his professional authority which reaches into the whole community. She can only achieve class equality because of her intelligence. She opens up the circle of his all-male dinner parties (dependent on the female cook's excellent labor) to the wives of Carlingford, and the doctor again reluctantly admires. The masculine sphere of wit and critical intelligence that requires the satisfaction of the body does not suffer for the inclusion of women. His laughter signifies the relinquishment of some of his own desire as his "civilized" self-containment: he never roars, never really lets loose. The enlargement of his dinners to Lucilla's "Thursday evenings," while it does not change the structure of class relations, begins to redefine boundaries and inclusions.

Mrs. Woodburn is the other influential critic of Lucilla; her laughter is explosive, unlike Dr. Marjoribanks's self-contained aloofness. She has ties to Becky Sharp in her brilliance of impersonation and caricature, but also to Amelia in the "hysterical" nearness of laughter to tears and stress. Oliphant inscribes the "release" theory of laughter in the observation that it is a "safety-valve" for Mrs. Woodburn, but it is not exactly her own laughter that is the valve. The whole community lives in terror of her, wondering how she "takes off" each neighbor when she is with all the others, but her talent, her insight, is only for "the tricks of the surface" (241). Faced with a fairly straightforward question from Lucilla about her brother's whereabouts, she attributes to her some hidden agenda, a threat and plot: "She could no more tell what this meant, than if she had been ... totally unacquainted with human motives"; as a result, all her "fun and mimicry collapsed" (243). When Lucilla leaves, however, "The mimic, with her nerves strung to desperation, burst into the wildest comic travesty of Miss Marjoribanks's looks and manners, ... and sent her unsuspicious husband into convulsions of laughter. He laughed until the tears ran down his cheeks — the unconscious simpleton; and all the time his wife could have liked to throw him down and trample on him, or put pins into him, or scratch his beaming, jovial countenance. Perhaps she would have gone into hysterics instead if she had not possessed that other safety-valve, for Mrs Woodburn had not that supreme composure and self-command which belonged to Lucilla's higher organisation" (244–45).

The "safety-valve" offers Mrs. Woodburn superficial connections to her objects of attack and to the circle of people to whom she gives the pleasure of a ridiculing comedy. Failing to make real attachments here, she also fails to "make any exertions for the good of the community" *except* in her comedy; she does not identify with a communal desire but in fact must remain aloof because she is a kind of impostor, trying, like Becky, to work her way into social empowerment, married to a man beneath her in class position and whom she does not love. Her mimicry allows her the exploration of other identities, other positions not available materially, but only symbolically and temporarily, from which she must "come to herself" to regain a center. Lucilla is the one person she almost wants to become, approaching her through "wild travesty" in her own out-of-body experience. She does not let go entirely, however, for even though she laughs hysterically at times, she doesn't cry or assault her husband except by indirectly levelling him with laughter, and putting him into convulsions. She works the dispersion of laughter on him; he is a real target.

Lucilla's own failure to laugh preserves her intactness, her seemingly material opacity, and even her limitation. She wants people to be amused and is quietly amused herself, sometimes both amused and exasperated, by her cousin Tom. She gives out "a little cry of alarm and wonder" (712) at things going wrong, at the comedy of the accident which starts as unlucky but turns out to be exactly right. Tom himself is such an accident in her life; he is always doing the wrong thing, his body wholly uncontainable, and he disrupts the order of her spaces, for which she holds him in contempt, saying it is "*so like Tom.*" He seems ridiculous to her, and she therefore comes closest to laughing at him. Although there is expediency in Oliphant's sending him away for much of the novel only to have him return and finally win Lucilla, the ending works the way laughter works by suddenly collapsing. Lucilla concedes, "It was to be Tom after all" (478) — notably, after much energy and guessing directed at other men. Oliphant resolves the comedy of the accident, a "happy fall," with Lucilla's discovery that the man near and known was all along the right choice. Lucilla's intuitive talent, greater even than her design, brings people near each other by a kind of metonymic social gravity that actually forms the community. Other old attachments need to be recognized and brought to light, but Lucilla's intuition is not split by self-consciousness and cannot prove its own ground. This comedy helps produce the laughter that flourishes around Lucilla without disrupting her desire in laughter. She is funny because she both has and does not have control. She does not have verbal wit but disposes of situations; seeing no division of mind and body, she enacts mind.

Meredith's Diana "[claims] a space for laughter" as "the breath of her soul" (7) that depends on "the liberty she [allows] herself in speech and action" (6). "She, especially, with her multitude of quick perceptions and imaginative avenues, her rapid summaries, her sense of the comic, demanded this aërial freedom" (7). Diana marries Augustus Warwick, however, to preserve the space of her physical freedom from the sexual advances of men, to whom she has twice been fair game, seized as an object without regard for her own desire. The marriage is a failure and Warwick destroys the freedom of her "soul": Diana "would let loose her silvery laugh in the intervals" of play at the whist-table; Warwick "burst out at last, with bitter mimicry, 'yang—yang—yang!' and killed the bright laugh, shot it dead. She had outraged the decorum of the square-table" (6).

Diana's laughter is not killed, however; it goes underground. It remains part of, and defines the boundaries of a better protected space, her friendship with Emma Dunstane, to whom she is not Diana but the "beloved Tony," inscribing a masculine position that both reconstructs and erases gender difference.[10] Diana provokes "laughing peals" in Emma over civilization and politics (118) and laughs herself. Laughter also characterizes Diana's relationship with her maid Danvers, who laughs so much that she thinks Diana "as good as a play" (much as Rawdon thinks Becky). As importantly, laughter is part of Diana's relationship with Thomas Redworth. On a carriage ride the latter three take, misadventurous because of the driver but full of hilarity, Diana has "some of her wildest seizures of iridescent humour" (102). Redworth sees into causes — Diana's winning her case against her husband's

charges of adultery is one, although she also wants to escape from the scene
and laughs in some desperation — but he is "nevertheless amazed by the airy
hawk-poise and pounce-down of her wit, as she ranged high and low, now
capriciously generalizing, now dropping bolt upon things of passage — the
postillion jogging from rum to gin, the rustics baconly agape, the horse-kneed
ostlers. She touched them to the life in similes and phrases; and next she was
aloft, derisively philosophizing, but with a comic afflatus that dispersed the
sharpness of her irony in mocking laughter" (102). Diana's lovely and
privileged, often "silvery" laughter minimizes the criticism of her "sparkling
wit," but her object here is primarily working-class men, ridiculed for their
bodies and their effect on her body, although "touched to life." We can read
this scene straightforwardly as Diana's and/or Meredith's class arrogance, or
as her animosity to men in general, but Meredith has early on seen the "animal
vivaciousness " and "ready roar" bubbling in the breasts of "our old yeomanry
farmers" (2) as a promising sign of wit to come in the English people, and
therefore on a continuum with the English/Irish Diana. She is quite possibly
attacking the *aristocratic* boorishness of her pursuers by displacing it on
laboring men.

Shortly afterwards, Diana concludes that she is independent "of her sex
and the passions"; that she is "a Diana of coldness, preferring friendship; she
could be the friend of man. There was another who could be the friend of
women. Her heart leapt to Redworth. Conjuring up his clear and trusty face,
at their grasp of hands when parting, she thought … he was the man to whom
she could have opened her heart for inspection… [She] burned with regret
that at their parting she had not broken down conventional barriers and given
her cheek to his lips … like a dear comrade" (137).

Judith Wilt asserts that Diana must come to recognize that she is not cold,
that friendship is not what she really wants; rather, she must accept her desire,
her disposition to "kindle," in Meredith's metaphor for the commitment of
the whole self — mind, spirit and body — to passion neither idealized nor
repudiated (MD and RP 70–72). Diana needs to get over her "sexual aversion." There is more support for this argument in Diana's relinquishing of her
girlhood idealization of romance, connected to her chastity as a safe space,
in exchange for the acceptance of her experience as a woman, but I want to
reclaim friendship and resituate it within the space of laughter, which breaks
down "conventional barriers," especially those barriers within the system of
desire that exist both between women and between women and men, in class
and gender.

In Irigaray's terms, the most restrictive system of desire for women is the
specular régime of the masculine gaze. Meredith's recognition of this coercion is one reason for which, in my reading, he both uses the language of
"obscurity" and actually seems to obscure Diana herself, dissolving her
within language, sometimes within the network of texts about her, especially

the opening "diaries and diarists touching the heroine" (1). Sometimes she even seems to recede *behind* language. Following the associative, metonymic motions of the mind, the narrator loses track of her as his original referent, the material being who is his subject. But Meredith was also proposing an alternative to the the visual realm by emphasizing the relation of touch, and language *as* touch. Diana's wit both touches and attacks, making contact; her laughter connects.

Meredith tries to construct language, and particularly laughter, as sound that touches, having both material and immaterial, or invisible effects. He anticipated Irigaray's theory of women and language as *near* but does not, I think, assert this as the privileged connection of women alone. In the effort to construct a narrator who lets Diana out of the visual realm, and yet keeps her as a subject-not-object within representation, he seems to dematerialize her in order to think of her in other terms. Hardy uses a similar strategy with Tess, but only holds her within or lets her elude a consistently narrative gaze, not giving her substance in another register.

Intensely conscious of the sphere in which women were required to move as gendered bodies, Meredith uses imagery of the moon both to illuminate and to obscure Diana and to characterize the intellectual difficulty of her perceptive wit that cultivates thought because its sense is also "obscure" — not readily apparent. Classical as is the imagery revolving around Diana as the chaste goddess of the moon and the hunt who protects wild creatures and wild spaces, it has the further advantage of reflecting the motion of a body as it comes into and goes out of view. The silveriness of Diana's laughter attaches to the obscure light of the moon, but this light also abates her continual sense of nakedness and exposure, because of her imputed "experience," her history. Allon White's essay on stylistic as well as thematic obscurity in Meredith (86–94) locates the issue of exposure in Meredith's experience of the public spectacle of his own failed marriage, but White also observes Meredith's point that a woman who has a "history," especially of sexual experience, has a "scent" that makes her liable and easy to be hunted by the "dog-world," including the men who originally pursue her because she is a virgin and unattached. Diana is safe from this world when she is with Emma, but Emma's own husband was one of Diana's grabbers, and his violation intrudes on the perfect candor and naturalness between the two women. If Diana eludes chase, and even avoids Emma, it is because of her swift motion, her receding from both touch and sight.

The inherent contradiction and final impossibility of keeping a character present and visually "absent" do not escape Meredith. Nor does he condemn pleasure in visual beauty and vision itself. He seeks to qualify its coercion to determine behavior and demand the "decorum" that restricts spontaneity and motion. Redworth watches Diana lighting a fire — kindling, as it were — and then says to himself of Warwick, "Owner of such a woman, and to lose her!" (88). The narrator remarks ironically that Redworth shares "the generosity of men speculating upon other men's possessions" (89) but Redworth, asserting his faith in Diana, turns "to look at her with the eyes of a friend." The regard of her as a possession is something he himself must lose, and he does so by realizing finally that she is not extra — a luxurious ornament — to him; she would "complete" him. He recognizes and accepts his own lack. Diana and Redworth tease each other, she gently criticizing him for his speculation and material calculations: "[M]editating railways, you scored our poor land of herds and flocks ... It was clever of you to find your way by the moonbeams" (92). She next intuitively touches without seeing that she hits him, regarding her marriage: "'You succeed in everything you aimed at, and broke your heart over one chance miss?' 'My heart is not of the stuff to break,' he said, and laughed off her fortuitous thrust straight into it." He then finds that it is easier to speak to her without facing her.

Gradually, Redworth becomes willing to look ridiculous in his love for Diana; he is willing to be laughed at. Percy Dacier, with whom Diana is entranced for much of the novel, and who, incidentally, has a "broad laugh" and loves burlesque, cannot stand the exposure of his own desire because that desire would then be exposed *as* lack, as his own lack. To be lacking is not manly. Diana, refusing to become his possession by two "accidents" — Emma's illness and the need for money that makes her, moving from the private to public spheres, expose Percy's political desire to an unscrupulous newspaper editor — shows him that he is lacking because his desire has failed, and he does not like failure, with the inevitable humiliation that should, but doesn't, civilize him. Moreover, he sees her wit as ornamentation, a luxury, as he sees Diana herself — "the mere finishing touches, not a part of the texture" of human nature, as she describes Warwick's attitude towards women (133).[11] Redworth, in contrast, accepts a possibly feminine position; he risks the spectacle of his own desire.

It is finally a touch of her own, not surprisingly, that allows Diana to recognize Redworth's passion for her, which she thinks the thing lacking in all his material successes and contradictorily radical politics. When he says he is going to her native Ireland, the independence of which is one of his progressive causes, "He could not have said sweeter to her ears or more touching" (403). Laughter, although it does not happen at this exact moment, is part of this space of friendship; it brings people near, and then into contact with each other, and it occurs near, and associated with, moments of touching. Both are metonymic because catching and contagious, passing quickly between one and the other. Touch is connection, of course — social and sexual connection — that cannot make the judgments of sight and which people must learn not to exercise simply because they see something they want. As Beer notes, Redworth's virtue has been not to pursue. Rather, he helps create the space for Diana's laughter, for her motion, and for her returning expressive touch and wish to be touched. He does still momentarily shock her "under eyes tolerably hawkish in their male glitter," and in his kiss she feels "her loss of self in the man" (406). However, she acknowledges "her subserviency to touch and pressure — and more, her readiness to kindle" (409). She puts a kiss on his arm and finds him "electrically alive to the act through a coat-sleeve" (411), and yet he holds back, drawing in his breath. This is what civilizes — not the ability to possess, but the ability to relinquish, to not hold onto — not the ability to laugh, but to be laughed at. His "expression and repression" win her utterly and she begins to create a metaphorical, but also material space for him. He widens and ramifies their interactions within their relation; ultimately he brings sociality into the sphere of desire and intimacy.

Like laughter, and the breath that is his soul this time, lightness of touch both dissolves boundaries and leaves "intact." Safeguarding a space for laughter and friendship within marriage, Meredith might be accused of providing momentary releases that allow the larger structure of desire, and the fact of marriage itself, to be reasserted. To dissolve boundaries within a space reestablishes boundaries around a space, and heterosexual marriage as a preserve also excludes. But I think Meredith also offers a prolonged critique of the institution. By constructing, in the space of fiction, an alternative sphere for women's independent laughter, language, and motion, and by safeguarding the independent subjectivity of his heroine, he also comes near her.

NOTES

1. Freud and Bergson (148) both argue that laughter intends to humiliate, and Freud expands the idea to define a sexual joke as the wish to expose what is sexual — i.e., the sexual parts. (The sexual joke, an exception to my argument, tries to promote, not deflate desire.) But the middle-class, presumably civilized and therefore "repressed" woman, with an "incapacity to tolerate undisguised sexuality" (101) might resist her exposure precisely as sexual parts, as object. Perhaps she just doesn't have the reverse desire of exposing a man as an object.

2. Gagnier seems to accept the thesis that for men "humor is functional, promoting group cohesion and intergroup conflict through disparagement, and social control through momentary releases that only serve to reinforce the status quo" (138). Judith Wilt, from a perspective on women's laughter, finds that it frustratingly has no long-term effect and even no use, although it allows women to cope (Wilt, LMCM). Both points resemble criticism of Bakhtin on carnival as an *allowed* reversal of power, after which things return to business as usual. But things happen in such spaces, and people pay attention to them. I think it is difficult to measure the degree and importance of release, and if such a release materially helps a real woman to live her life, it is unnecessary to ask for her individual sacrifice for the good of a group's political advancement.

3. Mary Russo gives a fine account of the implications of Bakhtin's theory of carnival for feminism in "Female Grotesques: Carnival and Theory," in which she discusses the construct of a feminine exhibitionism that makes a spectacle of itself. This applies to both Becky and Jos.

4. Neil Hertz has pointed to the currency of the Medusa's head particularly in nineteenth-century historiography to figure a political threat as a sexual threat, as, for example, in Victor Hugo's anxiety about the "monstrous and unknown forms" of the June 1848 workers' revolution associated with the exposure of a "public whore's" genitalia (Hertz 29). Hertz reads the Medusa from Freud, who argues that the multiplication of phalluses in the serpents of the Medusa's hair figures castration, therefore lack and femininity. The Medusa becomes the sign of male hysteria about the potential loss of his own body part as well as his property and power — what he can "hold onto," as opposed to a "center [that] will not hold," Hertz says, poking fun at Yeats. Thackeray makes Becky dangerously French. For her audacity in speaking French well and for refusing to do unpaid teaching, her headmistress "Minerva" Pinkerton (Minerva was the noted oppressor of the Medusa in classical mythology) finds it "necessary to remove this rebel, this monster, this serpent, this firebrand" (13).

5. Hélène Cixous contests the construction of female desire as lack, arguing that only when men look at the Medusa straight on (i.e., not in a mirror) will they see that the Medusa — that is, female desire — is "not deadly. She's beautiful and she's laughing" (255). A feminine *text*, however, is "more than subversive. It is volcanic; ... [A woman writing such a text shatters] the framework of institutions, [blows] up the law, [breaks] up the 'truth' with laughter" (258).

6. Oliphant's readers, according to Vineta and Robert A. Colby, found Lucilla too smug, and Blackwood found much of the humor too hard and biting (62–67).

7. As in so many Victorian novels, the death of the mother enables the daughter's independence, as Marianne Hirsch has argued in *The Mother/Daughter Plot*. But there is a poignant twist, for Oliphant's daughter had recently died, and the unfaltering representation of a strong daughter who could survive might have been a necessary fiction.

8. Pope, in *The Rape of the Lock*, uses masculine epic — i.e., the serious, heroic, and desiring — to describe a feminine and "trivial" sequence of events, giving the narrator the double perception; he plays the mode and object off each other. Oliphant works in the opposite direction, situating the mock heroic language in Lucilla's own desires and construction of the world.

9. "Lucilla" itself means "little light," a feminine light.

10. Gillian Beer observes that "Diana's intellect and emotions are unified only in her relationship with Emma" (150). She also raises but rejects the possibility that Meredith is representing an erotic relationship.

11. Touches are not *merely* finishing, although the novel "finishes" with Diana, held in "[Emma's] arms ... hands locked, in the unlighted room." Emma speaks of Diana's having a child, to which the silent response is "an involuntary little twitch of Tony's fingers" (145). Meredith's joke.

WORKS CITED

Barthes, Roland. *The Pleasure of the Text*, trans. Richard Miller. New York: Hill and Wang, 1975.

Beer, Gillian. *Meredith: A Change of Masks: A Study of the Novels*. London: University of London, Athlone Press, 1970.

Bergson, Henri. "Laughter," in: *Comedy*, ed. Wylie Sypher. Baltimore: Johns Hopkins University Press, 1980, 58–190.

Cixous, Hélène. "The Laugh of the Medusa," trans. Keith Cohen and Paula Cohen, in: *New French Feminisms: An Anthology*. New York: Schocken Books, 1981, 245–64.

Colby, Vineta, and Robert A. Colby. *The Equivocal Virtue: Mrs. Oliphant and the Victorian Literary Market Place*. [n.p.]: Archon Books, 1966.

de Man, Paul. *Allegories of Reading: Figural Language in Rousseau, Nietzsche, Rilke, and Proust*. New Haven: Yale University Press, 1979.

Freud, Sigmund. *Jokes and Their Relation to the Unconscious*, trans. James Strachey. New York: Norton, 1963.

_____. "Medusa's Head," in: *Sexuality and the Psychology of Love*, trans. Philip Rieff. New York: Macmillan/Collier, 1963, 212–13.

Fuss, Diana. *Essentially Speaking: Feminism, Nature & Difference*. New York: Routledge, 1989.

Gagnier, Regenia. "Between Women: A Cross-Class Analysis of Status and Anarchic Humor," in: *Last Laughs: Perspectives on Women and Comedy*, ed. Regina Barreca. New York: Gordon and Breach, 1988, 135–48.

Hardy, Barbara. *The Exposure of Luxury: Radical Themes in Thackeray*. Pittsburgh: Pittsburgh University Press, 1972.

Hertz, Neil. "Medusa's Head: Male Hysteria under Political Pressure." *Representations* 4 (Fall 1983): 27–54.

Hirsch, Marianne. *The Mother/Daughter Plot: Narrative, Psychoanalysis, Feminism*. Bloomington: Indiana University Press, 1989.

Irigaray, Luce. "This Sex Which Is Not One," in: *This Sex Which Is Not One*, trans. Catherine Porter with Carolyn Burke. Ithaca, NY: Cornell University Press, 1985, 23–33.

Kristeva, Julia. "From One Identity to an Other," in: *Desire in Language: A Semiotic Approach to Literature and Art*, ed. Leon S. Roudiez, trans. Thomas Gora, Alice Jardine, and Leon S. Roudiez. New York: Columbia University Press, 1980, 124–47.

Meredith, George. *Diana of the Crossways* (1885). New York: Charles Scribner's Sons, 1911.

Oliphant, Margaret. *Miss Marjoribanks*, ed. Penelope Fitzgerald (1866). New York: Penguin/Virago, 1989.

Russo, Mary. "Female Grotesques: Carnival and Theory," in: *Feminist Studies/Critical Studies*, ed. Teresa de Lauretis. Bloomington: Indiana University Press, 1986, 213–29.

Stubbs, Patricia. *Women and Fiction: Feminism and the Novel 1880–1920*. Brighton, Sussex: Harvester Press, 1979.

Thackeray, William Makepeace. *Vanity Fair: A Novel Without a Hero*, ed. Joseph Warren Beach (1848). New York: Modern Library, 1950.

White, Allon. "'Godiva to the Gossips': Meredith and the Language of Shame," in: *The Uses of Obscurity: The Fiction of Early Modernism*. London: Routledge & Kegan Paul, 1981, 79–107.

Wilt, Judith. "The Laughter of Maidens, the Cackle of Matriarchs: Notes on the Collision between Comedy and Feminism," in: *Gender and Literary Voice*, ed. Janet Todd. New York: Holmes & Meier, 1980, 173–96.

_____. "Meredith's Diana: Freedom, Fiction, and the Female." *Texas Studies in Literature and Language* 18:1 (Spring 1976): 42–62.

_____. *The Readable People of George Meredith*. Princeton: Princeton University Press, 1975.

9

The Feminine Laughter of No Return: James Joyce and Dorothy Richardson

KRISTIN BLUEMEL

Despite a history of popular and critical neglect, Dorothy Richardson's *Pilgrimage* has always attracted a small, cult-like following. Yet even Richardson's most vigorous defenders would have a hard time proving that her writing is not "impossibly obscure" were they required to rest their case on the following passage:

> A voyage, swift and transforming, a sense of passing in the midst of this marvel of flame-lit darkness, out of the world in glad solitary confidence with wildly, calmly beating morning heart.
>
> The encircling darkness grew still, spread wide about her; the moving flames drew together to a single glowing core. The sense of his presence returned in might. The rosy-hearted core of flame was within him, within the invisible substance of his breast. Tenderly transforming his intangible expansion to the familiar image of the man who knew her thoughts she moved to find him and marvel with him. (III, 192)[1]

Believe it or not, this is a description of a kiss. It is the first one ever received by Miriam Henderson, the heroine of *Pilgrimage*. In comparison to

James Joyce's description in *Ulysses* of Molly Bloom's adolescent sexual adventures, Richardson's strained lyricism seems prudish, boring, and rather ridiculous. In fact, it is easy to imagine Molly transforming Miriam's virginal epiphany into a joke that sends us into stitches of mocking laughter. This kind of mocking laughter — and the parodic wit that produces it — are the subjects of this essay. To be more exact, I'm going to discuss the relationship of the comedy of Molly Bloom's chapter, "Penelope," in terms of its formal stream-of-consciousness style and against the backdrop of Richardson's novel, written in a similar style.[2]

Why read "Penelope" alongside of *Pilgrimage*?[3] And why read either as part of a discussion on gender and comedy? One way to address these questions is through a consideration of the politics of humor. Within this more general framework, the critical-political question, "What is at stake here?" can be alternatively posed as, "What is at stake here for women, for literary critics, for laughing women, and especially laughing women critics?" Though I will not attempt to answer this third question directly, I hope it will become clear why it is important at least to pose it at the beginning of an investigation of gender and comedy in Joyce and Richardson.[4]

One reason we should read "Penelope" and *Pilgrimage* together is because Joyce and Richardson are contemporaries whose experimental novels share thematic and formal characteristics we have come to identify with modernism. More specifically, *Pilgrimage*'s bold rebellion against conventional language and narrative justify claims that it should be regarded as an alternative odyssey of modern British literature. For example, readers who put down *Ulysses* and take up *Pilgrimage* will find themselves exploring London instead of Dublin; their wandering "hero" is Miriam Henderson instead of Leopold Bloom; this "hero" is obsessed with memories of a mother's suicide instead of a father's; the work environment is that of dentistry instead of advertising; the settings are lecture halls, boarding houses, and A.B.C.s instead of a library, bar, and brothel; and the society consists of socialist, feminist, and exiled eccentrics instead of male intellectuals or professionals.

Aside from such thematic comparisons, the appeal of pairing Joyce and Richardson lies in the profound discrepancy between their statures in literary history and contemporary critical debate. Though Richardson pioneered the use of the so-called stream-of-consciousness style in her first book, *Pointed Roofs*, her particular innovations are largely forgotten and her books omitted from the modernist canon.[5] This difference in critical and popular reception may or may not be related to the fact that Richardson's radical enterprise is founded on a vigorous, uncompromising feminism.

By citing *Pilgrimage*'s feminism as a source of its unpopularity, I do not mean that the literary expectations of a generally sexist and benighted populace doomed the novel to obscurity on ideological grounds. Rather, I would like to suggest that the novel is limited or disabled by a contradiction between Richardson's feminist content and her feminist form. Paradoxically, *Pilgrimage* insists upon an inflexible "truth" of female superiority while using that feminist "truth" as the basis of a formal experimentation which effectively undermines the very possibility of natural and ultimate truths.[6]

Of course feminist ideology is not an integral part of Joyce's stream-of-consciousness style and his heroine is likely to inspire almost as much despair as love in the hearts of his feminist readers. Like a number of other critics, I am torn between Molly's distressing conventionality and her delightful unruliness. Richardson's blue-stocking heroine does not inspire such ambivalent feelings. On the other hand, neither does she inspire much laughter. By considering the ways Richardson's unambiguously feminist heroine deprives *Pilgrimage* of the comedy that might have "saved" it, I hope to recontextualize "Penelope" in order to better come to terms with its limitations as a feminist text.

If this is the "answer" to my question about the value of reading "Penelope" alongside of *Pilgrimage*, it lands us in familiar literary-critical terrain. To the extent that I am compelled to flaunt Richardson's colors as I explore the politics of her humor and to the extent that I do so at the expense of the canonical Joyce, I am working within the tradition of Anglo-American feminist criticism.[7] I am indebted to this feminist critical frame for establishing the connections between writing, politics, and gender that will allow me to move on to my questions about comedy. I'd like to formulate these questions by returning to that gap between the statures of Joyce and Richardson. Is it possible that the gap is related to the different novels' very different treatments of comedy? Furthermore, is it possible that the differences in stature and the differences in comedy are somehow related to Richardson's gender politics?

It is the ambition of this paper to demonstrate how interesting and complex the response to these questions should be. In a way, this ambition is inspired — and threatened — by the taunting claim, "Feminists have no sense of humor." What if my project only results in a reinstatement of the gap between Jolly Joyce and Dour Dorothy? What kind of feminist ally will Richardson prove if her feminist fiction refuses to let us laugh? I try to check the fears latent within these questions by regarding my own writing as an example of a literary alliance between feminism and humor. I present this essay as a challenge to the often rigid, short-tempered forms and styles of academe by refusing to abandon either the pleasures of reading or the rewards of a subversive criticism that dares to laugh.

* * *

Pointed Roofs, the first of thirteen books that make up the four-volume, 2000-page bulk of *Pilgrimage*, was published in 1915 when Richardson was forty-two years old. By the time *Ulysses* appeared in 1922, Richardson had published six books of her novel. In the following years, while Joyce was writing *Finnegans Wake*, Richardson continued to live a transient, impoverished life with her tubercular artist-husband. Such material challenges apparently did not spark her imagination since she never developed her method or her subject in any radically new direction. Nor, in fact, did she finish *Pilgrimage*. Its last volume was published posthumously in its unrevised form in 1967.

In the foreword to the 1938 edition of *Pilgrimage* Richardson concisely describes her aim: "To produce a feminine equivalent of the current masculine realism" (I, 9). In order to meet her own criteria for a feminine novel — criteria based on her belief in women's difference from and superiority to men — Richardson, like Joyce, breaks with narrative conventions of characterization, plot, and structure. *Pilgrimage* initially earned fame and notoriety for its uncompromising use of the single, limited point of view of its heroine as she seeks identity and a mystical "reality" of life in Edwardian England. The first paragraph of *Pointed Roofs* is characteristic of the unsettling, convention-flaunting forms Richardson would employ throughout the rest of her novel:

> Miriam left the gaslit hall and went slowly upstairs. The March twilight lay upon the landings, but the staircase was almost dark. The top landing was quite dark and silent. There was no one about. It would be quiet in her room. She could sit by the fire and be quiet and think things over until Eve and Harriett came back with the parcels. She would have time to think about the journey and decide what she was going to say to the Fräulein. (I, 15)

The kind of information readers expect at the beginning of a novel is entirely absent. We are deprived of details of time, place, identity, and context beyond those which are perceived by Miriam herself. In the paragraph quoted above, Miriam is conscious of light and shadow, her immediate physical surroundings, and apparently, forthcoming contacts with people related to a journey. Just as the reader of "Penelope"'s first words — "Yes because he never did a thing like that before as ask to get his breakfast in bed" — feels as though he or she has slipped into Molly's consciousness at an arbitrary moment in time, so too does the reader of *Pilgrimage* feel oddly adrift without an authorial or narrating presence providing signs of the significance of these first moments inside Richardson's novel. However, we are somewhat prepared for the scene and subject of Molly's mental wanderings by information in the previous chapter of *Ulysses*, while nothing but perseverance enables the reader of *Pilgrimage* to establish the context for Miriam's thoughts.

On the one hand, Richardson's text effectively unsettles and even alienates the poor reader who is desperately groping for a solid referent on which to pin Richardson's prose. On the other hand, readers who boldly and patiently push on through *Pilgrimage* are rewarded by a sense of having acceded to a unique position of intimacy with and knowledge of Richardson's heroine and her fictional world. Paradoxically, such intimacy is proof of the illusory nature of the controlling knowledge to which we lay claim. We may be close to Miriam, so close we feel as though we're lodged between her eyeballs and her brain, but that very closeness announces the extent of our dependence on her, our subjugation to her, and thus our distance from her. Rather than knowing Miriam or mastering *Pilgrimage*, we must surrender to every twist of language in order to gain any hold on the narrative's meaning or reality. The novel positions us precariously on the fringes of realism, taunting us with familiar images while depriving us of any sense of control over them.

In part, this is an effect of the stream-of-consciousness style, which erases the narrative medium and with it, any sense of a narrating consciousness.[8] For the critic aware of Richardson's own life story, it may also be a result of the text's status as autobiographical fiction.[9] Yet the clearly non-autobiographical "Penelope" achieves the same effect of denying the narrating consciousness its mediating function between reader and character and character and author. As with *Pilgrimage*, we are lured into the false position of presuming an intimate knowledge of the character's and text's truth that is fundamentally opposed to *Ulysses*'s otherwise uncontained and uncontainable movement. Our fall into complacency while reading *Pilgrimage* and "Penelope" suggests that the distance between Richardson and Joyce may, at certain points, be very small indeed.

One way we can measure this distance is by analyzing the forms and functions of parody in Joyce's and Richardson's texts. Though "Penelope" may have a parodic effect, Molly, unlike Leopold Bloom or Stephen Dedalus, is incapable of self-parody. For example, we are confident that the narrating consciousness joins in our laughter at the caricature of Bloom represented by these mocking words: "well hes beyond everything I declare somebody ought *to put him in the budget if I only could remember the 1 half of the things and write a book out of it the works of Master Poldy*" (18.578–80). Yet if we let that parodic laughter bounce back against the language of the narrating consciousness — as we would in any other chapter of *Ulysses* — we find that narrating consciousness assumes Molly's identity and that she is not laughing with us. To suggest, then, that Molly is incapable of self-parody does not mean that we will leave unrealized the multiple relations and meanings created by parody. Rather, it is to suggest that there is a reduction in *authorized* parodic visions and effects. In the other chapters of *Ulysses* we laugh at the characters, but we usually do so in the company of an equally amused narrating consciousness. In "Penelope" that chortling, authorizing narrative consciousness is absent and we find ourselves laughing alone.

For example, when Molly is speculating on Bloom's amorous strayings, her sharp tongue and sharper jealousy serve to heighten the parodic and comic effects of the text without ever consciously registering her own comic participation in and creation of the fabricated love triangle:

> she couldnt fool me but he might imagine he was and make a declaration to her with his plabbery kind of a manner like he did to me though I had the devils own job to get it out of him though I liked him for that it showed he could hold in and wasnt to be got for the asking. (18.194–98)

The force of Molly's mockery in this passage is directed at Bloom, who is reduced to a kind of overly enthusiastic adolescent whose "plabbery kind of a manner" betrays his hormonal excesses while revealing his shameful susceptibility to the machinations of women. Molly's parody of her husband doubles as a parody of her hapless, unknown rival since only a "fool" would try to seduce someone as ridiculous as Bloom. Of course this kind of logic ultimately requires Molly to reform the caricature of Bloom into more dignified, manly proportions in order to preserve her own superior stature as his wife. We derive great comic pleasure from the linguistic contortions Molly's excessive jealousy and vanity inspire. Yet the very fact that we identify her feelings and her reactions as "excessive" suggests that Molly's speech unintentionally creates for us a caricatured vision of herself. The difference between the way we respond to the comedy of "Penelope" in comparison to Ulysses's other chapters is that here our fears of patronizing the focal character work against the parodic impulses of the text. The irrepressible laughter that always accompanies a reading of "Penelope" justifies these fears; whenever we laugh with Molly, we are also laughing at her.[10]

Although Pilgrimage does not inspire the same kind of ready laughter as "Penelope," the attentive reader will be conscious of a gentle and subversive parody at work throughout Richardson's novel. As with Ulysses, the text's deployment of parody typically links its challenges to literary convention with the reader's participation in its humor. This can be seen in the following passage from Backwater, the second book of Pilgrimage, during a moment in which Miriam is contemplating relations between the sexes. Her thoughts are inspired by a reading binge on the sentimental novels of Rosa Nouchette Carey:

> Reading her at home, after tea by the breakfast-room fireside [...] it had seemed quite possible that life might suddenly develop into the thing the writer described. From somewhere would come an adoring man who believed in heaven and eternal life. One would grow very good; and after the excitement and interest had worn off one would go on, with firm happy lips being good and going to church and making happy matches for other girls or quietly disapproving of everybody who did

not believe just in the same way and think about good girls and happy
marriages and heaven. (I, 283–84)[11]

It is hard to believe that Miriam invests herself in this sentimental fantasy
of domestic bliss for even a moment. Not only does her yearning seem
radically disjointed from her typical value scheme, but the unpunctuated style
of the passage critiques its stated meaning. Irony, even parody, is implicit in
the formal creation of a bland, undifferentiated flow of words that mimes the
undifferentiated flow of days any such happy-lipped, matchmaking woman
might experience. When the domestic ideal is rejected in the next paragraph,
we are not surprised.

This rejection is accomplished through a renaming of the envisioned
domestic matrons as "Those awful, awful women," and a reassertion of the
novel's previous standard of valued femininity. The awkward, intellectual
Miriam exclaims:

> I never thought of all the *awful* women there would be in such a life. I
> only thought of myself and the house and the garden and the man. What
> an escape! [...] Far better to be alone and suffering and miserable here
> in the school, alive. (I, 284; emphasis in original)

The problem with this reassertion of a feminist standard of womanhood is
that the diminished figure of the domestic matron comparatively posits
Miriam as an absurdly heroic and exaggerated figure. If we acknowledge, or
worse yet, even grin over the pathetic last line — with its image of glorified
adolescent suffering and knowledge — a parodic image of Miriam threatens
to overtake the sincere pathos of her lament. Without a narrating consciousness to authorize our laughter, our mental fidgeting begins. Why does Miriam
persist in taking herself so seriously? Are we betraying Miriam by laughing
at her distress? Are we intended to ratify her sentiment?

Such questions have a dampening effect on our response to the text's
comedy, in part because our laughter tends to work against the feminist
ideology that the text attempts to maintain. The above passage is typical in
that the reverberations of our parodic laughter at Miriam's position of work-
ing-girl-hero necessarily undermine that otherwise valorized position as it is
articulated by the text's feminism. The effect is to affirm the radical status of
Richardson's text outside and beyond its feminism insofar as its own essentialist truths disintegrate beneath the weight of its narrative forms. Comedy
gives us a good healthy push out of our illusory armchair inside Miriam's
consciousness. What is most frightening about this situation is the fact that
there's no alternative narrating consciousness to catch us as we fall.

Our experience of reading "Penelope" affects us in similar ways. I'd like
to interpret this experience in terms of an economics of comedy. Both
Pilgrimage and "Penelope" are comic and parodic insofar as they self-consciously mock other characters in their narrative worlds. Yet neither Molly

nor Miriam, the characters whose voices generate that comedy, are able to
recycle the laughter the text produces at the level of self-parody. Their
laughter goes in only one direction: away. Thus both Molly and Miriam lose
out on the returns of their own comic production. The reader, on the other
hand, realizes a parodic vision of the narrating feminine characters, capitaliz-
ing on their comic losses. Ironically, upon profiting at the hands of our
heroines, we then feel ambivalently about them because we love them even
as we outwit them. An effaced narrating consciousness is the mediating force
that enables us to gain — almost at the characters' expense — a doubling of
parodic effect which we freely, if somewhat guiltily, laugh away.

Understanding the comic limitations of the feminine voice in Joyce may
help us come to terms with the discomfort feminist readers often experience
upon encountering Molly Bloom at the end of *Ulysses*. Reading "Penelope"
alongside of *Pilgrimage* complicates this understanding by reminding us that
Richardson's feminist, feminine odyssey also inspires ambivalence and exasperation, though in significantly different, and perhaps more damaging,
ways.

NOTES

1. *Pilgrimage* is made up of thirteen separate book-length "chapters." This passage
   appears in *Deadlock* (1921), the sixth book-chapter of *Pilgrimage*. The other
   twelve book-chapters include *Pointed Roofs* (1915), *Backwater* (1916),
   Honeycomb (1917), *The Tunnel* (1919), *Interim* (1919), *Revolving Lights*
   (1923), *The Trap* (1925), *Oberland* (1927), *Dawn's Left Hand* (1931), *Clear
   Horizon* (1935), *Dimple Hill* (1938), and *March Moonlight* (1967). The thirteen
   chapters were first published in a single edition by J.M. Dent in 1967. All page
   references to *Pilgrimage* in this essay are to the 1979 Virago edition.

2. Dorothy Richardson would have been irritated by my uncritical linking of her
   name with the phrase "stream-of-consciousness style." She lamented May
   Sinclair's application of the term to her writing but was never able to escape the
   term once it had been introduced to literary conversation. It is not the aim of
   this writer to enter into the debate on what "stream of consciousness" means
   within a literary context. Readers who are interested in literary-critical definitions of stream-of-consciousness writing should see Dorrit Cohn's *Transparent
   Minds*, Leon Edel's *The Modern Psychological Novel, 1900–1950*, Robert
   Humphrey's *Stream of Consciousness in the Modern Novel*, and Frederick R.
   Karl's *Modern and Modernism*.

3. I am not the first to link Joyce's name with that of Richardson. Given
   Richardson's identification with the stream-of-consciousness style, she was
   often compared by contemporary reviewers to Joyce. Richardson herself wrote
   one of the first reviews of *Finnegans Wake*.

4. My investigation of gender and comedy in Joyce could be seen as part of the growing body of feminist work by Joyceans such as Marilyn French, Suzette Henke, Bonnie Kime Scott, and Elaine Unkeless. As long as Joyce has been writing, there have been readers interested in his texts' relations to comedy. For an example of a good recent study, see Robert Bell's *Jocoserious Joyce*. Almost all recent criticism of *Pilgrimage* has been explicitly feminist in its approach. See for example studies by Rachel Blau DuPlessis, Ellen G. Friedman, Gillian E. Hanscombe, Sydney Janet Kaplan, Jean Radford, and Elaine Showalter. For non-feminist studies of Richardson, see Gloria G. Fromm, Horace Gregory, John Cowper Powys, John Rosenberg, and Thomas F. Staley. To date, there have been no studies — feminist or otherwise — that focus on the problem of comedy in Richardson's writing.

5. Modernist scholars recognize Richardson's name and innovations, but her books remain unavailable to American readers and her nonfiction prose remains unedited and uncollected. The recent attention paid by feminist literary critics to modernist writing by women has set the stage for a renewed examination of Richardson's literary contributions.

6. My reading of *Pilgrimage* is informed by kinds of poststructuralist thought that are foreign to most studies of Richardson's texts. Many studies of *Ulysses*, on the other hand, have concentrated on the critical possibilities provided by a poststructuralist (i.e., Derridian, Lacanian, Kristevan, etc.) approach; to my knowledge, only Ellen G. Friedman, Stephen Heath, Jean Radford, and Sarah Schuyler have attempted to explore *Pilgrimage* in the same way. In their introduction to *Breaking the Sequence*, Ellen G. Friedman and Miriam Fuchs address questions raised by the intersection of poststructuralist and feminist theory and they choose to emphasize the importance of Richardson in this critical context.

7. The hazards for the feminist reader who chooses to engage in a traditional "neglected woman writers" criticism have been forcefully articulated by Toril Moi, among others. As Moi points out, Anglo-American feminist criticism has, until recently, been dangerously under-theorized. In particular, it is troubled by the fundamental contradiction between its revolutionary political agenda and its conservative aesthetic values.

8. As Dorrit Cohn demonstrates in *Transparent Minds*, the odd effects of stream-of-consciousness prose may also be discussed in terms of free indirect discourse.

9. Most of Richardson's critics have interpreted *Pilgrimage* as autobiographical fiction. Avrom Fleishman's chapter on Richardson in *Figures of Autobiography* is an obvious example of such criticism. Gillian E. Hanscombe shares Fleishman's fascination with the connection between Richardson's art and life, as do critics Horace Gregory, John Rosenberg, and Thomas F. Staley. In her preface to Richardson's biography, Gloria Gliken Fromm notes that her 1963 essay in *PMLA* "showed that *Pilgrimage* was indeed an autobiographical novel and that any portrait of Dorothy Richardson (as she herself insisted) must take its fundamental lines from her own novel" (xiii).

10. 10 Elaine Unkeless raises but does not pursue this point in "The Conventional Molly Bloom," 155.

11. One of Richardson's most notorious formal innovations is her frequent use of
     ellipses and breaks to indicate interruptions in her heroine's consciousness. In
     keeping with other critical studies of *Pilgrimage*, this essay attempts to honor
     Richardson's distinctive style by using ellipses in brackets to mark omissions
     from the text.

WORKS CITED

Bell, Robert. *Jocoserious Joyce: The Fate of Folly in* Ulysses. Ithaca: Cornell Univer-
     sity Press, 1991.

Cohn, Dorrit. *Transparent Minds: Narrative Modes for Presenting Consciousness in
     Fiction*. Princeton: Princeton University Press, 1978.

DuPlessis, Rachel Blau. *Writing beyond the Ending: Narrative Strategies of Twen-
     tieth-Century Women Writers*. Bloomington: Indiana University Press, 1985.

Edel, Leon. *The Modern Psychological Novel 1900–1950*. New York: Lippincott,
     1955. Rev. ed., New York: Universal Library, 1964.

Fleishman, Avrom. *Figures of Autobiography*. Berkeley: University of California
     Press, 1983.

French, Marilyn. *The Book as World: James Joyce's* Ulysses. Cambridge: Harvard
     University Press, 1976.

Friedman, Ellen G. "'Utterly Other Discourse': The Anticanon of Experimental
     Women Writers from Dorothy Richardson to Christine Brooke-Rose." *Modern
     Fiction Studies* 34 (1988): 353–370.

Friedman, Ellen G., and Miriam Fuchs, eds. *Breaking the Sequence: Women's Ex-
     perimental Fiction*. Princeton: Princeton University Press, 1989.

Fromm, Gloria G[liken]. *Dorothy Richardson: A Biography*. Urbana: University of
     Illinois Press, 1977.

[Fromm], Gloria Gliken. "Dorothy M. Richardson: The Personal 'Pilgrimage.'" *PMLA*
     78 (1963): 586–600.

Gregory, Horace. *Dorothy Richardson: An Adventure in Self-Discovery*. New York:
     Holt, 1967.

Hanscombe, Gillian E. *The Art of Life: Dorothy Richardson and the Development of
     Feminist Consciousness*. Athens: Ohio University Press, 1982.

——————. "Dorothy Richardson Versus the Novvle," in: *Breaking the Sequence:
     Women's Experimental Fiction*, eds. Ellen G. Friedman and Miriam Fuchs.
     Princeton: Princeton University Press, 1989.

Heath, Stephen. "Writing for Silence: Dorothy Richardson and the Novel," in: *British
     Modernist Fiction 1920–1945*, ed. Harold Bloom. New York: Chelsea House,
     1986.

Henke, Suzette A. *James Joyce and the Politics of Desire*. New York: Routledge, 1990.

Henke, Suzette A., and Elaine Unkeless, eds. *Women in Joyce*. Urbana: University of Illinois Press, 1982.

Humphrey, Robert. *Stream of Consciousness in the Modern Novel* (1954). Berkeley: University of California Press, 1965.

Joyce, James. *Ulysses*, ed. Hans Walter Gabler. New York: Vintage, 1986.

Kaplan, Sydney Janet. *Feminine Consciousness in the Modern British Novel*. Urbana: University of Illinois Press, 1975.

Karl, Frederick R. *Modern and Modernism: The Sovereignty of the Artist 1885–1925*. New York: Atheneum, 1985.

Moi, Toril. *Sexual/Textual Politics: Feminist Literary Theory*. New York: Routledge, 1985.

Powys, John Cowper. *Dorothy M. Richardson*. London: Joiner and Steele, 1931.

Radford, Jean. "Coming to Terms: Dorothy Richardson, Modernism, and Women." *News From Nowhere* 7 (1989): 25–36.

_____. *Dorothy Richardson*. Bloomington: Indiana University Press, 1991.

Richardson, Dorothy M. *Pilgrimage, 1915–57*. 4 vols. London: J.M. Dent, 1967; Virago, 1979.

Rosenberg, John. *Dorothy Richardson: The Genius They Forgot*. London: Duckworth, 1973.

Schuyler, Sarah. "Double-Dealing Fictions." *Genders* 9 (1990): 75–92.

Scott, Bonnie Kime, ed. *The Gender of Modernism: A Critical Anthology*. Bloomington: Indiana University Press, 1990.

_____. *James Joyce*. Atlantic Highlands: Humanities, 1987.

_____. *Joyce and Feminism*. Bloomington: Indiana University Press, 1984.

Showalter, Elaine. *A Literature of Their Own: British Women Novelists from Brontë to Lessing*. Princeton: Princeton University Press, 1977.

Sinclair, May. "The Novels of Dorothy Richardson." Rev. of *Pointed Roofs, Backwater*, and *Honeycomb. The Egoist*. April 1918: 57–9.

Staley, Thomas F. *Dorothy Richardson*. Boston: Twayne, 1976.

Unkeless, Elaine. "The Conventional Molly Bloom," in: *Women in Joyce*, eds. Suzette Henke and Elaine Unkeless. Urbana: University of Illinois Press, 1982. 150–168.

10

Courtship, Comedy, and African-American Expressive Culture in Zora Neale Hurston's Fiction

BARBARA MONROE

In her introduction to *Mules and Men*, Hurston says, "As early as I could remember it was the habit of men folks particularly to gather on the store porch of evenings and swap stories." But she adds, "Even the women folks would stop and break a breath with them at times" (2). The word "even" suggests that the porch was an equal-access stage — even as it insinuates that women were generally not expected to perform publicly.

In Part One of *Mules and Men* (1935)[1] and *Their Eyes Were Watching God* (1937), many women do indeed "break a breath" with the men on the porch, but in culturally prescribed ways. We see them playing some of the same roles in humorous exchanges that their white counterparts play: as peace-keeping arbitrators (*MM* 24, 29); as "straight men" feeding lines to the main player (*MM* 21, 26); as appreciative audience (*MM* 170, 171, 173); and as cultural custodians of a rich tradition of stories, games, and songs passed on to children in the home (*MM* 72). But Hurston also dramatizes verbal duels between women and men in joking rituals that do not have exact equivalents in mainstream culture. These scenes are played out in the liminal land of the

173

porch, where the jurisdictions of the home and the street intersect.[2] In what may be generally categorized as mating duels, Hurston's women and men engage in mock-courtship and post-courtship routines, two speech events[3] that play off Western notions of chivalry. Alice Walker has praised Hurston's portraits of male-female relationships as "some of the most healthily rendered heterosexual loving in our literature" (xv). In light of Hurston's descriptions of domestic violence, both threatened and realized, we have to ask what is healthy (or loving) about Hurston's portrayals of sexual partners. For in the ritualistic play that surrounds African-American courtship, themes of domestic violence, financial competition, sexual bravado, and infidelity are all too routine.

From the position of "an inside" of things (*TE* 68), Hurston offers an empathetic view of African-American courtship rituals. In assessing this view, we must place Hurston inside the historical context of African-American expressive culture: to wit, antebellum minstrelsy, the man-and-wife acts of vaudeville, the blues tradition, and stand-up comedy. At the same time, comparisons with mainstream romantic comedy point up important racial and class differences in the humor practices of women generally. As Mary Helen Washington has suggested, Hurston's "uncritical depiction of violence toward women" deserves scholarly inquiry (xiv). Such an inquiry will yield a balanced assessment of the post-courtship ritual in Hurston's domestic comedy, measured not only by Freud but also by a more culturally specific model, the folktale cycle of the Signifying Monkey.

When the honeymoon is over, or (in Hurston's words) when the rhyming riddles of courtship stop (*TE* 25; 32), post-courtship begins. The post-courtship routine in fact plays off the mock-courtship, renegotiating the issue of dominance, both physical and economic. The dynamic interplay of these two routines is succinctly dramatized in the verbal duel between Big Sweet and Joe Willard in *Mules and Men*. By way of signifying, or indirect insult,[4] Big Sweet accuses Joe Willard of sleeping with another woman. Joe takes up her implicit challenge, complaining to his company of friends that he cannot even go fishing without her following him to the lake and nagging him. Big Sweet's come-back — in the form of a *maternal fuss*[5] — replays the romantic notion of following the prince anywhere and reminds him of his love offerings, however mundane: "You didn't figger Ah was draggin' behind you when you was bringin' dat Sears and Roebuck catalogue over to my house and beggin' me to choose my ruthers. Lemme tell *you* something, *any* time Ah shack up wid any man Ah gives myself de privilege to go wherever he might be, night or day. Ah got the law in my mouth" (*MM* 124). By way of rebuttal, Willard performs this lament, which he both mocks[6] and means at the same time: "'Lawd ... My people, my people,' as de monkey said. 'You fool wid Aunt Hagar's chillun and they'll sho distriminate you and put yo' name in de streets'" (*MM* 124). Jim Allen enters the fray, striking a familiar theme in mating duels, dominance and control, recast in the sexual terms of "strad-dling" a cow, although the cow nonetheless controls its rider: "Well, you know what they say — a man can cackerlate [calculate] his life till he git mixed up wid a woman or git straddle of a cow" (*MM* 124). Jim's signifying connection is not lost on Big Sweet, whose retribution is quick — both fast and clever: "Big Sweet turned viciously upon the old man. 'Who you callin' a cow, fool? Ah know you ain't namin' *my* mama's daughter no cow'" (*MM* 124–25). Big Sweet's verbal riposte — a version of *playing the dozens* where participants insult each other's mothers[7] — hits its mark and silences the old man.

Instead of thinking of such speech events as primarily speech,[8] perhaps we can consider them as primarily events, as drama. For this "scene," like other scenes played between couples in *Mules and Men* as well as in *Their Eyes*, also enacts routines traditionally played between mates in this perfor-mative culture, both on stage and off. These routines are strikingly like those of many man-and-wife teams in Negro vaudeville that flourished in the 1920s as a specialty of the southern circuit. Folkways inspired the man-and-wife routine, where a smart-talking wife challenges the swagger of a hen-pecked husband (Stearns and Stearns 614).

One such team, Stringbeans and Sweetie May, enjoyed top-billing as early as 1915. Stringbeans would sing, dance, and play the piano (standing up), "like an early Ray Charles" (Stearns and Stearns 615): "Listen no-good womens/Stop kickin' us men aroun'" (qtd. in Stearns and Stearns 615). Another team, Butterbeans and Susie thrived much longer, cutting a series of recordings from 1922 to 1962. In their routine on stage, Susie cakewalked and sang the blues, and Butterbeans did the Heebie Jeebies and the Itch. They alternately sang, interrupted, and insulted each other. One of their numbers "Get Yourself a Monkey Man," a smart-talking Susie sings, "the man I got he's a hard-workin' man, he works hard all the time; and on Saturday night when he brings me his pay, he better not be short one dime" (qtd. in Stearns and Stearns 616). Butterbeans would reply that she must want a "Monkey Man" but that is not what she needs: "I'd whip your head every time you breathe; rough treatment, Susie, is 'zactly what you need" (qtd. in Stearns and Stearns 616). The visual performance added irony to his words: Butter-beans had a baby face and "timorous bearing" (Stearns and Stearns 616). These culturally-specific performance values were also prevalent in big-band shows such as Duke Ellington's. Ivy Anderson sang the blues, center stage, while drummer Sonny Greer heckled her from the comparative safety of the percussion section. "I got the blues," Ivy would sing, and Sonny would interject, "That ain't the worst you gonna get, Baby!" (qtd. in Stearns and Stearns 617).

Because these man-woman interactions are couched in comic terms, the aggressiveness of the intent can be denied, as Gene says in *Mules and Men*:

"'We ain't mad wid one 'nother... 'We jus' jokin'" (*MM* 24). But the aggressiveness of the content cannot be denied, for the theme of domestic violence is all too familiar, especially when compared to white domestic comedy. In one episode of *I Love Lucy*, Ricky spanks Lucy, as if she were a child; in *The Honeymooners*, Ralph Kramden routinely threatens to send Alice "to the moon," winding up his fist and swinging his arm like a golf club. The nagging wife and the hen-pecked husband are stock characters in European folk tradition, but being chased with a broom is usually as battered as the husband gets. Such comic fare in television and film has progressively passed from view. In African-American comedy, this slapstick violence is upstaged by sophisticated verbal performance unsurpassed in American humor, as we see in Hurston's work.

In *Their Eyes*, Hurston describes how Tea Cake slaps Janie around for the purpose of showing the community who is boss. Tea Cake and Janie perform their dominant and submissive roles after the beating; the stage effect of Tea Cake's pampering and Janie's hanging-on is not lost on the communal audience: "Everybody talked about it next day in the fields. It aroused a sort of envy in both men and women. The way he petted and pampered her as if those two or three face slaps had nearly killed her made the women see visions and the helpless way she hung on him made men dream dreams" (140). Hurston then recontextualizes this scene for her reader by turning immediately to Sop-de-Bottom's comic evaluation. Moving from praise and appreciation of Tea Cake's relationship with Janie to a mock-lament of his relationship with his wife, Sop-de-Bottom explains why he quit beating his wife:

> "Tea Cake, yo sho is a lucky man," Sop-de-Bottom told him. "Uh person can see every place you hit her. Ah bet she never raised her hand tuh hit yuh back, neither. Take some un dese ol' rusty black women and dey would fight yuh all night long and next day nobody couldn't tell you ever hit 'em. Dat's de reason Ah done quit beatin' mah woman. You can't make no mark on'em at all... Mah woman would spread her lungs all over Palm Beach County, let alone knock out mah jaw teeth. You don't know dat woman uh mine. She got ninety-nine rows un jaw teeth and git her good and mad, she'll wade through solid rock up to her hip pockets." (140–141).

Sop-de-Bottom's comic reversal typifies many scenes where the man is on the receiving end of the woman's fist, a comic strategy that domesticates the violence between mates. Strong enough to use her fist without aid of broom, the husband-beater is usually characterized as a Mouth Almighty,[9] who "spreads her lungs," as in the case of the Turners in *Their Eyes*. When Tea Cake and his friends stage a fight aimed at destroying Mrs. Turner's eating establishment, Mrs. Turner retrieves her husband to relieve her distress and protect her interests. "He came in, took a look and squinched down into a chair in an off corner and didn't open his mouth" (*TE* 144). After the brawl, she calls him into account:

> "What kinda man is you, Turner? You see dese no count niggers come in heah and break up mah place! How kin you set and see yo' wife all trompled on? You ain't no kinda man at all. You seen dat Tea Cake shove me down! Yes you did! You ain't raised yo' hand tuh do nothin' about it."
>
> Turner removed his pipe and answered: "Yeah, and you see how Ah did swell up too, didn't yuh? You tell Tea Cake he better be keerful Ah don't swell up again." At that Turner crossed his legs the other way and kept right on smoking his pipe. Mrs. Turner hit at him the best she could with her hurt hand and then spoke her mind for half an hour. (*TE* 145)[10]

But at many points in *Their Eyes*, violence against women is not played for laughs. When Janie tries to tell her grandmother than she does not love Logan, Nanny jumps to the conclusion that "dat grass-gut, liver-lipt nigger ... done took and beat mah baby already!" (*TE* 21). When Janie smart-talks Logan, he threatens to "take holt un dat ax and come in dere and kill" her (*TE* 30). Jody "slapped Janie until she had a ringing sound in her ears and told her about her brains before he stalked on back to the store" (*TE* 67). To exact revenge against Mrs. Turner for telling Janie to leave Tea Cake because he is too black, Tea Cake's friends first suggest that he

> "Tell her husband on her."
> "Shucks! Ah b'lieve he's skeered of her."
> "Knock her teeth down her throat."
> "Dat would look like she had some influence when she ain't. Ah jus' let her see dat Ah got control." (*TE* 141)

In another instance, the men on the porch take offense at Mrs. Tony's complaining that Tony does not provide for her and their children. They locate the problem in Tony's refusal to beat her to keep her in line: "'Tony won't never hit her. He says beatin' women is just like steppin' on baby chickens. He claims 'tain't no place on uh woman tuh hit,' Joe Lindsay said with scornful disapproval." Jim Stone agrees. "'Dat's de God's truth.'" Their remarks touch off Janie, who does what "she had never done before, that is, thrust herself into the conversation" (*TE* 70). But Jody Starks has the last word: "'You gettin' too moufy, Janie'" (*TE* 71).

Janie's open performance of submission to Tea Cake after his beating stands in stark contrast to her refusal to submit to her first husband, Logan, and her reluctance to submit to her second husband, Joe Starks. This variance suggests that love is an interplay of power, renegotiated as an intimate relationship evolves from courtship to marriage. In *Their Eyes*, Nanny warns

Janie that the most difficult stage of a marriage is that transition from "foot-kissin'" to "mouf-kissin." Janie's grandmother always associated sitting in the "high chair" on the porch with the privilege of the white mistress, protected from the world of work and male violence (*TE* 109). Although Janie is protected from neither, she must still pay the price of that nominal protection: a corresponding loss of self-dramatization and hence social power in this performative culture.

A comparison with mainstream romantic comedy once again illuminates some of the economic factors involved in women's comic behavior, inextricably linked to the power to speak. The Depression revised the economy of white middle-class marriage in a way that approximated the long-standing material conditions of African-American families. When men no longer were able to provide for their families, women shared (or assumed) the role of bread-winner. World War II exacerbated this trend, as women entered the work force in unprecedented numbers. The shift in the relative status of men and women strained the fault lines underlying bourgeois notions of gallantry, an attitudinal shift that romantic comedy proved responsive to. During these decades, mainstream audiences appreciated the give-and-take banter of romantic comedy pairs Tracey-Hepburn and Bogart-Bacall, whose overt antagonism was a measure of their love, based on mutual economic status and verbal agility. When women moved back to the home front after the war, a vapid "couplism" replaced this kind of comic routine between lovers, with the likes of Doris Day in the 1950s and Marlo ("That Girl") Thomas in the 1960s, who played sputtering, eyelash-batting, "cute-when-she's-mad," virginal types to their leading men. Mary Tyler Moore, the prominent comic heroine in the 1970s, was comically inarticulate when confronting Mr. Grant on such issues as equal pay. When words failed her, she would screw up her courage by mechanistically circling her arms and nodding her head, like a wind-up doll, performing a Bergsonian sense of comedy as the mechanical encrusted on the living.

The case of Mary Tyler Moore also illustrates that the comic enterprise is not just a matter of money but also of racial difference. White comic heroines historically have made comic fare out of inarticulateness, a lack of verbal skill associated with children, whose linguistic resources are understandably limited. Such regressive speech behavior would cost a woman respect in the African-American community. The two racially-marked traditions do converge in some respects, but only in very qualified ways. The low-income woman in both black and white communities has enjoyed a greater license to joke in public, a license that generally carries more restrictions as a woman moves up the class ladder, as we have seen in the case of Janie in *Their Eyes*. Further, white comic women in recent television situation comedy (e.g., *Designing Women*) employ a verbal wit that has been heretofore the forte of black women. Nonetheless, Claire Huxtable speaks with a body English (as well as code-switches to Black English Vernacular) foreign to Murphy Brown. The physical comedy of Lucille Ball was remarkable in part because her gift was so unusual for white comic actresses. Even so, slapstick is a performance style that African-American women have not traditionally valued. The stiffness of actresses like Margaret Dumont literally performs the part of the "straight man." Such rigidity and verticality draws the comic fire of anarchy and zaniness that the Marx Brothers played so well.

To roughly compare the relationship between any of the verbal combatants in Hurston's work to a white equivalent, we would have to imagine pitting Andrew Dice Clay against Roseanne (Barr) Arnold. My exaggerated comparison intends to place in (comic) relief the ambivalent cultural evaluation of women jesting and jousting in public, in what is perceived as decidedly unladylike — even masculine — ways. When a heckler shouted "You're fat!" during Roseanne's stand-up act, Roseanne skewered him with "Yeah, I am fat, but you'd crawl on your belly to fuck me!" (qtd. in Varian 182). Roseanne's come-back would not be seen as sufficiently sophisticated to merit applause for the African-American community that holds that subtlety is the soul of wit. Yet in both black and white communities, comic behavior is generally marked as masculine and therefore ambivalently valued when women presume to clown in public.

Unlike her white counterpart, however, the African-American woman has the force of history to back her claim to comic performance. Culturally endowed with a rich comic tradition, the African-American woman may, in fact, be playing a role historically played by males, dating back to the days of minstrelsy. Contrary to popular belief, minstrelsy was first created by slaves in the eighteenth century, not by whites in the nineteenth century. An anonymous watercolor painted circa 1790 documents slaves performing recognizable elements of a minstrel show; another painting, called "The Bones Player," shows a man using the rib-bones of a sheep as castanets (Isaacs 23). Probably slaves were made to perform for northern visitors, who took the concept back home with them. As early as 1843, the (white) Virginia Minstrels were performing to packed houses, a popularity the minstrel form enjoyed for fifty years (Isaacs 23).

During the antebellum period, the essential elements of minstrelsy became conventionalized: seventeen men in a half-circle, with a master of ceremony in the middle of the line, playing the straight man. At either end of the line, made up of various kinds of performers (singers, dancers, monologists), were the "end-men," the comic leads of the troupe, traditionally named Mr. Bones, who played bones as castanets, and Tambo, who played tambourine (Mitchell 18). A band provided musical accompaniment for the many dances, which included the soft-shoe, buck-and-wing, and cakewalk (Isaacs 23). A walkaround closed the first half of the show. The second half featured sketches with "'wenches'" played by men (Isaacs 25). Since no African

Americans were allowed to play professionally, all the parts were played by whites, with burnt cork on their faces and thickened lips. After the Civil War, African Americans reappropriated the minstrel and kept all its conventions, including the burnt cork and thickened lips (Isaacs 25). As the minstrel men, the black actor became, in the words of James Weldon Johnson, "a caricature of a caricature" (qtd. by Isaacs 20). From the end men of the old minstrel show evolved the two-man act, immortalized by (Bert) Williams and (George) Walker and later by Amos 'n' Andy.

It is within this tradition that the man-and-wife act developed. One of the earliest teams appeared in the early 1890s, with Ernest Hogan who is "credited with having changed the comic tradition from the 'silly end-man into a character with a slight, very slight, quality of the Harlequin'" (Isaacs 30). Hogan toured the country with Sissieretta Jones, whose stage-name was Black Patti, the first important team to tour both the North and South successfully. *The Creole Show*, which opened in 1891, also altered the minstrel show by substituting sixteen women for the line (Isaacs 31). By the 1920s, they were caricaturing white women costumed in blonde wigs in a play called *Chocolate Blondes* (Mitchell 91), an ironical turn of events when one remembers the burnt-cork days of minstrelsy. Hence women entered the fold of legitimate theatre, however uneasy the embrace.[11]

In the late 1920s, the man-and-wife acts were upstaged by the two-man team once again, and in the 1950s, the two-man team gave way, in turn, to stand-up comics, such as Redd Foxx and Jackie "Moms" Mabley (Stearns and Stearns 617–19). The case of Moms may not be as special as it seems, given her wanton persona and the nature of her routines. In the course of her career, which spanned the greater part of this century, Moms Mabley played largely to African-American audiences. Although many of her jokes were original and topical, she worked within the contours of folk humor recognized by her audience. Her appetite for cornbread and greens — and young men — was a staple of her subject matter: playing the lewd widow, she would smart-talk those who would question why she had a fifteen-year-old child when her husband had been dead twenty years, "*He's* dead, I ain't" (qtd. in Levine 363). Ritualistic insult structured her routines. She sparred with her pianist — "One of my thoughts would bust your head wide open" — and signified on old men — "Old man can't do nothin' for me but bring me a message from a young one" (qtd. in Levine 365).[12]

The man-wife acts of vaudeville provided historical precedence for women blues singers as well. Just as the man-wife teams dueled in song, exchanging verses or single lines, sometimes competing to see who could sing the larger number of obscene stanzas (Evans 155), solo performers in the blues tradition continued to signify on the sexual performance of the opposite sex. Both male and female singers celebrated the sexual enterprise, sometimes seen as a cooperative effort, but more often as a competitive one.

In "It Ain't the Meat, It's the Motion," the male singer made clear that it was his partner's motion "that makes your Daddy want to rock."[13] While the tradition is rife with songs praising male sexual potency, women blues singers stood ready to cap the claim: "Red Rooster say: Cock-a-doodle do/Richland woman say: Any dude'll do."[14] Lucille Bogan especially knew how to put out the brags, as in the unexpurgated version of a test pressing of "Shave 'Em Dry":[15] "I got nipples on my titties/Big as the end of my thumb/I got something 'tween my legs/That'll make a dead man come." Accompanied by Walter Roland's walking bass and encouraged by his verbal calls, Bogan performed with whoops and hollers, bragging with a swagger, "My back is made of whalebone/And my cock[16] is made of brass" (Oliver 230–231).

Such unladylike posturing caused Bessie Smith to get fired from her first recording connection when she stopped and said, "Hol' on a moment while I spit" (qtd. in Niles 35). In *Mules and Men*, Ella Wall is proud of her reputation, "[rotating] her hips with her hands": "'I'm raggedy, but right; patchey but tight; stringy, but I *will* hang on'" (*MM* 150). In *Dust Tracks on the Road*, Hurston strikes a similar posture of defiance and independence on the typical blues subject of love lost: "Songs are born out of feelings with an old beat-up piano, or a guitar for a mid-wife. Lovemade and unmade. Who put out dat lie, it was supposed to last forever? Love is when it is. No more here? Plenty more down the road" (189). Or in the words of Billie Holliday: "Don't want no trouble/I've got to be the boss/And if you can't play it my way/Well now, baby get lost" (qtd. in Ellison 9). In verbal agility as well as sexual bravado, the woman blues singer was a worthy match for any man.[17]

While the blues certainly bears rhetorical resemblances to vaudeville, the tradition enjoys its own distinct history. In 1902, Gertrude "Ma" Rainey, a minstrel and tent-show performer, heard a woman in Missouri sing, put the song in her act, and called it "the blues" (Evans 34). As "the Mother of the Blues," Rainey provides the earliest link between the rural folksong tradition and the classic female blues singers of the 1920s and 30s (Ellison 6). Although almost entirely a folk product of the twentieth century (Evans 32), the blues derives from a mixed ancestry of work songs and field hollers that antedate the Civil War (Ellison 2). As early as 1892, ethnomusicologists noted that women droned while working, singing "'neither A nor yet A flat, but between the two,' in other words, a blue note" (Evans 42). Because women worked side-by-side with men in the fields, their contribution to the roots and rhetoric of the blues should not be overlooked. As Mance Lipscombe, a Texas bluesman, points out, "You might call them blues but they were just made up things. Like a fella be workin', or most likely some gal be workin' near and you want to say somethin' to 'em. So you holler it, sing it. Or maybe to your mule or something" (qtd. in Ellison 3).

The epithets of the classic female blues singers pay homage to their role in blues history: Bessie Smith, Empress of the Blues, and Clara Smith, the

World's Greatest Moaner (Niles 35). The sexual double entendre of the latter
is also consonant with the image of the female blues singer, as I discussed
earlier. Musically, the blues note and signature instrumentals, such as the
slide, are traceable to African origins; lyrically, they borrow from old
European songs that feature the wily wives and cuckolded husbands (Oliver
193). Because of the "extraordinarily high" number of sexual songs in blues
repertoire that feature themes of abuse and bawdry (Oliver 249; Evans 28),
it is viewed as a "devil's music" by church-going, middle-class African
Americans who want to distance themselves from this musical tradition
(Oliver 12; 23), the historical roots of which clearly mark it as a working-class
phenomenon.

The man-and-wife acts, stand-up comedy, and the blues — all provided
expressive outlets for African-American women in the course of this century.
But in all these formats, the woman played the role of the antagonist of the
man. As wife, she is domineering; as stand-up comic, she is a lusty widow;
as a "lady" who sings the blues, she can rock her rider. What is the status of
the "talk" in African-American expressive tradition generally and in
Hurston's domestic humor specifically? Is it just "talk"?

While Freud has theorized that joking is a socially-sanctioned outlet for
aggression, jokes *about* aggression may carry different affect. The overt
antagonism in such routines may be a covert declaration of the affection
between the combatants, like saying "please don't throw me in the briar
patch" and meaning the opposite. In Hurston's "The Gilded Six-Bits," the
narrator explains that the ritualistic banter between Joe and Missy May
"pretended to deny affection but in reality flaunted it" (57). By unspoken
mutual assent, joking relationships assume a symmetry of status between
duelers.

Rather than reading Hurston by way of Freud, however, the folktale cycle
of the Signifying Monkey might provide a more culturally appropriate model
for understanding what is going on behind Hurston's domestic scenes. The
Signifying Monkey always uses the same rhetorical strategy to beat the Lion:
he always tricks the Lion into believing that he has spoken literally when he
has spoken figuratively. Time and again in these tales, the Lion is literally
beaten by the Elephant, but he is also figuratively beaten by the Monkey
"because he fundamentally misunderstood the status of the Monkey's statements" (Gates, *Signifying Monkey* 57). Gates maintains that the Lion mis-
reads the Monkey's act of signifying because he fails to "distinguish between
manner and matter," fails to understand that "the play is the thing" (*Signifying
Monkey* 70).

But words do matter. The Monkey's rhetorical defeat of the Lion is a more
effective way of deflating his status as King of the Jungle than the Elephant's
physical defeat. This point is not lost on the Lion: "[The Lion say], 'I'm not
gonna whip your ass 'cause that Elephant whipped mine,/I'm gonna whip

your ass for signifyin'" (qtd. in Gates, *Signifying Monkey* 57). African-American performance "is not a thing but an aspect of an interactional process, and that process is likely to be regarded as co-terminous with life itself" (Abrahams, *Talking Black* 9). What is under negotiation in these tales in relational power, always in flux, between the Lion and the Monkey. The significant third term[18] in the Signifying Monkey tales is the Elephant, a trope for male sexuality[19] conjoined with physical violence. The Monkey combines the forces of "talk" and sexuality to defeat the Lion — but never definitively.

In like manner, talk and sexuality intersect to mark the site of the domestic struggle for dominance between men and women in this culture, where women have historically held the keys to both production and reproduction. Threatened by this imbalance of power, men overcorrect verbally, using "rap" to shore up their "rep." For in a culture where talk is not cheap, verbal dominance is a mark of power, sexual and social at the same time. And, refusing to cede ground, women want what is minimally their due: as Aretha Franklin spells it out, a little R-E-S-P-E-C-T.

Henry Louis Gates, Jr., has suggested some of problems that attend a "forceful feminist critique" in the face of an expressive tradition that values sexual antagonism:

> Lyrics by 1930s blues singers like Lucille Bogan are as raunchy as anything in 2 Live Crew, certainly no more sexually enlightened. Then as now, middle-class blacks and intellectuals were mortified. Today, some black stalwarts say if something is obscene, it isn't part of black culture. Conversely (this thinking goes), the claim that it is part of black culture is something exculpatory. Both implications have to be resisted. The sexism in street culture only reaffirms the need for a forceful feminist critique... There is no point in trying to whitewash a multifarious cultural heritage, casting it as a monolith of virtue. Like all cultures, black culture consists not only of the best that has been thought and said, but the worst as well. (4:18)

Clearly, Hurston fully participates in what Gates calls a "multifarious cultural heritage." While her message and methods hardly advance a forceful feminist critique appropriate for the 1990s, she nonetheless signifies on the constraints on women's speech in the 1930s, some of which are still in force. The issues of voice and silence[20] are central not only in *Their Eyes* but in *Mules and Men* as well. Of the seventy tales in the volume, only five are delivered by women, and two of those by Big Sweet. In chapters 4 and 5, the women do not participate in the conversation at all, except for the brief courtship exchange between Pitts and Zora. Only in chapter 9 in the jook joint, do women, albeit of questionable reputation, take center stage.

Although Hurston's work is no monolith of virtue, the singularity of her comic achievement does advance a feminist agenda, however inadvertently.

Her verbal and performative mastery sometimes called into question her heterosexual femininity: as a child, Hurston has been described as "a reconstructed tomboy" (Hemenway, *Zora Neale Hurston* 14); as an adult, she was rumored to be bisexual (Walker xv). Remembered as "a perfect mimic" and "a brilliant raconteur" (Hemenway, *Zora Neale Hurston* 22; 60), Hurston translated her considerable oral gifts to the written medium, "stylin' out" as a master of genres, stylistic registers, and linguistic codes. Her improvisations have become the riff that successive generations must, in turn, measure up to, play against, and ultimately surpass. As the first African-American woman comic writer of record, Hurston keeps true to her cultural tradition but renovates it with a personal flourish that has left its mark on that tradition, a mark that must be reckoned with.

NOTES

1. In Part One of *Mules and Men*, Hurston reports seventy folks in Black English Vernacular that she collected in 1927–32 in Florida. Part Two, entitled "Hoodoo," written largely in Standard English, was added later because her publisher needed a book worth $3.50. Although the folk tales represent the "scientific" core of Hurston's field research, she admits that she "inserted the between-story conversation and business" (qtd. in Hemenway, *Zora Neale Hurston* 163). Hurston's fictionalized context — rather than the tales themselves — is the focus of this study.

2. For an in-depth discussion of the kind of talk associated with street culture, public occasions, and the home, see Abrahams, "Joking: The Training of The Man of Words in Talking Broad." Abrahams also explains the gendered implications of *broad talk* and *sweet talk* in this same article.

3. The mock-courtship and post-courtship routines heretofore have not been formally identified as speech events, although the stylistic register has been noted as a species unto itself. See Abrahams, "Negotiating Respect: Patterns of Presentation Among Black Women" for a discussion of the role of *smart talk* in the repertoire of a woman of respect. For a study of the courtship ritual, see Hemenway, "Are You a Flying Lark or a Setting Dove?" This ritual is carnivalized in the Daisy scene in *Their Eyes*, in what I am calling a mock-courtship ritual. Hurston expanded the Daisy scene into the play *Mule Bone*, Hurston's collaborative project with Langston Hughes.

4. For a full discussion of *signifying* as a speech event, see Mitchell-Kernan.

5. For a discussion of the *maternal fuss* as a speech event, see Heath.

6. For a discussion of how any speech event can be *marked* or *mocked*, see Mitchell-Kernan.

7. For a useful discussion of *playing the dozens*, see Mitchell-Kernan. Also see Mitchell-Kernan for discussion of other African-American speech events, including *capping*, *sounding*, and *woofing*.

8. Henry Louis Gates, Jr., explains how *Their Eyes* is a "talking book," or "speakerly text" in *The Signifying Monkey*. Barbara Johnson reapplies Gates' notion to *Mules and Men*, showing how Hurston dramatizes the confrontation of the and written culture.

9. For the implications of this label for a woman, see Abrahams, "Negotiating Respect."

10. This scene is not without parallel in fiction by white authors, as in Faulkner's *The Hamlet*. The common ground here is the South, where a man's unflappable nonchalance measures his sense of honor and humor. See my "Reading Faulknerian Comedy: Humor and Honor in *The Hamlet*." While such similarities between white and black cultural practices (especially in the South) are striking, I do not mean to suggest here that they are coterminous. For a critical analysis of the theory of "a culture of poverty" (the theory that the cultural values of poor people are the same across national and racial boundaries), see Chapter 9 of Ulf Hannerz's *Soulside*.

11. When Whoopi Goldberg won the Academy Award for Best Supporting Actress in 1991 for her performance as the psychic go-between in *Ghost*, she was only the second African-American woman to win the Oscar. The first went to Hattie McDaniel for her 1939 supporting role as Scarlet's mammy in *Gone With the Wind*.

12. Stand-up comic women have yet to enjoy crossover success — except when they cross over to television situation comedy, as did Marsha Warfield, who played the bailiff on *Night Court*.

13. A very different meaning obtains in the white version of the song, sung by Maria Maldaur, who attributes to the male both the meat *and* the motion that "makes your Mamma want to rock." For the original version, consult "Risque Rhythm: Nasty 50s R & B" (Rhino, compact disc).

14. Linda Barnes attributes this blues lyric to Mississippi John Hurt in *Coyote*, p. 121.

15. A dry shave is sexual intercourse without foreplay (Oliver 225).

16. In the South, "cock" originally referred to the female pudendum, according to Webster's Third New International Dictionary.

17. An ultimate form of this sexual competition is lesbian love, as suggested in the first recorded version of "Shave 'Em Dry" (1924) by Ma Rainey. She half-hollers this last stanza:
    > Why don't you run here mama, lay back in my arms,
    > If your man catches you I don't mean no harm,
    > Mama let me holler, daddy let me shave 'em dry. (Oliver 226–227)

18. Here I am reassigning Gates' values. Gates sees the Monkey as the "term of (anti)mediation, as are all trickster figures, between two forces he seeks to oppose for his own contentious purposes, and then to reconcile" (*Signifying Monkey* 56).

19. For a discussion of the elephant joke cycle of the 1960s as a cultural response
     to the black power movement, see Dundes, *Cracking Jokes*, Chapter 4; the
     elephant is "the epitome of sexual power" (Dundes 44). Abrahams documents
     an epic toast about the lion and elephant wherein the elephant is sexually
     superior in *Deep Down in the Jungle* 136–47. Lucille Bogan also makes the
     association in the expurgated version of "Shave 'Em Dry," a Baboon (sig-
     nificantly) taking the place of the Lion:

> The Monkey and the baboon playin' in the grass
> Well the Monkey got mad and whupped his yas, yas, yas.
> …
> You know a elephant he's big and stout.
> He would be all right if it weren't for his snout.
> Talkin' 'bout shavin', mamma gonna shave 'em dry.
> And if you don't know, mama's gonna learn you how. (Oliver 230)

     The Baboon is more clearly female in a joke cycle called "The Party," wherein
     the Monkey seduces Mrs. Baboon, as reported by Abrahams, *Deep Down in the
     Jungle* 225–28. The Monkey, thus played, recalls the "monkey man" who
     figures prominently in blues lyrics as a "backdoor man," who cuckolds the male
     while he is at work (Oliver 258).

20. For the most recent discussion of these and other issues, see Awkward's collec-
     tion *New Essays on Their Eyes Were Watching God*.

WORKS CITED

Abrahams, Roger. *Deep Down In The Jungle: Negro Narrative Folklore from the
Streets of Philadelphia*. New York: Aldine Publishing Co., 1970.

_____. "Joking: The Training of The Man of Words in Talking Broad," in:
Rappin' and Stylin' Out: Communication in Urban Black America, ed. Thomas
Kochman. Urbana: University of Illinois Press, 1972, 215–240.

_____. "Negotiating Respect: Patterns of Presentation Among Black
Women," in: *Women and Folklore: Images and Genre*, ed. Claire R. Farrer.
Prospect Heights, IL: Waveland Press, 1975, 58–80.

_____. *Talking Black*. Rowley, Massachusetts: Newbury House Publishers,
1976.

Awkward, Michael, ed. *New Essays on Their Eyes Were Watching God*. Cambridge:
Cambridge University Press, 1990.

Barnes, Linda. *Coyote*. New York: Dell, 1991.

Dundes, Alan. *Cracking Jokes: Studies in Sick Humor Cycles and Stereotypes*.
Berkeley: Ten Speed Press, 1987.

Ellison, Mary. *Extensions of the Blues*. London: John Calder, 1989.

Evans, David. *Big Road Blues: Traditions and Creativity in the Folk Blues*. Berkeley:
University of California Press, 1982.

Gates, Henry Louis Jr. "The Case of 2 Live Crew Tells Much About the American Psyche." Letter. *New York Times*, 15 July 1990: IV, 18.

_____. *The Signifying Monkey: A Theory of African-American Literary Criticism*. New York: Oxford University Press, 1988.

Hannerz, Ulf. *Soulside: Inquiries into Ghetto Culture and Community*. New York: Columbia University Press, 1969.

Heath, Shirley Brice. "The Children of Trackton's Children," in: *Cultural Psychology: Essays on Comparative Human Development*, ed. James W. Stigler et al. Cambridge: Cambridge University Press, 1990, 496–517.

Hemenway, Robert. "Are You a Flying Lark or a Setting Dove?" in: *Afro-American Literature: The Reconstruction of Instruction*, eds. Dexter Fisher and Robert B. Stepto. New York: The Modern Language Association, 1979, 122–52.

_____. *Zora Neale Hurston: A Literary Biography*. Urbana: University of Illinois Press, 1977.

Hurston, Zora Neale. *Dust Tracks on the Road*. Newark: Arno Press, 1969.

_____. "The Gilded Six-Bits." *Spunk: The Selected Stories of Zora Neale Hurston*. Berkeley: Turtle Island Foundation, 1985, 54–68.

_____. *Mules and Men*. New York: Quality Paperback Books, 1990.

_____. *Their Eyes Were Watching God*. New York: Quality Paperback Books, 1990.

Isaacs, Edith J. R. *The Negro in the American Theatre*. New York: Theatre Arts, Inc., 1947.

Johnson, Barbara. "Thresholds of Difference: Structures of Address in Zora Neale Hurston," in: *Race, Writing, and Difference*, ed. Henry Louis Gates Jr. Chicago: University of Chicago Press, 1986, 317–328.

Levine, Lawrence W. *Black Culture and Black Consciousness: Afro-American Folk Thought from Slavery to Freedom*. New York: Oxford University Press, 1977.

Mitchell, Loften. *Voices of the Black Theatre*. Clifton, NJ: James T. White & Company, 1975.

Mitchell-Kernan, Claudia. "Signifying, Loud-Talking and Marking," in: *Rappin' and Stylin' Out: Communication in Urban Black America*, ed. Thomas Kochman. Urbana: University of Illinois Press, 1972, 315–335.

Monroe, Barbara. "Reading Faulknerian Comedy: Humor and Honor in *The Hamlet*." *Southern Quarterly* 26, no. 4 (Summer 1988): 33–56.

Niles, Abbe. *Blues: An Anthology*, ed. W. C. Handy. New York: Da Capo Press, 1985.

Oliver, Paul. *Screening the Blues: Aspects of the Blues Tradition*. London: Cassell, 1968.

"Risqué Rhythm: Nasty 50s R&B." Rhino, compact disc.

Stearns, Marshall, and Jean Stearns. "Frontiers of Humor: American Vernacular Dance," in: *Mother Wit from the Laughing Barrel*, ed. Alan Dundes. Englewood Cliffs, NJ: Prentice-Hall, 1973, 613–619.

Varian, Nanette. "Roseanne Barr." *Penthouse* (December 1990): 81–84; 177–186.

Walker, Alice. "Foreword." *Zora Neale Hurston: A Literary Biography,* by Robert E. Hemenway. Urbana: University of Illinois Press, 1977, xi–xviii.

Washington, Mary Helen. "Foreword." *Their Eyes Were Watching God*, by Zora Neale Hurston. New York: Quality Paperback Books, 1990, vii–xiv.

11

Feminism/Gender/Comedy: Meredith, Woolf, and the Reconfiguration of Comic Distance

DAVID McWHIRTER

Recent criticism on gender and comedy has been largely devoted to the project of recovering and defining women's distinctive comedic traditions. Arguing that, as Regina Barreca puts it, "for most women humor occupies a different space emotionally and socially than it does for men," literary and cultural critics working along these lines have tended to agree that women's laughter is a deeply transgressive, "confrontational and boundary breaking," force (*They Used to Call Me Snow White*, 14, 11) — that for women, the comic has historically served as a vehicle for exposing the "shams, hypocrisies, and incongruities" of patriarchal culture, and for challenging "the basic assumptions about women that have justified their public and private subordination" (Walker, 9, 183). Barreca's dictum — "anytime a woman breaks through a barrier set by society, she's making a feminist gesture of a sort, and every time a woman laughs, she's breaking through a barrier" (*Snow White*, 182) — thus adumbrates a widely shared assumption that women's laughter is inherently subversive, compatible with and perhaps even essential to feminist political struggle.

Feminist critics concerned with the patterns and conventions of comedy as a literary *form* or *genre*, however, have typically adopted a less sanguine viewpoint. Indeed, much of the recent gender/genre criticism devoted to comedy tends to support Judith Wilt's assessment that there is an inevitable "collision between comedy and feminism" (173). Even a critic like Linda Bamber, who argues forcefully that Shakespeare's comic heroines "are associated with what challenges the social order" and that "they invite us to suspend participation in the everyday social drama of class, power, money, and status," nevertheless acknowledges that "the festive, disruptive, disorderly moment of comedy" poses no real threat to "the natural order, the status quo, [which] is for men to rule women" (28–29). Bamber, in other words, ultimately partakes of what Barreca describes as the "growing awareness that comedy is an ideological construct" ("Introduction," 7),[1] and shares in the suspicion that the comic form, rooted in rituals designed to reaffirm the continuity and stability of nature and/or society, and marked by a "deeply conservative ability to absorb and defuse emotions that threaten fertility and community" (Wilt, 177), is somehow fundamentally at odds with feminist political agendas. Women's laughter may be subversive, but comedy as a genre, it would seem, is almost fatally overdetermined in its reinscription of fixed, traditional gender roles and hierarchies of power.

The suspicion that comedy is, structurally and ideologically, an inherently androcentric genre in part reflects a broader skepticism about literary forms, and a persistent hostility to formalist criticism within the feminist community. Instead of viewing comedy in terms of an unchanging archetypal generic model which is itself wholly resistant to historical process and adaptation, however, I want to begin with the assumption — a crucial one, I think, for a feminist practice that aims at transforming dominant gender constructions as well as exposing them — that literary forms, like the forms of language, knowledge and social organization, are always potentially in flux, open not only to reconfigurations of the same, but also to more fundamental reconstitutions of purpose and affect. While comedy's roots may well lie in fertility rituals designed to reaffirm the continuity and stability of nature and/or society, Bakhtin, Donaldson and others have shown that the discontinuities and excesses unleashed by the comic are not always so easily contained (Bakhtin, *Rabelais and His World*, 268–69; Donaldson, 183–206). A subversive or even revolutionary potential is often discerned in romantic and post-romantic comedy, where, it is argued, laughter is typically less a corrective aimed at the individual who deviates from societal or "natural" norms than an attack on those norms themselves. This is why Robert Polhemus can assert that "the best nineteenth-century comic novels express a deepening social need to supplement, broaden, mock, attack, revise, and transmute orthodox faith and the moral order established by traditional theological institutions" (4). When George Meredith, in his 1872 "Ode to the Comic Spirit," praises comedy's capacity for probing "Old institutions and establishments,/ Once fortresses against the floods of sin,/ For what their worth," and for challenging "the criers of foregone wisdom, who impose/ Its slough on live conditions" (*Poems*, I, 521, 529), he aligns himself with what George McFadden describes as modern comedy's critique of "the ethos that underlies customary response" (49).

While much of the criticism devoted to Meredith's comic novels clearly reflects the sense that feminism and comic form are fundamentally incompatible,[2] several commentators — among them Judy Little (23), Margaret Comstock (*passim*), and Lisa Merrill (271) — have been able to discern in the author of the *Essay on Comedy* (1877) a precursor of the more radical comic writing practiced by twentieth century women like Woolf and Muriel Spark: a kind of writing where, in Little's formulation, "rounded-off comic fiction in which the hero is ultimately reintegrated into society" gives way to a "renegade" laughter which "mocks the deepest possible norms," specifically, the archetypal norms of "sex identity" governed by our "primary socialization" (1, 7–8).[3] Meredith's *Essay* is in fact a key text for any approach to the problem of feminism and comedy, in part for the very reason that it draws so heavily on classical and neo-classical models in its attempt to define the nature of comedy as a genre. Most immediately, however, the *Essay*'s insistence that a critique of society's prevailing gender assumptions constitutes a necessary element in the best comic writing has never been sufficiently stressed. Comedy, Meredith argues, "lifts women to a station offering them free play for their wit": "the higher the comedy, the more prominent the part they enjoy in it" (14). As "an exhibition of their battle with men, and that of men with them," it offers images of women opposed to "the pretty idiot, the passive beauty, the adorable bundle of caprices, very feminine, very sympathetic, of romantic and sentimental fiction." For Meredith, however, comedy's feminism goes beyond its capacity for representing women who "use their wits, and are not wandering vessels crying for a captain or a pilot" (15). Most strikingly, he repeatedly asserts that "pure comedy" can only attain its full shapeliness in a society where "men ... consent to talk with ... women, and to listen to them" (55). Given this presumption, Meredith in fact judges all cultures to be more or less wanting in the social conditions which allow comedy to flourish. He nevertheless calls specifically on

> cultivated women to recognize that the comic Muse is one of their best friends... Let them look with their clearest vision abroad and at home. They will see that, where they have no social freedom, comedy is absent... But where women are on the road to an equal footing with men, in attainments and in liberty ... there, and only waiting to be transplanted from life to the stage, or the novel, or the poem, pure comedy flourishes. (32)

But while the *Essay* insists on a fundamental link between comedy and feminism, it also suggests why feminists continue to distrust Meredith's comedy as a formal construct. For when Meredith turns to a delineation of comedy's aesthetic, he draws heavily on classical and neo-classical models, and stresses qualities — symmetry, clarity and wholeness of design, and, most insistently, the cool, distanced objectivity of the comic perspective — which seem to be deeply at odds with the political motivations he ascribes to the genre. As defined in the *Essay*, comic vision is characterized most consistently by its "common aspect ... of unsolicitous observation" (48). With a detachment akin to the dramatist's objectifying distance from his characters, the Comic Spirit surveys life "from aloft" (47), exposing the follies, pretensions, and eccentricities of human beings to the chastening but humane judgment of an "impersonal" laughter (53). For Meredith, the comic vantage is that of "the mind hovering above congregated men and women" (10), where the mind is understood to be a "general mind" (45), a consensus of "many sane and solid minds" (48), the "high fellowship" of a "civilization ... founded in common sense" (49). As an idealized "collective supervision" (52) based in "sound reason" and reflecting what is natural and "permanently human" (10), it provides a stabilizing, all-encompassing perspective on the "ever-shifting soil" of our "rapidly revolving world" (52), diffuses the "vapors of unreason and sentimentalism," and brings "a bright and positive, clear Hellenic perception of facts" (37).

For Meredith, then, comedy is distinguished by its aspiration to what Thomas Nagel calls a "view from nowhere"[4] — by its apparent capacity for assuming a godlike perspective or unbiased objectivity capable of grasping and fixing the fundamental design of the "rapidly revolving world," of seeing life's essential pattern, whole and *sub specie aeternitatis*, and of discovering the structure of the same in and behind manifestations of apparent difference. Meredithian comic detachment thus might well be understood as a particularly oppressive instance of the "absolute epic distance" Bakhtin ascribes to "the classicism of all non-novel genres" — a distance which, as Bakhtin recognizes, entails a profound resistance to any social, cultural, or linguistic change. According to Bakhtin, the monological "completedness" of the classic genres — including comedy — implicitly and explicitly valorizes the past, representing the world as "an utterly finished thing ... completed and immutable." Reality is perceived as "an absolute distanced image, beyond the sphere of possible contact with the developing, incomplete, and therefore re-thinking and re-evaluating present." The distanced perspective of classic form thus shapes a world — and a conception of individual identity — that is whole but closed; it diagrams a "circle" inside of which "everything is finished, already over," in which everything is bound by the "prior discourse" of the "authoritative word ... the word of the fathers" (*Dialogic Imagination*, 16–17, 20, 342).

In Bakhtin's formulation, distance as an aesthetic category works to grant historically contingent social constructions — including those related to gender — the status of fixed, "natural" law. And so conceived, comic distance would indeed appear to play a central role in defining comedy's generic formal *and* political conservatism. Moreover, feminist theory and practice have tended to distrust the linked concepts of distance and objectivity, not only because "views from nowhere" so frequently turn out, upon closer examination, to be versions of a male gaze, but also because the very drive for distance and abstraction has increasingly been seen as a male-gendered epistemological strategy that is deeply implicated in androcentric culture's suppression of women's difference. Nancy Chodorow's influential gender-based model of personality development, for example, shows how the socialization processes and family structures prevalent in western societies define certain cognitive and evaluative modes — especially abstraction and the quest for objectivity — as masculine, while ways of knowing characterized by subjective and relational modes, and by an emphasis on concrete phenomena, are perceived as feminine (43–46). An analogous conceptualization emerges in Evelyn Fox Keller's exploration of modern science's masculinist biases. "The scientific mind," Keller writes,

> is set apart from what is to be known, i.e., from nature, and its autonomy is guaranteed ... by setting apart its modes of knowing from those in which the dichotomy is threatened. In this process, the characterization of both the scientific mind and its modes of access to knowledge as masculine is indeed significant. Masculine here connotes, as it so often does, autonomy, separation, and distance ... a radical rejection of any commingling of subject and object. (79)

Susan Bordo extends this line of thought even further, arguing persuasively that "the flight to objectivity" in the post-Cartesian metaphysical tradition also encompasses a "flight from the feminine" (*The Flight to Objectivity*, 97).[5] Seen in these contexts, Meredith's emphasis on comedy's "unsolicitous observation" and "impersonal" laughter — not to mention his reliance on concepts such as "common sense," "sound reason," and the "permanently human" — becomes disquieting. Whose "reason"? one wants to ask, suspecting that Meredith's comedy, like that of the neo-classical writers whose language he echoes here, is in part a formula for suppressing difference by containing it in the supposed objectivity of a "common sense" which is decidedly *not* common, but male. Indeed, traditional critics like Joseph Warren Beach have proven themselves all too ready to read Meredith's comic vision as an expression of patriarchy, where "common sense" is "reasoned nature," and nature is defined as "the very incarnation of law" (191).

In her recent study of feminist theory and the construction of knowledge, Lorraine Code summarizes and extends the feminist critique of distance,

arguing that the ideal of objectivity, with its insistence that "observers stand
— and *should* stand — dispassionately ... at a distance from the objects of
their observation," is in practice a "*masculine* epistemological stance" that
"for all its self-proclaimed objectivity ... is sustained by *subjective* forces: by
interests and self-interest" (48). And given the role that the ideals of detachment and "common sense" have played in sustaining the interests of patriarchy, it is hardly surprising that some feminist thinkers have been moved to
attack the possibility of objectivity as both dangerous and "illusory" (Susan
Griffin, 280). But Code's desire to "break[] the spell of timelessness, detachment, universality, and absoluteness" (46) leads her not to a rejection of the
epistemic value of objectivity, but to a recognition that the model of ideal
objectivity which characterizes Western philosophy and science is inadequate. Rather than simply denouncing objectivity as "an inherently male
construct" (35), Code attempts to deconstruct the traditional subjective/ob-
jective dichotomy, "to show that, often, objectivity requires taking subjectivity into account" (31), and to refigure "knowledge seeking as a communal,
dialogic activity marked by interdependence and intersubjective critique"
(123), but nevertheless still "*objectively* constrained by the (changing, openended, but roughly specifiable) possibilities of 'human nature' and by the
(also changing, but specifiable) nature of 'the world'" (42).

Code's effort to "produce epistemological positions that would accord
better with feminist purposes" (145) involves a rethinking of objectivity and
distance that can be discerned in Keller's critique as well. Keller proposes an
alternative model of "dynamic objectivity," a way of knowing distinguished
by its ability to "make use of subjective experience ... in the interests of a
more effective objectivity": her reimagined distance "recognizes difference
between self and other as an opportunity for a deeper and more articulated
kinship." Similarly, Carol Gilligan, extending Chodorow's insights, has
shown how women characteristically employ strategies of abstraction and
objectification which transpose "the image of hierarchy" into "the image of
web" — an image that reveals "an expanding network of connection" and
relationship rather than a fixed pattern or law (Gilligan, 62–63, 39).

These reconceptualizations of objectivity suggest that comedy's distanced
perspective — a distance which has in practice typically served to reinforce
patriarchy and its supposedly immutable laws — need not necessarily imply
the closed world of Bakhtin's "absolute epic distance." What is revealed when
we look at nature, human nature, and human history from an imagined
distance? The comic perspective Meredith theorizes in the *Essay* unquestionably *resembles* the detached, stable and containing perspective of classical comedy's conservative vision — where all difference, no matter how
powerful or disruptive, is ultimately reconciled in the reassertion of an *a
priori*, unchanging plot or pattern. But Meredith is also acutely aware of the
conservative and androcentric implications of the comic form he employs,

and the *Essay*, I believe, in fact hinges on a subtle but crucial reconfiguration of comic distance. Meredith asks us to rethink the uses of those abstractions we call literary forms, and to explore how the comic vision's distanced perspective might serve a feminist politics through the continuing projection and reimagination of its possibility. In this sense the *Essay* can be seen as a blueprint for what Bakhtin calls "the novelization of other genres," a process through which "the novelist inserts into these other genres" — in this case, comedy — "an indeterminacy, a certain semantic openendedness, a living contact with unfinished, still-evolving, contemporary reality (the openended present)" (*Dialogic*, 6–7).

The key to understanding Meredith's re-visioning of comic distance lies in his deliberate acknowledgment of the hypothetical status of the Comic Spirit's objective vision. For Meredith, "pure comedy" is in fact an unrealized ideal. "Good comedies," he asserts, "are such rare productions" precisely because the "great comic poet" is "repel[led]" by "a state of marked social inequality of the sexes" (3); we recall, moreover, his belief that comedy can only flourish in a society where "men ... consent to talk on equal terms with ... women, and to listen to them." Now Meredith knows that Victorian England is not such a society. But the genius of comedy, as Meredith theorizes it, is its projection of a representational perspective outside or beyond the horizon of society as it is currently constituted. The most crucial quality of the comic perspective lies in its acknowledged status as an as yet unrealized possibility, a projected or imagined *common* sense of educated men *and* women which, he is at pains to emphasize, does not and cannot exist within the current construction of bourgeois society. I am suggesting, in other words, that when Meredith speaks of the Comic Spirit as a "collective supervision," founded in "common sense" and "born of our united social intelligence," he means what he says: the "impersonal" laughter of pure comedy *must* be a "laugh of men and women in concert." Such a dialogic consensus — what Meredith calls, in the penultimate line of his "Ode to the Comic Spirit," "the music of the meaning of Accord" (*Poems*, I, 529) — has not yet been forged, in England or anywhere else. Comedy thus requires a special kind of suspension of disbelief: *in theory*, "you must ... believe that our state of society is founded in common sense, otherwise you will not be struck by the contrasts the Comic Spirit perceives" (48). But Meredith does not hesitate to remind us that "our English school has not clearly imagined society; and of the mind hovering above congregated men and women" — the "general mind" of the Comic Spirit — "it has imagined nothing" (10).

Comedy's imagination of a distance is, then, for Meredith, a kind of necessary science fiction, an abstract figuration of a possible and still-to-be-defined future perspective, rather than an essentialist embodiment of an existing social consensus or an unalterable law of nature. Although it springs from the "prior discourse" of the old world's "authoritative word," comedy dialogizes that word by imaginatively enacting the possibility of a truer, non-sexist objectivity; its laughter is aimed at the present from the vantage of a conjectured future, at society from an imagined space above and beyond its existing confines. The Comic Spirit images the possibility of a perspective reflecting the common sense of men and women. What comedy's distance discerns, however, is not monological unity, but polyphonic wholeness, the wholeness — to draw on Bakhtin once more — of "the world become historical," where "there is no first word (no ideal word), and the final word has not yet been spoken," where everything is grasped "as an uninterrupted movement into a real future, as a unified, all-embracing and unconcluded process" (*Dialogic*, 30). Thus if comedy's formal strategies of distance and abstraction have been used to discern "essential" or "universal" patterns and "natural laws," they are also, in Meredith's revision, capable of revealing unanticipated networks of difference, connection, and relationship — of opening up a space in which the "natural" can be rehistoricized, in which we can grasp the truth that nature exists and finds its forms only in and through human history.

Meredith's "novelization" of comedy, theorized in the *Essay* and embodied in such feminist comic fictions as *The Egoist* and *Diana of the Crossways*, helps to explain his importance for Virginia Woolf, who acknowledged her debt to her predecessor in a series of essays that spanned her career.[6] Woolf believed that the "chief task" of the modern novelist is to convey the "incessantly varying" movements of the mind "with whatever stress or sudden deviation it may display" (*Essays*, 3: 33), to represent the self as an entity enmeshed in mental and historical process. But Woolf's fiction is also deeply rooted in the traditions of English comedy; like Meredith, she was fascinated with literary modes and figures — Elizabethan and Restoration drama, comic opera, Austen, Pope, and Congreve — that reflect an alternative impulse towards comic distance and formal perfection. Woolf thus praises Goldsmith's "detached attitude and width of view" (*Collected Essays*, 1: 108), and valorizes "the finely shaped mould of *The Rape of the Lock*," "the repose, the distinction, the reserve" which characterize "the sense of form which seems to have prevailed in the eighteenth century." What Woolf admires in the neo-classical writers is "the completedness with which they triumphed, imposing shape upon the tumult of their material"; but she also wonders, "did they not perhaps leave out too much, and sacrifice so devoutly at the shrine of form that some very important qualities were excluded" (*Essays*, 2: 324–25)?

Woolf recognizes, moreover, that the comic writers she admires "leave out too much" in part because they are so sure of what to put in. The great comic writers achieve their sense of "tranquility," "security" and "certainty" by excluding difference, complexity, and history: "they know the relations of human beings towards each other and towards the universe" — hence their ability to create "that complete statement which is literature" (*Collected Essays*, 2: 158–59).[7] Thus while Woolf values classical comedy's detachment, she also shares Bahktin's suspicion of its monological "completedness," its vision of reality as an ahistorical, "absolute distanced image" (*Dialogic Imagination*, 17). When Woolf argues in *A Room of One's Own* that the older, "hardened and set" literary genres — "the form of the epic or of the poetic play" — are not "rightly shaped" for the woman writer (80), she articulates her reservations about comedy as well.

In Meredith, whom she once described as a "dramatist of the Restoration" born "out of his due time" (*Collected Essays*, 1: 236), Woolf found a precursor who shared not only her high valuation of comedy, but also her feminist wariness of its closed, completed vision. For Woolf, Meredith is "a great innovator" whose "experimental" comic fictions anticipate her own quest for a fictional form capable of fusing detachment and penetration, pattern and contingency, abstraction and empathy — the imperatives of comic form and novelistic insight (*Collected Essays*, 1: 231). It is no accident, I think, that Meredith figures so prominently in Woolf's 1927 essay, "The Narrow Bridge of Art," where she prophesies the future development of modern fiction along lines which, as several critics have remarked, anticipate the hybrid, seriocomic form of her last novel, *Between the Acts* (1941). In her essay, Woolf finds the closest approximation to the inclusive, carnivalesque form she seeks in "the poetic drama of the Elizabethan age," where the possession of "some general shaping power, some conception which lends the whole harmony and force," does not preclude historical complexity and "psychological subtlety." The new form, she speculates, "will differ from the novel as we know it now ... in that it will stand further back from life. It will give ... the outline rather than the detail"; but it will also retain the novel's capacity to "express the feeling and ideas of the characters closely and vividly" (*Collected Essays*, 224–26).

Between the Acts, a text Woolf referred to as her "Elizabethan play" (*Diary*, 5: 356), is quite literally both a novel *and* a play, for its action consists mainly in the characters' attendance at the comic pageant written and staged by Miss La Trobe. Like Meredith, Woolf is engaged, quite consciously, in the novelization of comedy here, unless we understand, as I think we should, that she is attempting to reinsert the burgeoning content of the modern novel — the unarticulated desires, oppressive self-consciousness, emotional paralysis, and thwarted lives of her characters, as well as the impending historical horror of World War II that shapes and haunts those lives — back into the container of comic form. David Daiches has remarked that "no careful reader" could fail to recognize *Between the Acts* as fundamentally tragic (122). And it is certainly true that Woolf's novel — as opposed to La Trobe's pageant — for the most part portrays characters who are variously "caught and caged" (*Between* [*B*], 176), "pegged down" (*B*, 180), and "pressed ... flat" (*B*, 47) by the oppressive social scripts in which they are trapped, especially the stifling gender roles that imprison Giles and Isa Oliver in a ghastly parody of the heterosexual marriage plot, and the larger more disturbing structure of power relations those roles reflect. The self-destructive homophobia internalized by the homosexual William Dodge, the restrictive identity (wife, mother, "Sir Richard's daughter" [*B*, 15]) to which Isa is manacled, and the gender conventions which have transformed Giles into an emotionally crippled loner, estranged from his wife and children, and barely able to contain his rage at his own impotence, exemplify, for Woolf, the patriarchal forces that have produced not only the characters' collective sense of hanging "suspended, without being, in limbo" (*B*, 178), but also the larger historical impasse in which they are caught. In this purgatorial modern landscape, personal relations have become an arena of mutual tyranny and destruction, while group relations — whether between men and women, social classes, or nations — are increasingly governed by the logic of exclusion, victimization, and violence, even, as Woolf's ominous references to Mussolini suggest, by the ideology of fascism.

Yet Woolf's "tragic" novel, with its disturbing vision from within consciousness and history, occupies the same textual space as Miss La Trobe's comic play, which looks at history, individual and collective, past and present, from a vantage of extreme detachment. Even if we understand that it is contained within the novel's narrated discourse, the pageant allows us, in effect, to turn our perspective on the novel's characters inside out. In addition to experiencing their personal and historical predicament from within, we also see them from without, as actors in a drama which we view from the third balcony, a drama in which their "part," as we are repeatedly reminded, "is to be the audience" (*B*, 58). Sallie Sears thus remarks on "the degree to which [*Between the Acts*] distances us from the lives it parades before our eyes" (212). For all our involvement in those lives, the characters also appear to us as figures in an intricate and highly abstract pattern — a pattern that we discern through the distanced and distancing lens of the pageant's comedy.

The pageant reads history primarily in terms of the history of artistic forms and conventions, with a particular emphasis on the traditions of English comedy. Thus each of the pageant's first three acts consists of a characteristically motley combination of elements — prologue and epilogue, song, dance and masque — which frame respective parodies of an Elizabethan romance, a Restoration comedy, and a Victorian melodrama, the last of which modulates into a comic opera worthy of Gilbert and Sullivan. This pattern cannot help but encourage us, when we reach the fourth act ("The Present Time. Ourselves" [*B*, 178]), to read the "abortive" desires and actions of the novel's characters — Isa, Giles, and the others — *into* the comic frame of the pageant, and thus to see what transpires between the acts of Miss La Trobe's creation as still another play within her play.

Woolf thus encourages us to double our empathetic experience of the characters' thwarted lives with a detachment that sees those lives as pieces of a larger whole. But what is the nature of that whole? What is the shape of the self and the pattern of history we discern when we view them through the distancing frame of comedy? The pageant's long view of English history — a view which ranges from prehistory to the present day, condensing whole epochs into brief scenes — has led some critics to conclude that La Trobe and perhaps even Woolf are trying to transcend history altogether, to achieve a perspective in which the contingencies of self and history are ultimately absorbed into a natural or divine comedy, a romance pattern of eternal recurrence. Marilyn Zorn thus argues that "the pageant is, first of all, the world without time" (33), while Nora Eisenberg asserts that the choral interludes that periodically punctuate it evoke "a timeless world" of communal values, a world where historical inessentials such as "costume and name" change, "but the people beneath," nature and human nature, "remain the same" (256–57). Richard Lyons goes even further, arguing that the repeated comic patterns and plot motifs of the pageant's dramatic scenes serve "to undercut any sense of real change": "the apparent movement back in time is really a movement out of time," in effect "a negation of history" (153–54). Woolf in fact incorporates this line of interpretation of the pageant as a vision of history *sub specie aeternitatis* into her novel in the figure of Reverend Streatfield, the village clergyman. In his "official" closing remarks, Streatfield points to the fact that the amateur actors play multiple roles from different historical eras in order to support his reading of the pageant as an affirmation of the underlying truth that "we act different parts, but are the same" (*B*, 192).

But if the pageant at moments appears to evoke a timeless world of eternal values that is in effect a negation of history, I would argue that it functions more consistently as a transgressive comic ritual which serves to disrupt the social and cultural categories which oppress and distort the novel's characters and which have produced the historical nightmare of 1939. The counter to Reverend Streatfield in *Between the Acts* is Miss La Trobe, the vaguely foreign, classless, lesbian outsider who is the pageant's author and director. Referred to by her audience as "Miss Whatshername," Miss La Trobe pointedly chooses, at the end of the day, "to remain anonymous" (*B*, 194); and she uses her outsider's privilege to satirize the wholly historical forces — capitalism, imperialism, racism, and sexism — that are inseparable from the fascism and war they have produced. Indeed, many elements in the pageant's content recapitulate the novel's plot of personal and social collapse. In this view, the pageant's comedy is more subversive, its detachment less from history than from the social and cultural forces which have dominated that history and determined, in Alex Zwerdling's formulation, "the gradual but persistent decay of the sense of community" that culminates in "the fragmented present-day world" (317).[8] La Trobe thus mocks Britain's phal-

Woolf saw Meredith as a "spiritual godfather" (29), and explores the personal and political as well as the aesthetic connections between the two novelists.

7. For a helpful discussion of Woolf's ambivalence about comedy and its tendency to reflect a "solid norm" or "settled code of morals," see Little (22–98, *passim*, and especially 24–27). Little stresses Woolf's awareness of the need for a transformed comedic structure capable of reflecting changes in "society's notion of what is good and reasonable," especially changes in "the code that govern[s] behavior between men and women" (25).

8. In one of her last diary entries, Woolf remarks on her own "growing detachment from the hierarchy, the patriarchy" (*Diary*, 5: 347).

WORKS CITED

Bakhtin, Mikhail. *The Dialogic Imagination*, ed. Michael Holquist; trans. Caryl Emerson and Michael Holquist. Austin: University of Texas Press, 1981.

_____. *Problems of Dostoevsky's Poetics*, ed. and trans. Caryl Emerson. Minneapolis: University of Minnesota Press, 1984.

_____. *Rabelais and His World*, trans. Helene Iswolsky. Cambridge: MIT Press, 1968.

Bamber, Linda. *Comic Women, Tragic Men: A Study of Gender and Genre in Shakespeare*. Stanford: Stanford University Press, 1982.

Barreca, Regina. "Introduction," in: *Last Laughs: Perspectives on Women and Comedy,* ed. Regina Barreca. New York: Gordon and Breach, 1988, 3–22.

_____. *They Used to Call Me Snow White ... But I Drifted: Women's Strategic Use of Humor*. New York: Viking Penguin, 1991.

Beach, Joseph Warren. *The Comic Spirit in George Meredith: An Interpretation*. New York: Longmans, Green, & Company, 1911.

Boone, Joseph Allen. *Tradition Counter Tradition: Love and the Form of Fiction*. Chicago: University of Chicago Press, 1987.

Bordo, Susan. *The Flight to Objectivity: Essays on Cartesianism and Culture*. Albany: State University of New York Press, 1987.

Bordo, Susan, and Alison M. Jaggar, eds. *Gender/Body/Knowledge: Feminist Reconstructions of Being and Knowing*. New Brunswick: Rutgers University Press, 1989.

Chodorow, Nancy. "Family Structure and Feminine Personality," in: *Women, Culture, and Society*, eds. Michelle Zimbalist Rosaldo and Louis Lamphere. Stanford: Stanford University Press, 1974. 43–66.

Code, Lorraine. *What Can She Know? Feminist Theory and the Construction of Knowledge*. Ithaca: Cornell University Press, 1991.

Comstock, Margaret. "George Meredith, Virginia Woolf, and Their Feminist Comedy." PhD dissertation: Stanford University, 1975.

Daiches, David. *Virginia Woolf.* Norfolk, CT: New Directions, 1942.

Donaldson, Ian. *The World Upside Down: Comedy from Jonson to Fielding.* Oxford: Clarendon Press, 1970.

Eisenberg, Nora. "Virginia Woolf's Last Word on Words: *Between the Acts* and 'Anon,'" in: *New Feminist Essays on Virginia Woolf,* ed. Jane Marcus. Lincoln: University of Nebraska Press, 1981. 253–66.

Gilligan, Carol. *In a Different Voice: Psychological Theory and Women's Development.* Cambridge: Harvard University Press, 1982.

Griffin, Susan. "The Way of All Ideology," in: *Feminist Theory: A Critique of Ideology,* in: eds. Nannerl O. Keohane, Michelle Z. Rosaldo, and Barbara C. Gelpi. Chicago: University of Chicago Press, 1982. 273–92.

Keller, Evelyn Fox. *Reflections on Gender and Science.* New Haven: Yale University Press, 1985.

Little, Judy. *Comedy and the Woman Writer: Woolf, Spark, and Feminism.* Lincoln: University of Nebraska Press, 1983.

Lyons, Richard. "The Intellectual Structure of Virginia Woolf's *Between the Acts.*" *Modern Language Quarterly* 38 (1977): 149–66.

Marcus, Jane. *Art and Anger: Reading Like a Woman.* Columbus: Ohio State University Press, 1988.

McFadden, George. *Discovering the Comic.* Princeton: Princeton University Press, 1982.

Meredith, George. *An Essay on Comedy,* ed. Wylie Sypher. Garden City: Doubleday Anchor, 1956, 1–57.

_____. *The Poems of George Meredith,* ed. Phyllis B. Bartlett. Vol. 1. New Haven: Yale University Press, 1978.

Merrill, Lisa. "Feminist Humor: Rebellious and Self-Affirming," in: *Last Laughs: Perspectives on Women and Comedy,* ed. Regina Barreca. New York: Gordon & Breach, 1988, 271–80.

Millett, Kate. *Sexual Politics.* New York: Doubleday, 1970.

Nagel, Thomas. *The View From Nowhere.* New York: Oxford University Press, 1986.

Polhemus, Robert M. *Comic Faith: The Great Tradition from Austen to Joyce.* Chicago: University of Chicago Press, 1980.

Sears, Sallie. "Theater of War: Virginia Woolf's *Between the Acts,*" in: *Virginia Woolf: A Feminist Slant,* ed. Jane Marcus. Lincoln: University of Nebraska Press, 1983, 212–35.

Sochen, June. *Women's Comic Visions.* Detroit: Wayne State University Press, 1991.

Stubbs, Patricia. *Women and Fiction: Feminism and the Novel, 1890–1920.* Sussex: The Harvester Press, 1979.

Walker, Nancy A. *A Very Serious Thing: Women's Humor and American Culture.* Minneapolis: University of Minnesota Press, 1988.

Wilt, Judith. "The Laughter of Maidens, The Cackle of Matriarchs: Notes on the Collision Between Comedy and Feminism," in: *Gender and Literary Voice,* ed. Janet Todd. New York: Holmes & Meier, 1980, 173–96.

Woolf, Virginia. *Between the Acts*. New York: Harcourt Brace Jovanovich, 1969.

_____. *Collected Essays*. 4 vols. London: Hogarth Press, 1966–67.

_____. *The Diary of Virginia Woolf*. 5 vols. Ed. Anne Olivier Bell. London: The Hogarth Press, 1978–83.

_____. *The Essays of Virginia Woolf*. Vols. 1–3. Ed. Andrew McNeillie. New York: Harcourt Brace Jovanovich, 1986–88.

_____. *A Room of One's Own*. New York: Harcourt Brace Jovanovich, 1957.

Zorn, Marilyn. "The Pageant in *Between the Acts*." *Modern Fiction Studies* 2 (1956): 31–35.

Zwerdling, Alex. *Virginia Woolf and the Real World*. Berkeley: University of California Press, 1986.

12

"Between the Gaps": Sex, Class and Anarchy in the British Comic Novel of World War II

PHYLLIS LASSNER

The fiftieth year commemoration of World War II coincides with the end of communism and the Cold War. If the threat of a nuclear holocaust is past, the present is endangered by a revival of older wars. Nationalistic rivalries in the Balkans recall World War I, while campaigns of "ethnic cleansing" reawaken terrors of World War II. Prompted by the congruence of these events and fears, interest in war literature has intensified but remains vexed. Whereas the Great War is considered a watershed in the history of modernism, except for such American writers as Norman Mailer and Thomas Pyncheon, the fiction of World War II gets little attention.[1]

Far from the terrors of the death camps and yet threatened by Hitler's plans for world conquest, England remained an island in the European war. Although the Luftwaffe rained death and destruction on 60,000 Britains, the Battle of Britain was rivalled by a different kind of struggle on the home front. With factories and farms producing goods for the troops, domestic consumers endured shortages that included not only luxuries, but necessities like heating, cooking, and automobile fuel. The destruction of homes and shops in the blitz kept communities rootless and fragile, and although this provoked the government into noticing the destitute state of the poor, little could be done while the war effort took priority.

Between fear and privation, the British on the homefront fulfilled their own image as a stalwart and heroic people. Rich and poor muddled through, coping with humor that satirized the ineptness and indifference of their leaders and mocked their own conformity to a peculiarly British way of following orders. It is this tension in the character of a united yet divided people that became the grounds for a comic literature of this terrible war. True to their island natures, the English remained xenophobic, not only about the enemy and even the victims they sheltered, but about each other even as barriers of social class and region dissolved. While rich and poor joined forces in underground shelters, conversing with those whose eyes they had never before met, deep mistrust of the other fortified other British stereotypes about class, regional, and cultural differences.

These irreconcilable tensions constitute the subject and forms of British comedies of World War II. Among the many novels I could have chosen for this discussion, the following illustrate a range of attitudes towards these tensions which also produce different comic forms.[2] In Evelyn Waugh's *Put Out More Flags* (1942), Marghanita Laski's *Love on the Supertax* (1944) and Beryl Bainbridge's *Young Adolf* (1978), a nation is threatened not only by Hitler's armies but by internal economic and class conflicts. The comic forms of these novels interrogate those ideologies which may have united and propelled Britain to victory, but whose rhetorics also reified social divisions. Policies such as evacuation from the cities, produced by a Conservative governments were intended to protect women and children. In Waugh's novel, however, this policy backfires by producing an internal siege on the social fabric of the nation. *Love On The Supertax* appropriates the sonorous tones of Churchill's Macaulayesque oratory to deflate the rhetoric of the old and new guard of "the People's War." Beryl Bainbridge's *Young Adolf* (1978) imagines the rise of Hitler as Chaplinesque farce, parodying the Nazi campaign to dehumanize "the other" by submitting the future Fuhrer to the same fate and exposing England's prevailing social discordances.

Unlike postmodern comedy, which Lance Olsen defines as "generating alternate worlds," each of these novels is a comic fantasy that generates alternate visions of a world already known and all too well (61). To raise questions about the origins and destiny of that world, these novels use its familiar signifiers to defamiliarize it through satire, parody, and mockery. With varying results, these comedies investigate an England constructed in a language system whose arbitrary dualities keep its populace as divided and conflicted as the world at war. Like contemporary artists cited by Olsen, writers of the British homefront and those who remain haunted by it found comedy a way "of responding to a situation that [was], literally, fantastic"

(61). But differently, they deploy "the discontinuity and inherent otherness of the self, language, and the world" in order to affirm the authority of historical experience while questioning its meaning (Olsen 62).

> Most of war seems to consist of hanging about ... Let's at least hang about with our own friends. (*Flags* (284)

Evelyn Waugh's *Put Out More Flags* takes place at the surrealistic moment when war has been declared and invasion is imminent, but does not come. Later called "the phoney war," the period of waiting to beat back the enemy was at the time called the "Great Bore War," a pun that also assuaged the anxiety produced by government estimates of six hundred thousand casualties.[3] In 1939, when immediate invasion was anticipated, three million people left the cities for rural areas and small towns, half of them children (Calder 37). The cultural and psychological shock of leaving families and familiar urban neighborhoods was intensified by the unbridgable gulf between middle and upper-class hosts and their less advantaged guests. Within the year, most children returned to their homes, and when the Germans began bombing in earnest, most families felt that evacuation was a worse danger than keeping the children at home.

Despite the best intentions of billeting officials, the mostly poor urban children were often mismatched with hosts in small towns and rural villages, and the culture shock was mutual. Evelyn Waugh was not exempt from this experience. His intolerance of evacuees who "spend their leisure scattering waste paper round my gates" was perhaps heightened by frustration with "that odd, dead period" (*Diaries*, 8 September 1939).[4] Anxious to offer his "patriotic services," Waugh was ignored by wartime bureaucracy until he received a commission with the Royal Marines (*Diaries*, 6 September 1939). His dismay is transformed into a delicious revenge that forms the comic core of his novel.[5] Waugh noted in his preface to the 1966 Second Uniform Edition that this was "the only book I have written purely for pleasure."

Revenge is mutual in *Put Out More Flags*. Anarchic children from the London slums subvert the bureaucratic guardianship that marks a patriarchy's hegemony over public and private space. Only when an adolescent girl takes the role of commando does the home front become a battleground highlighting the impotence of government policy. In Waugh's domestic battle, however, women gain the high ground only long enough for men to gear up for victory. From the moment they descend on the manors of the gentry, the dreadful Connolly children, led by "ripely pubescent" Doris, wreak havoc on the staid village of Malfrey (*Flags* 97,98). Parodying the Dionysiac fates, the Connollies appear "as an act of God apparently without human agency; their names did not appear on any list; they carried no credentials; no one was responsible for them" (96). In a society shaped by continuity and decorum, the "leering, lowering, and drooling" Connollies are free agents, bound to no socially acceptable ethos or custom (98). Literally breaking up houses and evacuating on them, these evacuees respect no boundaries, expressing all bodily and psychic urges — proximity their only code of conduct. Using their body language as weapons, they become a fifth column of manners, and their invasion is so disruptive to the social order, even Whitehall is forced to take notice of this unaccountable internal danger.

Waugh mocks the misguided good intentions of a paternalistic government in its defeat by these children. The Connollies are defused not by official policing, but by the machinations of an anti-hero of the just war, Basil Seal. In his dedication to Randolph Churchill, Waugh contextualizes his comic anti-hero as suspended between an uneasy peace and a purposeful war. Basil Seal, like Waugh and his friends, is shaped by tensions between the failures of the first world war and hopes for the second:

> These characters are no longer contemporary in sympathy; they were forgotten even before the war; but they lived on delightfully in holes and corners and, like everyone else, they have been disturbed in their habits by the rough intrusion of current history.

For Basil, the false alarms of air raid sirens sound like a dirge to the world that made him. Now that Britain must pay the price for "bungled" peace terms, he is marginalized (15). Basil is a problem because his "individuality" exposes spurious connections between definitions of manhood and politics in his class (22). His mother's certainty that "There are just *men*" collapses differences between the heroic gestures of the last war and the unheroic self-interest of the reigning tories. These are men who rationalize their politics of appeasement by labeling Hitler's siege "the economic war of attrition" (19). Such doublespeak is used by the ruling class in this novel to justify either entertaining or rejecting von Ribbentrop and his compatriots only because they are "vulgar" (16). Before the war, this value system could also support Basil in his vocation as an elegant parasite, that is, an amusing if unscrupulous son and lover. Once war is declared, the failure to channel his energy into heroic service mocks and challenges the ethos of his class. Basil's loyalty to his own well-being questions the paradoxical politics of self-interest that made it possible for a ruling class to fight heroically in a war they feared would unseat them (18).

Waugh mocks the ruling class and yet supports it by gleefully making his anti-hero an agent provocateur in its "economic war." Basil outsmarts expectations not only of his family, but of the government, that he should become a hero. He usurps his sister's volunteer job as billeting officer and turns a profit by pawning the Connollies off on unsuspecting hosts who pay him to take them away. His elegant ploys, carried off with the sang-froid inherited from his class, are also, however, tantamount to a "system of push, appeasement, agitation and blackmail" (56). Unfortunately, this runs "parallel to Nazi diplomacy" and therefore mocks the ethos and politics designed to placate the "vulgar" enemy (56). At the same time that Basil's connivances foreground the vulgar profit motive, they parody the codes of heroism that win the "war for democracy" and the propaganda that unites a class-ridden England. He warns a potential victim: "It looks awfully bad if the rich seem to be shirking their responsibilities" (118). His self-interest reflects his class while making him its traitor; after all, his war work keeps peace on the home front by deploying tactics that put him in league with the Connollies. Unlike them, however, his origins account only too well for his character.

Basil's exploitation of the Connollies exposes British xenophobia about its own populace, but not as a flaw in the social fabric, for Waugh

> believe[d] that inequalities of wealth and position are inevitable and that it is therefore meaningless to discuss the advantages of their elimination; that men naturally arrange themselves in a system of classes; that such a system is necessary for any form of cooperative work, more particularly the work of keeping a nation together. (Appendix, "Conservative Manifesto" 160)

Waugh's relegation of Doris Connolly as "naturally" unequal supports the incestuous, exclusionary relations of the ruling class. Only Doris notices Basil's seductive, narcissistic relationship with his sister, but the perspective of this quintessential "other" is mocked. In contrast with the novel's derision of Doris's attraction to Basil, his affair with Angela Lyne is validated despite her "shuttered facade" and their "morbid" and "squalid" relationship (25,26). Whereas Doris's aggressive sexuality keeps her in her place in an underclass, Angela's dispassion and dependency on Basil ensures her redemption.[6] Their marriage at the end also coincides with his regeneration as a commando fighter on the European front. Though tempered by Angela's chastened optimism, this traditionally romantic ending is further supported by Basil's manipulation of another "other," one who has no access to plots which either mock or reaffirm heroism. Ambrose Silk, "cosmopolitan, Jewish pansy," is not only a foil for hypocritical British values, but a victim of Waugh's ambivalence towards them (87). As Heath notes, Waugh laments the anomalous aesthete who "represents the softness which in time of war is a liability" (154). Though portrayed with affection, Ambrose is also mocked for being a "degenerate" whose art cannot save him (87).[7] His fictionalized account of an aborted love affair with a young Nazi is transformed into farce when Basil convinces him to revise it because it sounds too much like propaganda. The result, in Basil's favor, is that the story is read as the "triumphant paean of Hitler youth" (246).

However sympathetically Ambrose's homosexual relationship is treated, he is duped by insisting on being an outsider, an identity that merges his sexuality with "his race": "the flair ... for comfort and for enviable possessions" (250). And though it is Basil's vanity which manipulates Ambrose, only the latter is forced into exile, while Basil moves into Ambrose's flat, not to mention his silk underwear. Basil's triumph and the novel's comedy have been bought at the expense of one of Hitler's real victims; the joke is on the Jew who's been targeted as a nazi. Basil's gambits, however, are sympathetic to an audience both supportive and critical of the very institutions he deflates. This novel, after all, debunks inflated myths of glory at a time when domestic suffering was being rationalized away. Taking nothing very seriously, Basil cannot be accused of malice of forethought, but only of outmaneuvering the very policies his readers endured. Ambrose, on the other hand, is also stigmatized for the link between his sexual, intellectual, and Jewish identity. Judy Little has observed that when the voices of two characters "collide and evaluate each other," the result may be the "ridicule of one of the voices and of the ideology it brings along" ("Humoring" 20). In the literature of World War II, such a gesture is paticularly problematic because of the objective correlative in the fate of actual victims. The effect here is not carnival, but the very vulgarity Waugh deplored. If, as Lance Olsen claims, "Laughter ... momentarily frees up a forbidden idea or emotion," this novel raises questions about the ethics of such release (21):

> thc decadence of the capital-owning classes — they're beyond all help.
> If you gave them DAS KAPITAL, they'd only tear it up and wrap their
> salmon in it. (Love 26)

Marghanita Laski's satire, *Love On the Supertax* assumes the form of a battle of class and sex whose sides are represented by a Mayfair debutante and an East End communist.[8] Embedded in their divisions of social status and ideology are intractible gender roles which like "stagnant pools of static water," defy any sense that war brings change (6). It is this sense of rigid stability that assures England of internal safety while being attacked by an external enemy. Despite and indeed within their mutual hostility is the promise that upper and lower classes enjoy their duty to their nation even as they conceive of it differently. The novel's conflicts between class, gender, and ideology are turned inside-out when a well-mannered working-class is feminized by its passivity while a debutante challenges the patriarchy. Forgoing patriotism for class loyalties, Laski's characters ultimately reinscribe the gender roles that sustain the armies of this internal war. With inequalities for both women and working-class, their "quarrel" is generative, in Bakhtin's terms because even as the status quo is maintained, their juxtaposed voices suggest "new linkages of ideas ... and changes in the arrangement" of class and gender in a society so committed to keeping itself intact (91). Unlike Waugh, whose satire serves his nostalgia for a traditional past, Laski satirizes such nostalgia.

Love On The Supertax takes place in the year it was written, reflecting Britain's feeling about her fifth year in the war. Like the war, people carry on relentlessly, but they are also weary and wary as victory is in sight, but the substance and shape of peace and the nation's future are not. Thus Laski's opening words reflect the people's mood, but with a twist that exposes divisions that would divide the nation even when the enemy was defeated: "This is not a story of that spring of 1944 as it came to strong vigorous citizens with an ample present and an assurance of the future, but of spring as it came to the needy and the dispirited, to the fallen and the dispossessed, spring as it came to Mayfair" (5). Laski mocks the gentry who mourn their decaying homes while denying that responsibility lies more with their own moral and social disintegration than with the blitz. The real homefront victims, silenced by their employers' obtuse and relentless complaints, is the working class who live "between the gaps, among the rubble and the destruction" and who unlike their down-at-the-heels betters, sustain the belief that England's "static" aristocracy is vibrant, not "stagnant" (6).

Laski's method of comic inversions involves her characters and plot in an intertextual play with her own literary history. The Second World War thus becomes the battleground for a class and sex war dramatized as a clash of Fieldingesque comedy and Richardsonian tragedy. Down on their luck in a nation whose class divisions are eroded by the war effort, an aristocratic family use their daughter Clarissa to revive their fortunes. Like the scions of the Harlowe family, Eustace, a ducal heir, is ultimately betrayed by self-interest, but not before he uses his sister to ingratiate himself with the entrepreneurial Sir Hubert Porkington. Like Richardson's heroine, this Clarissa escapes her family's clutches only long enough to highlight their self-delusions, but Laski forfeits tragedy so that her heroine can discover her own illusions and institute her own power. She rebels against her family by joining forces first with a young member of the British Communist Party and when she becomes disillusioned with him, joins up with Sir Hubert, who plots to restore power to the old order after the war by appropriating the methods of the rising middle classes.

The novel begins by marking the blissful fantasies of a discomforted gentry as the cause of their defeat: if only they had been born into "inherited poverty," they would be cozened by "dirt and disorder" and cheered by luxuries bought with "war-inflated wages" instead of being chilled and depressed by their crumbling and putrefying mansion (8,9). Ensnared in a system custom-made for self-importance, they see shortages of cash, domestic servants, and goods as an affront to their divine right of caste instead of an occasion to adjust to the historical emergency. They are caught between exercising their privilege by retreating into cold comfort or expressing loss of power by pawning themselves to the world of parvenus. Nowhere is this

dilemma more evident than in Clarissa's cooptation by either Sir Hubert's
capitalist finesse or Sid Barker's socialist passion.

Sir Hubert challenges Clarissa's class loyalties with threats about
"traitors," explaining that real victory will belong to "a nameless army" that
will "rebuild an Old England" based on the ideals of "Property, Privilege,
Domestic Servants," not to mention "the old School Tie [and] the Harley
Street Specialist" (*Love* 70, 71). Despite the rallying call to her class,
Clarissa's greater urge is to escape, and so like a radical Sleeping Beauty, she
awakens to the kiss of a communist worker who treats her to a world the
antithesis of her own. Like Alice through a tarnished and cracked looking-
glass, Clarissa accompanies Sid to workers' cafes that serve sacher tortes
rather than the "Boeuf haché à l'Americane — spam" offered by the Savoy,
whose dance floor is rejected for a chance to write political graffiti (*Love* 62).
But just as Alice is rebuffed by the white queen for lack of decorum, so
Clarissa is derogated for her tweeds and table manners, both of which testify
to her lack of politics, according to Sid's parents.

Clarissa's escape from sophistries on both sides lies in her challenges not
only to Hubert's politics, but Sid's. Shocked at Sid's rejection of the progressive Beveridge Plan when her parents also oppose it, she challenges him for
rejecting precisely what he has been lobbying for. But as she gains strength
from lampooning his argument that only "extreme social discontent" is "socially productive," he patronizes her (*Love* 75). What ultimately drives the
class-crossed lovers apart is Sid's orthodox view of marriage as sharing class
values and background, the very loyalties Clarissa defied in preferring him
to Sir Hubert. With a dual irony that allies communist and aristocrat, the Duke
and Duchess appreciate Sid's traditional class and gender values. His dream
of a classless society verifies the Duchess's hope that Clarissa has "a right to
her chance" of escaping the "sinking ships" of Mayfair with a working-class
man (*Love* 100).

Clarissa's rebellion returns her to her own class, but only after being
rejected for war work. Her interview demonstrates that class status is immutable in a world where every reversal is the mirror image of the original.
The welfare officer who interviews Clarissa is a renegade from the aristocracy
who argues that escape is impossible because "the other girls sneered at my
clothes, at my accent," and because of being "ashamed of your family, of
your mother's diamond bracelets and your father's Rolls Royce" (*Love* 107).
Her conclusion is all too reminiscent of those who try to rise from the lower
orders: "People of our sort can never really be accepted" (*Love* 107). Like
Richardson's heroine, the body of the duke's daughter is ultimately retrieved
by her class but in a way that destroys her will by coopting it. More subtle
than Lovelace, Sir Hubert eschews sexual violence for the seductive power
of upper-class elan; his political and sexual discourse seals Clarissa's fate
when he so confidently expropriates the rhetoric of his socialist rival: "the

Cause is and must always be of greater importance than the individual" (*Love* 117).

The "Cause" turns out to be "the establishment of the Second Capitalist International" (*L* 118). More universal than that of the workers', Sir Hubert's slogan, "Owners of all lands unite if you want to hang on to your gains," represents a plan that not only rivals that of the communists, but is its mirror image (*L* 119). Contrary to the communists' belief about a long war serving capitalist goals, Sir Hubert's "International" would end the war quickly, but with means and goals the opposite of the workers. Like the liberals, Sir Hubert recognizes good Germans as well as bad, but their value is reversed as it is the reactionaries who will be enlisted in his International. Among his goals is "the emasculation of the Socialists through continued coalition Government," but this will serve a "really reactionary peace whereby the German Army is firmly established as a bulkwark against Russian Imperialist expansion" (*L* 120,121). The most complex inversion defines Sir Hubert's propaganda campaign. His group will surreptitiously buy control of a liberal newspaper and influence its readers by planting reactionary ideas in cartoons, letters, and ads that promote consumerism, features that appeal to readers more than the editorial statements which will maintain the progressive slant of the paper. Swept away by such revolutionary gestures, Clarissa at the end is literally boxed into her betrothed's arms, "looking backwards, fearless and unafraid, into the Past" (*L* 127).

In contrast to Waugh, who despite many ironies, reifies female stereotypes, Laski ironizes those stereotypes. Waugh masculinizes the sexually voracious Doris and feminizes the artist/outsider, Ambrose Silk, in order to heroicize Basil Seal. Laski hyper-feminizes Clarissa to highlight how rigid class boundaries detour any possibility for redefining women's roles. What June Sochen observes about American culture is also true in these novels, that women are not encouraged, raised, or trained to express themselves aggressively (14). Feminist critics of comedy have invoked Bakhtin's theories of the dialogic style to argue that social hierarchies can be deconstructed by "juxtaposing the male voice of solemn formality and the female voice of buoyant hysteria" (Little, "Humoring" 20). Laski challenges hierarchies of both gender and class in such juxtapositions. The equally solemn voices of Sid and Sir Hubert deconstruct the authority claimed by the ideologies of both socialism and conservatism while Clarissa's equally rapturous infatuation with both men subverts the allure and power of masculinity as it is defined in their opposing social classes.

> Never in all my life, thought Adolf, under torture or interrogation, will
> I mention that I have been to this accursed city, visited this lunatic
> island. (*YA* 158)

Beryl Bainbridge's comedy derives from two interlocking perspectives.
Written thirty years after the Allies victory over Hitler, her retrospective view
registers like a cheer, mocking the origins of the Fuhrer whose own victory
endangered the world.[9] Playing against this threat is what Olsen calls a "post
modern fantasy" that "produces an 'ontological dialogue'" raising "questions
of existence: Which world is this? What is to be done in it? Which of my
selves is to do it?" (61). Bainbridge's humor derives from imagining such
questions for Adolf Hitler as he is forced into an epistemological and ontological nightmare over which he has no control. The man who controlled
the fate of untold millions is controlled in this novel by a writer who situates
him in the island that so defamiliarizes his grounding in reality, it is no wonder
that he will want to conquer it from the air and that it remains beyond his
grasp.

As the title suggests, the novel imagines the Fuhrer years before he has
recreated himself as world conquerer. Visiting an older half-brother, Alois, in
1912 Liverpool, young Adolf is a mess of a man. Wearing shapeless, tattered
clothing, with no vocation or sense of purpose or even self, he can either be
shaped or dissolve. Underlying this portrayal are questions about the construction of a masculinity that will be resolved as a diabolical masculinist war
machine. The obsessions that defined Hitler's plans for aryan supremacy are
explained as a postmodern fiction; they are shown to derive from a clash
between his unstable, inchoate selfhood and the chaos and inequities of a
nation that never doubts its superiority. However Hitler's perceptions and
experience evolved into *Mein Kampf*, the randomness of his experience in
England belies any causal relationship between his character or ideology and
social and political realities. The vision of dystopic Liverpool may prefigure
the depressed Germany of twenty years into the future, but the novel subverts
any causality between Hitler's plans for a German utopia and his fictional
odyssey. Likewise, the carefully wrought persona of the leader of the Third
Reich is deconstructed by dramatizing its genesis in the art of burlesque and
the artlessness of pure chance. His sister-in-law Bridget cannot help but laugh
at "that funny walk and his ridiculously shrunken jacket" which remind her
of "a pantomime" (*YA* 45). On the other hand, his brown shirt is created out
of a rag that happens to be the only salvagable cloth to dress him for a job
interview as a waiter.

Bainbridge's comedy defeats Hitler's demonic character by portraying him
as crazy with fear of the "other," "ranting incomprehensibly about vermin
and redskins and men with beards," each of whom is presented as projections
of his own nightmares about a mad stranger whose existence remains ques-

tionable (*YA* 33–34). With greater risk, she projects our worst nightmare onto his fears. His dehumanization and extermination of "the other" are shown to derive from his earlier abjection when his "entire life, with its small triumphs and disasters, its boundless hopes and aspirations" was reduced to a "puny dossier ... stamped with a row of figures that effectively obliterated his name" and produce the terror that he is "[n]o longer a man" (*YA* 32). His terror and ours part company as he recalls being "led to a large room and told to undress. The ceiling was covered in intricate lengths of piping and the floor was tiled. Here he bathed in public... He was now like a walking weather-vane — the least hint of dampness ... and an unmistakable reek of lysol instantly emanated from him" (*YA* 32–33).

Bainbridge runs the risk of trivializing the Holocaust with her comedy but instead creates an appropriate commemoration. The moral and mimetic dilemma of representing the Holocaust is resolved by the comic fantasy of inflicting upon Hitler the unresolvable fear of the dissolution he inflicts on others. By shaping him with a psychological model of history, Bainbridge refuses to reduce Hitler to either a cartoon or grotesque that would replicate his dehumanization of others. In this way, *Young Adolf* escapes a problematic of postmodern comedy in its self-reflexive meta-fantastic mode. Olsen explains this as occurring when historical and purely textual features of postmodern comedy clash. Apolitical obsessions with "surface-oriented concerns" clash with "modern mimetic holocaust fiction obsessed with the history of a people, the history of Western civilization, the practical morality of praxis, and the final connection between personal and collective tragedy" (134). Bringing young Adolf to England constructs a moral and political stance by valorizing and historicizing the inherent courage of all "others" in Hitler's path.

Young Adolf connects the character and fate of the self-styled superman with that of "others" he might have decimated were he not defeated. The people of Liverpool are portrayed as disconnected from the priorities and purposes of a distant heart of a nation. An unmanaged economic and social disaster, Liverpool appears ripe for either revolution or disintegration, options signified by a group of anarchists who are presented as opposing an indifferent government, but who bungle their own best intentions. These ineffectual political agents are feminized as they plot to rescue a group of impoverished children from the poor laws of the British government. The hundreds of anarchists, their leader "brandishing his shillelagh," lose to under a dozen civil servants armed only with lanterns because they are "caught off balance" between their maternal role and their "heroic pose" (*YA* 133). Identified with the women who yield their children, the dissidents are "the majority [who] walk like lambs to the slaughter" when "the minority act with enough authority" (*YA* 134).

This scene is both poignant and comic because it cannot escape the shadows of the Second World War which reverses the authority of English politicians, civil servants, and generals as well as that of the Fuhrer and grants it to the people. We can laugh at a young Adolf perplexed by the "nation of fearfully dangerous eccentrics" because when he grew up to actually besiege Britain (136),

> the people surged forward to fight their own war, forcing their masters into retreat, rejecting their nominal leaders and representatives and paying homage to leaders almost of their own imagination... The war was fought with the willing brains and hearts of the most vigorous elements in the community, the educated, the skilled, the bold, the active, the young, who worked more and more consciously towards a transformed post-war world. (Calder 18)[10]

Situating a fearful and paranoid young Adolf in 1912 Liverpool unmans his rhetoric in the shadows of his real defeat and provides the evidence that he is defeated by the combined belief of the English and himself in their national character. Despite its homage to fixed boundaries of gender and class and internal conflicts and confusions, the English defy coherent definition and rally to a united purpose.[11] In her retrospective fiction, Bainbridge cuts the monstrous Hitler down to size by demystifying him in the light of the cultural myths that propelled a heroic people to victory.[12]

In each of these three novels, comic forms decenter deeply entrenched ideologies of class and gender in a society that managed to sustain its traditional social infrastructures despite the dislocations of a second world war. The deep conservatism that rallied a disunited people to defend their nation is both undercut and maintained by these novels. They interrogate and critique the destructive implications of traditionalism through comedies that resonate with the literary traditions that underwrite it. Most radically, perhaps, they question our contemporary literary and political categories by dramatizing moments of historical crisis as defamiliarizing events.

NOTES

1. See Fussell, Tylee, Klein, and Cadogan and Craig.

2. Most British wartime comedy were memoirs and letters published serially in women's magazines to inspire endurance of homefront privations and fears of invasion. See, for example: E.M. Delafield, Joyce Dennys, and Dorothy Ratcliffe, as well as *Women in Wartime: The Role of Women's Magazines 1939–1945, The Home Front: The Best of Good Housekeeping 1939–1945*, and *Bombers & Mash*.

3. Angus Calder reports that estimates were based on miscalculations of bombing effects in 1917–18.

4. Letter dedicating *Put Out More Flags* to Randolph Churchill. Phillips interviewed Waugh's oldest daughter, who verified her father's irritation (44).

5. Heath notes Waugh's patriotic hopes and disenchantment.

6. McDonnell ascribes Waugh's treatment of Angela to his later explanation "that the character ran out of control" (84).

7. Carens sees the conflict between the aesthete and man of action as Waugh's own, but that Ambrose pays by being ridiculed. Phillips observes that though Ambrose is likeable, Brian Howard, Waugh's homosexual friend, was upset about the portrayal. Hopely claims that Waugh's "subtle" treatment "encourages" the reader's "delight," but then targets Ambrose's aestheticism as inappropriate at a time when Britain is retreating from Dunkirk and Norway (88).

8. Laski's novel is a send-up of Walter Greenwood's 1933 *Love on the Dole*, a pessimistic proletarian novel in which romance and social realism defeat each other when the heroine rebels against poverty through prostitution and the socialist hero dies in vain. In 1987, Laski discussed the relationship between genre, characters' social class, and popular and "art" novels: "Of the minor strands, the farcical has had a spasmodically continuing life ... notably written by men, and with, in England, usually an upper-class ambience" (21). Little analyzes Woolf's and Spark's "renegade comedy" as mocking traditional social norms by unresolved "imagery of revolt and inversion" (1). Laski's mockery and revolt continues into her heroine's reintegration into society.

9. Cadogan and Craig ascribe "retrospective fiction" of the War to Tom Harrisson's informational surveys of the period (272).

10. Johnson sees *Young Adolf* as retrospective prophesy: "when the real horror comes, it will have had its origin in the England of 1912" where the powerless cannot "defeat authority" (103).

11. Orwell explored national character in "The English People": "During the bad period of 1940 it became clear that in Britain national solidarity is stronger than class antagonism ... it is probable that the stolid behaviour of the British town populations under the bombing was partly due to the existence of the national 'persona' — that is, to their preconceived idea of themselves" (21).

12. Glendinning faults the novel for not solving the "mystery" of Hitler's character while *The Atlantic* praised its juxtaposition of humanity and pitilessness. Prescott found it offensive in the light of history. Rosenfeld argues that fictonalizing Hitler frees his actual deeds from historical consciousness, that Bainbridge's irony grants Hitler the pity he did not show "to the peoples of Europe" (32,33).

WORKS CITED

Bainbridge, Beryl. *Young Adolf*. London: Fontana, 1979.

Bakhtin, Mikhail. *Problems of Dostoevsky's Poetics*, ed. and trans. Caryl Emerson. Minneapolis: University Press Minnesota Press, 1984.

Braithwaite, Brain, Noelle Walsh, and Glyn Davies, eds. *The Home Front: The Best of Good Housekeeping 1939–1945*. London: Ebury, 1987.

Cadogan, Mary, and Patricia Craig. *Women and Children First: The Fiction of Two World Wars*. London: Gollancz, 1978.

Calder, Angus. *The People's War: Britain 1939–45*. London: Cape, 1986.

Carens, James F. *The Satiric Art of Evelyn Waugh*. Seattle: University of Washington Press, 1966.

Delafield, E.M. *The Provincial Lady in Wartime*. Chicago: Academy Chicago, 1986.

Dennys, Joyce. *Henrietta Sees It Through: More News from the Home Front 1942–1945*. London: Andre Deutsch, 1986.

Fussell, Paul. *The Great War and Modern Memory*. New York: Oxford University Press, 1975.

Garnett, Robert R. *From Grimes to Brideshead: The Early Novels of Evelyn Waugh*. Lewisburg: Bucknell University Press, 1990.

Glendinning, Victoria. "Hitler in England 1912." *The New York Times Book Review* (11 March 1979): 15.

Greenwood, Wlater. *Love on the Dole*. London: Cape, 1933.

Harrisson, Tom. "War Books." *Horizon* (December 1941): 416–437.

Heath, Jeffrey, *The Picturesque Prison: Evelyn Waugh and His Writing*. Montreal: Queen's University Press, 1982.

Hopley, Claire. "The Significance of Exhilaration and Silence in *Put Out More Flags*." *Modern Fiction Studies* 30 (Spring 1984): 83–93.

Johnson, Diane. "Young Adolf Goes to Beryl Bainbridge's England," in: *Terrorists and Novelists*. New York: Knopf, 1982, 97–104.

Kakutani, Michiko. "Noverlists Are News Again." *The New York Times Book Review* (14 August 1983): 22–23.

Klein, Holger. *The Second World War in Fiction*. Houndmills: Macmillan, 1983.

Laski, Marghanita. *Love on the Supertax*. London: Cresset, 1944.

_____. "Only a Thriller or Where Does the Mainstream FLow?" *PN Review* 14 (1987): 20–22.

Little, Judy. "Humoring the Sentence." *Women's Comic Visions*, 19–32.

_____. *Comedy and the Woman Writer: Woolf, Spark, and Feminism*. Lincoln: University of Nebraska Press, 1983.

McDonnell, Jacqueline. *Evelyn Waugh*. Houndmills: Macmillan, 1988.

Minns, Raynes. *Bombers & Mash: The Domestic Front 1939–1945*. London: Virago, 1980.

Olsen, Lance. Circus of the Mind in Motion: Postmodernism and the Comic Vision. Detroit: Wayne State University Press, 1990.

Orwell, George. "The English People," in: The Collected Essays, Journalism and Letters of George Orwell, Vol. 3: As I Please: 1943–1945. Eds. Sonia Orwell and Ian Angus. Harmondsworth: Penguin, 1987, 15–55.

Phillips, Gene D. Evelyn Waugh's Officers, Gentlemen, and Rogues: The Fact Behind His Fiction. Chicago: Nelson-Hall, 1975.

Prescott, P.S. "Review of Young Adolf." Newsweek (19 March 1979): 90.

Ratcliffe, Dorothy Una. Mrs. Buffey in Wartime. London: Nelson, 1942.

"Review: Young Adolf." Atlantic (March 1979): 133.

Rosenfeld, Alvin. Imagining Hitler. Bloomington: Indiana University Press, 1985.

Sheppard, Alice. "Social Cognition and Gender Roles." Women's Comic Visions, 33–56.

Sochen, June., ed. Women's Comic Visions. Detroit: Wayne State University Press, 1991.

Tylee, Claire. The Great War and Women's Consciousness. Houndmills: Macmillan, 1990.

Waller, Jane, and Michael Vaughan-Rees. Women in Wartime: The Role of Women's Magazines 1939–1945. London: Optima, 1986.

Waugh, Evelyn. Put Out More Flags. Boston: Little, Brown, 1955.

_____. "Preface." Put Out More Flags. Second Uniform Edition. London: Chapman and Hall, 1966.

_____. The Diaries of Evelyn Waugh. London: Weidenfeld and Nicolsen, 1976.

_____. The Letters of Evelyn Waugh, ed. Mark Amory. New Haven: Ticknor & Fields, 1980.

_____. Appendix: "Conservative Manifesto," in: The Essays, Articles and Reviews of Evelyn Waugh, ed. Donat Gallagher. Boston: Little, Brown, 1984, 161–162.

13

Alice Childress's
Like One of the Family:
Domestic and Undomesticated
Domestic Humor

ZITA Z. DRESNER

What has been termed "domestic" or "housewife" humor emerged in post-World War II America in response to the back-to-the-home antifeminist sentiment engendered by the political conservatism that considered any threat to the *status quo* a sign of creeping Communism. Characterized as a body of humorous writing in which the autobiographical *persona* of a harried, white middle-class housewife describes her frantic and often unsuccessful efforts to cope with life in the slow lane — in the family and home-centered environment of the new postwar suburbs — the domestic or housewife humor popularized by such writers as Shirley Jackson, Jean Kerr, and Erma Bombeck has been castigated by some feminist critics for encouraging women to accept the home as their proper place in the culture and for supporting the notion that domesticity (in the pre-modern sense of the word) offers women adequate outlets for satisfying their needs and utilizing their talents. My own work on domestic humor, however, has led me to a different conclusion — that this humor functions covertly in a number of ways to inspire rebelliousness.

This rebelliousness is the major link between the humor written from the perspective of the white suburban housewife and the humor of Alice Childress's *Like One of the Family: Conversations from a Domestic's Life*, published in 1956 after appearing as columns in Paul Robeson's *Freedom* and the *Baltimore Afro-American*. Developed in sixty-two "conversations" between Mildred, "a sassy, defiant day worker" (Harris DLB 67) and her friend, Marge, a neighbor and sister domestic worker whose voice is never actually heard, Childress presents Mildred as an undomesticated domestic — a black woman who refuses to feel degraded or to allow herself to be denigrated because her work is what others would consider menial, who fights for civil rights and for her own right to be respected. Because Mildred, as a single, black working-class woman doing domestic work in white women's homes, represents a very different *persona* from that of a white middle-class housewife doing domestic work for her own family in her own home, important differences exist between Childress's work and that of the white "domestic" writers, but the humor that emerges from these two angles of vision also has a number of provocative commonalities in spite of the different significations of the adjective "domestic" used to describe it.

Structurally, the books of housewife humor by Kerr and Bombeck, like Childress's book, reveal their origins as columns in newspapers and magazines. They consist of short chapters in the form of brief, informal disquisitions on a variety of topics pertaining mainly to the speaker's role as housewife or domestic worker but also to her place in the world. In Kerr's and Bombeck's collections, those pieces that do not directly deal with childcare, household duties, and the role of wife tend to concern the treatment of women in American popular culture — in particular, the way in which the media manipulate stereotyped and idealized feminine images to make women, in general, and housewives, in particular, feel inadequate, guilty, and docile. Self-help books, advertisements directed to women (especially for household products, cosmetics, and apparel), and self-proclaimed experts on such topics as women's psychology, husband-wife relationships, and child-rearing are especially taken to task and satirized by these humorists — not only for pomposity and falsity, but, more important, for undermining women's sense of autonomy and fostering an anxious dependence on "society's" measures of what constitutes self-worth. This humor, therefore, encourages readers to question society's model of woman's image and roles.

In Childress's book, the conversations that do not directly recount Mildred's experiences as a domestic worker often concern the graver social issues surrounding the racial struggles of the 1950s, especially anti-Negro violence and blatant discrimination. "Ridin' the Bus," for example, deals with the Jim Crow laws in the South; "What Does Africa Want?" discusses the burgeoning black liberation movements in Africa; and "A new Kind of Prayer" is a plea for the end of racial violence. In addition, Childress selects topics that enable her to satirize those of both races, black and white, who exhibit hypocrisy, ignorance, pretentiousness, or greed. "Ain't You Mad?" and "Northerners Can Be So Smug" are two examples of many pieces that illustrate this point. In "Ain't You Mad?" Mildred's white employer looks up from the newspaper and says to her, "Isn't it too bad about this girl tryin' to get into Alabama University?" He goes on to exclaim that "you people" must be angry and asks Mildred what "you people" are going to do about it (Childress 171). Mildred explodes at his hypocrisy, exclaiming "Ain't you mad?" and continuing, "If you ain't got the grace to stand up and fight for your own decency and good name, don't you dare ask me what *I'm* gonna do, because as long as *you* ain't *doin'* I ain't gonna tell you" (Childress 172). In "Northerners Can Be So Smug," Mildred takes her fellow black churchgoers to task for lambasting the South for its racial discrimination while "forgettin' that this land also has a North, East and West to it!" (Childress 178). "To hear us talk, anyone would think the North was some kind of promiseland come true," she continues, but "All is not sweetness and light just 'cause we're on the North side of the Mason and Dixon line!" (Childress 179).

In contrast to housewife humor, then, which is only gently rebellious and only covertly political, these examples of Childress's work support John O. Killens' assertion, in comparing Mildred to Langston Hughes' Jesse B. Simple, that "Childress's humor is in the profoundest tradition, i.e., humor with a political vengeance" (131). Both Kerr and Bombeck, as noted, when they stray from the arena of home, still focus on personal rather than political change. Their message to housewives is to resist the social and commercial pressures that try to control who they are and what they do within the parameters of woman's role rather than to reject that role altogether or to examine and/ or challenge the economic system and political institutions that define and reinforce that role. Childress, on the other hand, seeks to promote a revolution in both the white and black communities of America in order to achieve a transformation of American institutions that will finally provide Afro-Americans with the rights, opportunities, and protections they are owed. As Mildred avers in response to a disquisition on the beauty of "separate but equal," provided by her employer's redneck visitor from Alabama: "I got a message for you. We gonna change *all* these laws 'til there ain't a piece or a smithereen of Jim Crow left" (Childress 189).

What nevertheless connects these "political" pieces with the "softer" social commentary pieces of the housewife humorists is that Childress, like these writers, uses the devices of humor, especially incongruous contrasting images, to satirize those behaviors and precepts promoted by American culture to demean and oppress a particular group of people — blacks in her work, instead of housewives. Moreover, while Childress has been criticized for creating a character whose assertiveness is too unrealistic to emulate and the housewife humorists have been attacked for creating characters whose passivity engenders acceptance of a meaningless role, in fact both Mildred and the *personae* of housewife humor encourage their readers (albeit, in different ways) to change the stereotypes and defy the myths attached by the culture to the signs — i.e., housewife or domestic — used to define their being and, thereby, to enlarge the boundaries of the possible in their lives. Consequently, both Childress and the housewife humorists call for a reexamination of stereotypes and ideologies.

Another link between the work of housewife humorists and Childress is that the style of both is conversational and the tone, informal, presupposing a reader who is a peer of and who identifies with the speaker. The housewife *persona* speaks to the reader as she would to a friend, sharing her frustrations and anxieties, her subterfuges and strategies for coping. There is a confidentiality about her discourse that includes the reader in the "I," transforming the singular into the plural "we," and creating between the reader and writer the sense of intimacy that Joan Rivers sought to evoke with her opening stand-up line, "Can we talk here?" Similarly, Childress's *persona*, Mildred, opens each of her "conversations" with a greeting to her friend Marge — for example, "Marge ... Day's work is an education," or "Marge, ain't it strange how the two of us get along so well?" or "Hey, Marge, come on in and live a while" — thus setting up an intimate relaxed atmosphere for a talk between friends that also establishes a tone of confidentiality. Although the reader is never provided with any of Marge's actual words — the "conversations" are actually Mildred's monologues — the reader is nevertheless drawn actively into the narrative by, in a sense, becoming Marge, by filling in from her own experience what Marge would say and how Marge would react to Mildred's stories. In both Childress's work and that of the housewife humorists, then, the writers elicit from their readers a sympathetic ear for their speakers and a conspiratorial approval of their speaker's actions and thoughts, thus achieving one of the major social functions of humor: the fostering of group solidarity.

In creating a sense of solidarity, both Childress and writers like Kerr and Bombeck use humor to debunk myths about the group that the *persona* represents. In housewife humor, the popular image of the happy, successful homemaker — who cheerfully and expertly performs her myriad roles of cook, cleaner, laundress, interior decorator, chauffeur, nurturer, guidance counselor, tutor, hostess, caterer, moral support, mistress, model, mother, wife, etc. — is countermanded by the *persona* of the frustrated, imperfect housewife, who is depicted as the "real" norm. Kerr, for instance, despite her professional accomplishments, depicts her *persona* as being insecure, vulnerable to the opinions of others, and as incapable of keeping her household under control as her weight. Bombeck describes her *persona*'s house as a disaster area and her ego as under constant attack from family members, as well as the media. In identifying with a housewife whose life is an unending and often unsuccessful struggle to bring order out of chaos, the reader can exorcise her own anxieties about her own imperfections as a wife, mother, and homemaker. The housewife humorists also poke fun at the activities that form the housewife's daily existence and, by extension, at the notion that a woman's value as a human being is determined by the dedication and talent with which she executes these activities. By enabling the reader to recognize and laugh at the incongruity between the idealized image of the housewife promoted by the culture and the authentic individual represented by the humorous *persona*, the housewife humorist encourages her readers to believe that they can deviate from the standards for women imposed by the culture's ideology without suffering the consequences of this deviation: guilt and shame.

In a similar manner, Childress challenges basic assumptions that the dominant white culture has promoted about blacks, in general, and about black domestic workers, in particular. As Trudier Harris writes, "Instead of a handkerchief-headed black woman, or one bowing and scraping before her 'quality white folks,' Mildred stood up straight and tall" (Intro. xv). This defiance, expressed in the first "conversation" in the book, the title piece, sets the tone for the work as a whole and establishes Mildred as the negation of the Aunt Jemima stereotype, of the docile, domesticated domestic. By directly confronting her white employer in "a violation of the expected behavior of domestics" (Harris, Intro. xix), Mildred refutes the myth propounded by the employer that Mildred is "like one of the family." "I am *not* just like one of the family at all!" Mildred retorts, and she cites as evidence the facts that the family eats in the dining room and she eats in the kitchen, that she does not "just adore" the employer's children, who are spoiled, and that while the employer thinks it a compliment to say that the family doesn't think of her as a servant, she sure feels like a servant after all the work she performs (Childress 2). Moreover, Mildred ends not by apologizing for her outburst or by backing down in any way but, instead, by asking her employer for a raise which, she says, *will* make her feel that she is appreciated as much as the employer's words imply.

"Debunking myths and demanding change ... [is] a pattern of interaction throughout *Like One of the Family*" (Harris, Intro. xx). In "If You Want to Get Along with Me," for example, Mildred exposes the hypocrisy of the white employer who pretends to be her friend only to exploit her. In "The Pocketbook Game," where Childress pokes fun at a white employer's assumption that Mildred, being black, is by nature dishonest, and in "The Health Card," where Childress satirizes the employer's fear that Mildred, because she is black, may be diseased, Childress uses a standard device of "out-group" humor — role reversal — to empower Mildred while at the same time disempowering the white employer who would disparage her. By refusing to allow herself to be used or manipulated by her employers, by asserting her integrity and autonomy, Mildred provides a new, more "real" norm or model of black womanhood for other black women and working-class women to emulate while allowing Childress to poke fun at the prejudices and delusions of whites. By allowing Mildred "to violate all the requirements for silence and invisibility that were historically characteristic of domestics" (Harris, Intro. xx), and to do so without being fired from her jobs, Childress encourages her readers also to question the presumed authority of whites and to force white people to confront the stereotypes they have about black people. Thus, Childress, like the housewife humorists, suggests in her work that one can deviate from the norm of expected behavior (here, the behavior imposed by whites on blacks) without suffering the consequences of this deviation: physical injury or financial deprivation rather than guilt or shame.

While Childress's Mildred serves functions similar to those of the *personae* of Kerr and Bombeck, *Childress contrasts with the housewife* humorists in that, as John O. Killens has noted and as the remarks of Trudier Harris imply, she does not achieve her effects by directing laughter at, as well as with, her *persona*. Mildred never plays the fool, and her difference from the traditional "wise fool" character is that Childress' pointed humor arises not from the discrepancy between the character's overt foolishness and her covert wisdom but from the discrepancy between white people's foolish stereotypes about blacks and the reality Mildred embodies. This discrepancy continually creates the irony that reveals the whites as the fools. Mildred is also different from traditional Afro-American "tricksters" in that she assumes no mask herself. Rather, she continually repudiates the mask that whites attempt to impose on her and compels them to confront the incongruity between their preconceptions and the reality of who she is. In doing so, she turns the disparagement directed at her into laughter at the disparagers and acquires an aura of at least personal invulnerability.

While the *personae* of the housewife humorists may appear to be more vulnerable than Mildred to the opinions and preconceptions of others and are often depicted by their authors as ridiculous in their efforts to mold themselves into stereotyped images that are patently absurd, one way in which Kerr and Bombeck encourage their readers to be more autonomous is by giving the lie to the notion that homemaking is and should be a housewife's only *raison d'etre*. As a playwright, in addition to a homemaker, Kerr's autobiographical *persona* is shown in other venues than the home and as interested in pursuits other than keeping house. Bombeck's *persona* is also presented as having interests in activities other than housekeeping and childrearing, if she only had the time to pursue them, and as seeking not only to develop her own abilities while taking care of the family but also to prepare for life after the children are on their own. Moreover, Bombeck's stated purpose for writing her first book was to counter the "bum rap" given housewives in the media — the image of insular, trivial people properly obsessed with cleaning products, deodorants, and appliances.

Childress, too, challenges the stereotype of women, in general, and black women — especially working-class black women — in particular, as devoid of intellectual aspirations and social interests. Not only does Childress characterize Mildred as self-assertive and willing to risk suffering the potential economic consequences of her assertive behavior — perhaps, in part, because she is single and without children to support — but Childress also challenges the stereotype of the "dumb" domestic by having Mildred discuss "a range of topics that others might judge antithetical to a domestic's intellectual ken" and "that others would probably prefer to have her overlook" (Harris, Intro. xvii). Childress represents Mildred as someone who is concerned about the social and economic discrimination faced by blacks, both in America and overseas, and who is also active in organizations that promote civil rights, equal opportunity for blacks, and an awareness of and pride in black history and black achievement. In various conversations, she defends her nephew's political activism for civil rights ("Bubba"), demands respect for domestic work ("All About My Job"), criticizes black preachers for discouraging rather than inspiring their congregations ("I Go to Church"), defends Paul Robeson against the attacks of the white press as embodied in the character of a white employer ("Story Tellin' Time"), laments the stereotypical portrayals of blacks in movies and plays ("About Those Colored Movies"), and argues for a union for domestic workers ("We Need a Union Too"). Finally, Childress uses the topics of some "conversations" to promote a simple but humanistic philosophy of life that includes respect for age, appreciation of human labor, abhorrence of war and violence of any kind, contempt for pretense and snobbery, and appreciation for the good things that life can offer: a fine meal, a beautiful sunset, a kind gesture, a moment of intimacy with friends or family. The conscience and concern displayed by Mildred often contrast with the insensitivity and condescension of her white employers, but these same qualities also allow her to express appreciation for a particular white employer's respect and friendship ("I Liked Workin' at that Place") or for a group of white South African women who protested for Negro rights ("Somehow I'd Like to Thank Them").

In challenging the stereotypes of housewives and domestics as women with no other interests, skills, or concerns but those connected to activities that serve their own or their employer's households, housewife humorists and Childress both endow their speakers with dreams and aspirations to do something and be something more than what their present circumstances prescribe. Thus, Kerr presents her narrative self as someone who seeks a way to balance a playwriting career with her homemaking responsibilities, who wants to integrate the pleasures of family life, however chaotic, with the excitement of the theatre, however nerve-wracking, without shortchanging either. While

Bombeck tends to generalize the desire to be something more than just a household drudge, she attributes to housewives as a group an after-the-children-are-grown wish to utilize in the world whatever talents they believe they have had to subordinate to homemaking.

Childress's Mildred also has dreams of being something other than a domestic. In "I Wish I Was a Poet," she prefaces her narration of an experience that moved her by telling Marge that she wishes she were a poet not because she wants to be famous but because "sometimes there are poetry things that I see and I'd like to tell people about them in a poetry way; only I don't know how, and when I tell it, it's just a plain flat story" (Childress 102). Of course, Mildred, by virtue of her story-telling ability, displays throughout the book — especially in pieces like "Listen for the Music," "Hands," "Pretty Sights and Good Feelin's," and "All About Miss Tubman" — an artistic sensibility that enables her to manipulate language and create images that evoke from her listeners (employers, Marge, friends, children, etc.), as well as from the reader, the responses she desires. As Trudier Harris writes, "Creation begins with observation, and Mildred has the potential to see beyond the obvious, to look beneath the surface of things." "The interest … in making things comes unexpectedly to life," Harris continues, "is what defines Mildred as a budding artist. Her imagination has not been dulled by housework, and … for those who would question a maid becoming an artist [the passage from 'Hands' describing the power and beauty of things made by laboring hands] suffices to combat such objections. A short way from the statement that everyone who works is a servant is also the suggestion … that any servant can become an artist" ("'I Wish I Was A Poet': The Character as Artist in Alice Childress's *Like One of the Family*," 25). As the housewife humorists, by their own example, demonstrate to their readers that women need not be condemned by their decision to marry and have children to a life of unremitting subordination of their own needs and dreams to the demands of homemaking, Childress demonstrates through Mildred that the necessity of doing domestic work, or any other labor, to survive economically need not destroy an individual's creativity or prevent her from finding other outlets for artistic expression.

As artists themselves, of course, the housewife humorists and Childress have different interconnections with American literary and humor traditions and different "roots." As Harris develops in her analyses of Childress in *From Mammies to Militants* and other articles, Mildred's language is tied to traditional Afro-American written and oral forms, as well as to Afro-American conceptions of art and the artist. In contrast, housewife humor is connected to a body of predominantly white women's humor in America, which defines itself within and against a tradition of white male humor. Just as Kerr and Bombeck, in their *personae*, reproduce the tone and idiom of the white middle class and adapt to their purposes techniques that have characterized American humor since the 19th century, Childress's Mildred represents the cadences and idiom of Afro-American speech, and Mildred's "conversations" reflect basic patterns of ethnic humor that involve defiance and deflation of the oppressor through linguistic deconstructions and comic reversal. In addition, while the emphasis in housewife humor is on the liberation of the individual from the constraints of the nuclear family, the focus in Childress's work is on the liberation of the Afro-American community from the political, social, and economic oppression imposed by the dominant culture.

While recognizing the significant differences between the nature, functions, and impact of the humor created by Childress and by the housewife humorists, this paper, in focusing on the intersections between the works of these writers, seeks not only to enlarge our notion of "domestic" humor but also to serve one of Childress's own purposes. In a piece called "In the Laundry Room," Mildred pushes a white houseworker to overcome her racial prejudices by pointing out to her that what they have in common (their work, their class, their status, and, consequently, their problems and concerns) transcends racial differences and provides a basis for mutual support. By examining some of the similarities between Childress and the white purveyors of "domestic humor," by focusing on what unites as well as separates them, we can locate areas of common concern in our own lives and perhaps discover ways in which we can form alliances and utilize the devices of humor to fight our common prejudices and oppressions.

WORKS CITED

Childress, Alice. *Like One of the Family*. Boston: Beacon, 1986.

Dresner, Zita Z. "Domestic Comic Writers," in: *Women's Comic Visions*, ed. June Sochen. Detroit: Wayne State University Press, 1991, 93–114.

Harris, Trudier. "Introduction" to *Like One of Family* by Alice Childress. Boston: Beacon, 1986, xi–xxxiii.

_____. *From Mammies to Militants*. Philadelphia: Temple University Press, 1982, 3–33.

_____. "'I Wish I Was a Poet': The Character as Artist in Alice Childress's *Like One of the Family*." *Black American Literature Forum* 14/1 (Spring 1980): 24–30,

Killens, John O. "The Literary Genius of Alice Childress," in: *Black Women Writers*, ed. Mari Evans. New York: Doubleday, 1983, 129–33.

14

Funny, Isn't It?: Testing the Boundaries of Gender and Genre in Women's Detective Fiction

GLORIA A. BIAMONTE

LAUGHTER AMONG THE CORPSES

> My theory of detection resembles Julia Child's approach to cooking: Grab a lot of ingredients from the shelves, put them in a pot and stir, and see what happens.
>
> V.I. Warshawski, *Killing Orders*

Surviving the numerous attempts on her life and the nearly ritual demolition of her apartment and car, private investigator V.I. Warshawski, better known as Vic to those close to her, is a bit more careful about her detecting than her glibly stated theory might suggest. With intelligence, toughness, tenderness, and, yes, a sense of humor, V.I. confronts corruption in the emotionally charged world of urban Chicago — a confrontation that brings her face to face with insurance companies, the medical establishment, the Catholic Church, building contractors, and, of course, local politicians. But V.I.'s success is often made sweeter because of the ongoing resistance she meets from the Chicago police, particularly her deceased parents' old friend,

Lieutenant Bobby Mallory. Though she finds herself in brutal and terrifying situations — bound in a ratty blanket that is floundering in a chemical-infested swamp (*Blood Shot* 1988); dragging her unconscious aunt through a burning building while her own eyes glaze over from the pain of a battered skull (*Burn Marks* 1990); experiencing the emotional devastation triggered by her growing awareness that a local hospital is complicit in the deaths of a young mother and her new-born child (*Bitter Medicine* 1987) — V.I. injects humor into these most gruesome of experiences with her comic perspective and her poignant wisecracking.

V.I.'s unflagging and penetrating wit does not, however, solely evoke the nervous laughter associated with black humor — the sort of humor that might seem most appropriate to the horrors she confronts:

> What I wanted was to decamp for some remote corner of the globe where human misery didn't take such naked forms. Lacking funds for that, I could retire to my bed for a month. But then my mortgage bill would come and go without payment and eventually the bank would kick me out and then I'd have some naked misery of my own, sitting in front of my building with a bottle of Ripple to keep it all out of my head. (*Burn Marks* 121)

Neither are her, at times, scathing comments primarily noted for their sarcasm: "'I've been trying to get you to tell me a few things for the last two weeks and you've been acting as though English was your second language and you weren't too fluent in it'" (*Blood Shot* 263). Nor are they simple attempts at comic relief, both for herself and the others involved in the grim brutalities of murder, fraud, deception, and poverty — as evidenced by V.I.'s flippant response when questioned about her role in an old man's suicide: "'Thanks, Max. I appreciate the compliment. Most days I don't feel that powerful'" (*Blood Shot* 188). Rather, V.I.'s wit, while providing the distancing essential to these forms of humor, accomplishes a wider range of purposes, often acting as a form of social critique and serving as a vehicle for genre renovation.

Disguised as a monk in her attempt to understand the connection between Corpus Christi and the Ajax Insurance Company, V.I. tries to convince herself that she is unafraid:

> Of course, a hard-boiled detective is never scared. So what I was feeling couldn't be fear. Perhaps nervous excitement at the threats in store for me. Even so, when Roger asked me, tentatively, if I wanted to go back to the Hancock with him, I assented without hesitation. (*Killing Orders* 215)

Self-mocking as these comments may seem, their sole purpose is not to elicit the reader's sympathy for this likeable detective's vulnerability. The comments verge on parody as they become genre-mocking, placing V.I. in a tradition, that of the hard-boiled detective, and then removing her from it by her ready assent to abscond with Roger. As Lizabeth Paravisini and Carlos Yorio suggest in their discussion of the duality of parodic detective fiction, parody offers

> two texts within one: the parody itself and the parodied or target text: both present within the new text in a dialogical relationship ... in parody we find two languages crossed with each other, two styles, two linguistic points of view — in short two speaking subjects. (182)

By creating a dialogue between the traditionally perceived hard-boiled detective and the newly evolving, socially conscious professional, Sara Paretsky, V.I.'s creator, glances back while moving forward and, in so doing, transforms the detective figure — a transformation that her humor subtly encourages.

However, the hard-boiled detective is not the only aspect of the genre that undergoes change in V.I.'s world — change again demarcated by humor. Sara Paretsky admits that she is no Agatha Christie, nor does V.I. bear any resemblance to Sherlock Holmes. In trying to determine if a crime of passion is the motivating force behind Nancy Cleghorn's murder, V.I. ponders the facts: "Who waits two years to revenge himself on love gone sour? Outside Agatha Christie, that is" (*Blood Shot* 113). And while searching for clues through the toxic swamp surrounding Dead Stick Pond, V.I. decides

> [t]here was nothing to be seen here, no trace of life or death. I headed slowly back down the path, stopping every few feet to inspect the bushes and grasses. It was a futile gesture. Sherlock Holmes would no doubt have spotted the telltale cigarette butt, the gravel from another county that didn't belong here, the fragment of a missing envelope. All I saw was the endless array of bottles, potato-chip bags, old shoes, coats, proving that Nancy was only one of many discarded bundles in the swamp. (*Blood Shot* 117)

Even though there are times when V.I. wishes for a "selfless Bunter" to "suffer hideous hardships" for her, she does not hope to emulate Peter Wimsey; rather, she would like to resemble Kinsey Milhone, a nod of sisterhood to Sue Grafton's contemporary private investigator:

> To entertain myself while I waited I tried to calculate the expenses I'd incurred since starting to look for Caroline Dijak's old man. I've always been a little jealous of Kinsey Milhone's immaculate record-keeping; I didn't have receipts for meals or gas. Certainly not for cleaning up the Magli pumps, which was going to run close to thirty dollars. (*Blood Shot* 342, 159)

Here the humor not only links V.I. to an alternate, evolving tradition of female investigators, but also removes her from the refined, aristocratic world of

Dorothy L. Sayer's Wimsey, and places her in the middle-class world of
dry-cleaning and budget-keeping.

V.I.'s self-conscious participation in the rejuvenated genre of detective
fiction is only one of the areas highlighted by her penetrating wit. Her
investigations take her throughout Chicago and its bordering neighborhoods
— a charged landscape that cannot evade the transformative power of her
observant gaze and reflections:

> The decimation of Lebanon was showing up in Chicago as a series of
> restaurants and little shops, just as the destruction of Vietnam had been
> visible here a decade earlier. If you never read the news but ate out a lot
> you should be able to tell who was getting beaten up around the world.
> (*Killing Orders* 36)

First seeming funny, V.I.'s unusual idea of gleaning information on imperialist
activity simply by choosing to dine out frequently provokes serious reflection
on one of the less-touted reasons for America's growing multi-ethnic, multi-
racial population. Clever but grimly humorous in her observations, V.I. suggests a connection between the shifting face of America's cultural diversity
and the oppression experienced by Third World people across the globe.

An example from Paretsky's sixth novel, *Burn Marks* (1990), demonstrates
the range of potentially rich terrain that humor can explore. While attempting
to visit one of her Aunt Elena's hospitalized friends, V.I. receives "help" from
Lotty's assistant who gets her into the hospital as a social worker:

> I made a face as I thanked her. Social worker! It was an apt description
> of how I'd spent my time since Elena showed up at my door last week.
> Maybe it was time for me to turn Republican and copy Nancy Reagan.
> From now on when alcoholic or addicted pregnant strays showed up at
> my door, I would just say no. (*Burn Marks* 71)

Even imagining V.I. and Nancy Reagan together in the same room can evoke
laughter without considering the absurdity of V.I. using Mrs. Reagan as a
more-than-curious role model. But Paretsky takes the amusement caused by
this bizarre juxtaposition of dissimilar women one step further by having V.I.
incorporate Mrs. Reagan's drug prevention slogan "Just say No" into her
thoughts. V.I.'s integrity would balk at the idea of just saying no to someone
approaching her for help, just as her mind, in calmer moments, would be
repulsed by the thought of turning Republican. Highlighting the nearly complete ineffectiveness of the "Just Say No" campaign to halt drug usage among
young people, the serious edge to V.I.'s "humorous" thoughts cannot go
unnoticed, for even V.I. recognizes that she is a wit, "but with good judgment"
(*Burn Marks* 140).

Clearly, Paretsky's humor functions on multiple levels, *from* the distancing
of comic relief *to* the rejuvenation of parodied genre conventions *to* the highly

politicized nature of her penetrating social commentary *to* the provocative self-examination of her biting sarcasm. The dialogue between "two speaking selves" created by parody evolves into several dialogues for Paretsky — dialogues not only between the traditionally perceived hard-boiled detective and the alternate, evolving tradition of female investigators, but also between V.I.'s feminist consciousness and the destructive and often morally bankrupt authority of monolithic institutions, and, finally, between V.I. and her continually evolving self. Working outward as social critique and inward as analytic tool, humor allows V.I. to enter into conversation with society and with herself, creating the multiple dialogues which function as "emancipatory strategies" in Paretsky's fiction.[1]

Sara Paretsky is not, of course, the first writer of detective fiction to employ humor. From the cheerful ineptitude of Doyle's Watson to the bumbling self-effacement of Christie's Miss Marple to the wisecracking indifference of Hammett's Spade to the literary witticisms of Cross's Kate Fansler, humor has found a central place in a fiction marked by death, violence, and unimaginable atrocities.[2] Even one of the very earliest female detectives, Anna Katharine Green's Miss Butterworth, a precursor of Christie's Miss Marple, uses her seemingly self-effacing comments to poke fun at her adventurous nature while simultaneously stressing the value of her observations. The double-edged nature of much of this humor reflects the duality that characterizes detective fiction. Moving back into the past to *uncover* a crime while moving stealthily into the future to *recreate* the story of its detection, writers of detective fiction must perform a careful balancing act — a delicate juggling of mystification and enlightenment. Describing this dual movement of detective fiction, Dennis Porter explores how in

> the process of telling one tale a classic detective story uncovers another. It purports to narrate the course of an investigation, but the "open" story of the investigation gradually unravels the "hidden" story of the crime. In other words, the initial crime on which the tale of detection is predicated is an end as well as a beginning. It concludes the 'hidden' story of the events leading up to itself at the same time that it initiates the story of the process of detection. (29)

Thus, detective fiction provides two stories: one absent but real, the other present but relatively insignificant.

Humor, too, often tells two tales, and it is the double-edged quality of humor that Emily Toth and Nancy A. Walker address in their discussions of American women's tradition of humorous writing, a tradition that dates back to the poetry of Anne Bradstreet. Though detective fiction does not, of course, belong squarely within the definition of humorous fiction, the elements of humor used by many of the female practitioners of the genre share several of the attributes delineated by Toth and Walker. Walker emphasizes the point that "to be a woman and a humorist is to confront and subvert the very power that keeps women powerless" (9). One way in which women humorists have confronted "this delicate balance between power and powerlessness" is by employing familiar stereotypes of women for the purpose of mocking those stereotypes (9). In doing so, the texts function, as do the texts of detective fiction, on two levels, "one that appears to endorse popular stereotypes of women, and another that points to the origins of these stereotypes in a culture that defines women in terms of their relationships with men" (Walker 12). With the double text of humor challenging cultural assumptions, women's humor is often used subversively to lay bare the forces of the dominant culture — the forces that have led to women's marginalization. Emily Toth describes this dual nature of women's humor as "a weapon, and as communion" (212). In this sense, humor acts to unite women against the social roles that imprison them.

Taking the discussion further is Judy Little's exploration of what she calls "renegade comedy," comedy which "mocks the deepest possible norms," comedy which

> implies, or perhaps even advocates, a permanently inverted world, a radical reordering of social structures, a real rather than temporary and merely playful redefinition of sex identity, a relentless mocking of truths otherwise taken to be self-evident or even sacred. (2, 3)

Implicitly, agreeing with Walker's characterization of women's humor as "seek[ing] to correct a cultural imbalance" by emphasizing the "disparity between the 'official' conduct of women's lives and their 'unofficial' response to that conduct," Little attempts to understand the origin of women's humorous impulse:

> We can expect ... especially in a time of social change, that the work of writers who perceive themselves as 'outsiders,' as persons assigned to the threshold of a world that is not theirs, will manifest the distinctive features of inversion, mocked hierarchies, communal festivity, and redefinition of sex identity. If the work of such writers is comic, it will be comedy that mocks the norm radically and perhaps generates hints and symbols of new myths. (6)

Most interesting is Little's description of these women as on "the threshold," a phrase that echoes William Stowe's description of detective fiction as "a literature of crisis, of borders, of the extreme" ("Popular" 661). Consciously or unconsciously, detective fiction attempts to render several fluctuating borders — borders where the pursuit of the criminal becomes a pursuit of self; where the numerous authorized and unauthorized "readings" of the absent story overlap, contradict, or create glaring gaps; where the text's ambiguity allows for the subversive speculations of author, detective, and reader. What Little proposes is that those on "the threshold" — in her case, women — create humor that extends beyond the targeting of the far-from-perfect rules of their culture to the creation of a new and different order. Laughter, evoked by blatant attack or subtle ridicule, threatens to become an act of creation. Humor that tests boundaries can establish them as well and, in so doing, create dis-ease in its listener/reader/watcher by altering the very space that it brings to its audience's attention.

The humor of those on "the threshold" serves to heighten this dis-ease and, when employed in detective fiction, a genre already well-equipped to render fluctuating boundaries, produces a richness only suggested in the opening discussion of Sara Paretsky's fiction. Not only does detective fiction infused with humor contain the abundant possibilities of the genre's double storyline and the pregnant uncertainty of determining who is pursuing whom, but the humorous vision adds to this potential "the ability to hold two contradictory realities in suspension simultaneously — to perform a mental balancing act that superimposes a comic version of life on the observable 'facts'" (Walker 82). Clearly, exploring humor within detective fiction creates the possibility of multilayered readings — readings where the inherent doubleness of the genre is repeatedly magnified by the gaze from "the threshold," sometimes "distorted" by the fun-house mirror of humor, and always made rich by an attentiveness to the female signature.

CLAIMING A SPACE OF HER OWN

V.I. Warshawski's nod of sisterhood to Kinsey Milhone is a gesture worth investigating, for among those whom this nod could acknowledge are the early female investigators of Mary Roberts Rinehart. Rinehart began writing detective fiction when the genre was fully established as a fictional form — so established that Mark Twain was able to parody its conventions in his 1902 tale "A Double-Barrelled Detective Story." Employing the humor that her biographer Jan Cohn describes as the "trademark" of all her mysteries, Rinehart's first novel in book form, The Circular Staircase (1908), launched her popular success (Cohn 36).[3] Rinehart, in fact, intended The Circular Staircase to be "a semi-satire on the usual pompous self-important crime story" (My Story 92). Demonstrating her belief in the rejuvenating power of humor, Rinehart hoped that The Circular Staircase would help "the crime story to grow up" — a growing up that would shift the emphasis away from the puzzling clues to "people and their motivations" (qtd. in Breit 228). But Rinehart goes further than she hoped. In The Circular Staircase, Rinehart succeeds in using her humor to interrupt the text, create a newly defined narrative space, and initiate a dialogue about cultural assumptions concerning gender. Most important among Rinehart's contributions to the genre is her creation of amateur detective, Rachel Innes, a middle-aged, unmarried woman, whose proclivity toward involvement in mysterious events makes her an obvious descendant of Anna Katharine Green's Amelia Butterworth.[4]

Rachel Innes steps into the literary world with a "let's set the record straight" tone — a tone that immediately places her story in dialogue with the "garbled and incomplete" newspaper accounts surrounding the Sunnyside mysteries (6). But the confrontational mode that could easily erupt from Rachel's annoyance at her exclusion from the public record is quickly lost in the detached, almost fairy-tale like opening of her story:

> This is the story of how a middle-aged spinster lost her mind, deserted her domestic gods in the city, took a furnished house for the summer out of town, and found herself involved in one of those mysterious crimes that keep our newspapers and detective agencies happy and prosperous. (5)

Significantly, Rachel's adventures begin with a move — a move which this "objective" opening voice deems somewhat insane for it involves the desertion of domesticity and the involvement in crimes that, strangely enough, result in happiness and prosperity for some. That Rachel Innes intends ridicule in these lines grows clear as she quickly abandons this detached mode of recitation and opens the second paragraph with the urgency of her individual voice: "And then the madness seized me" (5). Rachel's abrupt switch from the third person to the first hints at the two realms of experience that simultaneously inform her narrative — two realms which include not only the public demeanor and the private response, but, important to this discussion, the dialogue between the anticipated and the actual, between the observable "facts" and Rachel's comic vision of them.

But Rachel's actual feelings about her summer "vacation" at the rented Sunnyside estate remain initially hidden within the sarcastic tone of her narrative. Though she informs us of her luck in surviving the summer months and of her repeated threats to return to Sunnyside when her nerve-frayed servant Liddy "begins to go around with a lump in her throat," we do not immediately grasp the extent to which humor or seriousness dominates Rachel's tone (6). Even Rachel's emphasis on her duty "to tell what [she] knows" and her ease with the narrative convention of re-telling the tale is somewhat undermined by the caricature-like portraits she paints of herself and her rather untraditional family (6).

At the center of this "family" is Rachel's comic "marriage" to her servant Liddy — a relationship held together by an incessant bickering that results in Liddy's numerous threats to leave and Rachel's equally numerous threats to discharge her.[5] Like Rachel, Liddy is never at a loss for words and clearly does not hesitate to state her mind, even, or perhaps especially, when she knows her pointed comments will irritate Rachel. Liddy is only too happy to "oracularly" inform Rachel that she has been tricked into leaving the room by two young lovers — something Rachel refuses to believe:

> 'Nonsense!' I said brusquely. 'I must have known enough to leave them. It's a long time since you and I were in love, Liddy, and I suppose we forget.'
> Liddy sniffed.
> 'No man ever made a fool of me,' she replied virtuously.
> 'Well, something did,' I retorted. (156)

Marking the characteristic note of their relationship, Rachel and Liddy's verbal jostling provides the unrelenting background "music" of the narrative. But even though Liddy informs Rachel that people who move to strange houses with unknown servants "needn't be surprised if they wake up some morning and find their throats cut," and Rachel instructs Liddy that the liquid diet she required after Rachel applied carbolic acid to her toothache provided "a splendid rest for her stomach," these two women cannot "get along for an hour without the other" (59, 235, 189). Transgressing the anticipated boundary between employer and employee, between the wealthy and the working class, Rachel and Liddy form an unusual alliance, using their sarcastic humor to create a dialogue where none might exist.

Completing this family group are Rachel's nephew and niece, Halsey and Gertrude, whom she has cared for since her brother died — an undertaking that suggests an ableness at assuming maternal responsibilities. However, we are once again left to question our expectation of this ableness, as we learn that with motherhood, as she says, "thrust" upon her, Rachel sends her niece and nephew away to good schools, making her responsibility "chiefly postal" (6). Summers are then transformed into the time of a rather unique spring cleaning — a time when Rachel takes her "foster motherhood out of its nine months' retirement in camphor" (6, 7). This unorthodox description of motherhood, even "foster motherhood," causes us, at first, to doubt the genuine warmth Rachel feels toward her adopted children, but soon it becomes obvious that rather than suggesting ambivalent feelings about Halsey and Gertrude, Rachel desires to amuse her listeners with the seductive allure of her increasingly communal humor and, in so doing, gain an audience for her alternative tale of the summer's events — a tale that transforms already circulated texts while it emerges as a vehicle for Rachel's self-definition.

Creation of her amusing persona is essential to Rachel's skillful development of a relationship with her readers. Added to her bickerings with her maid — "Liddy's nerves are gone, she said, since that awful summer, but she has enough left, goodness knows!" — and her awareness of the shortcomings of her "foster motherhood" are Rachel's funny observations about herself as well as human nature generally (6). Driving with Halsey has been an education for Rachel: "I learned how to keep my eyes off the speedometer, and, after a time, never to stop to look at the dogs one has run down. People are apt to be unpleasant about their dogs" (7). Hardly expressing appropriate empathy over the possible injury and loss of loved pets, Rachel shields her fear of Halsey's excessive speed with her somewhat grim humor while simultaneously tearing down the expectations of her increasingly amused readers. Exceeding the goal of amusement, Rachel's skillfully woven narrative gradually but purposefully erodes our expectations of her, for later in the narrative Rachel's actions contradict these earlier words when we find her standing on the roof yelling at the newspaper boy, who has just thrown a rock at her adored cat Beulah. Rachel's seeming disassociation from herself is funny in this rather harmless instance. But this clever disassociation transforms the humor of this situation into a disembodied voice, an "unauthorized" discourse that whispers along the margins of the text, circulates between the previously circulated newspaper accounts of the summer's events, and slowly reconstitutes its speaking self and, consequently, her listeners/readers' perceptions of her.

Unlike Paretsky's contemporary professional detective, Rachel needs humor to protect and to create her evolving self. In a sense, humor becomes her expanding cocoon, enabling her to create a larger space within which to survive as a woman. V.I., possessing a more fully evolved sense of herself and a developed social consciousness, employs humor quite differently, using it to cut through the protective veneer that encases corrupt social and political institutions. As much a tool as a weapon, V.I.'s humor allows her to critique her progressively destructive society and to evaluate her own potential for changing this threatening environment. V.I.'s humor moves her both outward and inward; Rachel's, however, moves her, understandably, in one direction, for Rachel still needs to create livable parameters within which to thrive — only then will she be able to determine upon what ground to exercise her newly discovered self.

As Rachel becomes the target of her own mocking thoughts, the seemingly unreflective or disembodied nature of her words becomes suspect, transforming our once spontaneous smiles into more doubtful expressions of humor. Continually thrown off guard, unable to decide whether Rachel is the unconscious or conscious target of her mocking thoughts, we begin to wonder if this "D.A.R." and "Colonial Dame" is not shrewdly nodding at our, by now, uneasy laughter (50). Though Rachel suggests that she may have lost her head — "Never after that night did I put my head on my pillow with any assurance how long it would be there; or on my shoulders, for that matter" — we soon learn that this is rather unlikely, that there is more to Rachel Innes than her amusing demeanor reveals, and that, perhaps, losing her head is just what Rachel desires (10). Not unreliable, and certainly not insane, Rachel is simply enjoying the ambiguity of her clever humor — an ambiguity that grants her the freedom of growth while placing her reader on shaky interpretative ground.

Does this "very intelligent woman," who, according to Detective Jamieson, is clever enough to murder without leaving clues behind, want to minimize the effect of her words — want to remove the serious edge of her tone (48)? Though she may not know which bird is which — "they all look alike to me, unless they have the hallmark of some bright color" — or what crickets do at sunset — "chirp, or scrape their legs together, or whatever it is they do" — what Rachel does know is that she has never been given enough credit in print for helping to solve the Sunnyside mysteries. Detective Jamieson's private words of thanks, stressing that he could not have solved the case without her, do not satisfy Rachel who desires public recognition. But if, in fact, her purpose is simply to gain "credit in print," Rachel's rebuttal is rather extensive and, at times, seemingly digressive.(6).

We begin to wonder if Rachel desires to gain more than a knowledgeable, sympathetic public by telling her story. Perhaps, Rachel is aware of the importance of expression, of women's need to score "their feats in written and oral language" — for, as Hélène Cixous expresses nearly seventy years later, "writing is precisely *the very possibility of change*, the space that can serve as a springboard for subversive thought, the precursory movement of a transformation of social and cultural structures" (880, 879). It is this "very possibility of change" that triggers the humor of Rachel's narrative — a humor that attempts to shield the very thoughts and actions it most vividly brings to light.

Rachel, of course, writes her story so that her readers will witness the summer's events through her eyes. She wants us to experience both her fright and her bravery as she and Liddy discover the bloodied body of Arnold Armstrong at the foot of the circular staircase at the newly rented Sunnyside — a residence that does everything but live up to the peacefulness its name suggests. Murdered by an unknown assailant, Arnold, the black sheep son of the house's owner, the banker Paul Armstrong, has cultivated many enemies — a fact that provides Detective Jamieson with three primary murder suspects: Halsey, who may have been angry at Arnold's unwelcomed advances to Gertrude; Jack Bailey, Gertrude's lover and the teller at Paul Armstrong's bank, who uncovered Arnold's earlier forgery of his father's name; and lastly Gertrude herself, who is fearful of Arnold's advances and who also wants to protect Jack from Arnold's anger. Of course, none of these young people is the actual murderer. Rather, Mrs. Watson, the housekeeper, killed Arnold, who was the uncaring father of her deceased sister's child — a child Mrs. Watson has been caring for while being cruelly blackmailed by Arnold's threats to gain custody of the young boy.

However, murder is not the only mystery to be solved during Rachel's Sunnyside summer. Robbery is also very much an issue, for Armstrong's bank has declared bankruptcy, and the stolen money, stolen by Armstrong himself, is hidden somewhere — of course, in the very house Rachel has rented. Thus, after Arnold is found dead, the hoped-for peace of a summer retreat is shattered by strange tappings, nocturnal visits, and the eventual deaths of four more people. Complicated romance, lying not far beneath the surface, also adds to this murky environment. Will Louise Armstrong's father allow her to marry Halsey, even though his inherited wealth seems far from sufficient? If Gertrude's fiancé is not convicted for Arnold's murder, will he be convicted of robbing Paul Armstrong's bank? Who is the woman that the chauffeur Warner overhears arguing with Halsey on the afternoon of Halsey's disappearance?

Though Rachel's narrative answers all these questions and more, her investigations do not uncover the murderer even though she is the only person to whom Mrs. Watson confesses before she dies. Rather, as Rachel says in her final burst of annoyance, the newspapers "have been singularly silent" in revealing her "share in discovering the secret chamber... The inner history has never been told" (279). For Rachel, the mystery is not discovering who fired the bullet that ended Arnold's life, but, significantly, the mystery is *uncovering an unknown space*, a "secret chamber": "The murder of Arnold Armstrong was a beginning, not an end, I'm sure of that" (149). Rachel's desire to tell her story is also a beginning, not simply a rebuttal to set the facts straight; but, infused with humor, Rachel's narrative creates the space that "can serve as springboard for subversive thought."[6]

Though Rachel's repeated "as you know" implies that we are privy to the newspaper accounts she is rebutting, their contents are only grudgingly mentioned rather than explored in detail (101). Yet, she hopes we, like Gertrude, will "crumple the newspaper into a ball and fl[i]ng it to the floor" (84). Or, take our cue from Rachel herself, who has the newspaper clippings "somewhere, but just now [she] can remember only the essentials" (85). Rather than engage in a quarrel with the newspapers — the confrontational tone hinted at but not taken up in the opening — Rachel evidently wants us to ignore these accounts and witness her exploration of an as yet unexplored territory — an exploration that ends in the literal discovery of a "secret chamber" and the figurative acquisition of emotional, psychological, imaginative, and rhetorical ground. It is the boundaries of this newly defined space that Rachel's humor subtly demarcates — a suggestive, spatial elsewhere.[7]

Suggesting the psychological and emotional shifting of boundaries that accompanies Rachel's expanding world is her initial move to a temporary house.[8] From the opening of her narrative, space and how it is defined is important, for what bothers Rachel is that one of the newspaper accounts simply refers to her as "the tenant" at Sunnyside (6). Rachel rebels at the idea that she simply occupied or inhabited this house; rather, she has actively participated in solving the mystery and in so doing created a new space to accommodate her growing self-awareness, her reconstituted self:

> If the series of catastrophes there did nothing else it taught me one thing, that somehow, somewhere, from perhaps a half-civilized ancestor who wore a sheepskin garment and trailed his food or his prey, I have in me the instinct of the chase. Were I a man I should be a trapper of criminals, trailing them as relentlessly as no doubt my sheepskin-clad ancestor did his wild boar. But being an unmarried woman, with the handicap of my sex, my first acquaintance with crime will probably be my last. Indeed it came near enough to being my last acquaintance with anything. (8–9)

The wry humor of Rachel's last statement serves several purposes. First, it highlights Rinehart's parody by deliberately and rather heavy-handedly pointing to the upcoming horrors that our poor narrator will encounter. Exhibiting no subtlety, Rinehart takes the genre's notion of fairness to the reader a bit far, assuming that nothing less than bold signposts will prevent the suspenseful atmosphere from going unnoticed. Secondly, with Rachel's self-reflection focusing on the late discovery of her adventuresome nature, Rinehart touches upon the issues of women's freedom and power in relation to societal restrictions — "the handicap of my sex" — while neutralizing these very words with Rachel's humor and a quick retreat back to the resolvable story line of the murder.

Multiple dialogues occur within Rachel's layered narrative. Rachel taunts her readers' expectations of an "unmarried woman, with the handicap of [her] sex," while we question her behavior when, "like a dog on a scent, like [her] bearskin progenitor with his spear and his wild boar," Rachel throws herself quite enthusiastically into "the frenzy of pursuit, and dust of battle" (269). Rachel ridicules the woman she is slowly becoming — "Certainly I cut a peculiar figure, in my bare feet and dressing gown, with a gun in my hand... I had gone berserk" — while this newly evolving self responds by doing as she pleases: "I am not fond of a height... yet I climbed out onto the Sunnyside roof without a second's hesitation" (194, 269). Rachel mocks the socially sanctioned roles that have demanded her limited self-awareness — "to Gertrude and me was left the woman's part, to watch and wait" — while these roles continue to define her allotted space — "this is hardly a woman's affair" (217, 101). Rachel's multivalent humor involves us in a dialogue with our own expectations of her, allows Rachel a freeing ambiguity (for who is responsible for a seemingly disembodied discourse?), and questions the limits placed on Rachel as a woman. Yet, it is this same humor that undercuts the involvement, the allowance, and the questions by undermining their seriousness.

Comparing Rachel's dialogues with V.I.'s once again underlines the vastly different intents of their humor, in large part a reflection of the eighty years which separate them. Rachel's dialogues are self-referential, often focusing on how we, as readers, will perceive her in relation to societal expectations of her behavior. V.I., using her humor to advertise rather than shield what some may perceive as her "transgressions," and never employing humor to neutralize her ideas, behavior, or beliefs, directs our thoughts to larger issues, yet issues that directly affect both her and us — is health care truly healthy and does that care extend to everyone?; is the Catholic Church involved in an unholy communion with big business?; is political influence playing a deadly game close to home? Unlike Rachel's, the dialogues which V.I.'s wit initiates do not always, or even often, revert back to her. Rachel's dialogues must, however, for unlike V.I., Rachel needs to understand, create, and determine her own potential as a free-moving self before she can direct her gaze and her conversation elsewhere.

Added to the multiple dialogues *within* Rachel's narrative is the dialogical nature of Rinehart's parody of detective fiction — the two speaking selves that Paravisini and Yorio describe in their discussion of parodic detective fiction. Rinehart pushes at the boundaries of her parodied genre, while Rachel pushes at the boundaries that limit her growth — both determined to create space for a newly evolving woman. In a sense, author and character mirror each other as they "gain new life by parodying ... older forms, and stretching them beyond their former limits" (Paravisini 181). As Rachel's storytelling enters the oral tradition and she redefines herself for her apparently misled audience, Rinehart transforms Rachel's telling into a text and creates herself as a writer and, as her comments on her readers suggest — "they call me Mary, as though they had known me for a very long time. And perhaps they have" — creates her own story as well (*My Story* 570).

Humor does not, therefore, simply neutralize the potentially subversive content of Rachel's thoughts; nor does it erase the revitalization suggested by Rinehart's heavy-handed use of detective fiction's conventions. Rather than do as her words suggest, Rachel does participate in the chase, and does so rather relentlessly, while Rinehart writes prolifically in the face of her own protests. That Rachel hopes to alter the parameters of her allotted space, a space determined by gender as well as class, is evident in that she never loses a chance to leave the house no matter what the hour or under what auspicious conditions. Recognizing early on that "the house seemed to choke" her, Rachel takes the cue from her cat Beulah and gets "back to nature": "[W]hen Beulah, my cat and most intelligent animal, found some early catnip on a bank near the house and rolled in it in a feline ecstasy, I decided that getting back to nature was the thing to do" (35, 22).

Rachel's route back to her own nature, however, is not as easily accessible as Beulah's seems to be. Feeling "under surveillance" at the Sunnyside estate,

Rachel is also under the watchful eye of her ingrained sense of who she should be as well as the limiting vision of those around her (15). As Liddy wisely notes: "There's some things you can't handcuff" (153). Among the ghosts that Rachel must give shape to are the internal preconceptions that limit vision to what has only been seen before, block hearing to what has only been heard before, and confine imaginings to the realm of the expected. But Rachel persists in the hope of an elsewhere beyond this expected realm — a hope evident not only in the actions she narrates but also in the form her narrative takes, for Rachel's sarcastically humorous tone is as much for herself as it is for us. The humor softens the impact of her discoveries while it enables the slow erosion of constraining limits that have prevented Rachel's more accurate knowledge of herself and her potential.

To accomplish this dual goal, Rachel's actions as well as her narration of them require a careful balancing act — a balancing enabled by the humor that allows Rachel to feign disinterest as she is in the very act of tearing down traditional expectations of her behavior. Rachel performs this tight-rope walking while enthusiastically strolling through the uncut grass to Thomas's lodge, making sure the readers of her "heavy-handed" genre do not miss another CLUE, and all the while proving herself to be a proper "Colonial Dame":

> I record this scrap of conversation, just as I have tried to put down anything and everything that had a bearing on what followed, because the gardener Halsey sent the next day *played an important part in the events* of the next few weeks. Events which culminated *as you know* by stirring the country profoundly. At that time, however, I was *busy trying to keep my feet dry*, and *paid little or no attention.* (101, emphasis added)

Rachel's words are riddled with contradictions that are, in this instance, the source of her humor. Obviously, she has paid more than a "little or no attention" in order to record "anything and everything" including a mere "scrap of conversation." And though we do not know, as Rachel suggests, how the events culminated, we only momentarily shift our attention to the newly introduced gardener — a diversionary tactic by our narrator who is not yet comfortable with her increasing ability to leave "the strait and narrow way," and by our author who highlights the clue in order to shift our attention away from it and back to Rachel (50).

Rachel's seeming disinterest at this point in the narrative coupled with her over-concern with keeping her feet dry amounts to what Mary Russo in her discussion of female grotesques describes as a "flaunting of the feminine" (224). In describing the "power of masquerade," Russo suggests the difference between men and women who assume femininity as a mask:

> Deliberately assumed and foregrounded, femininity as a mask, for a man, is a take-it-or-leave-it proposition; for a woman, a similar flaunt-

ing of the feminine is a take-it-*and*-leave-it *possibility*. To put on
femininity with a vengeance suggests the power of taking it off. (224)

Rachel's humor suggests the power of taking off this mask of femininity while
she shields herself behind it most securely by fretting over her damp feet.

However, Rachel's assumed caution concerning her damp feet ends
abruptly as she and Halsey reach the servants' lodge, and Halsey attempts to
take dubious control over the situation: "[t]his is hardly a woman's affair. If
there's a scrap of any kind, you scram in a hurry" (101). Not only does Rachel
quickly cross the veranda and hammer on the door, but she informs Halsey
of her intentions to "stay right here," while she translates his command that,
she says, reflects "Halsey's solicitous care for me put into vernacular" (101).
Assuming the need to translate Halsey's words suggests the oddity of his
demand as well the versatility of our narrator, who is able to maneuver
gracefully through the tangled syntax of two "languages." But Rinehart's use
of humor does not end by poking fun at the unreasonable limits placed upon
our narrator.

Unknown to Halsey and to Rachel is the fact that Louise Armstrong has
been hiding in the servants' lodge for fear of being found by an undesired
suitor, who is also a partner in her father's burglary. Upon entering the lodge,
Thomas, the butler, immediately beckons Rachel upstairs, quietly informing
Halsey: "You bettah sit down, suh... It's a place for a woman, suh" (102).
Rachel cannot refrain from underlining the unexpected turn of events:
"Things were not turning out the way Halsey expected" (102). Not only do
events not meet Halsey's expectations, but when Rachel sends for him and
he hysterically assumes Louise is dying, Rachel orders him out of the room,
this time using her own vernacular: "'Fudge!' I snapped ... 'She's doing
nothing of the sort. And don't pinch my arm. If you want something to do,
go and choke Thomas'" (104). Angry at Halsey's supposition that she does
not belong in the lodge and Thomas's deceit in keeping Louise's presence a
secret, Rachel claims a space — where she can actively participate in the
strange events surrounding her — by disarming Halsey with the quaintness
of her exclamation, "Fudge," and the absurdity of her demand "go and choke
Thomas." Why not set the men against each other while she gathers more
information from the ailing Louise? Keeping her feet dry has lost its priority,
if, in fact, it ever truly had any.

With Rachel's eviction of Halsey, the shifting of male space becomes
essential to the creation of her own space. This shifting is less pointedly but
more humorously suggested when Rachel speaks with Louise's undesired
suitor, Dr. Walker. Though he ostensibly comes to Sunnyside to discuss what
must be done with "the butler's body," it is Dr. Walker's body that Rachel
cannot refrain from observing and commenting upon as he sits down rather
awkwardly: "The chair was lower than expected, and his dignity required

collecting before he went on" (167). Walker's "space" is so radically altered by the end of the narrative that, in order to avoid arrest, he must escape to South America without the stolen money. Driven out of the country, Walker is also successfully squeezed out of Rachel's narrative.

Detective Jamieson also deals with shifting terrain when he realizes that his ability to detect, or as Rachel describes it "twist ... circumstances and motives to suit himself," is severely limited — a limitation that arouses his frustration with Rachel: "But as long as I learn only bits of the truth from both you and her [Gertrude] what can I do?" (150, 64). What, indeed, can any of these men do, for as Rachel's space increases and her self-referential humor marks its shifting boundaries, Halsey cannot find comfortable ground in his lover's sickroom, Dr. Walker cannot expect to be at ease seated in Rachel's living room or surviving in her narrative, and poor Jamieson is reduced to learning "about the events at Sunnyside in some occult way" (150).

Imaginative flexibility, something that both Halsey and Walker lack but Rachel slowly gains, constitutes an essential aspect of Rachel's newly gained terrain. Stymied in her attempts to figure out who Warner, the chauffeur, overheard speaking with Halsey in the library, Rachel initially finds herself "working in a circle" (222). The unknown woman's words, which send Halsey out of the house and nearly to his demise, indicate that she was questioning Paul Armstrong's sudden death. Unable to imagine who this woman could be, Rachel's primary problem is an inability to visualize Halsey sharing emotion-filled confidences with the scar-faced cook; nor can she imagine this woman possessing important information. Blocked by misconceptions based on rigid class and gender definitions, Rachel does, however, recognize that in Warner's reticence to look within the room and see whom Halsey was speaking with, he has lost "the key to everything" (219). Rachel is more correct than she may realize, for acquiring the imaginative flexibility to allow for the cook's ability to participate in a distressing as well as informative conversation with Halsey, is possessing the key to an unmapped and potentially rich territory.

Even Halsey is aware that Rachel has gained imaginative ground during her Sunnyside summer, for, as Rachel informs us, he often interrupts her narrative with his new maxim: "'Trust a woman to add two and two together, and make six'" (268). Rachel, however, elevates her new imaginative freedom to a credo with her retort: "if two and two plus x make six, then to discover the unknown quantity is the simplest thing in the world. That a houseful of detectives missed it entirely was because they were busy trying to prove that two and two makes four" (268). Amusing in its simplicity, Rachel's response leaves no doubt that she has left "the strait and narrow way," for she can now imaginatively envision the existence of an unknown quantity that does not fit the once expected outcomes or act in accordance with prescribed rules (50).

Halsey begins to learn from his aunt as he describes the situation as he perceives it — a description interesting in its spatial suggestions:

> 'I have the feeling that we three outsiders [himself, Rachel, and Gertrude], who have paid our money for the privilege of staying in this spook factory, are living on the very top of things. We're on the lid, so to speak. Now and then we get a sight of the things inside, but we are not a part of them.' (100)

The power with which his class and gender once endowed him is removed. In "this spook factory," Liddy finds the clue that leads to the stolen money; Warner overhears the conversation between Halsey and the cook whose knowledge precipitates many of the narrative's events; and Mrs. Watson is the one person who carries around the knowledge of the buried story — a story which has already led to Arnold Armstrong's death. Once not having to pay much attention to the servants, Halsey must now "under pretense of examining his injury ... watch [Mrs. Watston] through the mirror" (99). For the first time consciously aware of her existence, he must also, with physical as well as psychic discomfort, perceive her from a different angle of vision. Just as the mirror in the old mansion "reflects [Rachel and Liddy] from unexpected corners," we must also shift our gaze and, in turn, our expectations of the characters and of the shifting conventions of Rinehart's parodied genre (13).

Literalizing Rachel's discovery of new space, Rinehart parodies yet another convention of detective fiction, the secret room. Paul Armstrong and Dr. Walker's attempts to enter Sunnyside and retrieve the stolen money, hidden in a safe in the "secret chamber," are, like much else in this narrative, far from subtle. Leaving gaping apertures in walls, apertures that Rachel wishes she knew how to read, flinging steel rods through walls onto an unsuspecting servant's head, and hammering none too quietly throughout the night, Walker searches for the secret chamber while Armstrong, knowledge-able of its whereabouts, attempts to find a way to remove the hidden safe. Rachel, unwilling to accept the woman's part "to watch and wait," grows in her conviction "that somewhere behind its handsomely papered walls there lay a hidden space, with the possibilities it would involve" (255).

Significantly, Rachel's thoughts move in this new direction after she has been invited by Jamieson to witness the removal of Paul Armstrong's coffin that, it is learned, contains the body of a pauper rather than that of the bank president. Even the finality of the grave seems doubtful as Rachel notes "the sense of desecration, of a reversal of the everlasting fitness of things, in resurrecting a body from its mother earth" (252). But it is this very reversal, causing Rachel to question her own identity, that allows her the freedom to expand beyond constraining boundaries. The nighttime trip to the graveyard even erases Rachel's desire to feign disinterest and to worry about damp feet:

> Once when through a miscalculation I jumped a little short over a ditch and landed above my shoe tops in the water and ooze I remember wondering if this was really I, and if I had ever tasted life until that summer. I walked along with the water sloshing in my shoes, and I was actually cheerful. I remember whispering to Jamieson that I had never seen the stars so lovely, and that it was a mistake, when the Lord had made the night so beautiful, to sleep through it! (250)

The literal expansion of her traversable terrain liberates Rachel's inner censor; she can now enthusiastically revel in her new taste of life. Yet, a small unconvinced piece of our narrator still feels compelled to attribute her exalted feeling to the loveliness of stars — a far more acceptable cause than the powerful sense of freedom in which she clearly revels. Getting back to nature, as her cat Beulah does, suggests the larger territory that Rachel is beginning to claim and experience.

Having evolved beyond feigning disinterest in adventure, Rachel can now call architects and begin to carve out more rhetorical space for herself: "Just now I want to ask you a question about something that is none of my business" (126). Rachel has tried this earlier with the Armstrong's lawyer, Mr. Harton: "I am going to ask you some questions, and I hope you will answer them. I feel that I am entitled to some knowledge, because my family and I myself are in a most ambiguous position" (45). The ambiguity of her position frees Rachel's tongue but clouds Harton's perception, for, as Rachel comments: "I don't know whether he understood me or not" (45). Though not understanding, Harton does answer, but Rachel does not have such success with the architects who are unable or unwilling to provide her with information on a hidden room at Sunnyside. But, of course, Rachel's failure fuels her desire.

Armed with a tape measure, Rachel begins her quest for the hidden room — a quest that renders her quite laughable, as we find her on the roof like her "bearskin progenitor with his spear and his wild boar" (269). Rachel, "a spinster, a granddaughter of old John Innes of Revolutionary day, a D.A.R., a Colonial Dame," is barely recognizable: "[T]he wind belled my dressing gown out like a sail. I had torn a great strip of the silk loose, and now I ruthlessly finished the destruction of the thing by jerking the strip free and tying it around my head" (50, 269). Destroying the clothing that confines her, Rachel ties the transformed silk into a warrior's headdress, securely keeping intact the very head she repeatedly informs us she is losing. Clearly, a transformation has occurred, forcing us to reconsider laughing at our narrator's "antics."

Even after Rachel discovers the hidden room and finds herself locked within it, she cannot help but humorously depict her desire to explore the parameters of this new space, "according to the time-honored rule of people shut in unknown and ink-black prisons" (272). But Rachel is given little time for exploration, for she is soon joined by the pursued Paul Armstrong, who recoils upon feeling a cold, clammy hand in this supposedly secret chamber. Though once the others "liberate" her, Rachel exalts at being "a free woman again" — "I wanted to laugh and cry in the same breath, to crawl into bed and have a cup of tea and scold Liddy and do any of the thousand natural things that I had never expected to do again" — her narrative suggests, of course, the contrary (277).

Though Rinehart resolves the murder mystery and the burglary mystery, the open space that humor has created primarily for Rachel to move into — crossing the lines that have rigidly held and defined her — still remains open at the novel's end. The mystery is over, but the woman's life continues. In fact, Rachel's closing words, spoken with the utter frankness that she now feels comfortable expressing, suggest a future that may provide undiscovered space rich in new possibilities: "To be perfectly frank, I never really lived until that summer... But Liddy or no Liddy, I shall advertise tomorrow for a house in the country, and I don't care if it has a Circular Staircase" (286). There is little doubt that Rachel hopes it will, and that Liddy may be "afraid to come" but will "not dar[e] to stay behind" (29).

Evidently Detective Jamieson is correct in believing that "not everybody is an electrician who wears rubber gloves"; we can confidently supplement these words with our knowledge that not every D.A.R. is a self-mocking, bumbling spinster, and that not all humor is simply funny (241). Rachel informs us that certain deceptions are "like telling a necessary lie. One ought not to be found out" (79). Yet the rich ambiguity of Rachel's humorous narrative suggests that Rachel avoids detection, but very much harbors the desire *to be found out*. Revealing the "inner history" of the secret chamber, Rachel also discovers/uncovers herself, and will continue on this path of rediscovery. Demonstrating an awareness of her audience and an ease with the narrative convention of re-telling, Rachel clearly has shared her story before and will continue to retell it: "At this point in my story, Halsey always says ... and Liddy always screams and puts her fingers in her ears at his point" (268, 275). Punctured with new asides, each recitation will, consequently, contain potentially rich future dialogues.

While Rachel's narrative carves a place for her story in an oral tradition — "We were no longer onlookers who saw a battle passing around them. We were the center of action" — Rinehart's novel *The Circular Staircase* begins her movement into literary tradition (213). Just as the tramp, who uses "a strange argot, in which familiar words took unfamiliar meanings," is eventually understood by the Innes's family, so Rachel's reconstituted self, finding its shape within her humorous narrative, is "gradually made clear to us" (232). Perhaps, we will even find ourselves nodding in agreement with V.I. Warshawski's witty self-reflection on the likelihood of the police following a promising lead: "Maybe I'd be the first woman on the moon — stranger things have happened" (*Burn Marks* 25). And they do.

NOTES

1. See Patricia Yaeger's brilliant discussion of women writers' use of "emancipatory strategies" in making language work *for* rather than *against* them — inventing "language games that challenge and change linguistic codes," and, in so doing, writing new possibilities into the language (15).

2. For an early discussion of humor and detective fiction see Craig Rice's "Murder Makes Merry" in Haycraft's *The Art of the Mystery Story*. Also see Earl Bargainner's *Comic Crime*. Especially interesting is Lizabeth Paravisini and Carlos Yorio's essay, "Is It or Isn't It?: The Duality of Parodic Detective Fiction" which examines how humor forces the reader to determine whether the fictional work is "to be read as a 'straight' novel or as a parody" (181). Dennis Porter examines the irony that establishes "an ambience of play" in Christie's fiction, and the American stylistic feature of the wisecrack in Hammett and Chandler (130–145).

3. Jan Cohn provides the best biographical information on Rinehart in *Improbable Fiction: The Life of Mary Roberts Rinehart*. Also see *Mary Roberts Rinehart* by Dorothy Cameron Disney and Milton MacKaye, who suggest that an analysis of Rinehart's work "will show the conflicts, the inconsistencies, the many different people in the one person who produced it" (16).

4. A. E. Murch cites the connection between Rachel Innes and Miss Butterworth, describing Innes as "largely a re-incarnation of Miss Green's Amelia Butterworth in her personal qualities, social position and habits of thought, her relationship with her long-suffering maid, her sympathy with young lovers, as well as in her detective methods and her facility for 'happening' to discover important information by accident" (212–213). Rachel, however, gives voice to Miss Butterworth's subtly humorous thoughts, using the transformative power of humor in a way Miss Butterworth would most definitely approve. In her autobiography, Rinehart tells the story of picking a publisher for *The Circular Staircase* "by the simple method of taking a story by Anna Katherine Green from the book case, not[ing] the name Bobbs-Merrill of Indianapolis, and sen[ding] it off" (94).

5. The necessity of placing "family" and "marriage" within quotation marks suggests the different slant these words are given in Rachel's humorous narrative.

6. The space created by Rachel's narrative is comparable to William W. Stowe's "hypothetical space" — the space he believes popular fiction opens up for the "manipulation and criticism" of cultural and social values ("Popular" 660). In

this sense, the text itself becomes a space for the readers "to affirm or to modify or to reject some of their culture's conventional values and structures," in short, to entertain ideas they might not otherwise have considered (661). Rachel's created space is both for herself and her audience.

7. Interestingly, the 1908 *New York Times* review of *The Circular Staircase* first describes the novel as being "all about an old house with an unsuspected secret chamber" (460). The murders are, in fact, sixth on this reviewer's list of plots and subplots. The most recent 1985 paperback reprint of *The Circular Staircase*, however, depicts a dead man at the foot of a staircase on its blue-tone cover, highlighting the murder rather than the hidden room.

8. Many of Rinehart's novels begin with a move to a summer home, sometimes rented, sometimes owned. See in particular *The Confession* (1921), *The Wall* (1938), and *The Yellow Room* (1945).

WORKS CITED

Bargainnier, Earl F., ed. *Comic Crime*. Bowling Green: Bowling Green State University Popular Press, 1987.

Breit, Harvey. "Mary Roberts Rinehart." *The Writer Observed*. New York: World, 1956, 227–229.

Cixous, Hélène. "The Laugh of the Medusa." Trans. Keith Cohen and Paula Cohen. *Signs* 1 (Summer 1976): 875–893.

Cohn, Jan. *Improbable Fiction: The Life of Mary Roberts Rinehart*. Pittsburgh: University of Pittsburgh Press, 1980.

Disney, Dorothy Cameron, and Milton MacKaye. *Mary Roberts Rinehart*. New York: Rinehart and Co., 1948.

Eco, Umberto. "Frames of Comic Freedom." *Carnival!*, eds. Thomas A. Sebeok and Marcia E. Erickson. Berlin: Mouton, 1984, 1–9.

"Entertaining Mystery." *New York Times Book Review* 22 Aug. 1908: 460.

Grafton, Sue. *'F' is for Fugitive*. New York: Bantam, 1989.

Green, Anna Katharine. *The Circular Study* (1900). Garden City, NY: Garden City P, 1926.

Haycraft, Howard, ed. *The Art of the Mystery Story: A Collection of Critical Essays*. New York: Simon, 1946.

_____. *Murder for Pleasure: The Life and Times of the Detective Story*. New York: Appleton, 1941.

Klein, Kathleen Gregory. *The Woman Detective: Gender and Genre*. Chicago: University of Illinois Press, 1988.

Little, Judy. *Comedy and the Woman Writer: Woolf, Spark, and Feminism*. Lincoln: University of Nebraska Press, 1983.

Paravisini, Lizabeth, and Carlos Yorio. "Is It or Isn't It?: The Duality of Parodic Detective Fiction," in: *Comic Crime*, ed. Earl F. Bargainnier. Bowling Green: Bowling Green State University Popular Press, 1987, 181–193.

Paretsky, Sara. *Bitter Medicine*. New York: Dell, 1987.

_____. *Blood Shot*. New York: Dell, 1988.

_____. *Burn Marks*. New York: Dell, 1990.

_____. *Guardian Angel*. New York: Delacorte, 1992.

_____. *Indemnity Only*. New York: Ballantine, 1982.

_____. *Killing Orders*. New York: Ballantine, 1985.

Porter, Dennis. *The Pursuit of Crime: Art and Ideology in Detective Fiction*. New Haven: Yale University Press, 1981.

Rinehart, Mary Roberts. *The After House* (1914). New York: Zebra, 1989.

_____. *The Album*. 1933. New York: Zebra, 1988.

_____. *The Case of Jennie Brice*. 1913. New York: Zebra, 1987.

_____. *The Circular Staircase*. 1908. New York: Zebra, 1985.

_____. *The Confession*. 1921. New York: Zebra, 1989.

_____. "The Detective Story." *Munsey's Magazine* May 1904: 319–20.

_____. *The Door* (1930). New York: Zebra, 1986.

_____. *The Haunted Lady* (1942). New York: Zebra, 1987.

_____. "His Other Self" ("The Alter Ego"). *Munsey's Magazine* Dec. 1904: 403–05.

_____. *The Man in the Lower Ten* (1906). New York: Zebra, 1990.

_____. *Miss Pinkerton*. New York: Farrar and Rinehart, 1932.

_____. *My Story: A New Edition and Seventeen Years Later*. New York: Rinehart, 1948.

_____. "The Repute of the Crime Story." *Publishers' Weekly* 1 Feb. 1930: 563–66.

_____. *The Swimming Pool* (1952). New York: Dell, 1962.

_____. "Thoughts." *The Ladies' Home Journal* May 1931: 3, 179.

_____. *The Wall*. 1938. New York: Zebra, 1989.

_____. *The Yellow Room*. 1945. New York: Zebra, 1988.

Russo, Mary. "Female Grotesques: Carnival and Theory," in: *Carnival!*, eds. Thomas A. Sebeok and Marcia E. Erickson. New York: Mouton, 1984, 213–229.

Stowe, William W. "Popular Fiction as Liberal Art." *College English* Nov. 1986: 646–63.

Todorov, Tzvetan. "The Typology of Detective Fiction," in: *The Poetics of Prose*. Ithaca: Cornell University Press, 1977, 42–52.

Toth, Emily. "A Laughter of Their Own: Women's Humor in the United States," in: *Critical Essays on American Humor*, eds. William Bedford Clark and W. Craig Turner. Boston: G. K. Hall, 1984, 199–215.

Walker, Nancy A. *A Very Serious Thing: Women's Humor and American Culture.*
    Minneapolis: University of Minnesota Press, 1988.
Yaeger, Patricia. *Honey-Mad Women: Emancipatory Strategies in Women's Writing.*
    New York: Columbia University Press, 1988.

III.
FILM, STAND-UP COMEDY, AND CARTOON ART

15

Hollywood, 1934: "Inventing" Romantic Comedy

KAY YOUNG

Joel McCrea: "I mean sex didn't even enter into it!"
Claudette Colbert: "Oh, but of course it did, darling...
                Sex *always* has something to do with it."
                           (The Palm Beach Story, 1942)

1. BACKGROUNDS TO A FORM

Preston Sturges opens *The Palm Beach Story* with a series of silent shots: of a hysterical, fainting maid, minister kept waiting at the altar, groom being dressed by the best man in a taxi, two Claudette Colberts — one locked, tied, and gagged in a closet, and one in full bridal regalia leaping over the body of the maid and running outside — and the union of bride and groom as they meet each other in mid-flight down the aisle, accompanied by the *William Tell* Overture mixed with Mendelssohn's bridal march, frozen into sporadic stills with projected credits. As the finale of the prologue, the camera zooms back from the couple joined at the altar and two cursive doilies come into view reading, "and they lived happily ever after," followed by, "or did they?"

Credits and background complete, the acted present of the film begins five years subsequent to the wedding with the wife walking out on the husband.

The orchestrated, frenetic pantomime of the opening does more than pay homage to the silent film era: it plays an intertextual joke with yet another, earlier image of Claudette Colbert. She has worn the same veil and had the wind in her heels before. As the bride who laboriously dresses for her impending marriage to King Wesley and forebodingly walks down the aisle to join him in marriage, Colbert in *It Happened One Night* suddenly bolts. In running from this marriage and choosing the real King, Clark Gable's Peter Warne, Colbert/Ellie Andrews jumps into a marriage that the narrative of *It Happened One Night* suggests (in the course of their previous interaction together) is a model of living "happily ever after." Elizabeth Kendall's provocative study, *The Runaway Bride*, focuses on this moment of the Capra film and this image as a way to locate the beginnings of a genre of Hollywood filmmaking — the romantic comedy — and with it a new conceptualization of America. However, if the 1934 *It Happened One Night* closes with a leap into the suggested possibility of a new form of comedy, the 1942 *The Palm Beach Story* opens with a leap into its closure. Kendall's recognition of the "runaway bride" locates the woman as the primary site of wonder of these comedies — she problematizes marriage by risking running away from and toward it; she discovers and expresses a sense of self-determination and freedom in this act of running toward and away from her object of desire.[1] Yet, what the woman comes to risk — both her self-discovery and self-protection — find themselves matched in her partner's responses to her in these films. If this new woman runs, this new man stands still wearing an apron. Brought together by a shared talent for play and a shared desire for each other, the coupling partners of these films discover more of who each is by virtue of sometimes keeping and sometimes running away from the company of the other. It is, I would suggest, the display of a partnership which allows for strong, independent selves joined with the mutual desire to couple and to work at trying to understand what that means that makes these films romantic comedies and that makes them remarkable.

From 1934 to 1945, Hollywood invented narratives which did more than distract the country through the worst of the depression years and World War II. While dramas, melodramas, westerns, musicals, adventure tales, science fiction, and comedies of solo and male teams had been portrayed in silent and then "talking" films, comedies that found their energy in the interactions of a romantic couple did not appear until the 1930s. They then dominated Hollywood for a decade. Frank Capra's *It Happened One Night*, Woody Van Dyke's *The Thin Man*, Howard Hawks' *Twentieth Century*, and Mark Sandrich's *The Gay Divorcee* opened in 1934 and collectively transformed how the narrative of movies constructed the intimacy of romance — through a comedy that invented itself before it knew what it was.[2] Shot in a scant four weeks, *It Happened One Night* was taken neither by its creators nor by its reviewers to be a watershed work in the evolution of Hollywood filmmaking. However, within a month of its release audiences were flocking to it, the Greyhound Bus Company came back to life after near bankruptcy, and the makers of men's undershirts lost substantial business after Gable revealed himself to be bare chested when he scared Claudette Colbert to her side of "the walls of Jericho" before they were wed.[3] What the "It" was that happened was what the studios sought to reproduce, the "it" which enabled the transformation of Carole Lombard from the "Orchid Lady" of weeper films to "the first beautiful woman comic,"[4] prompted a national desire to see repeated portrayals of the marriage of Nick and Nora, and the marriage in movement of Fred Astaire and Ginger Rogers. With the institutionalization of the Production Code in Hollywood in 1934 (a response within the industry to a growing desire among the clergy to censor and control the "unhealthy" influence of films), which subjected all movies to a considerable fine if released without the Code's stamp of approval, the sultry, libidinous presence of Mae West, Jean Harlow, and Marlene Dietrich went underground. The platinum blonde seductress languishing in satin in the bedroom of the 1920s and early 30s was replaced by the working woman, or independent heiress whose common sense or need to break free from her dominating father or crazy family leads her to flee home. With restrictions placed on the explicit expression of desire, desire reinscribed its presence in the 1930s comedy through allusion or sublimation. If sex was to become aggression, then the sexual partners would become physical and verbal combatants; and if sex was to be couched in metaphor and humor, then it required a partnership where the joke could be shared. What the presence of the Production Code encouraged, therefore, was that women become active players in their portrayals, that their words and actions be as vibrant and playful as their male partners. Rather than being the vamp whose seductive powers overwhelm a necessarily diminished male, or being the passive woman against whom a male acts and from whom he gains his assertion of self in the denial of hers, the woman of these 30s comedies is set squarely in the position of equal in wit, energy, and resourcefulness to her male partner. Yet, the surprise of these films comes not just from their notions of what it means to be a woman, but as well from what occurs while the couple is the midst of going at it with one another: each attains a deepened understanding of his or herself and a more complicated appreciation of the other as a result of being in this partnership. Molly Haskell writes of the couples of these films:

> [T]here is an equalization of obstacles and a matching of temperaments.
> A man and a woman seem to prickle and blossom at each other's touch,
> seem to rub each other with and against the grain simultaneously, and,

in the friction, in the light of each other's eyes, to know themselves for
the first time.[5]

If the presence of the Production Code helped to take the woman out of
the bedroom as her primary place of residence, get her a career (or if she is
an heiress locate her on the road), and put her into a partnership with the man,
the Depression made her the representative of a beleaguered, yet determined,
even madcap possibility of America. The women stars who were surviving
the Depression offered a sense of endurance, skepticism, wit, and common
sense. Claudette Colbert, Barbara Stanwyck, Ginger Rogers, Rosalind Russell, Jean Arthur, Myrna Loy, Carole Lombard, Katharine Hepburn, Irene
Dunne portrayed varying roles from the "party girl" who endures anything
to survive, to the heiress who tries anything to find meaning, even if that just
means learning how to dunk doughnuts. Cary Grant, Clark Gable, Gary
Cooper, William Powell, Fred Astaire, Jimmy Stewart, Spencer Tracy, Robert
Montgomery, Joel McCrea, and Henry Fonda display an energy equal to their
co-stars, but most often act as the ones in the partnership to whom things are
done. They learn what it means to be the "dupes" of the woman's jokes, and
in so doing discover their own vulnerability. Dressed in women's robes,
cooking breakfast, tongue-tied, playing the servant, befuddled, disastrously
clumsy, these men find themselves unhinged by the sheer presence of these
women and too discover their own desire for irreverence and screwiness by
being in relation to them. While Vaudeville had introduced the male-female
comedy team to America as a "domesticated" humor in response to the
growing numbers of women in the audience from the 1890s on, never did it
portray the couple as equals in the ability to jest, and never did the woman
gain a comedic role as wise-cracking, sexual and strong. When the Palace
could no longer support the playing of Vaudeville because its audiences had
migrated to movie theaters by 1932, Vaudeville's departing image ofthe
woman in male-female comedy was of the character Gracie — an illogical,
childlike figure in her own world — a world into which the audience could
peer with husband George and wonder knowingly how she could be so
idiotic.[6] The model of the woman comic as "dumb" was not the one followed
in the films of romantic comedy: Carole Lombard in *My Man Godfrey* and
Katharine Hepburn in *Bringing Up Baby* may be "screwy," but they are not
without the ability to discern how to use a situation to their own best advantage. The women of the films of romantic comedy rely on the quickness
of their wits to bring their partners to the recognition that they have met their
equals and can at best hope for a draw.

Where Vaudeville left off in its initiation of the male-female comedy team,
these films pressed forward in their re-invention of coupling as the shared
site for the mutual production of comedy. Superficially, what emerged was a
reversing of roles: a seeming "feminization" of the man and "masculiniza-

tion" of the woman. However, more provocatively the woman offered the Depression audience a catharsis which the man could not; and the woman and the man teamed together worked through what neither could address alone.[7] If the Depression emasculated the man by removing his traditional sites of status and of power — his work and his body — (where could he assert himself economically and against whom could he vent his rage?), it invented within the woman an emotional and intellectual resourcefulness Further, in softening his edges and defining hers more, the impact of the Depression reinvented the couple to be the site for expressing rage/passion and for redefining the self in relation to the self's partner. Coupling, therefore, became the arena which not only endured the Depression but flourished as an entity of romantic comedy: marriage found a narrative for its expression.

George Meredith's "Essay on Comedy" provides a theoretical frame which suggests that Capra's adaptation of Samuel Hopkins Adams "Night Bus" embodies comedy's highest form. In Meredith's model, comedy depends upon the freedom and equality of the woman to the man. His description of the evolved woman of comedy and the comedy which emerges as a result of this evolution stands as a working definition of the form which Hollywood's romantic comedies of the 30s takes:

> The heroines of comedy are like women of the world, not necessarily heartless from being clear-sighted; they seem so to the sentimentally reared, only for the reason that they use their wits, and are not wandering vessels crying for a captain or pilot. Comedy is an exhibition of their battle with men, and that of men with them; and as the two, however, divergent, both look on one object, namely, life, the gradual similarity of their impressions must bring them to some resemblance. The comic poet dares to show us men and women coming to this mutual likeness; he is for saying that when they draw together in social life their minds grow liker; just as the philosopher discerns the similarity of boy and girl, until the girl is marched away to the nursery. Philosopher and comic poet are of a cousinship in the eye they cast on life.[8]

Frank Capra (*If Happened One Night, Mr. Deeds Goes to Town, Mr. Smith Goes to Washington, You Can't Take It With You*), Leo McCarey (*The Awful Truth, Love Affair*), George Stevens (*Alice Adams, Swing Time, Penny Serenade*) Gregory La Cava (*My Man Godfrey, Stage Door, Fifth Avenue Girl*), Howard Hawks (*Twentieth Century, Bringing Up Baby, His Girl Friday*), George Cukor (*Holiday, The Philadelphia Story*), Preston Sturges (*The Lady Eve, The Palm Beach Story*) are Meredith's comic poets. The directors, working in collaboration with the screenwriters and the stars themselves, created narratives which recreate the partners of a marriage. As a childless couple (though often with a dog: William Powell and Myrna Loy's "Asta," Cary Grant and Irene Dunne's "Mr. Smith," Cary Grant and Katharine

Hepburn's "George" [all played by the same scotch terrier]) freed from domestic drudgery, each person of the couple is liberated to assert him or herself, discover the other, and experience a passion which translates not into a blissful harmony, but rather into a kind of struggle between giving oneself over to the other and resisting that offering. While there is not a woman among the directors of this genre (which is I think more a comment on the impossibility of being a woman director of the day than a reflection on the genre's resistance to female direction), various women writers — Vina Delmar (*The Awful Truth*), Gladys Lehman (*There's Always a Woman, Good Girls go to Paris, Hired Wife*), Dorothy Parker (with Alan Campbell) (*The Moon's Our Home, Woman Chases Man, Weekend for Three*), Bella Spewack (with Samuel Spewack) (*My Favorite Wife*), and Virginia Van Upp (*Café Society, Honeymoon in Bali*) — made names for themselves scripting these films and brought their felt presence to the shaping of the language of the films. While the focus of the comedy relied on what happened between the starring couple, Capra, Stevens, La Cava, McCarey, and Sturges entered into creative partnerships with their women stars. Informal collaborations emerged between them which helped to enable the film's vision of these women to be not just constructions of male fantasy, but companions, co-creators of their own comedy and their own visions of themselves.[9]

The activity of "inventing" by naming a genre insists on recognition of a new form of narrative. That the coinage of the phrase "screwball comedy" has been traced to Paramount Studios (in their efforts to make identifiable and therefore to sell their new productions) and to a reviewer of or publicist for *My Man Godfrey* (1936)[10] makes apparent the self-consciousness of those connected with the films of their radical difference and how that difference needed to be accounted for by name. And yet that difference was to be marked by a word borrowed from baseball — "screwball."[11] Here was a distinctly American genre making itself up. These films are thick with the language of voices — rapid exchanges where dialogue overlaps and produces, as if chemically from an attraction of opposites, responsive sparks, and memorable one-liners. Extended, uninterrupted speeches are absent. Prolonged tracking shots without words are rare. Verbal intercourse is the primary distinguishing feature of this new form — conversations work as displays of vibrant, uncontrolled, interactive, sublimated sexuality. Slapstick, cross-dressing, fetishizing of body parts, are additional markers of the form that, like the frenetic outpouring of language, fall into the narrative not from requirements of logical plotting but from the sexual energy of coupling. And while courtship proves to be a time of ordeal, the ordeal is not resolved in marriage. Marriage is a state that screwball comedy depicts as frequently as courtship, but without acknowledging victors of or solutions to conflict. Instead, these films understand marriage as a condition of discord and of passion, which does not lead to marriage's end, but rather to its continued return. Hence,

Stanley Cavell in *Pursuits of Happiness* defines a genre related to screwball to be the comedy of remarriage, where in *Bringing Up Baby* (along with *The Lady Eve, It Happened One Night, The Philadelphia Story, His Girl Friday, Adam's Rib,* and *The Awful Truth*):

> [T]he validity of marriage takes a willingness for repetition, the willing-ness for remarriage. The task of the conclusion is to get the pair back into a particular moment of their past lives together. No new vow is required, merely the picking up of an action which has been, as it were, interrupted; not starting over, but starting again, finding and picking up the thread. Put a bit more metaphysically: only those can genuinely marry who are already married. It is though you know you are married when you come to see that you cannot divorce, that is, when you find your lives simply will not disentangle. If your love is lucky, this knowledge will be greeted with laughter.[12]

If comedy is fundamentally a festival of renewal, then the marriage ac-tively chosen and desired over time works as a site for its display in being about the willing renewal of itself. The clown comedy of Chaplin, Keaton, Lloyd and Langdon sets off the male comic as alone in and victimized by an indifferent, at times malevolent, world where accident forces him to submit to the beatings of a universe over which he has little control.[13] Rising again after suffering stinging pratfalls and physical humiliations, the clown comics display the renewal of endurance and reciprocation — they stand up and return to others the blows that were delivered to them. The talking comedy of a pair of lovers borrows the physical blows and pranks, but pares them down to the size of jest between domestic partners and adds to them the verbal games which makes each speaker dependent on the presence of the other to talk back.[14] After the technological advances of the 1927 *The Jazz Singer,* where sound is synchronized with image, the talkers of these films defined what it means to be a "talkie," namely a movie about talking. The choice by these partners to continue to play together, to construct together a world which they make with the interaction of their voices, hands, and bodies, then destroy and again remake, fashions their marriage to be a joint-alive-creation, more their own than a child, more renewable because changeable than the repertoire of acts of a solitary figure facing the world alone. Yet, if the silent male comic is set loose in the world which works as the backdrop against which he can showcase his comedy, the comic couple is by no means set off in isolation, much as they may at times desire it. The world, whether it be a neutral ground like the road, the sea, or Connecticut, or places of attachment and identification like the home, place of work, or New York City, function as the settings for these marriages which are not confined to a home or private space. With at least one partner wealthy enough not to worry about a steady income (or if they work, it functions as another setting for marriage), the boundary between public and private blurs enabling the marriage to spill into unexpected locations. The life of the marriage fills the narrative with itself.

Why, though, is it that these marriages justify or enable these films? In commenting that comedy "celebrates the sense of adequacy,"[15] Morse Peckham's observation leads me to wonder, what makes these marriages adequate? What precludes the narrative's following through on abandoning the old partnership for the unknown possibility of the new? What creates in these films a sense that this comedy is good enough?

2. MODELS OF A FORM

As a way into considering what makes screwball comedy "adequate," which is another way of asking what makes its marriages adequate, I turn to the openings of two of its films to bring us closer to the particularity of screwball's comedy. I am interested in the initial moments of a couple in romantic comedies, how the films portray the couple's introductions to each other and to us, their initial looks and sounds, and what they do when first together, because that opening structure sets the pattern against which the variations of their comedy will be mapped over the course of the film. It is particularly illuminating to examine the opening scenes of meeting in *The Thin Man* and *Top Hat* for their displays of what it means to be a couple making comedy/making a marriage. Woody Van Dyke's *The Thin Man* (1934) and Mark Sandrich's *Top Hat* (1935) helped not just to define a genre of comic narrative, but as well to define partnerships which, like the teaming of Hepburn and Tracy, created marriages on film through multiple films over many years. Subsequent to *The Thin Man*, William Powell and Myrna Loy would star together in thirteen films, including five more in the *Thin Man* series; likewise, in response to the audience excitement at their dancing of the "Carioca" in *Flying Down to Rio*, Fred Astaire and Ginger Rogers would do ten movie musicals together. These performers' early appearances in *The Thin Man* and *Top Hat* defined their images as couples on film: Powell and Loy are sophisticated, wealthy, and bemused together in the face of a surrounding world of corruption, Astaire's arch theatricality is tempered by Rogers's version of American pragmatism and lack of pretension, and Rogers's sexiness is made elegant by Astaire's dancing. However, while solving crimes and performing in shows, they are primarily couples who play together. And it is how they play, their different forms of couple's play in the midst of how they work which transforms their world and lives together to be comic, to insist on their marriages' renewal, to reveal models for how to see and differentiate their form of comedy and its romance.

Jokes require a verbal or visual feedline to set them up and a punchline to "punch out" their resolution, or reveal the joke.[16] There is a kind of violent energy required in joking if it is to "knock" us as its overhearers into the recognition that this is play. William Powell and Myrna Loy perform such a knocking in their separate joke entrances to *The Thin Man*. The camera removes Nick and Nora from the linear plot-telling of the film by introducing each from the back. Powell's three bartenders, who mirror us as his audience (though we only get to see his back), watch and listen as he provides the punchline to his own joke:

> Powell: "You see Vic, the importance is in the rhythm. You should
> always have rhythm to your shaking. A Manhattan you shake to foxtrot,
> a Bronx to two-step, a dry martini you always shake to waltz time."

Delivering a monologue, Powell shakes and pontificates on dancing rhythms (the punchline), not to dance (as is everyone else around him — the feedline), but to drink. Rituals complete — shaking, giving the drink to the waiter, being given the drink by the waiter — he at last drinks. Surrounded by shouting hotel attendants dropping packages, led by Asta, Myrna Loy's entrance to us and to Powell presents her from back to front, but in a reversal of roles. While there were no great slapstick female comics like Chaplin, or teams like Laurel and Hardy, Loy when at last filmed from the front falls forward, drops packages (the feedline), and brushes herself off with, "Women and children first, boys" (the punchline, countering the mayhem of her entrance with an ambiguous assertion of command and aplomb: is she asking to be rescued or to be left alone?). Singly, each is capable of telling his or her own joke; each, therefore, is a comic, which makes one an appropriate match for the other. Yet, neither is as funny alone as they are together. The elegant Loy collapses while the equally elegant Powell gazes on, offering neither to assist her nor to disown her. The delay of their full frontal appearances asserts that these two will turn their backs on this plot, that the detective plot is not ultimately the one which most interests them; and that it is coming into the presence of the other that prompts or merits the full, "frontal" attention of each, which means the offering of a joke.

With the arrival of a worthy partner, a dialogue can begin. Nick is ultimately alone when in the company of fawning bartenders and sweet ingenues; Nora has no need of hotel men gathering around her as if like a child she needs assistance. His response, "Say, what is the score?" reveals that he is the one in the room who knows what to say and do, which makes him her partner. Nick does not act the part of the husband who insists on the fragility of his wife, and Nora insists that her fall act as the feedline to their ensuing joke which they construct together:

> Loy: "Oh, so it was you he was after."
> Powell: "Hello, sugah."
> Loy: "He dragged me into every ginmill on the block."
> Powell: "I had him out this morning."

Using the terse rhythm of almost uniformly monosyllabic Vaudeville patter,
the two construct a kind of song out of their bantering in which gaining
information is not the object of their speech. Rather, it is the pleasure which
each takes in knowing how to respond and in hearing the other's response
that drives the conversation, gives it the ring of private delight which the
voices of Powell and Loy make so evident in their delivery as the ones who
have the good fortune to be the players of this comedy team. The pleasure of
hearing their verbal juggling comes from its marked difference to the ordinarily slow, irregular exchanges of words in a conversation, from the sense
of excitement which brevity and a fast pace generate. Whereas a slow rhythm
creates the thoughtful, plaintive adagio and sonata, quicker tempos inspire
spritely allegros — the musical display of comedy. The rapid, rhythmic beat
of Powell's and Loy's speech sharpens the comedy of their words' meanings
with a comedy of sound.

Finding puns, jesting at jealousy, using each other's body as a mirror of
their own, the two continue their routine after the departure of the ingenue
who has brought with her to the table the problems of the plot, which they
immediately dismiss in the fast, edged dialogue introduced in Dashiell
Hammett's novel and developed further in the film's remaking of the couple:

Loy:	"Pretty Girl."
Powell:	"Very nice type."
Loy:	"You got types?"
Powell:	"Only you darling. Lanky brunettes with wicked jaws."
Loy:	"Who is she?"
Powell:	"Oh darling, I was hoping I wouldn't have to answer that."
Loy:	"Go on."
Powell:	"Dorothy is really my daughter. You see it was spring in Venice, and I really didn't know what I was doing. We're all like that on my father's side."
Loy:	"By the way, how is your father's side?"
Powell:	"Oh, it's much better, thanks, and yours?"
Loy:	"Say, how many drinks have you had?"
Powell:	"This will make six martinis."
Loy:	"All right. Will you bring me five more martinis, Leo, and line them up right here."
Powell:	"Hmmm."

Dismissing along with the detective plot of the film the sexual threat of a
"pretty girl," the two reduce her to an old joke ("Dorothy is really my
daughter"), and then to a pun ("How is your father's side?"); the gendered
roles, therefore, of "jealous wife" and "duplicitous husband" are undone. This
is not about a threatened marriage, but it is about playing with the elements
of a context, working them over to discover what games can be constructed
from them. Without their mutual presence as a team, there could be no play

about the "sexual threat" of a third interrupting their partnering; similarly, punning requires two voices to work the transformation in a word from one of its meanings to another with the repetition of the word in a different context. If Loy plays the "straight man" who questions here, and allows Powell the verbal freedom to design his own fun in response, she is the partner who through finding the pun turns over the joke to her benefit. They both therefore "score," and their making of comedy is an ongoing game where the role of "winner" repeatedly changes and shifts.

If the language game of joking between two people necessarily places one in the position of laying the groundwork for the context and topic of the joke and the other in the position of making the joke from out of those elements, then the joke must work as a joint production, like a conversation. Yet, it also works as a physical creation designed between the team who must present their bodies to each other as other elements of the joke. When Loy and Powell face each other to speak the above lines, the camera films them from the side and watches their mirroring acts of first leaning their heads into their hands and then lowering their hands to signal the end of the fantasized reverie. Their play insists that one's physical identity be brought into line with the other's, that that much care be paid to recognizing the motions of the other as a way to signal how completely the joke is understood, how mutually constructed it is. Loy's act of lining up the five martinis to equal Powell's brings an embodied closure to this scene about their balancing act of wit in words, gesture, and inebriation, a scene which finds itself mimicked and redesigned (though less powerfully) throughout the five films to follow.

If the gestures of Powell and Loy suggest a way in which a joke works as a mutually derived, physical construction in the mirroring of bodies, the films of Fred Astaire and Ginger Rogers bring that element of team comedy to its full flowering. In *Top Hat*, the opening scene of this couple together occurs when they dance for the first time to Irving Berlin's "Isn't it a Lovely Day," modeling what the movie will take as the way Astaire and Rogers play out their marriage. They perform a "routine" — an elaborately staged joke built from a sketch about an idea that gets repeated in varying guises as "their" routine. Its repetition makes it routine (Astaire's and Roger's routine is, of course, the wooing of the woman in dance), as does its being a dance (something that must be staged, learned from repeated practice), but what could feel *less* routine, less like the everyday than the experience of watching a couple break into dance? There is a magic to this routine that stems from its un-routineness. Whereas the aura of Powell and Loy's unroutine-routine comes from their ability to trade remarks and the delight they take in doing so, Rogers and Astaire offer instead the trade they make between their bodies. Their feet sound their wit, creativity and talent. Powell's and Loy's quick, abbreviated rhythm of exchanged speech becomes with Astaire and Rogers the bantering of taps which at a faster, more intensified, more athletic pace translate the voice-swapping of a talking comedy team to the tap-swapping of a dancing comedy team.

Tap dancing above all forms of Western dance partnering insists on a noisy, talkative interaction of bodies, where gendered movements (like that of a woman performing on toe or a man leaping) are bypassed for the androgynous noise-making and motions of the taps. Wearing the same shoes and equally free to explore the same moves, both partners challenge one another to see how far the taps of the other will lead each to perform. Tap finds its great era of expression in films of the thirties with the "talkies" that highlight its sound, the depth of talent of tappers available to be filmed from Vaudeville and Broadway, and the desire by contemporaries to see this fashionable, American invention of dancers "having it out" romantically in tap. Astaire and Rogers, using the choreography of Hermes Pan, appropriate this as their form of expression, their way of making romantic comedy.

In the Rogers and Astaire routine, repetition is a fundamental romantic comedy device that joins the two into a couple. First Rogers whistles the second stanza of "Isn't it a Lovely Day" after Astaire has finished whistling the first stanza. When he saunters away from her to trace a circle before her, an act beckoning her to join him, she does so behind him, putting first one hand in her pocket to match his and then the other as he does so. The repetition here of the joke, "Walk this way, " (uttered by the butler whom guests follow imitating the butler's gait), becomes an unspoken jest here. It is not a trope of deprecation to the imitated Astaire, but the signal that what he does she can do, that she is not there to be passively entertained, but to join him as his partner in this act of play. Imitation in step acts like the rhyming of a song. There's a kind of giddiness that accompanies rhyming words and rhyming feet, something madcap that gets at the nature of play, its desire for the screwy.

We can think of their dances as the other side of slapstick — the nonviolent comedic choreographing of bodies interacting — which engage not in dueling acts of escalating destruction but in competing feats of art. Prompted by the number of taps, the degree of diffculty of tapping at the toe or heel in relation to the position of the body, the intermingling of tapping to turning, the speed of execution, Astaire and Rogers throughout their routine modify their individual motions according to what the other is doing. They trade off who leads a step and who follows, whether to initiate a new move or to imitate what the other has done. Staging the opening bars of "Isn't it a Lovely Day" as a dialogue in imitation and in one-upmanship, the two circle around each other, but resist touching. This activity of challenge tapping is a variation of doing a play on words, where the sounds of words themselves, their double meanings, their foreignness become the grounds for generating a routine out of confusion, as in Abbott and Costello's "Who's on First?," or out of private understanding, as in Sid Caesar's imitation Japanese and its comprehension by Imogene Coco. A play on words works here as a play on the sounds of shoes through replication and transformation, games which challenge one pair of shoes first to understand the other's delivery, and then to do the same or better. The two only break into unison movements which face front to the camera, side by side to each other, when the music escalates into a crescendo, as if this is where the music/their moving have been leading — a collapsing of the dialogue into a monologue of sounds.

With claps of thunder and the music's arrival at its fastest tempo and most intense, complete execution of its melody, the dancers at last touch with a fury that sets them swinging in dance position across the stage. Unlike his partnering with Rita Hayworth, Audrey Hepburn, Leslie Caron, or even Cyd Charisse, there is a fullness to the force Astaire uses in his partnering with Rogers. This is as much about co-partnered sex as it is about strength. He throws her around him and she sturdily continues; what they create between them is not about modifying energy or treating the other as less than one's equal in force, presence or passion. Toward the close of the dance, Rogers even lifts Astaire in a knee-height turn about her as he has done to her. Their ability to mime one another in unison dancing, their responsive motions back and forth between them, their repetitions in delay of one another make their bodies seem tied to a string, tied to each other. What we see is their under-standing of their own and each other's body. This understanding is not just about how another body looks or feels against one's own, but about how it moves, how it takes shape in the world, joined through a deep connection within to knowing how to match one's own body with it to create a third body in motion composed out of the two, a sexualized body in dance.

The sound humor of the taps merges with a sight humor of the bodies discovering themselves and each other to create, like Powell and Loy, a comedy that is mutually constructed and embodied in contrasting visual and aural forms. And like Powell and Loy, Astaire and Roger's mutual knowledge of how the other plays and well-matched talent for being able to run with the joke enables them to create a shared comedy constructed from their equaliz-ing talent and desire. With whom would each member of the team more want to be than the partner who challenges and forces a deeper discovery of him or herself by virtue of being in the other's presence? When Astaire and Rogers shake hands as the final act of their dance, they introduce themselves to each other, congratulate each other on their performances, and contract themselves to a binding relationship — a marriage in dance.

The movies take these opening encounters between Powell and Loy, As-taire and Rogers as models for what their marriages are, and then recast them by discovering variations on how they play. Each film's comedy finds its source in the couple's interactive creation and recreation of this repartee; the film's romance asserts itself in its wonder that these two have found each other, and that they are able to do so easily what no one else in their narrative universes can even attempt, let alone see in the case of Astaire and Rogers or hear in that of Loy and Powell. What these couples do together is private. Huizinga writes in *Homo Ludens* that those engaged in play purposefully remove themselves from others to free themselves to create a world apart, a world of their own:

> The exceptional and special position of play is most tellingly illustrated by the fact that it loves to surround itself with an air of secrecy. Even in early childhood the charm of play is enhanced by making a 'secret' out of it. This is for *us* not for the 'others.' What the 'others' do 'outside' is no concern of ours at the moment. Inside the circle of the game the laws and customs of ordinary life no longer count. We are different and do things differently.[17]

Whether it be the athleticism of Hepburn and Grant, the desire to con and be conned of Fonda and Stanwyck, the talent for slapstick and for laughter of Grant and Dunne, the ability to argue of Tracy and Hepburn, the delight in banter of Powell and Loy, the pleasure of making a dance between Rogers and Astaire — these couples separate themselves from the others of their worlds by virtue of their gifts for what they can do together, and out of a desire to be alone with each other to "be different and do things differently." Apart from one another they are not what they are together, and together they are not only adequate as a marriage/comedy act, but unmatched, which is to say, perfectly matched.

3. CONCLUSIONS

What the films of romantic comedy want to tell, the drive of their narratives, is of marriage spilling out frenetically into all locations, making all spaces available for its playing out, as in Hitchcock's *Mr. and Mrs. Smith*; of marriage incorporating public events into its privacy and working itself out between the bedroom and the courtroom, as in Cukor's revival of the form in *Adam's Rib*; of marriage over cocktails and witty repartee set against a world of crime, as in W.S. Van Dyke's *The Thin Man*; and of marriage on the dance floor working through the miscommunications by word in dance as in Mark Sandrich's *Top Hat*. The films find their narratives of marriage of continuous interest: marriage either constitutes the plot's focus, or the text repeatedly returns to the marriage regardless of its connection to the plot. Letting go of the desire for a linear progression of storytelling — where the known is left behind, the novel is sought, and the energy of the narrative is sustained in a movement of "progress" by the individual — screwball comedies create a desire for circles of familiarity. Figuring the woman and the man as a community of two set against or within a larger community, screwball comedy joins highly defined and differentiated individuals in an interactive relation of sexual opposition and attraction. This charged interaction of the woman and man creates an ongoing sense of energy, surprise and movement in the narrative from the couple's continuous playing out of themselves when set side by side. However, the movement progresses around a series of knowns — the same partners, the same conflicts, the same settings, the same story. As the couple repeats its interaction, something gets worked through without the movement ending; where one cycle ends another begins as the marriage explores itself and the partners explore themselves in a middle realm somewhere between beginnings and ends.

When a narrative allows repetitions and returns to the known, it reveals a distinctive form of narrative desire, the wish for more, the pleasure of that more; the screwball comedy discovers happiness in an intimacy found pleasurable and returned to. Taking delight in marriage, the screwball film portrays the pleasure found in the performances of married people, of their play together as a couple and as individuals in response to one another, and the sustaining power of that delight. That it took an economy of privilege and of focus in these films to enable the luxury of exploring marriage without financial worry, without children, makes this exploration a site of privilege, not of the everyday. And yet marriage defines itself to be a site of the everyday; Kierkegaard asserts this when he asks in *Stages on Life's Way*, "What is as plain and everyday as marriage?"[18] Extraordinary times, the Depression, the coming into being of the talkies, and the instituting of the Production code in the film industry, collaborated to make marriage a location of the fantasy of filmmaking, transforming it from a story so ordinary it could not be told to an everyday story laced with the possibility of the remarkable. "You see, every once in a while I find myself dancing," Fred Astaire tells Ginger Rogers when they first meet in *Top Hat* — an ordinary feeling made extraordinary in the performance of a couple at play.

NOTES

1. These running brides on film connect themselves to earlier women in narratives — to Jane Eyre for one, whose ultimate act of self-expression is to walk as a bride away or toward a home and a husband as her assertion of the right to choose where or if she will place herself sexually and as whose partner. Emma Bovary runs away from marriage when she tosses her bridal bouquet into the fire and runs outdoors toward her first lover with whom she discovers sexual freedom, an act which can never return her to her husband. However, it is Jane Eyre's running back to Rochester to choose to be his bride as she has come to understand what that means which presages something of the story these films

tell, of the woman who reframes marriage as a ground for her freedom, sexuality, and self-expression.

2. For a more extensive reading of these four films and the cultural moment in which they arose, see James Harvey's *Romantic Comedy* (New York: Alfred A. Knopf, 1987), in particular Chapter 6: "1934: Turning Point," 107–139.

3. Ed Sikov, *Screwball* (New York: Crown Publishers, 1989) 84.

4. Elizabeth Kendall, *The Runaway Bride* (New York: Alfred A. Knopf, 1990) 138.

5. Molly Haskell, *From Reverence to Rape: The Treatment of Women in the Movies* (Chicago: Chicago University Press, 1987) 127.

6. The development of the male-female comedy team in Vaudeville from the 1890s to 1932 charts a course from the immigrant humor of ethnic marriage routines of, for example, John and Maggie Fielding doing sketch acts like "The Tipperary Couple," to the enactment in song and dance of courtship in elegant evening clothes by Hallan and Hart (like those to be featured by Ziegfeld), to the carping, shrewish wife and defenseless husband in the "talking acts" of Melville and Higgins, to the routines of Ryan and Lee which first featured the woman's "stupidity" as the primary force of the couple's comedy. The dividing of "straight man" from comic in the team always made the humor be at one partner's expense; vaudeville did not produce a couple who shared the ability for "smart" talk and for being the butt or creator of the joke. Shirley Staples' *Male-Female Comedy Teams in Ameican Vaudeville 1865–1932* (Ann Arbor: UMI Research Press, 1984) provides a sweeping overview of the evolution and decline of the male-female comedy team in Vaudeville.

7. For an extended discussion on how the woman of these films embodied an image for the American audience of endurance and hope in the Depression, see Kendall chapter 3, "Romantic Comedy Settles In" 50–65.

8. George Meredith, "An Essay on Comedy" in *Comedy*, ed. and intro. Wylie Sypher (Baltimore: The Johns Hopkins University Press, 1986) 15.

9. It is one of Kendall's primary narratives to tell how this collaboration was achieved between the central directors and women stars of these films.

10. Fittingly it was in 1934 that Carl Hubbell, pitcher for the New York Giants, struck out the future members of the Hall of Fame Babe Ruth, Lou Gehrig, Jimmie Foxx, Al Simmons, and Joe Cronin with a pitch he mastered and then called the "screwball." Sikov 19.

11. See Duane Byrge and Robert Milton Miller's *The Screwball Comedy Films* (Jefferson, North Carolina: McFarland and Co., 1991) 8; Wes D. Gerhring's *Screwball Comedy: A Genre of Madcap Romance* (New York: Greenwood Press, 1986) 7; and Kendall 88.

12. Stanley Cavell, *Pursuits of Happiness* (Cambridge: Harvard University Press, 1981) 126–127.

13. Leland A. Poague, *The Cinema of Frank Capra: An Approach to Film Comedy* (New York: A.S. Barnes and Co., 1975) 34. Poague has interesting things to say about the clown comedy of Aristophanes and its reappearance in silent film comedy and the plot comedy of Shakespeare and its reformulation in the cinema of Frank Capra in his chapter, "Capra and the Comic Tradition."

14. It is significant that Mae West is the only model of the solo female "clown" from the early films of Hollywood, and that her routine was about talking sex. West works as the bridge between these eras of comedy to suggest how the woman could be brought into comedy, as dangerous and wonderful in speech and as a sexual presence, as the male clown had been in visual jest. Similarly, the absence of female comedy teams in Vaudeville and early film with the exception of Hal Roach's "creation" of the female Laurel and Hardy in Thelma Todd and ZaSu Pitts, (Pitts is later replaced by Patsy Kelly; see Leonard Maltin's *Movie Comedy Teams* [New York: New American Library, 1970] for a more detailed account of this female movie comedy team), reveals how the role of the woman comic revolved around her sexual interaction with the real or imagined presence of a male partner. Screwball comedy uses and moves past this sexualized partnering by giving the woman and the man the freedom both to exploit and to dispense with a sexually determined rendering of their comic roles.

15. Morse Peckham, *Man's Rage for Chaos* (New York: Schocken Books, 1967).

16. Milt Josefsberg, *Comedy Writing* (New York: Harper and Row, 1987) 1. I am indebted to Josefsberg's delineation of the elements of humor in writing.

17. Johan Huizinga, *Homo Ludens* (Boston: The Beacon Press, 1955) 12.

18. Søren Kierkegaard, *Stages on Life's Way*, ed. and trans. Howard V. Hong and Edna H. Hong (Princeton: Princeton University Press, 1988) 118.

WORKS CITED

Byrge, Duane, and Robert Milton Miller. *The Screwball Comedy Films*. Jefferson, NC: McFarland and Co., 1991.

Cavell, Stanley. *Pursuits of Happiness*. Cambridge: Harvard University Press, 1981.

Gerhring, Wes D. *Screwball Comedy: A Genre of Madcap Romance*. New York: Greenwood Press, 1986.

Harvey, James. *Romantic Comedy*. New York: Alfred A. Knopf, 1987.

Haskell, Molly. *From Reverence to Rape: The Treatment of Women in the Movies*. Chicago: Chicago University Press, 1987.

Huizinga, Johans. *Homo Ludens*. Boston: Beacon Press, 1955.

It Happened One Night. Dir. Frank Capra. With Claudette Colbert, Clark Gable, Walter Connolly, Jameson Thomas. Screenplay Robert Riskin. Based on the short story "Night Bus" by Samuel Hopkins Adams. Columbia, 1934.

Josefsberg, Milt. *Comedy Writing*. New York: Harper and Row, 1987.

Kendall, Elizabeth. *The Runaway Bride*. New York: Alfred A. Knopf, 1990.

Kierkegaard, Søren. *Stages on Life's Way*. Ed. and Trans. Howard V. Hong and Edna H. Hong. Princeton: Princeton University Press, 1988.

Maltin, Leonard. *Movie Comedy Teams*. New York: New American Library, 1970.

Meredith, George. "An Essay on Comedy," in: *Comedy*, ed. Wylie Sypher. Baltimore: The Johns Hopkins University Press, 1986.

The Palm Beach Story. Dir. Preston Sturges. With Claudette Colbert, Joel McCrea, Mary Astor, Rudy Vallee. Screenplay Preston Sturges. Paramount, 1942.

Peckham, Morse. *Man's Rage for Chaos*. New York: Schocken Books, 1967.

Poague, Leland A. *The Cinema of Frank Capra: An Approach to Film Comedy*. New York: A.S. Barnes and Co., 1975.

Sikov, E. *Screwball*. New York: Crown Publishers, 1989.

Staples, Shirley. *Male-Female Comedy Teams in American Vaudeville 1865–1932*. Ann Arbor: UMI Research Press, 1984.

The Thin Man. Dir. Woody Van Dyke. With Myrna Loy, William Powell, Maureen O'Sullivan, Asta. Screenplay Albert Hackett and Frances Goodrich. Based on the novel by Dashiell Hammett. MGM, 1934.

Top Hat. Dir. Mark Sandrich. With Fred Astaire, Ginger Rogers, Edward Everett Horton, Helen Broderick. Screenplay Dwight Taylor and Allan Scott. Choreography Hermes Pan. Music and Lyrics Irving Berlin. RKO, 1935.

16

Mae West Was Not a Man: Sexual Parody and Genre in the Plays and Films of Mae West

ANDREA J. IVANOV

I. PERSONA AND PARODY

I am an example — rare I hear — of a writer who performed her function perfectly, in the sense that I was both the creator and the consumer of my own basic literary material...

Yes, I first had to create myself, and to create the fully mature image I had to write it out to begin with. I admit that my writing is only for the theatre, that my ideas and my texts were from the first for the stage, through the secret doors of my personal life. But no one has clearly created himself in the public eye as I have, unless it's George Bernard Shaw or Flagpole Kelly.

Mae West, *Goodness Had Nothing to Do With It* (72)

The comedy of Mae West began with the authoring of "Mae West." Notoriety from her early vaudeville and stage career shaped the figure created through playscripts, films, and ephemera such as theatre reviews, studio releases and publicity clippings. Long before the advent of her film career, Mae West was writing and performing in off-Broadway plays and productions usually seen as offensive, vulgar and cheap by current moral and legal interests. Theatrical reviewers, until the debut of *Diamond Lil* in 1928, consistently panned her plays and excoriated her. In 1927, Mae West was sentenced to, and served ten days in prison for producing an "immoral play"; *Sex*, her melodramatic tale about a waterfront prostitute, ran for 383 performances before it was raided by police and forcibly closed. That she reaped a million or more dollars worth of free publicity from such legal actions was hardly a surprise to any of the parties involved. "When girls go wrong," Lady Lou informs the fallen Sally in Paramount's 1933 film, *She Done Him Wrong*, "men go right after 'em."

West enacted "herself" strategically — the "self-parody" involved in "doing herself" having been read as "camp" and as masquerade. Several critics find West engaging in the masquerade of sexual identity, whether this be as female female impersonator, as "phallic" woman, or both. In "'The Kinda Comedy That Imitates Me:' Mae West's Identification with the Feminist Camp," Pamela Robertson argues that West's female female impersonation works to hyperbolize the feminine through masquerade; it parodies drag, avoiding the denigration of women that, as some critics argue, is entailed in female impersonation. West "recuperates" the female impersonator aesthetic as a "female aesthetic" (63). West's female fans of the 1930s identified with her and therefore this identification was a camp practice — a "feminist camp" (63). In "The Power and Allure: The Mediation of Sexual Difference in the Star Image of Mae West," Ramona Curry argues that "contemporary gay male and feminist interests in this cultural icon" do not clash; rather they are "reconcilable, even complementary: these audiences have common cause in understanding the sign as a parody of gender as a social construction" (2). I agree with both Robertson and Curry, but contend that West's performance or parody — her "camp" — must also be understood in terms of her persona's construction in comedic and melodramatic genres. Parody as a mode of comedy interacts with West's gender parody through modes of excess. The sexual identity of West's persona was alternatively questioned or "confirmed" through forms of gender(ed) and generic excess.

In this essay, I examine the discursive "authorship" of West's persona, and the sexual parody or "camp" that made West's comedy more than self-mockery and allowed her to manipulate constraints of gender and body. Secondly, I analyze the dialectic between persona and genre. The "masquerading," parodying, and "camping" persona enters the genre — mask, and all — most prominently through the theme of multiple lovers. This theme marks the excess that constituted much of her parody of gender roles and sexualities. The premise of West's promiscuity also appears to forestall comedy's traditional closure in marital union. Pressure to "get Mae married" emanated from the Hays Office as well as from the demands of narrative comedy.[1] However, West's persona was also constructed through hybrid genres, such as the comic melodrama and Western, in which the modes of parodic and melodramatic excess provided the persona means for controlling humor and deconstructing obstacles to the play of her sexual desire.

Readings of Mae West's persona and, ultimately, of her parodic practices, are often understood in light of, or in the wake of vaudeville stars Eva Tanguay and Sophie Tucker. Martin and Segrave describe Tanguay as the "biggest star in vaudeville's history," interpreting her blend of raucous antics, lewd ballads, and generally grotesque demeanor as symbolizing "the growing restlessness of women emerging from Victorian darkness"; she "was very much the forerunner of, and influence on, the liberated 1920s flapper" (68). Similarly, Tucker was "the bold brassy hunk of woman, flaunting her sexuality through bawdy songs" (79). In *Horrible Prettiness*, Robert Allen evaluates the West persona as becoming "less and less threatening as it became more and more difficult to take her expressive sexuality seriously" (281). Quoting Marjorie Rosen, Allen presents the image of a 40-year-old, overweight West in 1933 as a "turn-of-the-century sausage"; West "had come to resemble nothing so much as a female impersonator, parodying rather than exuding the vamp's controlling sexuality" (281). Fixing West in the Tanguay and Tucker tradition of the grotesque, Allen thus suggests that West's transgressive sexuality was a ruse. His discussion of her career follows the narrative of the sexually threatening female entertainer who eventually turns to parody when her body will no longer sustain the signs of a seamless, "serious" sexuality. By the time she emerged as a "star" in theatre — famous as Diamond Lil — this "unthinkable" sexuality was on the verge of being exposed. But what was actually exposed, argues Allen, was a sexuality "unthinkable" in another sense. In the "history of burlesque since 1869," the denouement of West's career and persona may be — perhaps a little too neatly — summarized in the "final strategy" of this history: grotesque figures such as Tanguay's, Tucker's, and West's were "authorized to be transgressive because, by their fusing of incongruent cultural categories [such as age and sexuality], they had been 'disqualified' as objects of erotic desire" (281–282).

In the picture of the 1933 West, both Robert Allen and Marjorie Rosen suggest that West's comedy relied chiefly on self-parody. Since her sex appeal "was no longer obvious," this parody's implied target was West's own failure (largely as body, as physical image) to meet implicit standards for acceptance as a viably "sexy" woman. On the contrary, West and other diverse agents and media changed "norms" of sexual attractiveness. In 1933, the year after West made her debut in films, a number of articles discussing "Westian" influences appeared in local city papers. Despite her 40 years and full figure, or rather, because of them, West was altering fashion. "Light journalism," especially letters to "Mae" from columnists such as J.P. McEvoy appeared, thanking West for her eye-opening revision of the "fashionable" woman's body. "You see," writes McEvoy, "for years I've been looking at women and wondering in my artless fashion, what all the fuss was about. They were all kind of straight up and down, like men, only they didn't have nearly such good shoulders" (McEvoy 1933). *Motion Picture* ran a July 1933 article entitled, "Curves! Hollywood Wants Them — and So Will You!" It claims, among other things, that the "advent of beer," and "the influence of Mae West" led to an increased "avoirdupois — and curviness — of beauty on the screen" (Tildesley 34). Her "coup de gras" in this sense, then, might have been the type of headlines that read, "Physicians Endorse Mae West's Curves:"

> Milwaukee, Oct. 6, 1933 — Mae West, whose curves won her fame in the movies, has received the full approval of the Central Association of Obstetricians and Gynecologists...
> "If it is Mae West who is responsible for this new and yet age-old fashion, my hat is off to her," declared Dr. Holmes. "The return to pumpness [*sic*] in women is a boon to motherhood."

A month after this report, the following headlines appeared in the *Examiner*: "Will Mae West Make Us Fat?" Dr. Morris Fishbein, editor of the *Journal of the American Medical Association*, commented on the repeal of prohibition and the styles inspired by Mae West: "the Mae West renaissance and the cocktail will go hand in hand in adding pounds to the average American" (*Examiner* 11/1/33). The sanctions and concerns of the two medical associations weave the discourse back to J.P. McEvoy and his facetious remarks on viewing the Rubens paintings: "There must be a lot of inflation going on in here."[2]

To create a "fully mature image," Mae West claims that she had to "write it out to begin with" (*Goodness* 72). The written, or more precisely, discursive production of West's persona is more than evident in journalistic and star-system ephemera. West manipulated these texts to reinforce her viability as a sexual icon. The "self-parody" that critics such as Allen and Rosen note in West may also be read more accurately as a form of the "gender parody" theorized by Judith Butler. If, according to de Beauvoir, one "becomes a woman," Butler finds that "In this sense, gender is in no way a stable identity or locus of agency from which various acts proceed; rather, it is an identity tenuously constituted in time — an identity instituted through a *stylized repetition of acts*" ("Performative Acts and Gender Constitution" 270).[3]

Differences between West's self- and gender parody are illustrated by a scene from *My Little Chickadee* (Universal 1940). At the end of the film, W.C. Fields slyly repeats the invitation to "Come up 'n see me sometime," while West counters (in her best Fields voice), "I'll be sure and do that, my little chickadee." Following is a close-up of West's behind slowly sashaying up the stairs, "The End" cleverly superimposed over the image of her rear-end. As an instance of self-parody, this single image might suggest the loss of her sexual attractiveness and "the end" of her career. Indeed, her "end" is simply assimilated into the repetition of a piece of comic business clichéd since "the end" of the silent film era. In its "broadest" reading, this visual joke becomes a reader/spectator's inference of intertextuality. By 1940, the conflation/connection of the visual with the literal was a well-worn one, "ironized" only by the owner of "the end" being shown.

Alternatively, the close-up and subsequent enlargement of the Mae West behind serves as an extreme exaggeration, another instance of excess, after the already disorienting reversal of personas and genders. There is pleasure afforded in the erotic as well as in the comic spectacle; the seductive sway of West's behind and its size plays into certain values of sexual attractiveness. Consequently, a certain type of femininity is parodied. Indeed, it is chiefly this other instance of parody which seems to situate the West persona in light of Butler's theory. When Cuthbert J. Twillie extends the invitation from "the bottom" of the stairs, Flower Belle answers. Yet, to contemporary spectators familiar with the two famous personas, it is actually W.C. Fields who invites Mae West to "come up and see [him] sometime." Not only are the "stars" blatantly "breaking character" and emerging as "themselves," but they are performing the final gender reversal in a film already replete with them. Earlier in the film, we see Fields prancing around in a frilly robe, and West poised with pistols firing. The idea that an original is always already copy may well be exemplified by the illusion of the two stars "breaking character." Who are the two stars, W.C. Fields and Mae West, but "character"? The "characters" of Flower Belle and Twillie are never more than the "characters" of Mae West and W.C. Fields. Their final exchange is a polite and mutual "self" parody, intended, perhaps, to reveal their "true" selves while only exposing more of their "characters," and in turn, their status as constructs. The question becomes, of course, can we see past this act of legerdemain to the constructedness of the gender, or is it part of the "joke" that beneath that pink robe (and obviously so) there is *really* W.C. Fields, a *real* man, and a real gendered subject?

Mary Ann Doane writes, "Male transvestism is an occasion for laughter," whereas "female transvestism is only another occasion for desire" ("Film and Masquerade" 48). From this comment, and similar ones by Molly Haskell and other critics of drag and camp, we begin to see that the "joke" is aimed specifically at the (straight) male spectator. Andrew Ross quotes Rebecca Bell-Metereau's argument that the comic/erotic distinction relies on more than gender alignment. According to her, female impersonation may be seriously, 'willingly,' or 'sympathetically' received by the groups within the film (*No Respect* 157 n40). However, in *My Little Chickadee*, no such "sympathetic" group exists. In Freudian terms, the straight male spectator of this film becomes either that "second person" who finds what is comic in the object of ridicule, or that third person in the economy of the "tendentious" joke, who has witnessed an exposure.[4] W.C. Fields in a frilly, pink robe is comic for a number of reasons: bibulous, overblown, and bald, he is clearly a grotesque in the trappings of a beauty. Summarizing the viewpoints of those who hold that such a "comic" moment is indeed gynephobic or misogynistic, Carole-Anne Tyler quotes Alison Lurie: "'Although women in male clothes usually look like gentlemen, men who wear women's clothes, unless they are genuine transsexuals, seem to imitate the most vulgar and unattractive sort of female dress, as if in a spirit of deliberate and hostile parody'" ("Boys Will Be Girls" 41). Tyler analyzes a scene from *Pink Flamingos*, in which Raymond watches a "beautiful woman" who "lifts her skirts to reveal her penis" (44). The male spectator laughs only if he does not identify with Raymond's desire; "his laughter is a defensive response to the castration anxiety suddenly evoked and evaded by making what is literally a transvestic identification with the phallic woman" (44). However, the masquerade Fields dons is far from a "man-scare-ade." The male spectator's laughter becomes an anticipatory response to this very joke; he is relieved that should Fields remove the robe (an act which is imminent as he parades in front of the bathtub), he won't be surprised.

It is dubious, though, that Fields always "possesses" the phallus in *My Little Chickadee*. Misogyny and violence toward women and children were a staple theme of Fields's comedy, but often these themes worked to humiliate him, or else render him "feminine." In an earlier train scene, Flower Belle becomes Twillie's typical female nemesis, nonchalantly picking off Indians with her pistols as Fields cowers in the aisle; "You can't intimidate me," she tells them. Instances such as these challenge Fields's phallic status vis-à-vis his position in a "male" role, and as a "male" actor. Ramona Curry, for example, sees "'Mae West' as a sign of a phallic woman" ("Power and Allure" 282), chiefly insofar as that term encompasses a sense of "power." Curry acknowledges the term "'phallic's' association with the social category 'male,'" but believes this association to be made "historically, not physically or essentially" (282). I would argue, however, that the scene's context (comedic hyperbole) renders West's "maleness" as a comic pose. Despite his browbeaten status, Twillie's misogyny and sexual "ogling" of Flower Belle may do more to reassure the male spectator about the location of the phallus than do the posings of West.

Critics of camp and drag have often addressed the topic of the phallic woman, using it frequently in reference to Mae West. Much of the criticism addressing this topic was raised most influentially, if not first, by feminist film criticism of the seventies. In her discussion of the fetishization of the star, Claire Johnston finds "traces of phallic replacement" in the Mae West persona; "The voice itself is strongly masculine, suggesting the absence of the male, and establishes a male/non-male dichotomy" (211). The terms called forth by the sign that the star persona as "Woman" presents, therefore,

are prohibitive, and set up a binary system of inquiry that is self-reflexive —
even the "non-male" becomes a marker of the "male." Johnston does admit
a "female element" into the picture of the phallic dress, but this she dismisses
as an introduction of the "mother image," which simply works to express the
"male oedipal fantasy" (212). The West persona, in the end, mobilizes its
aggressive sexuality and elaborate dress in the interest of "sexist ideology"
(Johnston 212). Whether because it unconsciously allows men the privilege
to fetishize it, or because it sets an "anti-liberated" example of body bondage,
West's persona celebrates its male and "non-male" qualities, giving them
ultimate preference over a disturbing or occluded femininity.

The tendency of recent feminist and camp critics to see traces of the phallic
in the West persona finds its less sophisticated parallel in popular press of the
thirties. Even though that particular "occasion for desire," that moment of
actual transvestism, seldom occurred during the film career of Mae West,
charges that West was a man — or rather, the superlative female impersonator,
proliferated into the status of legend or famous apocrypha, ever since George
Davis's tribute to her in a 1934 *Vanity Fair* article. Photographs of a "masculine" Mae West certainly do exist, remnants of her early stint in vaudeville
as a male impersonator. Though she rarely — if ever — practiced formal male
impersonation or cross-dressing in her Hollywood career, other modes of
"troubling" gender (to borrow Butler's term) were open to her. The "camp"
for which Mae West is heralded is one dimension of this gender parody. Camp
often questions, provokes and denies the essential nature of the self; its
sexuality or gender is never beyond doubt "male" or "female." Its definition
is surprisingly elusive and exclusive; indeed, what seems to characterize
camp practitioners and critics alike is the assumption that one comes to know
it through lived experience. Ross calls camp a "subjective process," then
quotes Thomas Hess aptly stating that it "'exists in the smirk of the beholder'"
(*No Respect* 145).

As criticism within the last twenty years began to address camp as an
important cultural phenomenon, there were finer slants in appraisals of West's
"male impersonation." West was the "star who most professionally exploits
the ironies of artifice when, like a female drag queen, she represents a woman
who parodies a burlesque woman, and then seems to take on the role for real,
as a way of successfully fielding every kind of masculine response known to
woman" (Ross 160). Booth writes that "after watching Mae West or a drag
queen, we should feel less inclined to take, for example, coquettishness
seriously — more detached from the rituals of courtship in which we are
expected to participate" (59). Finally, referring to one of West's famous
homosexual "sexual allusions," Philip Core draws her into "the camp" by
calling her at once "'womanly,' and 'one of the lads'" (192).

After West's Hollywood career, and before serious critical attention was
given to camp, there were signs that occasional press was still occupied with

the problem of West's gender. Attempts were made to establish her unquestionable "womanliness." A 1949 *Life* article entitled "Mae's X-Ray" offers some fruitful evidence for those who discount West's viability as a (male) female impersonator, or for those who wish to quash the annoying rumors that "Mae was really a man." West performed this bit of publicity work to "set a good example," as it were, and encourage people to get chest x-rays for the early detection of tuberculosis. The writer of the article was well aware that a "detection" of another sort was really the occasion for the reference to West's anatomy. However, the findings of the medical imprint only revealed what everyone already suspected lay under those laced corsets: a shocking, scandalous extra roll of fat pinched neatly between her waist piece and bra.

Not surprisingly, critical opinion of West's place in the star system, as well as her popularity with camp and cross-dressing devotees, points to a fundamental ambivalence about West's femininity. That Mae West was and has been heralded as a camp phenomenon is indisputable. But her comedy was mediated through more than her clothing and mannerisms, or her "camping." West's persona depended on the idea of an excessive sexual desirability, and, at the same time, a control over that desirability. During her early stage and film career, Mae West debunked the traditional "feminine" more through the excess of (desirable) flesh and an outright enjoyment of sexuality.

But the "excesses" of Mae West's persona differ from those belonging to the whole of her comedy. The distinction I wish to make mirrors the difference between West's heady claim to "sole" self-creation and the warring signs of a more diffuse creative process: the persona — complete with ambivalent gender and guises, found so attractive to spectators who wished to shake up the sexual status quo — must act within, and with specific genres of comedy. West may have "created herself," but she was also created. Mark Booth writes that "where the aesthete makes his life a work of art, the camp person tries to do the same with his personality" (27). Of course, the "creation" of a personality is as much a convention of vaudeville (not to mention Hollywood's star system) as it is part of the camp aesthetic.[5] Despite the traces of "maleness" that pegged West as a female female impersonator, the way in which her persona is played out in the genres of her plays and films necessitates the full recognition of the "woman" underneath.

II. WHERE THE ONE
BECOMES THE MANY

I decided to go back to vaudeville before I had all the young men in the neighborhood playing at gang warfare. I saw the pattern of my relationship with the male sex that was to recur throughout my life, where the

one becomes the many, and without so much as my having to lift even
my voice. This is not ego, saying this; just a fact.

Mae West, *Goodness Had Nothing To do With It* (25)

The theme of multiple lovers functions as a genre convention as well as a
sign of sexual excess. When Tira (Mae West) encounters a fortune teller in
I'm No Angel (Paramount, 1934), he tells her that he sees a "man in her life."
She replies, "What, only one?" Mae West's one-liners often represent the
intersection of the persona's work on the genre; she predicts and "plots" the
course of her own films and "future." Before "the one" at film's end, we can
expect "the many."

The filmic "Mae West" evolved through figures of the golddigger, the
"femme amoureuse" and the prostitute, Diamond Lil, all of these requiring
an "excess" of paramours. The persona had to negotiate the fine line between
self-parody and gender parody, in addition to overcoming — or attempting
to overcome — the demand from both studio and genre to close her negotiations in marriage. Though the Hays code was largely responsible for attenuat-
ing the pasts of West's protagonists, the allusion was clear. West used a
"strategy" of multiple lovers to rewrite and recast the prostitute into a figure
of power instead of exploitation.

The premise for West's unpublished first play, *The Ruby Ring* (1921), is
based on the multiplicity of guises that its golddigger protagonist can assume.
The blond-haired toast of the party, Gloria, makes a bet with the frustrated
Irene and Alice, promising them that she can make five different men propose
to her in five minutes apiece. Successfully performing five different "acts,"
Gloria wins her bet; when her handsome husband beckons her home, she
shows him her new ruby ring — the ring of adulterous intention that replaces
the ring of marital fidelity.

In collaboration with Adrienne Leitzbach, Mae West authored another
unpublished play, *The Hussy* (1922), which incorporated the same "bet"
premise of *The Ruby Ring*. With Margie Lamont in *Sex* (1926), however, West
moves her authorship and characterization (both written and performative)
into the (il)legitimated place of the waterfront prostitute. Nora Ramsey of *The
Hussy* ultimately plays into the "true love" marriage contract, as does Margie
Lamont of *Sex*. But Margie's past is undisputed, as is the greater melodrama
involved in her sacrifice: instead of marrying the socialite's son and improv-
ing her lot, Margie chooses to marry her sailor boy lover, largely out of
kindness to the matronly socialite who has already unjustly accused Margie
of conspiracy to drug and rob her. Margie's marriage in the end hardly co-opts
or lessens the "power" of her position as prostitute; the majority of the humor
in the play comes from precisely this social-ethical "position." At the end of
a series of articles syndicated in 1933, feature writer Martin Sommers quotes

one of the court-deigned "objectionable" exchanges between Margie and one of her "vultures" in *Sex*:

> Rocky: Where's my collar button?
> Margie: They're your collar buttons. Find them yourself. Who do
> you think I am — your wife? (qtd. in Tuska 34–35)

In complementary ways, two other plays in West's canon bolster the position of women and their practice of sexuality. The 1928 play, *Pleasure Man* was a telling reversal of the multiple lover theme. Based on the lurid backstage romances of a vaudevillian actor, the play paid homage to a man's desire for several lovers (and the production to West's penchant for multiple variety-type acts). Yet Rodney Terrill's skills at and "unleashed" passion for seductions only lead to his castration and death.[6] The female characters of the play are thus "revenged," and a reverse double-standard is humorously implied. Though in many ways sympathetic to gay life, Mae West's exploration and production of homosexuality in *The Drag* (1927) may have been an effort to "normalize," "save," or empower the prostitute protagonist of Sex merely by virtue of her heterosexuality. *The Drag* opened in Connecticut on January 31, 1927, and thus played concurrently (if not in proximity) with *Sex*. A tolerant, if somewhat sensational, confrontation with homosexuality was far more controversial at the time than the depiction of the "oldest profession" (Ward 14).

The film adaptations of the plays *Diamond Lil* (1928) and *Frisco Kate* (1930), and of the novel, *The Constant Sinner* (1930) did not eliminate the multiple lover theme. In these films, the desire for (multiple) liaisons is allowed to flourish, even though the West character might temporarily favor one ("the best") over another. This partially explains the continual return to the Diamond Lil clone. Her generosity is stereotypical but lends her promiscuity an ethic (never take another woman's man, for instance), and a delight, rather than a self-effacing, self-destructive search for intimacy or gratification. The "razor edge" of this "delight" comes in an exchange from the film adaptation of *Diamond Lil*, *She Done Him Wrong* (Paramount, 1933). Lady Lou "rides into" the film in an open carriage, greeted by the upturned noses of the ladies on the sidewalks. She disembarks and is met by a mother and child:

> POOR IRISH MOTHER (holding hand of her little boy): Lady
> Lou, you're a fine gal, a fine woman.
> LOU: Finest woman that ever walked the streets!

West's 1930 novel, *The Constant Sinner* (originally titled *Babe Gordon*) lacks the woman of ambiguous profession, and notably, the one-liners and innuendo as well. Instead, we are embroiled in the very unambiguous and lurid environs, habits, and desires of a small-time hooker who makes good.

Regardless of their social standing, however, all of the Mae West characters participate, to some extent, in the following discourse of desire:

> Babe was born a *femme amoureuse*. Her idea was that if a man can have as many women as he wants, there is no reason why a woman should not do the same thing. She was one of those women who were put on this earth for men — not one man but many men. (15–16)

To the extent her liberal sexual practice is allowed to go unhampered, West's prostitute persona is not compromised. Based on the unpublished *Frisco Kate* (1930), the film *Klondike Annie* (Paramount, 1936) features Rose Carleton, the "San Francisco Doll." Like Frisco Kate, she is a woman "with a past," and boards a boat headed for Nome, Alaska, escaping night club owner Chan Lo and her confinement as his captive performer. After murdering Chan Lo, she hides from the law by impersonating a settlement worker, Annie Alden. "Klondike Annie" is then allowed to do good in the community in which she had first planned to seek anonymity and refuge. Her decision to return to San Francisco to clear her name is also a decision to choose ship captain and lover Bull Brackett, rather than the more "respectable" avenue of marriage with the policeman. Redeemed is her sense of self-esteem, not necessarily her licentious ways.

In an article entitled "Mae West as Censored Commodity: The Case of *Klondike Annie*," Ramona Curry argues that the "case history of *Klondike Annie* makes evident that it was West's unconfined *enjoyment* and control of her sexuality, rather than the depiction of outlaw sexuality itself, that was received as transgressive" (77). Curry's argument addresses the reasons for Mae West's declining box office success, pointing out that her devaluation as a "star" around 1936 was undertaken "*within* the industry," largely through the agency of the Production Code Administration (57). In so many words, "Mae West" had become an ideological threat to dominant political and economic hegemony (77).

The prostitute figure central to Mae West's films became the instituted, stereotypical agent of perverse enjoyment; the "legitimate" illegitimate practitioner of excessive sexuality. Unlike the oppressed prostitute, West's character was narcissistic, reveling in, and joking about her excessive admiration. The epitome of this narcissism is popularly recounted in the anecdote of the mirrors that lined the ceiling of her Rossmore apartment boudoir. "I like to see how I'm doin'," she would quip, and biographical accounts only confirm the more or less steady stream of sexual partners to this venue. Drawing from previous clinical practitioners, Freud defined narcissism as "the attitude of a person who treats his own body in the same way in which the body of a sexual object is ordinarily treated" ("On Narcissism" 14 *Stand. Ed.* 73).[7] The subject that fails to transfer his original narcissism to an object other than himself —

who fails to sexually overevaluate or fall "in love" — thus becomes prey to a secondary narcissism.

Theories of narcissism may also explain the mechanism of fusion whereby the image of the persona becomes indistinguishable from the image of the actress/performer. Defending her authorship of *Diamond Lil*, Mae West stated, "I have five men in love with me in 'Diamond Lil' and most authors can't keep up one love interest" (Mae West 81). In this statement, the conflation between the Mae West persona, the character Diamond Lil, the actress Mae West, and the "author" or playwright Mae West is so complete as to be vertiginous — a veritable whirlwind of identities. Contemporary practitioners and theorists of psychoanalysis note that the narcissistic woman often grafts the ideal self on to her physical body through the metaphor of the doll (Lowen 191; Kuhn 13). In naming her character, the "San Francisco Doll" in *Klondike Annie*, West suggests the unfeeling idol analogous to Freud's "type of female most frequently met with" ("On Narcissism" 89). Illustrating and inhabiting the narrative of the arch narcissist, the idol does not need to love, but to be loved.

For one reason, West's persona may be read as just such a type. The "intensity" of her self-love is manifest in the ubiquitousness of her lovers. But the altruistic actions of Klondike Annie, as well as the "romantic" love Tira or Lady Lou shows for the Cary Grant characters, contradict the idol caricature of West. Freud writes about "the importance of this type of woman for the erotic life of mankind" ("On Narcissism" 89). Once again, West was concerned with the erotic life of *woman*kind, though her persona inevitably acted on an understanding of her appeal to men. Further statements by Freud explain and anticipate the appeal of a Mae West. Recognizing the "charm" of the self-contented and inaccessible, he writes that "great criminals and humorists, as they are represented in literature, compel our interest by the narcissistic consistency with which they manage to keep away from their ego anything that would diminish it" (89). The panoply of West's comedic strategies, as well as the threat she posed in the enjoyment of sexuality, seems rooted in her attainment and perpetuation of that "unassailable libidinal position which we ourselves have since abandoned" (89).

In Sarah Kofman's reading of Freud, man finds the narcissistic woman so attractive out of a nostalgia for his own primary narcissism, that "lost paradise of childhood" (52). "The humorist," she writes," has in common with the great criminal the fact that he has succeeded in conquering his ego and holding it in contempt, thanks to his superego ... humor is particularly suited for freeing and exalting the ego" (55). A woman humorist often poses a double threat: she is not only content in her "unassailable" self-containment, but jokes about it.

The theme of many lovers, though suggestive of a potentially unfavorable narcissism, celebrates sexual enjoyment and desire. The "scare" behind Mae

West's "man-scare-ade" is produced by the compounding of West's "woman-liness" through such joyous excesses. Regina Barreca writes, "If the quality associated with Good Girls is control, then the quality most explicitly associated with Bad Girls is excess" (46). Furthermore, to be a woman who tells a joke that is not self-effacing is to be a woman who has access to power. Barreca quotes certain psychologists' findings, stating that it is the "witty person" in a "natural group" who is "among the most powerful members of the group" (110). She calls the "equation that makes women's humor subversive" that equation between "women using humor and women using power" (111). Thus, the power of the punch line becomes a form of control. "Mae West" exuded control both by punch lines and those other types of "lines." Witness the "control" of those "lines" through the metaphor of the corsets she popularized, the tight struggle against her body that was redeemable for her own uses.

Still, though the source of much of West's humor, the use of sexual pleasure may have its political limits. Luce Irigaray writes that woman cannot resort "to pleasure alone as the solution to her problem"; somehow, she must overcome her position as site of "rival exchange between two men" (350). She asks, "How can this object of transaction assert a right to pleasure without extricating itself from the established commercial system?" In *She Done Him Wrong*, Lady Lou/Diamond Lil is immediately "set up" as such an object in the first minutes of the film. Dan Flynn, local politician, schemes about exposing saloon owner Gus Jordan while he looks at a nude picture of Lou; it is no surprise that his motivation for such conspiracy is the attendant reward objectified in the picture. In *I'm No Angel*, circus owner Barton "frames" Tira as a "taken" object, discrediting her with her upper-class suitor Clayton, primarily in order to insure her continued performances for Barton. In both film scenarios, the Mae West character becomes an object of exchange between two men.

Yet, it is only a provisional "objectification"; the West character "becomes" the object in jest, and in mimicry, only "to become" the subject in a moment of double entendre, punning, or joking. She extricates herself from the "commercial" system by remaining the active, desiring subject. For it is indeed Tira who "wins" back Clayton, defeating Barton's scheme, and Lou who plays Flynn against her former lovers, enabling Captain Cummings (Cary Grant) to "win." Cummings' attempt to handcuff her at film's end ironically refers to the manipulation which made him the object of *her desire*. Lou objects to the cuffs, stating she "wasn't born with 'em." Cummings counters, "all those men would have been a lot safer if you had," and Lou replies, "I don't know. Hands ain't everythin.'" It is no coincidence that the "one-liner," a form of humor particularly solipsistic — or rather, apparently so, is among West's most potent allies. Unlike visual gags, comic business, or comic team dialogue, the one-liner stands alone. One persona delivers it.

Formally, West *seems* to need no one else, which contributes to the discourse of independence, control, and aggressive sexuality. West's comedy depends on the repeated assumption of the subject position, and the accompanying objectification of those who would objectify her.

Of Freud's classes of "tendentious" jokes, smut, in particular, illustrates the pattern West reversed. Directed towards women, smut "may be equated with attempts at seduction" (*Jokes* 97). Because it is motivated by the joke teller's or first person's sexual excitement, it works like the "exposure of the sexually different person to whom it is directed" (98). Freud's theorization firmly places man in the first (subject) position, and woman in the exposed or "object" position. Woman's embarrassment or her initial failure to become sexually excited is read by Freud as her "inflexibility"; as such, it is the "first condition to the development of smut" (99).

West's characters violate this "first condition" by assuming the teller's position of "sexually aggressive" jokes or double entendre, or by deliberately "exposing" themselves. In *She Done Him Wrong*, the picture Gus Jordan has hung in the saloon exposes and "objectifies" Lady Lou in the most common or traditional sense. Mary Ann Doane provides an analysis of another such incident of female exposure in a photograph by Robert Doisneau; only here the "exposed" female is contained in a painting which the man "eyes" over the bent head of his female companion whose gaze is otherwise occupied (53). A "dirty joke," as Doane reads Freud, "is always constructed at the expense of the woman" (53). But rather than laugh at the "exposed" Lady Lou, we observe what happens as the "objectified" subject of the painting waltzes in only to deliver the first of several double entendres in the picture ("Finest woman that walked the streets," "I've heard so much about you" — "Yeah, but you can't prove it"). Before she leaves the gathering of her onlookers, she "shows off" some more, passing around photographs of herself (additional "exposures"), and commenting on their effectiveness ("A little bit spicy, but not too raw, you know what I mean?"). In addition to becoming the spectator of her own image (and, in this way, simulating the position of the female narcissist), she has beaten her (male) joke tellers to the "punch" line: "I gotta admit that painting is a flash, but I wish Gus hadn't hung it over the 'Free Lunch.'" Lou's quick assumption of the subject position also controverts the idea of the woman's supposed "inflexibility"; she makes no pretense of modesty or embarrassment. Rather than rendering herself comic in the sense of Freud's degradation or "unmasking" (201), Lady Lou bypasses a complicit re-exposure of herself in exchange for an explicit demonstration of her desire for Sergei. Introduced as Rita's assistant, Lou asks him, "Day, or night work?"

Becoming an "unwitting" object was not in Mae West's game plan. The persona was always to eschew marital slavery and the type of the comic which would leave her ridiculed, or ridiculous. Mary Ann Doane's theorization of masquerade and the female film spectator explains one way in which West accomplished this. Doane's gloss on Christian Metz's explanation of voyeuristic desire — the "cinephile's" gap between desire and its object — leads her to posit the ways in which such a "gap" can be created. "The effectivity of masquerade lies precisely in its potential to manufacture a distance from the image, to generate a problematic within which the image is manipulable, producible, and readable by the woman" (55). Doane cites the female spectator's overidentification with the image, the moment at which the "female spectator's desire can be described only in terms of a kind of narcissism" (45). Interestingly, Mae West does become a "female spectator" when she looks at and comments upon the pictures of herself in *She Done Him Wrong*. Her verbal commentary, and her verbal "joking" create the ironic distance that separates her from her image. One might even sight traces of the "man" underneath the persona, claiming that in her joking commentary she is eroticizing her own image. But Mae West was not a "man." She is the female narcissist whose many lovers are the sign of her desire, not her neediness. The comedy that arises from such multiplicity not only results in the masquerade of femininity (as per Joan Riviére's and later, Judith Butler's formulations) but in the threat to "man," or more specifically, the male spectator.

In addition to masquerade, West's joking and humor was mostly aided — though sometimes hampered — by comedic genres. "Mae West" developed through vaudeville, which depended on multiple acts, a variety of discrete, sometimes "hodgepodge" musical, dramatic and comedic productions. "Comedy," argue Neale and Krutnik, "seems especially suited to hybridization, in large part because the local forms responsible for the deliberate generation of laughter can be inserted at some point into most other generic contexts without disturbing their conventions" (18). The films *She Done Him Wrong* and *My Little Chickadee* may be approached as comedic melodramas, or even comedic Westerns. Mae "always gets her *men*," which is not only a gender twist to the Western hero's motto, but a rescripting of the heterosexual union that ends most comedies. At the same time, this conventional ending is shared by melodrama. In their analysis of King Vidor's *Show People* (MGM 1928), Neale and Krutnik note the particular alliance of narrative comedy with melodrama, especially in reference to their endings (24–25).

For what is often pejoratively classified as cheap melodrama, or the sensationalism of Mae West's rather rickety "star vehicle," is actually part of a popularly and historically legible genre. Though the majority of West's films are commonly classified as comedies — or more accurately, though she is commonly understood as a comedienne — the rhetoric of excess often works in a purely melodramatic mode. In *The Melodramatic Imagination*, Peter Brooks describes this rhetoric as necessarily maintaining a "state of exaltation, a state where hyperbole is a 'natural' form of expression because anything less would convey only the apparent (naturalistic, banal) drama, not the true (moral, cosmic) drama" (40). In short, melodrama speaks the cosmic. Its purpose is to articulate the "moral occult," a "domain of operative spiritual values which is both indicated within and masked by the surface of reality" (5). Melodrama's abundance of "false faces," or theatrical "asides," make the stage enunciation of signs inherently dualistic. That virtue can be misprized, and evil disguised leads to a "conflict of signs" that Brooks notes must be "resolved in public trial" (45). Trial scenes, or rather, courtroom scenes in which a judgment is rendered are also common to comedy, and specifically, to West's films. Through such scenes, we can differentiate the "excess" of melodrama from the excess of parody, or from that which works in and through the multiple lover theme.

The excess in parody — basically, but not exclusively, understood as comic exaggeration — works differently from the excess in melodrama; the latter seeks to articulate a "truth," the former to render that "truth" ludicrous, or possibly, through some complex maneuver, to render the "truth" impossible. The judgment of the trial scene in *My Little Chickadee* is parodied by Flower Belle's sham marriage to Twillie. The Judge of her home town court has earlier exiled her from the town, ordering her not to return until she "can prove that [she is] respectable and married." Attempting to "have" Twillie and his abundance of (fake) currency, Flower Belle asks a con-man to pose as a minister and marry them aboard a moving train. Their vows are comically obscured by the blowing of the train whistle.

Linda Hutcheon's central definition of parody is "imitation characterized by ironic inversion" (6). *My Little Chickadee* is blatantly ironic as opposed to earlier films which tend to mask imitative strategies. For instance, the Production Code Correspondence for *She Done Him Wrong* indicates that the censors were expressly concerned in reducing the references to the number of men in Lady Lou's life (and past) (Letter, 1932). In her subsequent film, *I'm No Angel*, West was led to critique this aim while inverting diverse forms of patriarchal authority. The trial scene at film end does more than mock a court of "justice"; it works melodramatically by "prizing" virtue in Tira. The genres of comedy and melodrama are conflated as the trial scene genuinely enacts, parodies and finally deconstructs that concept of virtue.

I'm No Angel features Tira, the exotic veil dancer and lady lion tamer who brings a breach of promise suit against Clayton (Cary Grant). The upper-class fiancé leaves Tira before the wedding when he discovers the pajama-clad Slick Wiley lounging in Tira's apartment. Neither Clayton nor Tira know that Barton had sent Wiley over there to discourage Clayton and keep Tira as a performer. Tira prosecutes the case herself, openly recognizing the string of old boyfriends whom the defense has seated in the front row of the courtroom audience. Her own (advisory) lawyer remonstrates with her, and, as if it is not enough that her Brooklynese belies her "high-class" appearance,

Clayton's attorney, Bob, asks the court to "warn the jury not to be swayed by any theatricalism on the part of the plaintiff." Tira saunters up to the stand, and rightfully belittles the testimony of Brown, the man whose diamond ring had attracted her in the beginning of the film. Bob objects, calling the questioning "most irregular." The Judge allows Tira to continue as before, and Tira replies, "Thanks, Judge, you're regular. I'm doing my best to be legitimate."

In truth, Tira is doing her best not to be "legitimate," but to be "il-legitimately" legitimate. The attempt Tira makes to appropriate "class" is made visual, as well as aural. Dressed in pearls and a "tasteful" dress, not only does she appear to be the woman who has no need of the money she seeks, but she "puts on" the role of (male) attorney. The excess in the number of her lovers operates parodically, as does the excess involved in the con-tradiction between gender/role and speech/class. Both Tira and Clayton suffer from mistaken assumptions — those "knots" of confused identity which comedies always untie. Read melodramatically, however, these "knots" sug-gest that Tira's virtue has been "misprized." Questioning Slick Wiley, Tira reveals that he has spent most of his recent time behind bars. Bob objects, and claims she is "harassing the witness." She replies:

> Who's harassing who? I'm just askin' for a square deal. Don't take the
> word of an ex-convict against an honest, innocent, good woman.

At this moment, Tira has appropriated the rhetoric of melodrama, while at the same time "expressing" what is strictly true according to the "facts" of the plot: Tira is innocent of "cheating" on Clayton. This statement is not humorous or funny when it is read in this context; it is melodramatic — the moment at which Tira's Brooklynese and "substandard" diction, among other things, express the "truth" of her rightfully appropriated position of "wronged innocent." But in view of the men seated in the front row — the analogs of film spectators, the subjects of the gaze, as well as the objects of her desire — how can she be "innocent"? It just so happens that the most melodramatic moment of the scene is also its most parodic. Virtue has been "misprized," as well as "mis-prized" (overvalued, discarded or dismissed as an uncertain or irrelevant quality). A reporter asks Tira what she plans to do, now that she has "won" her case; Tira answers, "Carry on the same as before." In addition, one of her most famous one-liners parodically repeats the dialectic between the censors of *She Done Him Wrong* and its star:

> REPORTER: Why did you admit knowing so many men in your
> life?
> TIRA: Hmm! Well, it's not the men in your life that counts, it's the
> life in your men.

Through trial scenes, Peter Brooks tells us, melodrama begs the clarification and resolution of signs. Much the same thing may be said of comedy, and of narrative comedy especially. In most Mae West films, excess — that "too much" which by definition begs the question of original, imitation, and exaggeration — is often "signed," but not entirely subsumed by themes of the multiple. In fact, multiplicity becomes a generic strategy as well as a strategy of humor and masquerade insofar as it allows the simultaneous play of several, discrete genres. In comedy and melodrama, trials function not only as mediators of the "moral occult," or unravelers of comedic knots, but as signs themselves — indicators of the "legitimate," the "real." Parodic excess within comedy may seem to suggest that the non-excessive exists, that the original parodied is the "true" or "real." On the other hand, in most West films, simply by being rendered "signs," trials or other such institutions of the "real" are seriously questioned. The excess which writes or enacts "Mae West" might also render her body as sign. It is finally in this sense that Mae West engages in "self" parody. Through various signs of excess, she becomes the "woman's woman," who, as we know, cannot exist without ambiguity, scaring men off even while they desire her. Because West's films continually straddle and redefine the lines between comedy and melodrama, and because these genres also rely on excess, they shape the masquerade that, in "Mae West's" "hands," becomes a man-scare-ade.

NOTES

1. For an historical analysis of U.S. movie censorship and the comedy of Mae West, see Ramona Curry, "*Goin'to Town* and Beyond: Mae West, Film Censorship, and the Comedy of *Un*marriage," in *Film Comedy in History: Narrative, Performance, Ideology*, eds. Henry Jenkins and Kristine Karnick, forthcoming.

2. The typographical error "pumpness" in "Physicians Endorse Mae West's Curves" might be ignored both as a faulty transcription and as an editorial oversight. However, even as such, it indicates the suggestive, if admittedly perverse word play between "plumpness" and the inadvertent neologism "pumpness." Mae West's "plumpness" marked the "pumping up" of the thin woman of the twenties, or the "inflation" implied in the Rubens paintings. This word play becomes even more intriguing when we consider that during WWII the RAF christened their life-preserving jackets "Mae Wests." The slight difference between "plumpness" and "pumpness" parallels the challenge that the West persona brought to standards of beauty and sexuality (was she just pleasingly plump, or absurdly overblown?). Arguably, the West persona incited this query most as filmic object — or when the "movie camera exaggerated one's figure" (Davies 1). Mae West's body, as well as the image of her body, was constructed through — and by — connotations of fullness and buoyancy which were already widely

dispersed in American and British popular culture and discourse by WWII. Also at play is West's image as female bodybuilder, or the woman with "pumped up" muscles. In his studio release, Davies remarks that West could perform various muscle-hardening exercises "better and longer than the average man" (2). A "pumped up" West not only presented challenges to standards of feminine beauty, but repeated the challenge she was already bringing to gender construction.

3. Butler applies her formulations to performative activities within both gay and straight cultures. The "repetition of heterosexual constructs" is manifest in gay discourse and sexual practice as the "butch" and "femme" sexual styles; in fact, these constructs best reveal themselves as such when they are repeated in non-heterosexual contexts. Once the constructed status of the "original" is shown, performative proliferation of the "*idea* of the natural and original" is possible (*Gender Trouble* 31). West's humor is performed within straight contexts, but the thematic excesses of her humor question the idea of a "natural" woman similarly.

4. According to Freud, a "tendentious joke" requires three people: "in addition to the one who makes the joke, there must be a second who is taken as the object of the hostile or sexual aggressiveness, and a third in whom the joke's aim of producing pleasure is fulfilled" (*Jokes* 100).

5. A "true vaudevillian's art," stated a Yale Professor in 1933, is the development of a "stage personality so definite, rounded, unique and so entirely his own, that he would be recognized and hailed when he appeared on a stage — in New York or Kalamazoo" (qtd. in Ward 7).

6. In 1975, West published the short-lived production (it only lasted three days) as a novel, *Pleasure Man*. Rodney does not die, but lives on "successfully" as a eunuch. At the end of each chapter of the book, West printed her own handwritten "quips." At the book's conclusion, she writes, "And Rodney Terrill was as cocky as ever, although now he had nothing to back it up with" (*Pleasure Man* 251).

7. A full account of the history of Freud's development of the "narcissistic" or "ego-libido" is given in the Editor's Note to "Instincts and their Vicissitudes" (14 *Stand. Ed.* 113ff).

WORKS CITED

Allen, Robert. *Horrible Prettiness: Burlesque and American Culture*. Chapel Hill: University of North Carolina Press, 1991.

Anonymous. Letter, 1932. *She Done Him Wrong*: Production Code File, Mae West Collection. Library of Motion Picture Arts and Sciences. Beverly Hills, CA.

Barreca, Regina. *They Used to Call Me Snow White ... But I Drifted*. New York: Viking Press, 1991.

Booth, Mark. *Camp*. London: Quartet Books, 1983.

Brooks, Peter. *The Melodramatic Imagination.* New York: Columbia University Press, 1985.

Butler, Judith. *Gender Trouble: Feminism and the Subversion of Identity.* New York: Routledge, 1990.

_____. "Performative Acts and Gender Constitution: An Essay in Phenomenology and Feminist Theory," in: *Performing Feminisms*, ed. Sue-Ellen Case. Baltimore: The John Hopkins University Press, 1990, pp. 270–282.

Core, Philip. *Camp: The Lie That Tells the Truth.* New York: Delilah Books, 1984.

Curry, Ramona. "Goin' To Town and Beyond: Mae West, Film Censorship, and the Comedy of Unmarriage," in: *Film Comedy in History: Narrative, Performance, Ideology*, ed. Henry Jenkins and Kristine Karnick (forthcoming).

_____. "Mae West as Censored Commodity: The Case of Klondike Annie." *Cinema Journal* 31/1 (Fall 1991): 57–84.

_____. "Power and Allure: The Mediation of Sexual Difference in the Star Image of Mae West." PhD dissertation, Northwestern University, 1990.

Davies, Jim. "Mae West as I Know Her." Paramount Studio Press Release, 1933. Mae West Clippings File, 1930–39. Cinema Library, University of Southern California, Los Angeles.

Doane, Mary Ann. "Film and the Masquerade: Theorizing the Female Spectator," in: *Issues in Feminist Film Criticism*, ed. Patricia Erens. Bloomington: Indiana University Press, pp. 41–57.

Eells, George, and Stanley Musgrove. *Mae West: A Biography.* William Morrow and Company, Inc. 1982.

Freud, Sigmund. *Jokes and Their Relation to the Unconscious*, ed. and trans. James Strachey, 1960. New York: W.W. Norton & Company, 1963.

_____. "Narcissism: An Introduction (1914)," in: *Standard Edition*, Vol. XIV. Ed. James Strachey. London: Hogarth Press, 1957, pp. 73–102.

Hutcheon, Linda. *A Theory of Parody.* New York: Methuen, 1985.

Irigaray, Luce. "This Sex Which Is Not One." Trans. Claudia Reeder. *Essential Papers on the Psychology of Women*, ed. Claudia Zanardi. New York: New York University Press, 1990, pp. 344–351. Reprinted from *New French Feminisms*, eds. Elaine Marks and Isabelle de Courtivron. Amherst: University of Massachusetts Press, 1980.

Johnston, Claire. "Women's Cinema as Counter-Cinema," in: *Movies and Methods: An Anthology*, Vol. 1, ed. Bill Nichols. Los Angeles and Berkeley: University of California Press, 1976, pp. 211–219.

Kofman, Sarah. *The Enigma of Woman: Woman in Freud's Writings.* Trans. Catherine Porter. Ithaca: Cornell University Press, 1985. Published in France as *L'Enigme de la femme: La Femme dans les textes de Freud.* Editions Galilée, 1980.

Kuhn, Annette. *The Power of the Image: Essays on Representation and Sexuality.* Boston: Routledge & Kegan Paul, 1985.

Lowen, Alexander. *Narcissism: Denial of the True Self.* New York: Macmillan Publishing Company, 1983.

"Mae's X-Ray." *Life* 5 Sept. 1949: 28.

Martin, Linda, and Kerry Segrave. *Women In Comedy.* Secaucus, NJ: Citadel Press, 1986.

McEvoy, J.P. "Letter to Mae," n.p., n.d. Mae West Clippings File, Academy of Motion Picture Arts and Sciences Library, Beverly Hills, CA.

Neale, Steve, and Krutnik, Frank. *Popular Film and Television Comedy.* London and New York: Routledge, 1990.

"Physicians Endorse Mae West Curves." Milwaukee: n.p., 6 Oct. 1933. Mae West Clippings File, Academy of Motion Picture Arts and Sciences Library. Beverly Hills, CA.

Review of *Pleasure Man. New York Times,* 10/2/28: 34 (Littell Gabriel).

Riviére, Joan. "Womanliness as Masquerade," in: *Formations of Fantasy,* eds. Victor Burgin, James Donald, Cora Kaplan. London: Methuen, 1986. First published: *The International Journal of Psychoanalysis,* vol. 10, 1929, pp. 303–313.

Robertson, Pamela. "'The Kinda Comedy that Imitates Me': Mae West's Identification with the Feminist Camp." *Cinema Journal* 32/2 (Winter 1993): 57–72.

Rosen, Marjorie. *Popcorn Venus.* New York: Avon, 1974.

Ross, Andrew. *No Respect: Intellectuals and Popular Culture.* New York: Routledge, Chapman and Hall, Inc., 1989.

Sommers, Martin. "Welfare Island Fails to Tame the Wild West." *The News.* New York: News Syndicate Co., Inc. 1933. Reproduced in: Tuska, Jon. *The Films of Mae West.* Secaucus, NJ: Citadel Press, 1973, 34–35.

Tildesley, Ruth. "Curves! Hollywood Wants Them — And So Will You!" *Motion Picture,* July 1933, 34–35.

Tyler, Carole-Anne. "Boys Will Be Girls: The Politics of Gay Drag," in: *Inside/Out: Lesbian Theories,* by Gay Theories, ed. Diana Fuss. London: Routledge, 1991.

Tuska, Jon. *The Films of Mae West.* Secaucus, NJ: Citadel Press, 1973.

Ward, Carol. *Mae West: A Bio-Bibliography.* New York: Greenwood Press, 1989.

West, Mae. *The Constant Sinner* (Originally published as *Babe Gordon*). New York: Macaulay Company, 1930.

—————. *Goodness Had Nothing To Do With It.* Englewood Cliffs, NJ: Prentice Hall, 1959.

—————. *The Pleasure Man.* New York: Dell Publishing, 1975.

See also:

—————. *Diamond Lil.* New York: Macaulay, 1932. Reprint. New York: Sheridan House, 1949

—————. *Diamond Lil.* Unpublished Play, 1928. Library of Congress, Manuscript Division, Washington, DC

—————. *The Drag.* Unpublished Play, 1927. Library of Congress, Manuscript Division, Washington, DC

_____. *Frisco Kate*. Unpublished Play, 1930. Library of Congress, Manuscript Division, Washington, DC

_____. *The Hussy*. Unpublished Play, 1922. Library of Congress, Manuscript Division, Washington, DC

_____. *Pleasure Man*. Unpublished Play, 1928. Library of Congress, Manuscript Division, Washington, DC

_____. *The Ruby Ring*. Unpublished Play, 1921. Library of Congress, Manuscript Division, Washington, DC

_____. *Sex*. Unpublished Play, 1926. Library of Congress, Manuscript Division, Washington, DC

See also:

_____. *Chick*. Unpublished Play, 1924. Library of Congress, Manuscript Division, Washington, DC

_____. *The Wicked Age*. Unpublished Play, 1927. Library of Congress, Manuscript Division, Washington, DC

Films:

She Done Him Wrong (1933). Paramount. With Cary Grant and Gilbert Roland. Director: Lowell Sherman. Based on *Diamond Lil*; adapted by John Bright and Harvey Thew.

I'm No Angel (1933). Paramount. With Cary Grant. Director: Wesley Ruggles. Story, screenplay and dialogue: Mae West.

Belle of the Nineties (1934). Paramount. With Roger Pryor and John Mack Brown. Director: Leo McCarey. Screenplay: Mae West; based on her novel, *The Constant Sinner* (1930).

Klondike Annie (1936). Major Pictures (Paramount release). With Victor McLaglen. Director: Raoul Walsh. Screenplay: Mae West; based on her play, *Frisco Kate* (1930).

My Little Chickadee (1940). Universal. With W.C. Fields. Director: Edward Cline. Screenplay: Mae West and W.C. Fields.

See also:

Night After Night (1932). Paramount. With George Raft and Constance Cummings. Director: Archie Mayo. Additional Dialogue: Mae West.

Goin' To Town (1935). Major Pictures (Paramount release). With Paul Cavanaugh. Director: Alexander Hall. Screenplay: Mae West. Story: Marion Morgan, George B. Dowell.

Go West Young Man (1936). Major Pictures (Emanuel Cohen). With Warren William and Randolph Scott. Director: Henry Hathaway. Screenplay: Mae West; based on Lawrence Riley's *Personal Appearance*.

Every Day's A Holiday (1938). Major Pictures (Paramount release). With Edmund Lowe. Director: A. Edward Sutherland. Story and screenplay: Mae West.

The Heat's On (1943). Columbia. Director: Gregory Ratoff. No writing credit for West.

Myra Breckenridge (1970). Twentieth Century Fox. No writing credit for West.

Sextette (1978). Crown International Pictures. Based on play by Charlotte Francis, rewritten by West for Broadway in 1961.

"Will Mae West Make Us Fat?" n.p. Examiner, Nov. 1, 1933. Mae West Clippings File, Academy of Motion Picture Arts and Sciences Library. Beverly Hills, CA.

17

Women on the Verge of a Nervous Breakdown: *Sexism or Emancipation from Machismo?*

FLORENCE REDDING JESSUP

INTRODUCTION: MAY WE LAUGH?

Is Pedro Almodóvar's *Women on the Verge of a Nervous Breakdown* a sexist comedy about hysterical women or a story of liberation from machismo? Should our nerves jangle with Almodóvar's stereotypical treatment of women? Or, may we celebrate the happy ending and laugh with this comic film from Spain?

Even before we see *Women on the Verge of a Nervous Breakdown*, the title conjures up images of edgy, emotional, out-of-control women. Then, from the beginning until the final scenes we watch the female characters in a frenzy over men. Pepa (played by Carmen Maura) frantically searches for her lover Iván (Fernando Guillén), who has left her for another woman, to tell him she is pregnant and to get him back. Crazed Lucía (Julieta Serrano) hijacks a motorcycle in pursuit of the same Iván, to shoot him. Pepa's friend Candela (María Barranco) is in a panic fearing she will go to jail as an accomplice to her lover's plot to hijack the plane which Iván plans to take to Stockholm with his new paramour, Paulina (Kiti Manver). Before the end of the film, Candela and Iván's son Carlos (Antonio Banderas) flirt and kiss, while Carlos' financée, Marisa (Rossy de Palma), sleeps nearby. As Elvira Siruana notes, the women in this comedy behave as "neurotics" who chase after men, "competing" with each other as if they had "no other objective in their lives" (64).

The conclusion of the film, however, is not in the interest of the patriarchal power which such stereotypical images of women seem to justify. After all, irrational women need rational men to tell them what to do. But in the final scenes, Pepa is an independent career woman who says "*adiós*" to Iván. She also decides, as Murphy Brown will do four years later, to become a single parent. Clearly Pepa and her baby will be better off without Iván, a macho cad. As the comedy closes, phallocentric dualisms are upset. Pepa regains control of her life, and Iván remains irrationally subjugated to the macho role he plays. If the ending convincingly sums up Pedro Almodóvar's gender messages in this film, *Women on the Verge of a Nervous Breakdown* is a story about emancipation from machismo.

In Caryn James opinion, however, the endings of Almodóvar's films simply do not work. In "Almodóvar Adrift in Sexism," a New York Times article about *Women on the Verge of a Nervous Breakdown* (1988), *Tie Me Up! Tie Me Down!* (1990), and *High Heels* (1991), she sees the endings as "contrived, declared by authorial fiat." She finds "a definite trace of misogyny lurking beneath his apparently fond creations of women" because the conclusions are ineffective. "The undercurrent of sexism is directly tied to the bludgeoning control that wrecks the endings of Mr. Almodóvar's films," she explains. Women in *Women on the Verge of a Nervous Breakdown*, for example, "are suddenly made self-sufficient at the end; this is a neat feminist twist but not a convincing one." Hence viewers are left with the impression that women are "frenetic and silly" (H 11).

In contrast, Marvin D'Lugo believes that Almodóvar's female protagonists such as Pepa are "agents of radical cultural change" in films that reflect and further a "newly emerging social order." In his article "Heterogeneity and Spanish Cinema of the Eighties," he sums up the plot of *Women on the Verge of a Nervous Breakdown* in this way: "We trace the inner emancipation of the female who, having already achieved the outward marks of freedom and independence that have come with the social transformation of Spain, now struggles to achieve the inner liberation from a phallocentric past by means of her disengagement from the womanizing Iván." By the final scenes, in D'Lugo's opinion, Pepa represents a "cultural and social system in which the female has finally shed the ideological chains of her imprisonment in traditional Spanish patriarchy" (63–65).

Rather than a deus ex machina at the end of Almodóvar's films, D'Lugo writes that viewers participate in "the emancipating function of the specular ritual," which he defines as "the audience's bearing witness and tacitly legitimizing the cultural reordering that each filmic narrative chronicles" (66). In an analysis of the final scenes of *Law of Desire* (1987), the predecessor of *Women on the Verge of a Nervous Breakdown* (1988), D'Lugo notes the crowd of police and passersby who "look up to the window" where "the homosexual love scene is taking place." The audience joins spectators in the film in a "secular adoration scene" (56–57). As viewers affirm liberation from past intolerances, according to D'Lugo, they "rewrite the phallocentric and repressive scenarios of Franquismo" (64).

Pedro Almodóvar says that "his films are meant to deny even the memory of Franco," reports Vito Russo (14). Marvin D'Lugo identifies ironic images that negate the power over gender roles of institutions — the Church, the patriarchal family, and the police — used by Generalissimo Franco during his long dictatorship (1939–1975) to enforce conformity to gender hierarchy. Again in *Law of Desire*, D'Lugo notes the likeness to Michelangelo's *Pietà* of the final embrace of the homosexual lovers, Pablo and Antonio, in front of an "altar of pop-cultural artifacts" (56). Tina, Pablo's transsexual brother who turned woman to become the lover of her father — although the patriarch abandons her — stands by the police in the "adoration" scene. Undermining the patriarchal order of course reaches beyond dramatic changes in Spain. Almodóvar's humorous untying of old gender strictures has international appeal.

In 1988 *Women on the Verge of a Nervous Breakdown* topped box office records and received five Goya prizes in Spain and won awards in Toronto, in Venice, in Berlin and in New York. The next year it was a nominee for an Oscar. Its images of women chasing machos have entered many brains. Elvira Siurana's and Carlyn James' important concerns about the female characters' stereotypical behavior prompt a closer look at the film. As Alice Sheppard notes, "typical humor against women relies on stereotypes" (43). But in this analysis of gender in *Women on the Verge of a Nervous Breakdown*, I will try to show that Pedro Almodóvar uses stereotypes subversively, that he directs his humor against machismo, and that the ending confirms this humorous critique.

Because this essay views Almodóvar's gender messages from the vantage point of the end of the film, I will first focus on the final scene. Inspired by Marvin D'Lugo's baptism of the ending as the "annunciation," a beginning, I will share evidence that this finale is also a nativity scene that opens the ending with hope for better gender arrangements in the future. An epilogue to the plot, the final scene follows the closure of two parodic themes, Don Juan and stereotypical women in Hollywood comedies of the 1950s and 1960s. After analyzing these parodies, which involve the central characters and the main plot of the film, I will note contributions to gender themes by other scenes and characters. My conclusion will be that *Women on the Verge of a Nervous Breakdown* is about liberation from machismo.

Almodóvar's humor in this funny film renders machismo absurd. Yet our laughter has undertones of frustration as well as optimism. Pepa overcomes her subordination to the macho; the macho continues with someone else. Machismo roves around society throughout this film; the final scenes indicate that mañana it will go away.

ENDING: "ANNUNCIATION" AND NATIVITY SCENE

The final scene of *Women on the Verge of a Nervous Breakdown* follows the conclusion to the plot. In the penultimate scene, after two days and one sleepless night of frenetic searching, Pepa catches up with Iván at Madrid's Barajas Airport. By then she has nothing to say to him except "*adiós*." This leave-taking is a statement of emancipation from the macho, but there is one more scene. The last set is the terrace of Pepa's penthouse. Back from the airport, Pepa walks through her living room, past the police and others sleeping off drugged gazpacho, to reach the terrace just when Marisa wakes up. Then we watch the happy epilogue, called the "annunciation" by D'Lugo (66). Pepa announces her pregnancy to Marisa.

Marisa is one of seven people melodramatically entangled in Pepa's story who join Pepa in her penthouse during the second day in the fictional reality of the film. "*Sea precisamente al que tiene menos relación con ella al que le comunique su secreto*" ["it is exactly to the one with whom she has the least relationship that she communicates her secret"], points out Pedro Almodóvar (Vidal 268). But Marisa is part of the mesh. Carlos, Iván's son and Marisa's sweetheart when they enter the apartment, leaves Marisa for Candela, as his father discards Pepa for Paulina. Marisa is abandoned while she sleeps, dreaming sweet orgasmic dreams after consuming the gazpacho that Pepa concocted for Iván. Pepa has laced this nourishing cold soup with sleeping pills to keep Iván, even if asleep, with her. Iván does not come by, and almost everyone, including Marisa, relishes this delicious culinary symbol of Spanish summers. Thus Pepa announces her pregnancy to Marisa, who is there by a series of coincidences.

The names of the characters in this final scene are not accidental; they suggest the Holy Family. Pepa is a nickname for Josefina, the feminine form of José or Joseph; Marisa is derived from María. Pepa (Joseph) will be both father and mother to her child. Marisa (Mary), blessed with immaculate intercourse while sleeping on the terrace, is no longer a virgin. Pepa is pleased and calls virgins *antipáticas* [unpleasant]. This brief discourse, reversing the veneration of sweet innocent female virgins, does not appear in the original script. By adding it, Almodóvar debunks with a few phrases the age-old cult of women's purity and undoes an obsolete myth that helps sustain macho power. If female chastity is not fiercely defended, Don Juan's valiant conquests, the macho's "scores," are mere deceptions. If a female person is not an otherworldly virgin mother, does she need a worldly patriarch to rule her and the family? Happily the Mary at the ending of *Women on the Verge of a Nervous Breakdown* is not a virgin, and the family announced will not be patriarchal.

In the final scene on the terrace, a calm conversation between two women, Pepa is free from her submission to Iván, and the baby she plans to have will not grow up under the macho's influence. She has no worries about becoming a single mother, no concerns about social or political stigma, and no financial problems. (No Spanish politician, to my knowledge, nervously pointed to Pepa as a threat to "family values," that is, to "the importance of the father.") Well-to-do Pepa can afford a penthouse on Montalbán Street, in the beautiful *Los Jerónimos* neighborhood in Madrid, a few steps from the Prado museum and from the Retiro Park. Her economic advantage glows, if we contrast her with Gloria (also Carmen Maura) from Almodóvar's 1984 film *What Have I Done to Deserve This*? After Gloria frees herself from her macho husband by whacking him over the head with a ham and baking the fatal weapon, she is still financially stuck in an awful apartment overlooking traffic on Madrid's M30 beltway. For Gloria the "outward marks of freedom and independence," noted by D'Lugo in Pepa's case, are not so brilliant (65). Besides, Gloria's homosexual son who returns home to be the man of the house is already tainted by his father's machismo. But the carefree ending of *Women on the Verge of a Nervous Breakdown* predicts that machismo will not spoil Pepa's baby.

Venturing beyond the hopeful finale into the future — an epilogue invites us to do so — Pepa will continue her career, as Spanish women who work outside the home now commonly do when they have children. When she gives birth she will enjoy the Spanish sixteen-week parental leave with seventy-five percent of her salary. All Spaniards have both a paternal and a maternal surname, and Pepa's baby will carry on Pepa's maternal as well as her paternal family names. Spain's low birthrate, 1.3 children per woman in 1992, indicates that Pepa probably will choose to have one child. Perhaps, like Murphy Brown, she will hire a man to care for her baby until she or he goes to nursery school. The maid Pepa mentioned as she stepped over the spilled gazpacho in the last scene will help her clean the apartment, freeing her from the *la doble jornada* [double day's work] of many career women with children, not only in Spain. Also, the maps and planes in her apartment symbolize her freedom and imply she will travel. The film's ending encourages optimistic thoughts.

The hopeful finale suggests a nativity scene. The conversation between Pepa (Joseph) and Marisa (Mary) on the terrace with a view of Madrid's nighttime skies takes place close to a manger, or hints of one, and a light, like a star, winks above the Telephone Company building before the scene ends. Ducks and chickens are in the closing and opening sets. D'Lugo mentioned "the biblical intertext" of the "annunciation" and of the prologue (66). In the voice-over in the opening scene, Pepa said she, as a Noah, would have liked to have a pair of every animal but could not save the couple that mattered most to her. Happily, saving this couple, Iván and Pepa, is no longer a goal at the end of the film. Nor is this nativity scene, with Mary and Joseph and talk of a future baby, a "celebration of fertility," an element of comedy in traditional (androcentric) theory, noted by Regina Barreca (8). The glad tidings here are that Pepa is free from her submission to a Don Juan and that the baby will be a member of what D'Lugo calls the "presumably 'liberated' generation" (66).

"ON THE VERGE OF PARODY": DON JUAN

"*En mis películas todo está al borde de la parodia*" ["In my films everything is on the verge of parody"], Almodóvar tells us (qtd. in García de León and Maldonado 167). Throughout *Women on the Verge of a Nervous Breakdown* he parodies the legendary Don Juan. Although he does not mimic its style, Almodóvar implies actions, characters, and even the author of José Zorrilla's nineteenth-century *Don Juan Tenorio*, the drama that revitalizes the Don Juan myth with performances each year on All Saint's Day in Spain and in other Spanish-speaking countries.

The final scenes of *Women on the Verge of a Nervous Breakdown* suggest the ending of *Don Juan Tenorio*. At the end of the romantic drama, Doña Inés, willing to sacrifice her eternal life, saves Don Juan from hell. After Don Juan's last-minute repentance, the souls of Doña Inés and of Don Juan ascend into heaven in a whirl of flowers, angels, perfume and music. When Pepa saves Iván's life at the end of *Women on the Verge of a Nervous Breakdown*, Iván says "*estoy avergonzado*" ["I am ashamed"] and "*lo siento*" ["I am sorry"] and offers to talk with Pepa in the cafeteria. "*Ya es tarde*" ["It is too late"], Pepa responds. So, they go up into the sky on their separate ways. Iván prepares to board the plane to Stockholm to fly with his new lover Paulina to Beirut if the Shiite terrorists slip by the police. Pepa returns to her penthouse, to the terrace with a view of Madrid's heavenly skies.

The uplifting ending of *Women on the Verge of a Nervous Breakdown* brings the parody of the Don Juan legend to its ironic close. Pepa rejects Iván, but no woman leaves Don Juan Tenorio. He makes the decisions. Women, numbers to win a bet, matter only as helpmates to his ego. In contrast, Almodóvar's film is the story of a woman discarded by Iván who overcomes her subordination to him. In the end, Pepa completes the task stated in an early scene when the receptionist Cristina (Loles León) advises her, *"olvídale"* ["forget him"], and Pepa responds, *"dame más tiempo"* ["give me more time"]. Two days and one sleepless night later, she says good-bye to Iván.

Almodóvar signals Pepa's progress toward this *"adiós"* throughout the film. When she burns the bed, with Manuel de Falla's "Ritual Fire Dance" from "Love the Magician" playing in the background, she begins to purge the power memories of their lovemaking have over her. Then she packs up his clothes and gifts. After lugging the suitcase up and down the steps of her apartment, she finally heaves it into the trash, ridding herself of her subordination to him. She will no longer wait for him to come by for it. After flinging the telephone through the window in two moments of frustration and frantically running to answer it with each ring, she walks calmly to answer the call from Lucía. Almodóvar's stage instructions for this scene, the fifty-ninth of the eighty-four scenes in this eighty-eight minute film, are: *"Por primera vez Pepa se dirige al auricular como una persona normal, sin necesidad de batir un record de velocidad"* ["For the first time Pepa goes to the phone as a normal person, without the need to beat a speed record"] (Original Script 93). When she slings the record *"Soy infeliz"* ["I am unhappy"] through the window, with its slapstick landing on the neck of Paulina, she is freeing herself from the unhappiness Iván caused her. When she tosses the answering machine loaded with his lies through the window onto the hood of the car, just as Iván and Paulina are leaving, she throws his falsehoods back to him. This is a "ligera" [light] comedy, in Almodóvar's words (*Patty Diphusa* 146). We have little access to Pepa's deliberations, but scenes of visual and situational humor indicate her steps toward her liberation from Iván.

Names in *Women on the Verge of a Nervous Breakdown* bring to mind *Don Juan Tenorio*. As I have suggested, Iván is a Don Juan. Ana, Pepa's neighbor — the one who asks the panic-stricken driver of the mambo taxi if he sells guns — is an ironic namesake of Doña Ana who was seduced by Don Juan Tenorio in a case of mistaken identity. Ana in the film erroneously worries that Lucía is after her sweetheart Ambite instead of Iván. Pepa's paternal surname, Marcos, is the first name of Don Juan Tenorio's servant. We hear it only in her call to Lucía, early in the film when she is servile to her feelings for Iván. Pepa's first name implies the author of *Don Juan Tenorio*, José Zorrilla, as well as the biblical Joseph. D'Lugo notes how Almodóvar in the introductory voice-over "gives the voice of the creative author to Pepa" (65). Through Pepa, he creates a Don Juan from the perspective of a woman abandoned by the macho.

Point of view works ironies on the Don Juan myth. We see Iván through the problems he causes Pepa and Lucía. Invulnerable Don Juan Tenorio does not notice the suffering he brings about. With the exception of Doña Inés,

with whom he falls in love and whose father he then kills, women are objects
for seduction. Self-absorbed, after a conquest, he goes on to his next adventure. Similarly, Iván is not upset by Lucía's insanity. At the airport, even
though she tries to shoot him, he pays little attention to her — only a glance
and a mention of her name, as if reprimanding a little girl. If surprised by
Pepa's "*adios*," in the next moment he turns to his new lover and prepares to
board the flight to Stockholm. But we see Iván through Pepa's feelings, not
through his pride. He is a culprit.

Iván's machismo is to blame for Pepa's irrational actions; yet she is of
sounder mind than he. He first appears in Pepa's nightmare as he passes from
one woman to the next, pleased with the uninvited seductive phrases —
piropos, he playfully tells them. This introduction to Iván resembles Don Juan
bragging about his list of conquests, from one woman to the next, in the
opening scenes of *Don Juan Tenorio*. A one-dimensional macho from this
beginning of the film, Iván does not change or think. But Pepa, even when
"on the verge of a nervous breakdown," figures out, for example, where Lucía
lives and where Iván is going and with whom. Later, with pistols pointed at
her face, she is able to try to persuade Lucía not to kill Iván. In the end, Pepa's
rejection of Iván is a reasonable decision; Iván's machismo is unreasonable.

The mythic Don Juan, a fearless young hero, is reduced in *Women on the
Verge of a Nervous Breakdown* to a ridiculous liar in the figure of the
cowardly and middle-aged Iván. The most revealing scene of Iván's
prevarications occurs when he leaves this message on Pepa's answering
machine: "*No me voy de viaje, ni me voy con ninguna mujer*" ["I am not
going on a trip, nor am I going away with another woman"]. While he makes
the call from a phone booth because he is afraid to face Pepa, Paulina waits
in the car ready to go with him to Stockholm. Pepa walks by the phone booth
to put his suitcase in the trash, and Lucía passes by on her way to Pepa's
apartment. Pepa and Lucía move with determination, as does Paulina when
she yanks the suitcase from the dumpster and takes it to the car. Meanwhile,
Iván hides cowering behind the advertisement in the phone booth, afraid to
use his voice to tell the truth.

Pedro Almodóvar tells us that the inspiration for *Women on the Verge of
a Nervous Breakdown* was Jean Cocteau's *The Human Voice*. When
Almodóvar wrote the script, the only things remaining from Cocteau's
monologue were "*una mujer sola, el teléfono y una maleta*" ["a woman alone,
the telephone, and a suitcase"]. Then he added the voice of the lover and "*sus
mentiras*" ["his lies"]. Almodóvar also notes that Iván talks to machines —
telephones and an answering machine — that allow him to send lies without
looking at Pepa (qtd. in Boquerini 99). John Hopewell's comment about
Antonio in Carlos Saura's *Carmen* sums up Almodóvar's condemnation of
machismo in *Women on the Verge of a Nervous Breakdown*: "Machismo
impedes communication. It is also quite simply a lie" (154).

In addition to telling lies, Iván uses his voice to dub words into films, which evokes ideas about illusions of reality in the film within the film, in cinema, and in life. This early dubbing scene also hints at role-playing in machismo. Iván speaks, while the actors move their mouths, to delude future audiences who will think his voice pertains to someone else, which it does. It belongs to a beguiler. Iván is an impostor to himself.

The sad song "*Soy infeliz*" ["I am unhappy"] tells Iván, "*vive feliz en tu mundo de ilusiones*" ["live happily in your world of illusions"]. This song about hurtful delusion begins the film and later, on a record, flies through the window of Pepa's apartment. A sad bolero echoes the same message at the end of the film. Almodóvar's final commentary on machismo as represented by Iván is the song "*Teatro*" with its lyrics, "*lo tuyo es puro teatro*" ["yours is nothing but acting"].

"ON THE VERGE OF PARODY": HOLLYWOOD COMEDIES

Another parodic theme, visible throughout *Women on the Verge of a Nervous Breakdown* and brought to its ironic closure in the final scenes, is women's behavior in Hollywood comedies of the 1950s and 1960s. Generalissimo Franco's censors welcomed these films about happy subjugation, and Almodóvar saw many of them in Spain. Speaking of *Women on the Verge of a Nervous Breakdown*, he tells us:

> *He querido hacer una especie de alta comedia al estilo de las americanas de finales de los años 50, donde un grupo de mujeres están a punto de tirarse por el balcón o de ahorcarse con el cable del teléfono porque su novio no las llama. La película está basada en esos primeros momentos del abandono, en que pierden un poco el control de los nervios.* [I wanted to make a kind of high comedy in the style of the American ones at the end of the 1950s where a group of women are ready to throw themselves from the balcony or hang themselves with the telephone cord because their sweethearts do not call them. The film is based on those first moments of abandonment, when they lose some control of their nerves.] (qtd. in Bocquerini 104)

Pedro Almodóvar also makes clear, "*no quiero que sea una mirada complacienta sobre los sesenta, sino todo lo contrario.*" ["I do not want this to be a complaisant look at the sixties, but rather the opposite"] (Vidal 264).

In *Women on the Verge of a Nervous Breakdown* Pedro Almodóvar mimics and mocks women's stereotypical behavior in Hollywood comedies of decades past. But his message is not that women can act like funny little girls because in the end they will submit to their man who will take care of them. To the contrary, Pepa passes comically through the trauma of ending her relationship with Iván, who has discarded her. In the happy conclusion she is free to invent her own life. Significantly, the character in *Women on the Verge of a Nervous Breakdown* who remains completely dependent on her macho man is insane. Lucía, in her zany outfits from the 1960s, refuses to leave behind gender roles often prescribed by comedies of that decade and returns to the hospital. Pepa's denial of subordination, her declaration of independence, does not sanction stereotypical behavior of women as did many Hollywood happy endings of the fifties and sixties.

Almodóvar calls *Women on the Verge of a Nervous Breakdown* "*una comedia realista al estilo americano, o sea, muy falseada*" ["a realistic comedy in the American style, or, that is, very falsified"] (qtd in Bocquerini 98). Pauline Kael mentions the tone of the fifties of the plastic-like "cosmetic layouts" of the introduction (24). The main set, Pepa's apartment, resembles unreal Hollywood decor of decades past. The apartment building in the prologue is a bad painting, and its interior is impeccable. The kitchen, as María Asunción Balonga notes, is like one from "Homes and Gardens" (Caparrós Lera 324). The tomatoes for gazpacho are lustrous red; the colors inside and on the terrace are brilliant. Almodóvar explains that "*Lo que pretendo es que lo único auténtico y lo único verosímil sean los sentimientos de ella*" ["What I intend is that the only authentic thing and the only credible thing will be her feelings"] (Vidal 263). Against a backdrop of artificiality, Pepa's emotions are genuine from the beginning to the end.

We see Pepa's sincerity in an opening scene, the dialogue from Nicholas Ray's 1954 film *Johnny Guitar*. Iván first dubs Sterling Hayden's part into Spanish; later Pepa dubs Joan Crawford's words into Spanish. Iván, through Johnny Guitar's lines, asks for lies: "*Dime que siempre me has esperado.*" ["Tell me that you have always waited for me."] "*Dime que hubieras muerto si yo no hubiera vuelto.*" ["Tell me that you would have died if I had not returned."] "*Dime que todavía me quieres, como yo a ti.*" ["Tell me that you still love me as I love you."] Pepa says the lines with deep emotion, too heartfelt for the role Joan Crawford plays. Then she faints, which blends into the melodramatic pitch of the film. This clip shows that Iván, as a Don Juan, wants self-delusion; Pepa, authenticity.

As in *Johnny Guitar* and other Hollywood films of those decades, *Women on the Verge of a Nervous Breakdown* takes place with sudden shifts from the stage set to the streets. One of these switches from the set is to Almagro street in Madrid, and Almodóvar's choice is significant. This is the street where Pepa looks through an apartment window and watches a woman dance, an allusion to Alfred Hitchcock's 1954 film *Rear Window*, as noted by Patricia Hart. The name of this street lined with elegant buildings suggests the wonderful seventeenth-century theater, *Corral de Comedias*, in the town Almagro, where classical drama is still performed. It brings to mind Tirso de Molina's *El Burlador de Sevilla*, the seventeenth-century model for *Don Juan*

Tenorio. But Pedro Almodóvar chose this street for an additional purpose, one that states the underlying gender theme of the comedy.

The central office of the *Instituto de la Mujer* [The Women's Institute] is located at Almagro 36, and its telephone number is 410-51-12. Pepa reads its address when matching Lucía's phone number, 410-41-30, with street numbers in the Madrid directory arranged by addresses. She rushes through the numbers, "Almagro 30, 31, 32, 33, 34, 36," before arriving at Almagro 38, Lucía's address. The Center for Information on the Rights of Women, where women can receive advice on legal matters, is located at Almagro 30. Very close by on Almagro Street is the *Casa de la Mujer*, which houses various associations where women and men work for the cause of gender fairness. Lucía, ensnared in the past, lives on a street that symbolizes Spain's advances toward the goal of equality of opportunities. Her apartment is next door to the Women's Institute, a government agency dedicated to turning Spain's progressive constitutional rights for women into realities.

The Spanish government in 1983 created The Women's Institute "for the purpose of promoting the conditions necessary for equality between the sexes and for the participation of women in political, cultural, economic and social life" (Spain. Instituto de la Mujer). The Institute's work is inspired by the Spanish Constitution of 1978, which prohibits discrimination based on sex (article 14), specifically forbids discrimination based on sex at work (article 35), and declares marriage an institution based on equality (article 32). Moreover, the Constitution, in an aboutface from Generalissimo Franco's regime, promises that "the public powers" will remove obstacles in the path toward equality (art. 9.2). In the decade following its ratification, ending the year *Women on the Verge of a Nervous Breakdown* appeared, legislative and social reforms were dynamic. But, the Women's Institute notes "the difficulties in changing attitudes at the same speed as legislation" and says that "a profound change in social customs and individual behavior" is necessary (Spain. Instituto de la Mujer).

Almodóvar turns this need into comedy in *Women on the Verge of a Nervous Breakdown*. The ludicrous juxtaposition of Lucía's apartment next to the Women's Institute on Almagro Street is a serious social commentary. Moreover Iván has walked along this same street. There too is Iván's son Carlos, who according to Lucía "*ha salido como su padre*" ["has turned out like his father"]. During the first night of the film, Pepa stalks Almagro Street looking for Iván. She sits down across the street from Lucía's apartment and from the Women's Institute, waiting for her Don Juan. Women in 1988 engaged in behavior reminiscent of Hollywood comedies of decades past and Don Juans on a street that represents progress are absurd incongruities. But the optimistic ending justifies our smiles.

The protagonist Pepa conveys Almodóvar's messages of hope for women's progress. At the end of the film, Lucía, a foil to Pepa, trapped in the past, is put away. The macho Iván, also a crazy anachronism, roams free. Naive Candela, whose name implies *cándida*, ingenuous, still has much to learn. Her sexual desires blind her again — the scene with rabbits who like turnips and with a can of Seat car oil in the background has innuendos. She cuddles up to Carlos on the sofa, while his fiancée Marisa sleeps nearby. Where is female solidarity against machismo? By the final scenes, it is Pepa who advances from reactions reminiscent of Hollywood comedies of the fifties and sixties to actions suitable to the end of the eighties.

GENDER AND OTHER FUNNY SCENES AND CHARACTERS

Other scenes and characters corroborate Almodóvar's messages about gender in *Women on the Verge of a Nervous Breakdown*. They also add to the ludicrous situations and juxtapositions, the wild coincidences, the exaggerations, the caricatures, and the comic tone that make this film seem frivolous. But as Pedro Almodóvar asks, "*¿Qué es frívolo y qué es trascendente?*" ["What is frivolous and what is transcendental?"] (qtd. in García de Leon and Maldonado 168). Funny minor characters and scenes underline Almodóvar's portrayal of machismo as a lie.

Two television commercials are woven into this comedy. In the first spot, a priest puts a condom in the bride's bouquet during the wedding ceremony and warns her never to trust any man. María Barranco, the bride, later appears as Candela, deceived by a Shiite terrorist. Carmen Maura, Pepa, abandoned by Iván, dubs the words of the bride. We view the second commercial with Pepa who watches herself in the main role. "The mother of the murderer" combines detergent, murder, words of Pontius Pilate, a hint of Christ on the cross, police, and a housewife pleased with her clean wash. The advertisement for Ecce Homo laundry soap mocks housewives' delight in a clean shirt, as if it were a life or death issue, which in this case it is. Omo, by the way, was a "popular" detergent in Spain during the sixties (Boquerini 63). The police, no longer in a police state, are helpless before the stain-removing power of Ecce Homo. All blood and guts have vanished from the shirt. The mother has saved her son, the murderer. Television gives the word in the world of consumerism; detergent works miracles. The final sentence about the incredible detergent, "*Ecce Homo parece mentira*" ["Ecce Homo, it (or he) seems a lie"], suggests commercials deceive. These words can also mean, "behold, this man seems to be a lie."

Almodóvar plays with lies in this film. Chus, the Jehovah's Witness and concierge who cannot tell a falsehood, is a comic contrast to Iván and his prevarications. Lucía lies to herself about time not passing. Significantly, her mother wants to sell the outdated outfits to cure her daughter's self deception, but Lucía's affectionate father tells her she looks wonderful, *"estupenda,"* in an ugly wig. Lucía replies, *"Qué bien mientes, papá. Por eso te quiero."* ["How well you lie, father. That is why I love you."] Pepa lies to protect Candela. The police do not believe her when she tells the truth.

We do not hear the kind and funny mambo taxi driver lie, but he repeats sexist clichés. This sensitive taxi driver with his clown-like hair cries because Pepa cries and because he does not have eye drops for her. On the next trip he has the drops. Each time Pepa needs a cab, along comes the mambo taxi that offers magazines, newspapers, drinks, snacks, cigarettes, a sign *"Gracias por fumar"* ["Thank You for Smoking"], leopard seat covers, and mambo music. The taxi driver's sweetheart's sugary name, Azucena, reminds us of Don Quixote's illusory love for his sweet Dulcinea and hints at Pepa's love for Iván. Later, this Don Quixote in his Rocinante mambo cab says to Pepa that Azucena *"va a pensar que ... ja, ja"* ["will think we are ... ha ha"] because they meet so often. He also claims categorically that there are no dangerous women, *"si las sabe tratar"* ["if you know how to treat them"]. In the next moment he finds himself in the line of fire as perilous Lucia shoots at his mambo taxi.

In a reversal of a long-standing gender situation, women force men to partake in a wild taxi and motorcycle chase. They do not sit as companions to their crazed men who pursue each other until one car crashes — or the wheels fall off the stage coach. The mambo taxi driver, not a macho, wisely panics and gives up. He takes Pepa and Ana to the airport by a safer route. There Iván and Paulina are checking in for their flight.

Paulina, the supposedly feminist lawyer, is an ironic reversal of a feminist. She does not help women, is jealous of Pepa, and runs off with a Don Juan. Paulina Morales — her surname is also ironic — had represented Lucía in a suit against this Don Juan, Iván. Moreover, she is very "unlaughing," a term described by Regina Barreca in her introduction to *Last Laughs: Perspectives on Women and Comedy.* Barreca explains that this adjective can be "a weapon against both the 'pretty little girls' and the 'furious females' in order to negate whatever powers of humor they seem to possess" (15). But, Almodóvar, a feminist, does not label feminists humorless here. Rather, an implication is that feminists, not only in Spain, need humor as they further equality in masculine societies where machos still lurk.

SEXISM OR EMANCIPATION FROM MACHISMO?

Almodóvar would like to be thought of as "authentically feminist" and as "one of the least macho men in the world."

> *Quizá eso de que a mí me gusta la intimidad de las mujeres no deje de ser un reflejo machista. Pero espero que no, porque a mí me interesa la*

mujer y su mundo en todos sus aspectos... Yo creo que soy uno de los
hombres menos machistas del mundo, más autenticamente feminista. Lo
que no quiere decir que no vea la realidad. Defiendo a las mujeres,
pero no creo que sean unos arcangeles. Pero mi corazón suele estar
siempre con ellas. Aunque te salgan cosas de la educación. [Perhaps
the fact that I like the private lives of women is no more than a reflection of chauvinism. But I hope not, because I am interested in women
and their world in all its aspects... I believe that I am one of the least
macho men in the world, the most authentically feminist. That does not
mean that I do not see reality. I defend women, but I do not think they
are archangels. But my heart is almost always with them. Although
some things come out from one's upbringing.] (Vidal 35)

Pedro Almodóvar's messages about gender in *Women on the Verge of a
Nervous Breakdown* are feminist. Machismo is senseless and hurtful, they
say. Iván mindlessly plays the Don Juan role. Lucía's dependency on Iván to
give her life meaning is an anachronism and a complicity with the macho
charade. In contrast to Lucía and to Iván, Pepa, the hero, frees herself from
her subjugation to machismo. When Nancy Walker, in *A Very Serious Thing:
Women's Humor and American Culture*, identifies "the impulse of all feminist
humor" as "the fundamental absurdity of one gender oppressing the other,"
she expresses an underlying theme of this film (163).

Some of the aspects of women's humor described by Regina Barreca, Zita
Dresner, and Nancy Walker also fit Pedro Almodóvar's comic strategies. In
A Very Serious Thing, when discussing the subversion of stereotypes in
literature written by women, Walker notes "the purpose of mocking those
stereotypes and showing their absurdity" (9–10). In the same work she speaks
of the intent to "point to the origins of these stereotypes in a culture that
defines women in terms of relationships with men" and mentions portrayals
of "lovelorn women" as "victims of male indifference and the double standard" (12, 11). These comments describe Almodóvar's subversive use of
stereotypical behavior in *Women on the Verge of a Nervous Breakdown*. Also,
Almodóvar's meaningful scenes of Don Juans and dependent women on
Almagro Street, symbol of women's progress, come to mind when Nancy
Walker and Zita Dresner note women writers "exposing the discrepancies ...
between the inequities ... and the egalitarian ideals" (*Redressing the Balance*
xxii). Finally, the nativity scene on the terrace does "not, ultimately,
reproduce the expected hierarchies," a refusal which links it to "the ending
of comic works by women writers" discussed by Regina Barreca (12).

Yet *Women on the Verge of a Nervous Breakdown* is a film written and
directed by a man. Pedro Almodóvar, as he creates his humor, does not have
to deal with female social conditioning such as "standards of ladylike behavior," discussed by Walker (114). He, by the way, has mentioned, in
speaking about his sexual orientation, "we [gay men] keep on being what

they call masculine in behavior" (Russo 15). Identification of masculine stylistic traits would be a different study. But Almodóvar is a feminist and this film reflects the hope and the need for more progress as well as dramatic changes for women in Spain. As María Antonia García de León says, Almodóvar "*no tiene una visión androcéntrica*" ["does not have androcentric vision"] (Universidad Complutense 42).

Nor do I see macho control in *Women on the Verge of a Nervous Breakdown*. Almodóvar's presence is felt in his unique humor; in the wild series of significant surprises and incongruities; and in his signatures — taxis, telephones, television, not to mention the appearance of his mother and brother in minor roles. Also, we see *la Telefónica*, the Telephone Company building with its red clock, where Almodóvar once worked, from Pepa's terrace on Montalbán Street. Rather than dominating the audience, however, as Marvin D'Lugo discusses, he invites viewers' participation. As I have noted in this essay, Pedro Almodóvar offers suggestions in *Women on the Verge of a Nervous Breakdown* — a nativity scene with a Holy Family, parodic themes of Don Juan and of Hollywood comedies, Almagro Street, Ecce Homo, Azucena — for us to ponder beyond the visual images on the screen. After a laugh of recognition of his intentions, we collaborate in the gender messages.

Women on the Verge of a Nervous Breakdown, not a realistic comedy, reflects aspects of gender in contemporary society. Although Pepa's material comfort is Hollywood-like, her situation at the end of the film — a self-sufficient career women who decides to become a single parent — symbolizes real advances in the "outward marks of freedom and independence" for women, mentioned by D'Lugo (65). But the macho is still there. As Spanish women have said to me, "*queda mucho camino para andar*" ["there remains a long road to walk "], and not only in Spain. Machismo or its residues may be around in private lives and at work until women attain more "outward marks" of equality in societies, until they hold approximately half the decision-making positions, including those on the highest levels, for example. Meanwhile, machos are absurdly irrational, says Pedro Almodóvar, and ra-

Women on the Verge of a Nervous Breakdown is a story of emancipation from the macho. Pepa's independence and the epilogue, a nativity scene that undoes the patriarchal order, end the film with the hope that future generations will be able to laugh away machismo.

WORKS CITED

Almodóvar, Pedro, director and writer. *Mujeres al borde de un ataque de nervios* [*Women on the Verge of a Nervous Breakdown*]. Orion Home Video, 1989. (Original film produced by El Deseo S.A. and Lauren Films, Spain, 1988. Premiere, March 23, 1988)

_____. "Mujeres al borde de un ataque de nervios: Argumento original y guion." Original Script, 1987. Biblioteca Nacional, Madrid.

_____. *Patty Diphusa y otros textos*. Barcelona: Editorial Anagrama, 1991.

Barreca, Regina, ed. "Introduction," in: *Last Laughs: Perspectives on Women and Comedy*. New York, London: Gordon and Breach, 1988.

Boquerini (Blanco, Francisco). *Pedro Almodóvar*. Madrid: Ediciones JC, 1989.

Caparrós Lera, J.M. *El cine español de la democracia*. Barcelona: Anthropos, 1992.

D'Lugo, Marvin. "Heterogeneity and Spanish Cinema of the Eighties." *España Contemporánea* V (1992): 55–66.

Garcia de León, María Antonia. "Ecce Homo: Pedro Almodóvar. Tratamiento sociológico de una biografía." *El cine de Pedro Almodóvar y su mundo*. Cursos de Verano, el Escorial, 1989. Madrid: Universidad Complutense de Madrid, 1990, 15–62.

García de León, María Antonia, and Teresa Maldonado. *Pedro Almodóvar, la otra España cañí*. Ciudad Real: Biblioteca de Autores y Temas Manchegos, 1989.

Hart, Patricia. "Teachers on the Verge of a Nervous Breakdown: Film in the Foreign Language Classroom." Fall Conference of the Indiana Foreign Language Teachers Association. Indianapolis, 22 Oct. 1992.

Hopewell, John. *Out of the Past: Spanish Cinema After Franco*. London: BFI Books, 1986.

Instituto de la Mujer. *Instituto de la mujer/The Women's Institute*. Madrid: Ministerio de Cultura. (Ministerio de Asuntos Sociales, 1988), 1987.

James, Caryn. "Almodóvar, Adrift in Sexism." *New York Times* 12 Jan. 1992, natl. ed.: H11.

Kael, Pauline. *Movie Love*. New York: Plume, 1991.

Russo, Vito. "Man of La Mania." *Film Comment* 24 Nov./Dec. 1988: 13–17.

Sheppard, Alice. "Social Cognition, Gender Roles, and Women's Humor," in: *Women's Comic Visions*, ed. June Sochen. Detroit: Wayne State University Press, 1991, 33–56.

Siurana, Elvira. "Las mujeres de Pedro Almodóvar." *Poder y Libertad* 9 (1988): 64.

Vidal, Nuria. *El cine de Pedro Almodóvar*. Barcelona: Ediciones Destino, 1988.

Walker, Nancy A. *A Very Serious Thing: Women's Humor and American Culture*. Minneapolis: University of Minnesota Press, 1988.

Walker, Nancy A. and Zita Dresner, eds. "Introduction," in: *Redressing the Balance: American Women's Literary Humor from Colonial Times to the 1990s*. Jackson and London: University Press of Missouri, 1988.

18

Between the Laughter: Bridging Feminist Studies through Women's Stand-Up Comedy

ALLISON FRAIBERG

In a period of six months, I had two career choices staring me in the face. I wanted to be a writer, a serious writer, a serious feminist writer, and I wanted to be a stand up comic. I left it up to the fates. I did both, figuring the one I should follow would make itself known to me.

— Roseanne Barr (*My Life As a Woman* 193)

In my youth, I wanted to be a regular stand-up comedian, but in college I developed an unfortunate tendency to footnote and cross-reference my jokes, so I became a professor instead.

— Mary Klages, "Stand-Up Academic,"
English Department,
University of Colorado at Boulder (13)

Both Roseanne Barr (hereafter, Roseanne Arnold)[1] and Mary Klages recognize a crucial identification between what they do with comedy and who they are as feminists. While each has chosen a different path to express the intertwinings of comedy with unlikely counterparts, both maintain that the interconnection is basic to the ways in which they conduct their business. As

315

a famous comedian, Arnold's irony arises out of her recognition that one can
be a serious feminist writer by performing stand-up; Klages, on the other
hand, an established professor of English, speaks of the often unack-
nowledged similarities between academic performance and stand-up routines,
the difference being a certain sly propensity toward citation.

Both statements draw on a sense of irony: most "serious" feminist writers
aren't stand-up comedians, and most professors don't choose academics as a
safe alternative career choice to the stand-up circuits. But these feminist
theorists, Arnold and Klages, cannot dissociate their feminism from their
practices and performances of comedy. Stand-up is an intimate part of the
feminism each woman lives. Comedy is central to their lives and work, but
that intimate connection has been rendered invisible. The irony is based on
juxtaposing what are too often thought of as distinct and unrelated fields.

Arnold's and Klages' comments are funny because it's so rare to see
feminist issues bound up in the laughter of comedy. This essay is first about
making that critical connection between academic feminism and comedy
visible once again. It's about making that link, which has been broken,
explicit; it's about noticing that these opening passages from two feminists
fortunately aren't that funny after all.

From the nexus connecting academic women's studies with mainstream
women's comedy, I want to foreground the conditions that allow stand-up to
be seen as an important component within the larger practices and strategies
of women's studies. Stand-up comedy's context, its demand for an audience,
places audiences and performers in an unusual interactive dependency. I will
explore the work of comedians Paula Poundstone, Ellen DeGeneres, and
Margaret Cho because each, in her respective ways, self-consciously plays
off of that acknowledged interdependence in order to manipulate her cultural
critiques.

* * *

That foundational connection between comedy and academic women's
studies has only recently begun to be explored. With the appearance of such
important collections as Regina Barreca's *Last Laughs* (1988) and *New
Perspectives on Women and Comedy* (1992), June Sochen's *Women's Comic
Visions* (1991), and Nancy Walker's *A Very Serious Thing* (1988), feminists
in the humanities have started to explore the constitutive force of humor and
comedy in women's writings and experiences.[2] It was, of course, up to
feminist scholars to make visible both the comedic contributions made by
women and the reassurances women found in comedy, since literary and
critical traditions denied women recognition in this arena.[3]

In the introductions to her ground-breaking anthologies, Regina Barreca
takes on those male-dominated literary and cultural traditions. "Comedy
written by women," she argues, "is perceived by many critics as trivial, silly

and unworthy of serious attention" (*LL* 6). Four years later, in her follow-up anthology, Barreca's comments remain essentially the same. As her context widens from literary studies to critical studies in general, she finds that without "being defined as such, the study of comedy has been the study of male comedy" (*NP* 2). The clear goal of these critical anthologies is to bring to light the important contributions women have made on hyper-masculinized comedic codes. What I am interested in here, however, has less to do with working to incorporate women's comedy into male-defined comedic or cultural or literary studies, and more to do with how academic feminism has, and has not, approached the connections between stand-up comedy and women's experiences.

Aside from the few titles mentioned above, comedy has been a relatively low-key feature of academic women's cultural studies. In her review, for example, of Walker's and Dresner's *Redressing the Balance*, Jaye Berman inadvertently underscores the divide between academic women's studies and women's comedy. Speaking of the publication and value of Walker's book itself, Berman stresses that "*apart* from its scholarly function, it is a funny and fascinating compendium of American cultural history" (260, emphasis mine). The assumption that what is funny might not necessarily be scholarly is too strong a description of Berman's comment; still, the passage does indicate that the fit between what is considered funny and what is considered scholarly is at best an uncomfortable one. That uneasiness has characterized much of the discussion of women and comedy.[4]

While Barreca is certainly correct when she stresses the importance of placing "women at the center of a discussion of comedy because it has been done too rarely" (*NP* 2), I have to add my own spin on to the observation: it is important to place *comedy* at the center of a discussion of *women* because it has been done too rarely.[5] Comedian Paula Poundstone, for example, has headlined shows for years now, and is one of the best known comedians, male or female, in the country. She has a huge female following that is extraordinarily enthusiastic. Members of Poundstone's audiences regularly toss gifts on stage and, during performances, women interrupt the show with shouts of affection and excitement for Poundstone. If this reaction sounds a bit like the ones on the popular music scene, then that is exactly how it can feel for audiences at her comedy shows. Paula Poundstone's work has received no critical attention from women's studies scholars.

Because women's studies attends to the social and cultural inequities experienced by members of diverse groups and populations, it is not surprising that screening a Paula Poundstone performance isn't the first topic to pop into mind when designing syllabi, arranging colloquia, or preparing for curricular battles. Writer Fay Weldon accounts for the omission herself by explaining why she uses humor in her novels. She describes herself as "weak minded" for using comedy; not being funny is a compliment for Weldon because "rape, poverty, exploitation and so forth are *not* funny" (310–11). Of course these lived conditions are not funny, but some women, like Roseanne Arnold, have used comedy to talk about poverty and sexism; others, like Margaret Cho and Rhonda Hansome, use comedy to articulate seldom acknowledged perspectives on racism; still others, like Ellen DeGeneres, use comedy to create nodes of identification for large numbers of audience members.

Quite simply, many different women are using comedy in many different forms and ways. Because performance comedy is very popular both among women in the academy and the culture at large; because the incorporation of women's comedy into feminist curricula has been limited; and because critical attention has highlighted predominantly women's *literary* humor and comedy, I have chosen to focus on contemporary stand-up comedy by women.[6] While the field of stand-up comedy is still overwhelmingly male-defined, a large number of women nonetheless make their way performing, and headlining, stand-up acts. I want to talk about how these women in stand-up function to bridge the gaps between the theoretical positions of academic feminism and the experiences of women who attend stand-up performances, a bridge made quite visible by the passages from Klages and Arnold at the beginning of this essay.

Stand-up comedians have not traditionally fit well under a number of women's studies categories and disciplines. They are not particularly discussed in women's literary studies, and yet stand-up has not made much of a mark in feminist drama studies either. Feminist work in the social sciences has focused on the psychological issues of gender within social contexts, but with little attention to the cultural boom of comedy, especially stand-up. The scenario can begin to look like a game of disciplinary cat and mouse. Mainstream women's stand-up is too performance- or drama-oriented for the social sciences; it's not dramatic enough for drama studies; it's too popular and non-fictional for literary studies; and it's evidently too mainstream for feminist studies.

The scholarly work that has appeared on stand-up comedy by women has brought critical attention to such performers as Kate Clinton and the team of Kathy and Mo, comedians who, at least until recently, had played smaller, and decidedly less mainstream, venues to predominantly female audiences.[7] These comedians' material is explicitly feminist and, for that reason, more likely to be studied by feminists than DeGeneres' act which, at least on the surface, falls into the category of a kind of popular, observational humor.

Comedians who play predominantly to feminist audiences have had an enormous impact on popular feminism. Women's magazines such as *Ms.* and *Deneuve* regularly include articles on feminist comedians. On the rare occasions when academic feminism does study comedy, it looks to performers who work within a popular feminist arena such as Clinton, Karen Williams, or Marga Gomez. The work of these comedians is tremendously important, and it should certainly be the focus of much more study. At the same time, however, comedians such as DeGeneres or Poundstone, because they work on the national mainstream circuit, receive very little attention from women's magazines and none at all from academic feminism. While some work on Arnold has appeared — it is difficult to ignore the enormous impact she has had on popular culture — there is no mention of DeGeneres' or Poundstone's work, even though they attract huge audiences, even though they have each won Cable Ace awards for their work, and even though they each receive national network television coverage on a regular basis.[8]

There is no reason for these comedians to be so popular on and off campus — the mainstream stand-up circuit regularly includes campus visits — and yet be so unknown, at least officially, inside our halls and classrooms. Certainly one of the reasons for the lack of work on women stand-up comedians has to do with disciplinary criteria. Mainstream stand-up work, for the reasons above, just doesn't seem to fit very well into existing critical scenes. If women's studies is, however, to be an interdisciplinary field, then it not only has to be worked at in many disciplines; it must also be worked at outside, between, and even beyond those disciplines.

Feminist critics who study women's comedy in general have emphasized its subversive potential. Nancy Walker sees women's humorous writing as a "subversive protest against" the traditional powerlessness experienced by women (*Serious* 10). Barreca reinforces Walker's claim, but places the critique within a larger cultural frame. "Comedy," she argues, "is a way women writers can reflect the absurdity of the dominant ideology while undermining the very basis for its discourse" (*LL* 19). Here, Barreca locates subversion in terms of being both within the dominant ideology, reflecting it, and yet still being able to undermine it through humorous signifying.

Judy Little situates that double movement within a Bakhtinian frame of reference. Focusing on the "dialogics" of women's comedy, Little suggests that women have not only "humored the sentence," but that they have "carnivalized it" (19). Little emphasizes the playfulness of comedic subversions by contextualizing it in the revelry of carnival. Others, such as Linda Pershing, identify a more desperate effort in women's stand-up comedy. In her important work on lesbian stand-up comedian Kate Clinton, Pershing draws attention to women's use of comedy as no less than a "tool for survival" (195). Comedian Laura Kightlinger embraces both positions when she explains why she performs stand-up: "I just liked playing with knives" (85). Certainly her comments are delivered a little tongue in cheek, but her ambiguity highlights the double-edged efforts of stand-up comedy where, Walker points out, a woman runs the risk of "alienating rather than amusing her audience if she steps too far from conventionally conceived 'female' behavior" (*Serious* 79).

Walker's comments, in fact, run precisely counter to those of Poundstone, who responds with surprise to comments about the conditions for employment in stand-up made by another female comedian. "A comic was telling me," Poundstone explains, "that she thought she had started too late in life. I thought, Geez, this is one of the few areas where that doesn't mean a thing anymore. This has become an ageless, genderless job" (Kanfer 63). And while most comedians are still young and male, Poundstone, because of her relative level of success, has not felt the gendered pressures that Walker observes.

In keeping with this perspective, much of Poundstone's stand-up material focuses on easily accessible topics. *The Paula Poundstone Show*, which aired on HBO in June 1991, was organized, for example, around interviews of typically disliked public employees: postal workers, IRS agents, and parking meter attendants, to name a few. Poundstone would interview these workers and have them take questions from the audience which would serve as a kind of public, innocuous revenge on the service industry. In live performances, some of her favorite topics are equally benign. Poundstone is always asked about her cats, and she loves to talk about them. She even named one of her recent HBO specials "Cats, Cops, and Stuff."

Comedian Rita Rudner, however, says she doesn't much care for Poundstone's work because she sees it as being "too political." Rudner's comments may seem a little out of place. How political are cats, after all? Poundstone's politicized humor though has always been present in her work, mixed in with all the harmless observations. The 1992 presidential campaign solidified her political edge on a national level. When she was invited to perform at a White House Press lunch, she had to stand next to then-President Bush. When asked to introduce herself to the president, all she could muster was a polite, "Good luck in the private sector." From there, Poundstone took on the role of *Tonight Show* "White House correspondent," for which she attended both party conventions as well as the presidential inauguration. At the Republican convention, her political position became even clearer when she "reported" that a "cotillion of lesbians for Buchanan" had been formed, but only two women had joined. A fair share of Poundstone's audience is lesbian and the irony of her statement served to double back onto Buchanan's conservative positions.

When she covered the inauguration itself for *The Tonight Show*, she made a point of criticizing traditional women's roles in politics. With comedians Jay Leno and Larry Miller, Poundstone spoofed the film *Pretty Woman* as she and Leno went shopping at Miller's posh Beverly Hills mock-boutique for an inaugural gown. Poundstone muddled about the store in jeans and a sweatshirt, silent throughout, with Leno at the helm. Poundstone's critique was so effective precisely because she was so silent, a complete role-reversal for a stand-up comedian. The reversal was enhanced by Poundstone's reputation in stand-up: on what she calls a "good night," about a third of her performance is comprised of spontaneous interaction with her audience. In the *Pretty Woman* parody, the typical women's role in politics became a role explicitly incompatible with her own profession.

When Poundstone highlights these types of contradictions experienced by women, she generates a fundamental point of connection between the kinds of discussions held by academic feminist theorists and the daily experiences of women. She functions as a bridge of sorts between popular and academic women's cultural criticism, deconstructing gendered positions theorized in feminist classrooms. The fundamental difference lies in her offering the results to a national audience, opening a popular space, as Roseanne Arnold has done, that can serve as a critical focal point.

In contrast to Poundstone's content-based political criticism, comedian Ellen DeGeneres' cultural critique draws to a great extent on formalistic manipulations. As a stand-up performer, DeGeneres has worked steadily on a national level since she was featured in 1986 on an HBO *Young Comedians* special. Since then she has taped a number of specials for HBO and Lifetime Cable, and has appeared as a regular on network and cable comedy series.[9] She now appears regularly on late-night talk shows and headlines at all her performances. DeGeneres, interestingly enough, after establishing herself securely within the national mainstream circuit, has recently started to appear at women's festivals and fund-raisers. She has a sitcom slated for debut on ABC's fall 1993 schedule. At her live circuit performances, DeGeneres' audiences are predominantly white and commonly have about a two to one straight-lesbian ratio.[10]

DeGeneres performs observational comedy. The content of her work relies on acknowledging common experiences: that is, audience members are positioned to identify with her narratives. For the most part, she talks about situations to which audience members can relate. Unlike many of her colleagues in stand-up, she speaks rarely, if at all, about sexual relationships or specifically gendered contexts. In other words, she steers clear of what has been ripe terrain for both men and women in comedy: cultural observations based on gender and (hetero)sexuality.[11]

Instead, she tries to focus on the mannerisms and tendencies of as many listeners as she can, while, at the same time, grounding her observations in extended first-person narrations. Quite simply, she tells what seem to be embarrassing stories about herself, but then sutures audiences into a mass position of identification with her. The result is that DeGeneres manages to practice a coercive form of identification and displacement that actually inverts what could be seen as the self-deprecatory humor usually found in women's stand-up routines.

Her cultural observations often begin innocently enough. Almost stereotypically, DeGeneres often begins her shows with comments related to air travel. Speaking of the hostilities she harbors towards flight attendants, of the "disgusting" and "tiny" food served on flights, and of the ridiculous regulations observed during air travel, DeGeneres settles in, and settles her audiences into, a mainstay of stand-up discourse. It is certainly a class-based approach to modes of identification, but one that remains relatively accurate for audiences who attend live performances on a moderately regular basis. The comedy club crowd is generally white and middle-class, and DeGeneres works within this perspective.

DeGeneres soon complicates her mechanisms of identification though by invoking multiple perspectives. She regularly begins a segment of her routine from one perspective but shifts to another somewhere in the middle. Lisa Merrill, in her work on feminist humor, accurately and succinctly observes that comedy "depends on perspective" (276). For DeGeneres, comedy certainly depends on perspective, but perspective itself depends on where she is at any given moment in her act. At one point, she jumps from the point of view of someone who accidently hits a beehive with a stone, to that of the bees, back to the person who hit the bees, and finally to the people across the street watching the entire fiasco. The effect is dizzying, and the continual shifts work to undermine any stable, and therefore universalized, sense of perspective.

DeGeneres uses this structural technique when she ventures into more controversial territory. Her more charged material centers on commentary about her family and her childhood. The destabilized perspective is transposed onto an attempt to undercut narrative assumptions. During one sketch, she discusses a time she went into the kitchen to pour herself a glass of lemonade:

> I was in the back and I went to the kitchen to get some lemonade. And in the kitchen was my dad, my mom, all my brothers and sisters, standing there staring at me, about to start laughing. I was like, "what?" I was seven, I didn't know. And my dad said, "Ellen, honey, you were adopted and we've never liked you, so we've sold you to a tribe of Iroquois Indians. They'll be here to pick you up in about an hour. We're going to go to a movie. Bye-bye. Good luck."
>
> So I lived in the mountains for about nine years with the Iroquois, learning basket weaving and pottery. I taught them that noise you make under the arm. That was the skill I had. It was customary within the tribe to marry at thirteen and have several papooses, which I did. Anyway, nine years later, here comes trudging up the mountain, my dad, my mom, all my brothers and sisters, carrying a big thing of lemonade, going, "We were just kidding. We love you. You're ours." We went home and laughed and laughed and laughed.
>
> Funny thing is, they weren't even real Indians. They were just actors my dad had hired to play Indians. Just to fool me... He was always playing jokes on me (*HBO's One Night Stand*).

When DeGeneres takes the nuclear family to task, she uses the narrative assumptions that many of her audience members will invoke. Family members, who are supposed to love you, do not; children, who are supposed to be protected, are sold; and fathers, who are supposed to tell the truth, construct elaborate shams that terrorize the children. Every time a context begins to stabilize, DeGeneres cuts the frame out from under it, thereby undermining the stability of her central trope — power relations in a white, middle-class nuclear family.

Part of what enables DeGeneres to undermine traditional narrative structures involves the way she weaves tangential considerations into the core of her stories. Often, her asides begin to take over the story itself, shifting its focus, and shedding new light on "unimportant" distractions. She uses these unwieldy tangents for laughs, but they also serve to demonstrate how seemingly marginal concerns and perspectives can be drawn to the center of discussion. In one of her more elaborate narratives, DeGeneres offers an extended vision of what might actually be more frightening than putting your foot into a shoe with a spider in it. She meanders her way into thinking about how frightening life on a farm might be, but gets caught up in describing her aunt's life:

> Or, if you're on a farm, you know, cause you're visiting your aunt somebody. And you don't know her that well, but you knew her when you were a little girl, but you hadn't seen her in a long time. You just say, "Oh, I'll go to the farm to spend some time with my aunt." And so you're outside and she's like, "Sweetheart! Elly-Belly" — cause that's what she calls you even though you hate it. And she's like, "Would you go look for the, uh, thing I've misplaced?" So you're like, I don't care what it is even, you just want to stay outside cause that guy's inside that you hate and she wants you to call him Uncle Larry even though he's not your uncle and he's like drunk all the time and everything. But anyway, that's her life. (*Tonight Show*)

The particulars of her aunt's life, combined with DeGeneres' reaction to it, overwhelm the initial narrative. Lost in the complexities of this family structure is the original search for amusing, frightening experiences. DeGeneres tries to wipe away the intruding thoughts with the dismissive "anyway, that's her life," but the residual anger lingers throughout the sketch. DeGeneres' vagueness about her "aunt somebody" becomes a telling marker of the many women who have to deal on a daily basis with the "Uncle Larry" in their lives. In this sense, the comedic edge both diffuses and brings into the open the realities of abusive and dysfunctional family arrangements. Narrative tangents and insurgent perspectives emerge as the site of subversive gatherings. DeGeneres insidiously makes visible the often occluded space within traditionally defined story-telling modes for women audience members to nod their heads in collective recognition.

While DeGeneres focuses her narrative manipulations on the assumptions grounding the nuclear family, Margaret Cho takes a nexus of social relations and attacks them on two separate fronts. Cho identifies herself as Korean-American and began her stand-up career after realizing that the acting industry offered her little hope of ever getting parts that weren't stereotypical and racist. She began doing stand-up in San Francisco in 1989, worked the women's circuits, and has in the past year or so broken onto the national mainstream circuit. She was one the featured performers on last year's Bob Hope special called "Ladies of Laughter."

In an interview on CNN after the Los Angeles riots in 1992, Cho was asked about how she addresses racism in her work. "What I do," she responds, "is I take a stereotype and I enlarge it to the point where it seems ridiculous."[12] A large part of her routine draws on her experiences of racism and she presents those scenes to her audiences. When she is asked if a comedic forum makes it easier to deal with these issues, she emphasizes how comedy grants a certain sense of permission. Cho argues that "when you use humor people are less apt to be guarded." The comedic platform opens a door for Cho, but she is very clear that it is up to her to use the performance to keep it jarred open. She notes, for example, that early on when she was opening for other comedians she would always seem to follow someone who had just told a Chinese driver joke. To interrupt the lingering tone of the previous act, she would begin her own by introducing herself. "Hi, my name is Margaret Cho," she would say, "and I drive very well."

One of her most common opening routines currently focuses on a narrative mimicry of the problems she had when she was in the acting industry and the experiences she continues to have now that she works in comedy. Speaking of the casting agents who demand she play a certain stock role, Cho begins her act by explaining the difficulty they had with her:

> They had a real problem with me because I look this way but I talk this way [i.e., with "no accent"]. So it's like a problem. And they're trying to be sensitive about it and they're like, "Margaret, we don't want you to take this the wrong way, but could you be, I don't know, a little more Chinese?" Well, actually I'm Korean. "Whatever." (*Ladies of Laughter*)

Cho immediately addresses the racism she faces from the white entertainment industry. In the process, she confronts those in her audiences who hold those same expectations assuming some sort of contradiction between the way she looks and the way she speaks. Into one displaced context, Cho jams much of her mainstream audience's expectations.

Cho moves on though to complicate the simple deconstruction of racist assumptions by discussing the generational differences within her family.

I had to move out when I was really young because my mother is fully into Montgomery Wards. She used to make us go there every Saturday. She'd wake us up at seven standing outside going, "Kids! Kids! Let's go to Montgomery Ward. Let's go to Montgomery Ward." (*Ladies of Laughter*).

Cho begins the segment by isolating a cross-cultural moment of parent-child differences. She focuses initially on the embarrassment a teenager may feel being dragged off to a department store by her mother, on a Saturday no less. When she impersonates her mother calling them, however, Cho affects a very thick, exaggerated accent and squints her eyes, thereby signaling the end of the illusory universal moment.

At this point, Cho still refuses to let the image settle. She takes a break in the story to announce to her audience, "Isn't it incredible how when I squint my eyes I give the illusion of looking Asian?" Cho disturbs the cultural generation gap joke by mockingly assuming that her audience has forgotten that she "looks Asian." The ironic posture at once reinforces both the generational and cultural differences.

In the final stage of this part of her act, Cho pushes the cultural image to its limits. Again, she begins with an identifiable common denominator. "I felt sorry for my mother," she explains, "because I wasn't the easiest child to raise. I had a lot of problems." The address here is simple enough to garner a sense of mass identification. But Cho continues: "I had a lot of identity problems." Based on Cho's previous commentary, the implied assumption would involve a generational cultural conflict. How much, for example, did Cho identify with her Korean culture? How much with her California upbringing? Her explanation catches all off guard: "For a long time I thought that I was Jewish. I actually made all my friends call me Naomi. I was the Ori-yenta."

Once she cauterizes some of the initial assumptions about her identity at the beginning of her routine, Cho's strategy centers on isolating a moment with the greatest potential for identification. She takes that moment of connection as a starting point and then fragments it based on cultural expectations. And the process continues with each fragment reshaped into a new moment of identification, then shattered once again. Cho uses moments of generalized identification and forecloses on their potential to act as universal images. Her process of fragmentation doesn't just deconstruct universalizing impulses, but fragments the generalization to offer more localized nodes of connection. Each final image, in its temporary manifestation, offers a limited space for identification, a space accessible only to some. This strategy relies on drawing people into a moment of identification and then systematically restricting that space of connection.

In that fragmentation, Cho halts any proclivity towards universalism, but retains pockets of identification for members of her audiences who find themselves in similar positions. Cho's practice of fragmentation resembles, in some ways, the narrative theory behind DeGeneres performances. Both comedians invoke dominant cultural scenes in order to disturb the familiarity and assumed mass appeal associated with them. DeGeneres works her narratives into apparent dead-ends but then turns those dead-ends into the larger moments of identification that they are. Cho creates collective moments by destroying, through incessant fragmentation, the false collectivity of "universal humor." Poundstone's work isn't as formalistically aggressive as either Cho's or DeGeneres', but parodies *Pretty Woman* and offers critiques of gender by juxtaposing her political humor with the ostensibly benign humor for which she became famous. Poundstone offers herself as a human buffer to ease the jarring sensation of that juxtaposition. As in the *Pretty Woman* critique, she acts as the site of contradiction that undermines cultural assumptions.

Despite these similarities, Poundstone, DeGeneres, and Cho are comedians whose approaches are radically different from each other. Poundstone and DeGeneres, for example, do not confront issues of racism in their acts; Cho argues that dismantling racism is the first priority in her routines.[13] The work that each has produced repairs the perceived gap between women's concerns on and off campuses, and each works in her own way on the universalist imperative embedded in U.S. culture at large. But DeGeneres steers clear of the content-based political criticism that Poundstone is most closely associated with now after the 1992 election.[14] Both DeGeneres and Cho develop their political critiques from observations of family life, but DeGeneres' target is white, middle-class, nuclear arrangements and Cho works on cross-cultural and intra-cultural differences. The contrast between these comedians is important, and the temptation to resolve those differences under the rubric of mainstream performance comedy should be resisted. In their critiques, they each create different localized scenes of identification.

* * *

On a 1992 *Donahue* show focusing on women in (men's) drag, audiences were told that, while everyone had done men in drag repeatedly, this was the first of the talk shows to do an entire section on women in drag. Audiences at the men in drag shows usually respond favorably: most have a laugh and are 'entertained' — even those members of the audience who embark on moral diatribes serve as entertaining fodder for the others. When the women in drag were on, however, the responses were quite different. There seemed to be a much more hostile atmosphere overall and the most common comment had to do with the audience's feelings that these women 'just didn't look like men.' In other words, the women just weren't as good at drag as the men were, and consequently they were far less 'entertaining.'

Near the end of the show one of the guests made a comment that elicited hoots and howls from the audience as a whole. One of the women in drag was trying to allay the general attitude that the guests were not 'freaks' by claiming that gender is not something you are just born into, that it's something you play at or perform; in other words, that dressing like a man is just as arbitrary as dressing like a woman — both involve the donning of costumes. Quite simply, she argued, women don't naturally wear skirts and pluck their eyebrows. The audience would not tolerate her claim and drowned out her voice with their vocal rejection. What I find quite telling about this episode is that a Donahue audience, a fairly liberal New York crowd that recognizes oppression in the world, found absolutely ridiculous, even beyond consideration, a claim that, in academic feminist theory, is now a fairly benign assumption. This audience would have absolutely nothing to do with a simple deconstruction of gender.

On an episode of *Roseanne* in 1992, Roseanne Conner dressed in men's drag for a Halloween party. With her sister Jackie, she was delayed at the local pub where the Conners are regulars. Patrons repeatedly mistook her for a man, and the better part of the show dealt with Roseanne's experiences as a man in a bar. She stepped in to help her sister fend off the harassment of "another" man, and then insinuated herself into the on-going pool game. As a man, Roseanne passed and got some first-hand knowledge of displaced locker room banter. Roseanne, in her comedic context, fared much better than the women on Donahue. She was able to offer her deconstruction of gender relatively uninterrupted.

Like Roseanne Arnold, Paula Poundstone, Ellen DeGeneres, and Margaret Cho have offered their very different critiques of power and subordination. DeGeneres' formal subversions create a locus for identification in the dead-ends of traditional narrative structures. Poundstone's content-oriented deconstructions work to destabilize traditional stand-up contexts and discourses, all the while maintaining their mainstream popular appeal. Cho's strategy of generalizations and fragmentations creates a spiralling process of identification and displacement. The process enables Cho both to foreclose on any universalizing impulses members of her audience may harbor and to create a space for limited recognition.

The trick for each of them lies in how they get away with it all. Cho has suggested that people are "more apt to listen to you if you come to entertain them" (*CNN*). For Cho, the stand-up circuit allows her to talk about issues of race, gender, and in some cases, sexuality. When she was acting, she was never permitted the space to do anything but regurgitate the racist images instilled in the movie industry. Doing stand-up, Cho has remarked that she feels much more "in control" of her work. She manipulates the performative context by talking about the issues of power white audiences often have difficulty addressing in any substantial way.

After the 1992 L.A. riots, Cho felt the need to deal with riots in her work. She works a good deal of the time in California clubs and was finding her audiences very tense. She didn't talk about the looting or violence directly, but put forth her own sense of the enormous effects the riots would have on the country. "I would talk," Cho explains, "about how devastating the curfews were. I mean you'd go down the street at seven o'clock in the evening and all the 7–11's were closed. I mean, my God, is there anything that could affect America so much?" (CNN).

In many "serious" arenas, talk of the effects of power and oppression is dismissed as the unexamined banter of political correctness. Political pundits act like the casting agents of culture by dismissing any claims about the workings of domination. Like Cho who wasn't getting acting jobs because she didn't act "Chinese enough," feminists like Naomi Wolf are written off because she is conventionally attractive — she wasn't acting "plain enough" to have her beauty myth taken seriously. Bertice Berry was a sociologist at Kent State University; she also works as a stand-up comedian and plays colleges around the country. Like Cho, her primary topic of interest in her stand-up act is racism. Of the pressures she experiences talking about racism, Berry explains, "It's not a question of being politically correct; it's a question of being correct" (CNN). That transition in perception might best be attained through comedy, particularly stand-up.

An essential part of the joy and laughter women experience both perform-ing and watching stand-up is grounded, I believe, in these subversive effects produced by humor that gets away with something. DeGeneres, Poundstone, Arnold, and Cho each offers her own brand of woman-identified subversive comedy. Their enormous popularity serves first of all as a connective force bringing together the discourses of both popular and academic women's cultural criticism. Their work can bring to light the similarities between what we do in our feminist classrooms and what these women comedians do on their stages.

I do not want to suggest, however, that comedy has functioned to unify women's experiences and perspectives. The comedic work of these per-formers may, however, serve to highlight some of the similarities between women's cultural criticism both on and off campuses. It may gather together various women's thoughts, observations, and laughter. But none of these comics either works for or effects a unification among women. In fact, all their work tries to break down unexamined assumptions of mass identifica-tion. DeGeneres, Poundstone, Arnold, and Cho are very different women, performing radically different acts in front of varying and diverse audiences. The spaces they provide for recognition are just as diverse.

Stand-up comedians have captured women's attention while making us laugh; they have, in their own arenas, articulated complex arguments that comment on disparate cultural conditions. They reflect the discussions we have in academic settings while reinventing and making new available discursive territories. During the 1992–93 television season, comedian Elayne Boosler appeared on an episode of the NBC drama *Sisters*. On the show she played comedian Hildy Hirschberg who performs at main character Alex's breast-cancer support group. In her role, Boosler encourages members of the group to try their hands at stand-up because the experience might help them to cope with their situations in a therapeutic way. "We don't present it as a cure-all," says Boosler, "but comedy certainly makes a dire situation easier to deal with" (5). Boosler's follow-up statement is even more telling. After all, she explains, "who doesn't feel better after a big belly laugh?" True, but the stand-up performer isn't the one who's laughing. I don't think Boosler just made a mistake here; she implicitly identifies a moment of interaction.

Alex would feel better, Boosler assumes, not because she is in the audience laughing, but because she is transformed by hearing the laughter she may produce on stage. The laughter of stand-up produces more than the sum of its anecdotal laughs. In that vein, I want to argue that the laughter in stand-up can be more than something that happens to make someone feel better. It's not just a little comic relief.

In the interaction between audiences and stand-up performers, those laughs signal a lot more. Comedians may be able to get away with a lot of things on stage that would be unacceptable in other forums, but audiences, based on what they have heard, come away from performances with more than just a smile on their faces. Stand-up becomes a matter of agency when cultural critics begin to account for what the laughs mean, where they are coming from, and who is included. Cataloguing and accounting for the specifics and differences of these patterns offers feminist cultural criticism a strategy for turning a sense of comic relief into a matrix for agency grounded not just in contextualized social frames, but in a sense of pleasure as well.

The comedians I have talked about here are only a few members of an ever increasing group. Laura Kightlinger and Margaret Smith offer a feminism of cynicism; Brett Butler shares her views on being a feminist from Georgia; Sue Kolinsky, Elayne Boosler, and Cathy Ladman offer their own designs on heterosexuality; Carol Leifer and Ellen Cleghorne integrate characters into their stand-up routines; Marga Gomez, Karen Williams, and Suzanne Westenhoeffer base their stand-up in their diverse experiences as lesbians. There are so many more: Kathleen Madigan, Rhonda Hansome, Lea DeLaria, Robin Tyler, Jody Behar, Carol Siskind, Pam Stone, Mo Gaffney, and the list goes on. Each of these comedians approaches stand-up with a different vision; each of them plays to and gathers large groups of women together; and each of them creates spaces for agency embedded in the inter-

stices of their address and the shifting glances of recognition and acknowledged laughter.

In a personal essay on the business of stand-up, comedian Laura
Kightlinger urges women to, as she calls it, "return the favor" (88). Writing
specifically about the difficult treatment she received from agents and club
managers who were women, Kightlinger explains that returning the favor
involves a conscious effort to acknowledge and extend a hand to other women
in your business. "When you help other women," she argues, "then your head
is in the picture ... and they will return the favor just by re-establishing your
good judgement" (88). Kightlinger's argument is with club managers, book-
ing agents, and industry personnel who refuse to help out where they can. In
many ways, I have been like those women who refuse to extend a hand. I
have reveled in the laughter of audiences, snickered knowingly at the implicit
critiques and underhanded twists delivered, and taken immense pleasure in
the knowing glances I have shared with other women at performances. Not
until now, though, have I ever thought of returning the favor by bringing into
the classroom the diverse work of these women who stand up every day.

NOTES

1. The book *Roseanne: My Life as a Woman* was written under the name Roseanne
    Barr, but since her marriage to Tom Arnold, she has changed her name to
    Roseanne Arnold. I will refer to her as Roseanne Arnold throughout this essay.

2. For further reading on the subject of women in comedy see among others Judith
    Little, *Comedy and the Woman Writer: Woolf, Spark, and Feminism*; Deanna
    Stillman and Anne Beats, eds., *Titters: The First Collection of Humor by
    Women*; Judith Wilt, "The Laughter of Maidens, the Cackle of Matriarchs: Notes
    on the Collision Between Comedy and Feminism"; Elsie A. Williams, "Moms
    Mabley and the Afro-American Comic Performance"; Martha Bensley Bruere
    and Mary Ritter Beards, eds., *Laughing Their Way: Women's Humor in America*;
    Gloria Kaufman and Mary Kay Blakely, eds., *Pulling Our Own Strings:
    Feminist Humor and Satire*; Linda Martin and Kerry Segrave, *Women in Com-
    edy*; and Patricia Mellencamp, *High Anxiety: Catastrophe, Scandal, Age &
    Comedy*. All references appear in this bibliography.

3. Traditionally, women in literary and cultural studies were just seen as lacking a
    sense of humor. When women didn't laugh, it was assumed that they were
    humorless; there was not much consideration of the proposition that perhaps the
    humor involved was either sexist, degrading, or partial. For a historical account
    of critics' accusations see Regina Barreca's introduction to *Last Laughs*.

4. It has certainly been true of my own relationship to comedy. When I finally
    decided to tell my academic colleagues that I not only loved watching women

comedians perform, but actually wanted to make that pleasure my work, I began to hear from several women, and men, in my department who would tell me their stories about the comedic performances they enjoyed watching. People would actually stop me in the halls to talk about television and stand-up comedy; one of my colleagues and I would send electronic mail back and forth talking about the latest performances we attended. The conversations took on a tone of almost secretive confessional pleasure, somewhat similar to the kind that many academics feel when they enjoy a really popular mainstream film. In this sense, my experience differed from that of Barreca's who, when she told her colleagues she was editing a collection on women and comedy, was told "'*have* women done anything differently from Swift and Pope?'" (*NP* 1). The people I spoke with clearly loved the comedy they experienced and were quite well-acquainted with both mainstream and specialized comedians; they just didn't want to make it entirely public that they enjoyed this type of performance. When I would ask them if they had ever thought of producing some scholarly work on these comedians, the responses were all essentially the same: they would hesitate, think for a minute, and then say, "How interesting, but no, I haven't." The point I am trying to make here centers on the perceived inappropriateness of comedy, specifically, popular mainstream stand-up comedy, for scholarly attention.

5. The obvious exceptions are the wonderful collections and studies mentioned near the beginning of this essay and cited in the bibliography. Work on stand-up comedy has, however, been attended to less often than its more traditionally literary and dramatic counterparts.

6. Non-academic women's journals and magazines have noted the contributions of women stand-ups for years. One magazine in particular, *Deneuve*, even features one stand-up comedian in each issue.

7. See Brenda Gross' "The Parallel Lives of Kathy and Mo" in Barreca's *New Perspectives on Women and Comedy*, and Linda Pershing's "There's a Joker in the Menstrual Hut: A Performance Analysis of Comedian Kate Clinton" in Sochen's *Women's Comic Visions*. Many feminist comedians have consciously marketed themselves to feminist audiences, appearing regularly at Women's Music Festivals throughout the country. On that alternative circuit, comedians Lea DeLaria, Karen Williams, Marga Gomez, and many others have established themselves nationally.

8. One notable exception is Gail Singer's *Wisecracks*, a Canadian film produced by the Studio D of the NFB. In the film, Singer interviews women comedians and shows dozens of clips. To some extent, the film provides a historical base for women in comedy, but focuses primarily on contemporary stand-up comedians in Canada, Britain, and the U.S. DeGeneres and Poundstone are featured; Arnold is not. Both Poundstone and DeGeneres have received increasing attention from networks and cable stations in the past year. DeGeneres is currently taping a series for ABC, has appeared on at least three comedy specials for Lifetime, and can be seen regularly on *The Tonight Show* and *The Arsenio Hall Show*. Poundstone has had a series on HBO and is a regular guest on *The Tonight Show*.

9. Some of the specials include: *HBO's One Night Stand: Ellen DeGeneres* (1992);
    Six Comics in Search of a Generation (Lifetime, 1992); *Laughing Back*
    (Lifetime, 1991). The comedy series are *Open House* (Lifetime, 1989-90) and
    Laurie Hill (ABC 1992).

10. This observation is purely anecdotal, based in part on what I have seen at
    DeGeneres' stand-up performances both in person and televised. These com-
    ments are intended just to give an informal context to the performance situations
    in DeGeneres' shows.

11. In fact, DeGeneres' thoughts on this type of subjective positioning are quite
    clear. When asked in Gail Singer's film *Wisecracks* to comment on how she
    feels being a woman in comedy, she responded by ranking her preferred posi-
    tions of identification. She argued for being considered first "a person," then a
    "comedian," and then a "woman."

12. The interview took place on "Sonya Live," a daily current events talk show on
    CNN. The full reference for this interview appears in the bibliography. All
    non-performance quotes from Cho are from this interview. The performance
    citations are from her routine on the Hope special, also cited in the bibliography.

13. See Cho's interview in the magazine *Deneuve* cited in this bibliography. The
    discussion focuses on Cho's thoughts on racism and sexuality.

14. Poundstone has said in interviews that she finds it both disturbing and amusing
    that she now, after her stints at the conventions and the inaugural, regularly finds
    reporters camped on her doorstep waiting to ask her questions about the current
    administration. One of the questions she receives most often has to do with what
    she will do if Bill Clinton turns out not to be funny. Exasperated, Poundstone
    tells them that nothing would make her happier if the president of the United
    States *wasn't* funny. "If worse comes to worst," Poundstone tells them, "I'll
    reminisce about Bush" (*Larry King Live*).

WORKS CITED

Barr, Roseanne. *Roseanne Barr: My Life as a Woman*. New York: Harper & Row,
    1989.

Barreca, Regina, ed. *Last Laughs: Perspectives on Women and Comedy*. Philadelphia:
    Gordon and Breach, 1988.

_____, ed. *New Perspectives on Women and Comedy*. Philadelphia: Gordon
    and Breach, 1992.

Berman, Jaye. "Women's Humor." *Contemporary Literature* 31/2 (1990): 251–260.

Berry, Bertice. Interview. *Sonya Live*. CNN. April 7, 1992.

Bruere, Martha Bensley, and Mary Ritter Beards, eds. *Laughing Their Way: Women's
    Humor in America*. New York: Macmillan, 1934.

Cheh, Carol. "Comedian Margaret Cho." *Deneuve* 2/6 (Dec. 1992): 30.

Cho, Margaret. *The Ladies of Laughter*. NBC Entertainment, 1992.

_____. *Six Characters in Search of a Generation*. Lifetime Cable, 1992.

_____. Interview. *Sonya Live*. CNN. April 7, 1992.

DeGeneres, Ellen. *HBO's One Night Stand with Ellen DeGeneres*. Home Box Office, 1992.

_____. *The Tonight Show*. NBC Entertainment. January 12, 1993.

Gross, Brenda. "The Parallel Lives of Kathy and Mo," in: *New Perspectives on Women and Comedy*, ed. Regina Barreca. 89–99.

Kanfer, Stephen. "Sauce, Satire and Shtick." *Time* 136/19 (Fall 1990): 62–3.

Kaufman, Gloria, and Mary Kay Blakely, eds. *Pulling Our Own Strings: Feminist Humor and Satire*. Bloomington: Indiana University Press, 1980.

Kightlinger, Laura. "Return the Favor," in: *New Perspectives on Women and Comedy*, ed. Regina Barreca. 85–88.

Klages, Mary. "What To Do With Helen Keller Jokes: A Feminist Act," in: *New Perspectives on Women and Comedy*, ed. Regina Barreca. 13–22.

Little, Judith. *Comedy and the Woman Writer: Woolf, Spark, and Feminism*. Lincoln: University of Nebraska Press, 1983.

Martin, Linda, and Kerry Segrave. *Women in Comedy*. Secaucus, NJ: Citadel Press, 1986.

McNamara, Mary. "Laughing All the Way to the Revolution: The New Feminist Comics." *Ms.* (Jan.–Feb. 1992): 23–27.

Mellencamp, Patricia. *High Anxiety: Catastrophe, Scandal, Age & Comedy*. Bloomington: Indiana University Press, 1992.

Merrill, Lisa. "Feminist Humor: Rebellious and Self-Affirming," in: *Last Laughs: Perspectives on Women and Comedy*, ed. Regina Barreca. 271–280.

Pershing, Linda. "There's a Joker in the Menstrual Hut: A Performance Analysis of Comedian Kate Clinton," in: *Women's Comic Visions*, ed. June Sochen. 193–236.

Poundstone, Paula. *The Paula Poundstone Show*. Home Box Office, June 1992.

_____. *The Tonight Show*. NBC Entertainment. January 17–20, 1993.

Singer, Gail. *Wisecracks*. National Film Board of Canada, 1991.

Sochen, June, ed. *Women's Comic Visions*. Detroit: Wayne State University Press, 1991.

Stillman, Deanna, and Anne Beats, eds. *Titters: The First Collection of Humor by Women*. New York: Collier, 1976.

Walker, Nancy A. *A Very Serious Thing: Women's Humor and American Culture*. Minneapolis: University of Minnesota Press, 1988.

Walker, Nancy A., and Zita Dresner, eds. *Redressing the Balance: American Women's Literary Humor from Colonial Times to the 1980s*. Jackson and London: University Press of Mississippi, 1988.

Weldon, Fay. "Towards a Humorous View of the Universe," in: *Last Laughs: Perspectives on Women and Comedy*, ed. Regina Barreca. 309–311.

Williams, Elsie A. "Moms Mabley and the Afro-American Comic Performance," in: *Women's Comic Visions*, ed. June Sochen. 158–178.

Wilt, Judith. "The Laughter of Maidens, the Cackle of Matriarchs: Notes on the Collision Between Comedy and Feminism," in: *Gender and Literary Voice*, ed. Janet Todd. New York: Holmes and Meier, 1980. 173–196.

19

Comic Strip-Tease: A Revealing Look at Women Cartoon Artists

JAYE BERMAN MONTRESOR

An increasing number of women cartoonists have been joining the ranks of what was once an almost exclusively male field in this country, and as a result, the representation of women in comic strips has changed dramatically from the sexual fantasy figures familiar to readers of both mainstream and underground comics.[1] While one might expect women cartoonists to draw their female characters more realistically, it is often the case that their depictions are likewise exaggerations, albeit in a different direction. In both cases, women are presented as grotesques but to quite different effects, as can be seen in a number of contemporary women cartoon artists who are co-opting the grotesque image as a way of subverting conventional standards of feminine beauty.

The classical ideal or "aesthetics of the beautiful," which Mikhail Bakhtin associates with the high culture of the Renaissance, has also held sway in the low cultural genre of the American comic strip (Bakhtin 9). One can trace this type of idealized female beauty decade by decade from Mrs. Newlywed and her turn of the century "Gibson girl" good looks to Positive Polly, the "American girl-goddess" of the 1910s (Horn 41). The Roaring Twenties featured bobbed beauties, like Dumb Dora and Lillums Lovewell, who were

supplanted by the darkly dangerous *femmes fatales* of the thirties, like The
Dragon Lady and Ardala Valmar. Miss Lace, Wonder Woman, and other
pinups of the forties were especially popular with American soldiers, but by
the fifties, long-stemmed American beauties found themselves in competition
with exotic sirens, like Flamingo and South Sea Girl. Even in the sixties,
women characters did not really change much, since the glamorous career
women of that era, like "The Girls of Apartment 3-G," recall another popular
staple of comics since the twenties — the unmarried working girl. It wasn't
until 1970 that the liberation movements of the previous decade made their
way into mainstream comic strips, like "Doonesbury" (with its runaway
housewife, Joanie Caucus) and Friday Foster (the first black newspaper strip
heroine).

By contrast, since the emergence of women cartoonists in the seventies,
there has been a noticeable trend toward representing female characters in a
manner akin to the "grotesque realism" which Bakhtin identifies with the folk
culture of the Middle Ages (Bakhtin 18). This tendency is apparent in cartoonists whose work appears in a variety of publications: in mainstream
newspapers and magazines that feature cartoons by Cathy Guisewite, Nicole
Hollander, and Lynda Barry; in gay and lesbian newspapers that run cartoons
by Alison Bechdel and Jennifer Camper; and in underground "comix" in
which cartoonists Carol Lay, Phoebe Gloeckner, Diane Noomin, and other
fellow travellers of the Wimmen's Comix Collective display their art.

Bakhtin perceives a tension between these two ways of conceptualizing
the body — the finished body-as-product of the classical ideal vs. the unfinished body-in-process of grotesque realism — that can be traced to our
own time; witness, for example, our ambivalent cultural fascination with the
muscular make-overs of Madonna and Linda Hamilton on the one hand, and
the dieting ups and downs of Elizabeth Taylor and Oprah Winfrey on the
other. Similarly, the popularity of *zaftig* comedian Roseanne Barr Arnold's
abrasive, bawdy, working-class humor may be understood in terms of what
Bakhtin calls "the material bodily principle" of the folk (or "all-people"), who
laugh in celebration of "degraded" (in the sense of "down to earth") language
("abuses, oaths, and curses") and the activities of the lower body ("the genital
organs, the belly, and the buttocks") (Bakhtin 19–20, 27).[2]

While it is true that the audience for comics has been predominantly male,
even such potential role models for women as Sheena, Queen of the Jungle,
and Wonder Woman are more likely to produce alienation rather than identification on the part of female readers because of the way that they are drawn.
By contrast, characters drawn with a female audience in mind, such as
Hollander's Sylvia, or the cast of Bechdel's "Dykes to Watch Out For" strip
potentially serve a more feminist agenda by fostering a sense of wholeness
and connection among female fans.[3] Of particular interest are women cartoon
artists who promote a sense of community among women readers based on

shared strengths (as in Betty Swords' feminist cartoons for the M.C.P. calendar) rather than weaknesses (as in Cathy Guisewite's terminally insecure "Cathy" character).[4]

While male cartoonists have traditionally drawn from fantasy, female cartoonists have made it explicit in their strips that they are drawing from life — their own and those around them. This inscription of the female body in words and pictures may be more effective than a purely literary response to the call for an "écriture féminine" by such French feminists as Luce Irigaray, Hélène Cixous, Chantal Chawaf, and others for whom the final goal of writing is an articulation of the body (Chawaf 177). Such an articulation of the body is apparent, for instance, in cartoonist Lynda Barry's giant coloring book, *Naked Ladies, Naked Ladies, Naked Ladies*. Both the oversized dimensions of the book and its attention-getting title exhibit Barry's rebellious exuberance in defying her girlhood priest's attempt to make his young congregants promise not to look at naked women, a pledge that struck Barry as ridiculous even at the time. More to the point of this essay, her drawings call into question conventional definitions of female sexual attractiveness. The book is an extension of fifty-two of Barry's paintings which were inspired by a deck of risqué playing cards. Barry's version of the deck exalts the nude female in all her aspects, including aged, pregnant, and obese bodies. Barry says that her purpose was to show that all women are sexy, not just the ones featured in male pornography (Heil C5). By urging her readers to color (but not necessarily clothe) these naked ladies, Barry promotes active participation in place of the pornographic voyeurism so familiar in our culture. Thus (to borrow from film theory), instead of the usual case of men attaining pleasure by objectifying a monotypic female body with their gaze (and exiling all other types of female bodies to a kind of sexual Lower Slobovia), men are encouraged to relate to these "ladies" (and by extension human females) as subjects in all their infinite variety.[5] For women, the masochism said to be necessary for female viewing pleasure can be bypassed in favor of a carnivalesque celebration of every kind of body, including the Bakhtinian "grotesque body ... the open, protruding, extended, secreting body, the body of becoming, process and change" (Russo 219).[6] Mary Russo concludes her influential essay on female grotesques by asking how such bodies "might be used affirmatively to destabilize the idealizations of female beauty or to realign the mechanisms of desire" (Russo 221). Women cartoonists who draw attention to (but do not ridicule) female forms that deviate from the ideal dictated by the media and the beauty and fashion industries might have some answers. As Mary O'Connor asserts in her essay, "Subject, Voice, and Women," "the evocations of the grotesque, the portrayal of otherness, can produce a moment of utopian vision which relativizes the authoritative norm and thus produces the possibility of change" (O'Connor 201).

There is also a qualitative difference between the kind of laughter these cartoonists elicit and that produced by traditional male cartoonists, whose humor displays arrogant perception towards its target (usually consisting of less powerful groups in society, such as women or ethnic and religious minorities). This kind of humor corresponds to Sigmund Freud's observations in *Jokes and Their Relation to the Unconscious* that a witticism starts with an aggressive tendency or intent which becomes disguised through the work of the unconscious and combined with playful pleasure. Once the latent aggressive thought takes on more socially acceptable trappings, the energy originally activated to keep the hostility under repression is freed into laughter. Bakhtin has distinguished another kind of laughter, however, result-ing from his study of the carnival in Medieval and Renaissance Europe:

> Carnival laughter is the laughter of all the people. ... it is directed at all and everyone, including the carnival's participants... This is one of the essential differences of the people's festive laughter from the pure satire of modern times. The satirist whose laughter is negative places himself above the object of his mockery, he is opposed to it. The wholeness of the world's comic aspect is destroyed, and that which appears comic becomes a private reaction. The people's ambivalent laughter, on the other hand, expresses the point of view of the whole world; he who is laughing also belongs to it. (Bakhtin 11–12)

With regard to the women cartoonists of the past twenty years or so, the last sentence needs to be rewritten as "*she* who is laughing," since they elicit "carnival humor" by effecting identification on the part of the female reader and by willingly laughing at themselves as well as at others. Because humor that relies on the arrogant perception of traditional male humor to get laughs reinforces the fear, anger, and hatred that are at the root of so many of our social problems, sharing a laugh that promotes awareness and identification rather than arrogance and estrangement is one way that we can overcome such negative perceptions.

Barbara Brandon, who is notable as the first black woman cartoonist in national syndication, is notable as well for the way that she handles the problematic question of how to draw the female body. None of the black female characters who people her strip, "Where I'm Coming From," is shown below the neck. Although she jokes that "I'm not that good at drawing bodies," she seriously points out that "for too long in our society, women have been summed up by their body parts and not by their brains. I want to change that" (Thomas F8). For those who do not realize what a radical reversal of cartoon norms this posits even in our presumably "PC"-sensitive era, one need only consider underground guru Robert Crumb's recent strip, "Bitchin' Bod" (*Hup*, June 1992), in which his famous creation, Mr. Natural, magically removes the head of Devil Girl so that he and his buddies can enjoy her voluptuous body without troubling themselves with her personality. Unlike such products of misogynist male fantasy, the true-to-life voices of "the Girls," as Brandon collectively calls her characters, are based on people she actually knows (Hickey F4). Aware of her unique position as a cartoonist and woman of color, Brandon feels "a larger responsibility" than mere entertainment, and she uses humor to address such issues as race, gender, and class (Hickey F3). For example, in a strip reflecting the debate over multicultural education, the dread-locked Lekesha shares her thoughts with the reader:

> Looks like the public schools are adopting a multicultural curriculum. Whew! We've finally gotten to first base. Now I understand the big debate is what to teach. What's the problem? The answer is simple. Teach what wasn't taught when I was in school ... the *truth*, the whole *truth* and nothing but the *truth!* (Brandon 38)

Other strips have dealt with teenage pregnancy, gangs, and the Clarence Thomas hearings. The topical and often controversial nature of "Where I'm Coming From" has led to its placement on the editorial page rather than the comic section in some of the newspapers which carry the strip, which is fine with Brandon, since she is more concerned with provoking thought than getting laughs. Given the many issues of the day that Brandon addresses, it is understandable that she "cringes when people call her strip the 'Black Cathy,'" for she looks down on Cathy as a self-involved character who is "upset because she doesn't have a waistline" (Hickey F3).

Although "Cathy" has endorsed the Democratic party and addressed women's issues like sexual harassment in the workplace and the need for adequate daycare for children of working women, the dominant story line is Cathy's continuing struggle with her weight and body shape. For example, a recent strip shows Cathy reading her New Year's resolutions penned in her diet diary over the past twenty years:

> **1973 Plan**: Eat less. **Goal**: Lose 10 pounds. **Cost**: Free
> **1983 Plan**: Eat less, Join gym. **Goal**: Lose 10 pounds. **Cost**: $250.00
> **1993 Plan**: Enroll in Diet Group, Purchase diet food, Hire diet therapist, Buy workout videos, Buy workout weights, Buy workout clothes, Build home gym. **Goal**: Lose 10 pounds. **Cost**: $7,326.00. (Guisewite D10)

The final frame shows an exasperated Cathy collapsed on the couch with her diet diary covering her face. The text reads: "Here lies another victim of inflationary fat" (Guisewite D10). In fact, the pervasive portrayal of Cathy as victim in the strip ranks it among the most conventional of the comics drawn by women. "Cathy" features a single career woman who would be the exact cartoon counterpart of television's "That Girl" except that she is drawn decidedly dumpy by her creator, Cathy Guisewite. Unlike that of Nicole Hollander's Sylvia, a gutsy and deliberately unconventional character who celebrates eating as a form of pleasure and self-expression, Cathy's relation-ship with food is a losing battle fraught with guilt (food is, after all, one of the four basic guilt groups, according to Cathy, along with love, mother, and career).

While Cathy is a character with whom many modern women can readily identify, she buys into our cultural norms regarding beauty and boyfriends more than she questions them, and as a result, many feminists have found her wanting as a positive role model for women. As film maker Pamela Briggs says of a group of demonstrators who showed up to protest "Cathy" at the San Francisco premiere of *Funny Ladies*: "What they said was, they were tired of seeing a character that does seem like a victim, or feels like a victim on a fairly regular basis" (Kruh D2). Even "Cathy"'s resident feminist, Andrea, doesn't measure up according to *Working Mother*, which bashed her for being an "obnoxious, obsessive Yuppie who overanalyzes every move her overscheduled daughter, Zenith, makes" (*USA Today* D1). And Julianne Mal-veaux, a San Francisco labor economist who studies workplace issues says: "I'd like to see Cathy grow up... What irks me is, this woman is caught in a time warp. You get the sense she hasn't learned anything... Other characters have evolved. My take is, Cathy hasn't" (Kruh D2).

This view of Cathy renders the humor of the strip conservatively in keeping with Freud's theory of the comic. Freud notes that "persons become comic as a result of human dependence on external events, particularly on social factors" (Freud 199). What Freud calls the "comic of situation is mostly based on embarrassments in which we rediscover the child's helplessness" (Freud 226). And using "degradation" in a much more negative sense than Bakhtin, Freud concludes, "I am unable to decide whether degradation to being a child is only a special case of comic degradation, or whether every-thing comic is based fundamentally on degradation to being a child" (Freud 227). The latter case seems to be true of "Cathy," where the humor most often derives from Cathy's childlike helplessness and embarrassment vis-à-vis all her relationships. Consider, for example, the numerous strips in which she is manipulated by sales clerks, her boss, her mother, her boyfriend Irving, and even her dog, tellingly named Electra! Consider, too, her habitual recourse to binging on "junk food" as a response to her sense of powerlessness in these situations.

Viewing the humor of the strip as derivative of Cathy's essentially childlike state of development is especially relevant when one considers that the character originated as a kind of alter ego through which Guisewite communicated to her mother, Anne (Duly) Guisewite, a woman who en-couraged her three daughters to produce their own greeting cards and il-lustrate miniature books as gifts. It is Guisewite's mother, in fact, who may be seen in some sense as the creator of both the "real" and cartoon Cathys, since it was she who sent out Guisewite's early drawings to a greeting card company, researched comic-strip syndication in the public library, and urged her to dispatch samples of her work to Universal Press. As Guisewite wryly notes: "Most mothers tape their children's work to the refrigerator door... Mine would send them off to the Museum of Modern Art" ("Cathy Guisewite" 224). Here, too, one has the sense that even as an adult, Guisewite — like her cartoon double — is a helpless child in relation to her mother, for Guisewite notes that she sent her strips to Universal because she was "[a]pprehensive that her mother would submit the rough strips unless she herself took action" ("Cathy Guisewite" 225).

"Cathy"'s inability to attain an ideal body image can be interpreted psychologically as regression to the orality of the infant-mother bond as well as her ambivalence about letting go of her childlike state of arrested development. Is it her baby fat that refuses to budge or is it Cathy who isn't quite sure about giving up her dependency on externals, e.g., people, situations, and standards of physical attractiveness and success that exist outside of herself? It is notable that Guisewite carried more than fifty extra pounds on her own — now petite — frame for over ten years. In fact, Guisewite reports that the question most often posed to her by readers of the strip is, "Why aren't you fat?" ("Cathy Guisewite" 227). The answer may be that she still is fat, in her self-conception if not in actual fact. Cathy may represent Guisewite's "phantom body size," as weight counselor Sandy Daston calls the self-image distortion which occurs among people who still feel fat despite having lost a considerable amount of weight (Sandy Rovner C5). Guisewite claims that the essential difference between her alter ego and herself is that the cartoon Cathy "will eat an entire cheesecake, whereas I'll only eat half of one" but both Cathys still "turn to food to solve every problem" (Krier B2). Given that Cathy has failed at dieting for almost as long as Weight Watchers has been in existence, she seems an odd choice as celebrity spokesmodel for the Weight Watchers at Work program, the most recent marketing spin-off of the cartoon strip. Presumably, she was chosen as a non-threatening "before" image to whom would-be dieters could relate. Can we assume, then, that Cathy will necessarily follow through on the diet program and grow thin — and grow up — at last?

If only Cathy would look more to her cartoon kinswoman Sylvia as her role model, she could stop obsessing and start living.[7] Instead of creating a "body double," Hollander drew her inspiration for "Sylvia" from the witty women of her mother's generation as a way of creating a middle-aged role model for herself. Sylvia is a sensualist worthy of Rabelais, and like his giants, she seems to dwarf everything in her environment. Everything about Sylvia is exaggerated: body, nose, hair, hairbows, earrings, necklaces, makeup, hats, etc. But her most pronounced (and pronouncing!) feature is her mouth, because Sylvia is a very oral character. Unlike Cathy, who is in constant conflict over her oral impulses as she strives to attain a classical image of beauty, Sylvia can comfortably engage in such forbidden pleasures as eating, drinking, smoking, and speaking her mind, because she exemplifies the aesthetic of grotesque realism in which "the bodily element is deeply positive" and down-to-earth language is essential (Bakhtin 19, 27). This focus on earthy, material reality can be seen in a strip where Sylvia offers "healing hypnosis" to a Cathy-like ambivalent and insecure career woman, who is unable to resolve her conflict over home and career: "If I give up my career and stay home with my kids I'm afraid I'll regret it. If I have kids and keep working, I'll feel guilty. If I don't have kids I'll regret it ... Help!" (Hollander 68). Sylvia transposes this woman's whine to a jazzier key by giving her this post-hypnotic suggestion: "You will sleep now, and when you wake you will have only one regret ... that you will probably never take a shower with Mikhail Baryshnikov" (Hollander 68–69).

While Sylvia's appearance may be considered "ugly, monstrous, [or] hideous from the point of view of 'classic' aesthetics," as an avatar of the grotesque, her "gay and festive character" serves as a welcome contrast to "the drabness of everyday existence" (Bakhtin 19). Her loud, attention-getting appearance puts Sylvia in the category of the kind of woman Russo is talking about at the beginning of her essay, "Female Grotesques: Carnival and Theory," women who make spectacles of themselves, like "the possessors of large, aging, and dimpled thighs displayed at the public beach, of overly rouged cheeks, of a voice shrill in laughter, or of a sliding bra strap — a loose, dingy bra strap especially" (Russo 213). When others try to make the spectacular Sylvia feel ashamed of herself, she levels them with her humor, a weapon both sharp and blunt. For example, consider the following exchange in a coffee shop:

Waitress: "Syl, you have crumbs all over yourself."
Sylvia: "A few crumbs. Big deal."
Waitress: "A few?!"
Sylvia: "Beth-Ann, when I'm old, just cover me in plastic."
             (Hollander 42-43)

Some of Hollander's book titles — *I'm in Training to be Tall and Blond; My Weight Is Always Perfect for My Height — Which Varies*; and *Okay, Thinner Thighs for Everyone* — may seem interchangeable with the titles of some of Guisewite's books — *Eat Your Way to a Better Relationship; How to Get Rich, Fall in Love, Lose Weight, and Solve All Your Problems by Saying "No"*; and *Yes I Love Myself Enough to Stay on This Stupid Diet!!* — but while both cartoonists address the uneasy relationship women have with their bodies, they approach the issue from different perspectives. Unlike Cathy, who really doesn't love herself enough to either stay on or stay *off* a diet, Sylvia has self-esteem to spare. Even though she realizes that her body does not conform to the fashionable ideal, she prefers not to punish herself with dieting; instead, she wisely questions the value of conforming to the arbitrary and unnatural beauty dictates of the moment.[8] An example of this attitude can be seen in a cartoon where Sylvia, reading a book called *More's Better,* hears the news that "[a]t the turn of the century the average chorus girl was 5'4" and weighed 140 pounds, and people thought she was sexy." To which Sylvia wisecracks: "Where did we go wrong?" (Warren, *Women's Glibber* 161). Unlike Cathy, Sylvia does not worry about pleasing others — particularly men — with her appearance. When a man at the bar insists that women need men and asks her to imagine a world without them, Sylvia snappily responds: "No crime, and lots of happy, fat women" (Warren, *Women's Glib* 74).

Another of Hollander's titles, *That Woman Must Be on Drugs,* would seem to apply to all of the underground women cartoonists, for their work often has a hallucinatory intensity as can be seen in the eye-opening anthology, *Twisted Sisters: A Collection of Bad Girl Art.* Diane Noomin, the editor of the collection, is a bad girl herself, a founding mother of the underground comic book, *Twisted Sisters,* which she began in 1976 along with Aline Kominsky (the wife of Robert Crumb). In fact, with her dark glasses, dangling earrings, chunky bracelet, and beer, she bears an uncanny resemblance to Sylvia! Noomin says of the fourteen women in the collection that they provide "an uncompromising vision reflecting a female perspective. This is frequently expressed in deeply felt, autobiographical narratives. Often the art graphically reflects inner turmoil" (Noomin 7). Even among these radical women, most of whom were part of the anarchic San Francisco scene of the sixties and seventies, a common source of inner turmoil is the pain of feeling unattractive.

This is best expressed in Carol Lay's "Face the Facts of Love," a melodramatically written comic about an orphaned white American girl adopted by an African tribe which has its women undergo a beautification ritual called face-shaping. The resulting distortion is hideous by Western standards, and when the narrator eventually returns to America, she is at first repulsed by the "plain" faces of the women: "It wasn't long, though, before I learned it was *I* who was repulsive by their standard of beauty" (Lay 12). Even so, men flock to her because she is an heiress, but she withdraws from their insincere attentions. When she meets a handsome blind man who is ignorant of her wealth, we think that Irene will find true love at last. Lay undermines our romantic expectations, however, by showing the blind man to be appalled once he feels her face, afraid that her deformity will hinder his ambitions. Irene achieves total degradation by the last panel, as the once proud heroine wonders: "Maybe I should have told him I was rich" (Lay 18).

Dolores Mitchell also comments on the grotesque body images drawn by women cartoonists in her essay, "Humor in California Underground Women's Comix," noting that

> there is a tension present in much of the underground comix by women
> because of the fine line demarcating laughter that denigrates an image,
> such as that of a teenager with fat bulging in her sweater and jeans, and
> humanizing laughter inspired by a recognition of universal problems.
> (Mitchell 78)

Mitchell finds that the "most frequent departure from a physical ideal in these
books involves fat" and that consequently, "[m]uch humor in these books is
based on the contrast between ideal, socially conditioned expectations, and
the disillusioning reality that characters encounter" (Mitchell 82). For example, Chin Lyvely's "Those Perfectly Permeable Peters Sisters," features an
unhappy obese woman and Lee Marrs, whose comic "The Further Fattening
Adventures of PUDGE Girl Blimp" has as its heroine an unhappy obese
adolescent. Both the obese Peters sister and Pudge have romantic dreams
which remain unfulfilled as they encounter rejection after rejection by men
conditioned by conventional standards of beauty.

Another frequent feature of these underground comics is their emphasis
on the functions of the lower body, which as we have seen, Bakhtin identifies
with grotesque realism. These cartoonists are bad girls indeed as they graphically portray menstruation, pregnancy, elimination, copulation, and so forth.
These activities are made humorous through exaggeration, as in Julie
Doucet's "Heavy Flow," the story of a menstruating woman caught without
a tampon. Oozing obscene quantities of blood, she goes in search of Tampax,
terrorizing the citizenry as she upends cars and breaks down doors in her
fruitless search. Growing to monstrous proportions, she becomes a menstruating King Kong figure, towering above buildings and flooding the streets with
her flow. Finally, she reaches into a building and attains the object of her
quest, at which point she returns to normal size only to find herself the
embarrassed center of attention.

Bakhtin despaired that the modern world had lost its capacity for "a
regenerative, an affirmative, a healing — finally a politically progressive —
laughter" precisely because "the body, and especially the lower body, came
to be viewed as entirely negative and shameful" (Booth 62). Like the humor
of many women cartoon artists, the "[b]awdy, scatological laughter" that
Bakhtin saw in carnival "is ... a great progressive force, the expression of an
ideology that opposes the official and authoritarian languages that dominate
our surfaces" (Booth 61).

Russo ends her essay on female grotesques by asking why the figurines
of pregnant hags that Mikhail Bakhtin refers to in *Rabelais and His World*
are laughing. In a Freudian equation, they would be the objects of laughter,
the butt of the joke. But in Bakhtin's carnivalesque context, they have wrested
laughter — like Promethean fire — for themselves, the "all people." Like
Hélène Cixous' Medusa, they laugh in triumph, refusing to be objectified as

monsters, for they recognize that ugliness, like beauty, is in the eye of the beholder. Laughing at Perseus and the classical aesthetic he represents, they embody the truth of Cixous' enigmatic assertion: "You only have to look at the Medusa straight on to see her. And she's not deadly. She's beautiful and she's laughing" (255).

It is a pity that Perseus cannot look at the Medusa straight on. Like Robert Crumb, he finds it more convenient to cut off the disturbing head of this Devil Woman. But as more and more women inscribe themselves in comics and other texts and contexts, a Hydra effect might occur, so that for every head that men cut off, two will grow in its place and "laughs [will] exude from all our mouths" (Cixous 248).

NOTES

1. For a survey of how women have been portrayed throughout the history of American comics, see *Make Way!: 200 Years of American Women in Cartoons*, Ed. Monika Franzen and Nancy Ethiel (Chicago: Chicago Review P, 1988). See also *The Great American Comic Strip: One Hundred Years of Cartoon Art* by Judith O'Sullivan (Boston: Little, Brown & Co., 1990), which has a section devoted to women in the comics. For a more international perspective, see *Women in the Comics*, ed. Maurice Horn (New York: Chelsea House, 1977).

2. For more on Roseanne Barr Arnold vs. the feminine ideal, see Sian Mile's essay, "Roseanne Barr: Canned Laughter — Containing the Subject," in *New Perspectives on Women and Comedy*, ed. Regina Barreca (Philadelphia: Gordon and Breach, 1992), 39–46.

3. The following "explanation" by a self-styled expert on women in the comics (the title of his book on the subject [see note 1]) indicates the illogic men resort to when defending the status quo: "It would be foolish to see in all this [male-domination of the comics] the evidence of a deliberate male conspiracy. It is a *hard fact* that comic strips and comic book artists are, and have always been, men to an overwhelming extent. Women have never amounted to more than five per cent of the total roll of cartoonists at any given time... the mere presence of more women cartoonists would not, in my view, lead to any appreciable improvement in the image of women in the comics. (It is naive to believe that female cartoonists would be motivated by nobler goals than male cartoonists, *just as it was childish to assume that female politicians would be prompted by loftier ideals than male politicians, as recent history has clearly shown.*) ... The world of comics is unquestionably male-dominated because on the one hand society at large is *unquestionably* male dominated, and on the other hand the public of the comics is *unquestioningly* male-dominated. (*Study after study has borne the fact out*; furthermore one has only to visit one of the innumerable comic conventions taking place all around the country to see for oneself that

most of the attendance is male, as are most of the organizers and speakers.)" (Horn 10–12, emphasis mine).

4. For more on Betty Swords' cartoons, see her essay, "Why Women Cartoonists Are Rare, and Why That's Important" and sample cartoons in Barreca 65–84 (see note 2).

5. Although there are specialty magazines and videos which cater to men whose fantasies focus on obese bodies, aged bodies, and other deviations from the norm one associates with the women featured in *Playboy* or *Penthouse*, such tastes are considered perverse within the pornography industry. And, of course, these materials also effect objectification of the female body.

6. For more on feminist film theory, see the groundbreaking work that has been done in the last decade by such cultural critics as Teresa de Lauretis, Mary Ann Doane, Judith Mayne, Tania Modleski, Laura Mulvey, and Kaja Silverman. For other critics writing from an intersection of feminist and Bakhtinian theory see, for example, the collection of essays edited by Dale M. Bauer and S. Jaret McKinstry, *Feminism, Bakhtin, and the Dialogic* (Albany: State University of New York Press, 1991).

7. For more on "Sylvia," see Kayann Short's essay, "Sylvia Talks Back," in Barreca 57–63 (see note 2). For a comparison of Nicole Hollander and veteran *New Yorker* cartoonist Helen Hokinson, see Patricia Williams Alley's essay, "Hokinson and Hollander: Female Cartoonists and American Culture" in *Women's Comic Visions*, ed. June Sochen (Detroit: Wayne State UP, 1991). 115–138.

8. An example of how quickly and dramatically the winds of fashion can shift can be seen in the recent fashion magazine headlines declaring that "the waif" has replaced the fuller-figured models of the eighties. Wan, androgynous, and excruciatingly thin, the new models of the nineties are being compared to Twiggy, the body that launched a thousand eating disorders!

WORKS CITED

Bakhtin, Mikhail. *Rabelais and His World* (1965). Trans. Helene Iswolsky. Bloomington: Indiana University Press, 1984.

Booth, Wayne C. "Freedom of Interpretation: Bakhtin and the Challenge of Feminist Criticism." *Critical Inquiry* 9 (1982): 45–76.

Brandon, Barbara. "Where I'm Coming From." *Philadelphia News* 17 Feb. 1992: 38.

Chawaf, Chantal. "Linguistic Flesh." Trans. Yvonne Rochette– Ozzello. Marks 177–78.

Cixous, Hélène. "The Laugh of the Medusa." Trans. Keith Cohen and Paula Cohen. Marks 245–64.

Doucet, Julie. "Heavy Flow." Noomin 121–24.

Freud, Sigmund. *Jokes and Their Relation to the Unconscious* (1905). Trans. James Strachey. New York: Norton, 1960.

Guisewite, Cathy. "Cathy." *Philadelphia Inquirer* 2 Jan. 1993: D10.

"Guisewite, Cathy (Lee)." *Current Biography Yearbook* 50/2 (1989): 224–28.

Heil, Sharon. "Comic Tribulations: Lynda Barry Draws Humor from Life's Grim Moments." *Chicago Tribune* 9 Aug. 1987: C5.

Hickey, Elisabeth. "Black woman cartoonist is first to hit syndication." *Washington Times* 17 Sept. 1991: F3–F4.

Hollander, Nicole. *Never Take Your Cat to a Salad Bar*. New York: Vintage-Random House, 1987.

Horn, Maurice, ed. *Women in the Comics*. New York: Chelsea House, 1977.

Krier, Beth Ann. "Life Imitates Art for Cathy the Cartoonist." *Los Angeles Times* 7 May 1987: B2–B3.

Kruh, Nancy. "Cathy defuses issues with humor." *Dallas Morning News* 17 Nov. 1991: C14, D1–D2.

Lay, Carol. "Face the Facts of Love." Noomin 9–18.

Marks, Elaine, and Isabelle de Courtivron, eds. *New French Feminisms*. Amherst: University of Massachusetts Press, 1980.

Mitchell, Dolores. "Humor in California Underground Women's Comix," in: *Women's Culture: Renaissance of the Seventies*, ed. Gayle Kimball. Metuchen, NJ: The Scarecrow Press, 1981.

Noomin, Diane, ed. *Twisted Sisters: A Collection of Bad Girl Art*. New York: Penguin, 1991.

O'Connor, Mary. "Subject, Voice, and Women in Some Contemporary Black American Women's Writing," in: *Feminism, Bakhtin, and the Dialogic*, eds. Dale M. Bauer and S. Jaret McKinstry. Albany: State University of New York Press, 1991, 199–217.

Rovner, Sandy. "Health; Mirror, Mirror on the Wall … Did That Diet Accomplish Anything at All?" *Washington Post* 18 May 1979: C5.

Russo, Mary. "Female Grotesques: Carnival and Theory," in: *Feminist Studies/Critical Studies*, ed. Teresa de Lauretis. Bloomington: Indiana University Press, 1986, 213–229.

Thomas, Keith L. "Homegirls in 'Toon Town." *Atlanta Journal* 13 Jan. 1992: F8–F10.

Warren, Roz, ed. *Women's Glib: A Collection of Women's Humor*. Freedom, CA: The Crossing Press, 1991.

_____, ed. *Women's Glibber: State-of-the-Art Women's Humor*. Freedom, CA: The Crossing Press, 1992.

Index

A

About Those Colored Movies, 227
Academic feminism and comedy, 313–330
Acton, Harold, 133
Adam's Rib, 270
Adams, Samuel Hopkins, 261
African-American literature
  and courtship, 173–184
  and domestic humor, 221–229
Afternoon Teaparty, 126
Age of Reason, 200
Aggression in comedy, 10
Ain't You Mad?, 223
All About Miss Tubman, 228
All About My Job, 227
Allen, Robert, 277
All's Well that Ends Well, 36–38, 42–46
Almodovar, Pedro, 9, 299–313
Ambrose Silk, 209–210
Amelia, 146
Amos 'n Andy, 180
Amour courtois tradition, 108
Ana, 305
Anarchists, 215
Andrea, 340
Angela Lyne, 209
Angellica, 88, 91–92, 94–96
Animus/Anima, 54
Anna Matilda, 101
Annie Alden, 285
Annunciation scene, 302–303
Antonio, 301, 306
Anzola, 27–28

Aphra Behn and Sexual Politics: A Dramatist's Discourse with her Audience, 84
Apte, Mahadev, 3
Archaism, 104
Archetypal figures, 54–55, 72
Ardala Valmar, 336
Aretino, Pietro, 23, 26–27
Arimondo, Antonio, 19
Aristotle, 120
Arnold Armstrong, 241–242
Arnold, Roseanne Barr, 179, 315, 318, 336
Arranged marriage (See Marriage, arranged)
Artistic tendencies and women, 228
As We Like It: How a Girl Can be Smart and Still Popular, 57
Astaire, Fred, 259, 264, 267–269
Augustus Warwick, 153
Austen, Jane, 72
Author and heroine parallelism, 100–102
Azucena, 311

B

Babb, Howard, 73
Backwater, 166
Bainbridge, Beryl, 206, 214–216
Baker, Ernest, 83
Bakhtin, Mikhail, 6, 7, 11, 192–193, 195
Balla di capello, 22, 27
Balonga, Maria Asuncion, 308
Baltimore Afro-American, 222
Bamber, Linda, 190

Barber, C.L., 57
Barbara Hardy, 147
Barr, Roseanne (See Arnold,
    Roseanne Barr)
Barreca, Regina, 2, 10, 94, 96, 189,
    289, 311, 316–317, 319
Barry, Lynda, 336, 337
Barth, John, 126
Barthes, Roland, 143
Barton, 287, 290–291
Basil Seal, 208–210
Beach, Joseph Warren, 193
Beauman, Sally, 124
Beauty, redefinition of, 337
Bechdel, Alison, 336
Becky, 147–149
Bed-trick, 41–42, 45, 46–47
Beer, Gillian, 156
Beerbohm, Max, 121, 122, 129
Behn, Aphra, 10, 81–97
Belle's Strategem, 10, 99–116
Bell-Metereau, Rebecca, 279
Bembo, Zuan, 19
Bennet, Elizabeth, 55
Beolco, Angelo, 23, 25
Bergson, H., 140–141
Berry, Beatrice, 328
Bertram, 43–44, 46
Between the Acts, 11, 197–200
Beulah, 244
Biamonte, Gloria, 8
Big Sweet, 174–175
Bio, 23–25
Birdsall, Virginia, 68
Bitchin' Bod, 338
Bitter Medicine, 232
Black women, 8–9, 221–229
Blood Shot, 232
Bloom, Donald, 5, 166
Blow, 132
Bluemel, Kristin, 5
Blues, 181
    singers, 180–182

Blunt, 92
Blurt, Master Constable, 36–40, 43–46
    and the passage of time, 41–42
Bly, Mary, 8
Blyth, Reginald, 2
Bobby Mallory, 232
Body, lower, 344
Bogan, Lucille, 181
Bombeck, Erma, 4, 222, 223,
    224–226, 228
Boosler, Elayne, 329
Booth, Mark, 282
Bordello, 21
Bordo, Susan, 193
Brandon, Barbara, 9, 338–339
Braverman, Richard W.F., 68
Brechtian gestus, 95
Brexalu, Gasparo, 20
Briggs, Pamela, 340
Bringing Up Baby, 260
Bromwich, David, 121
Brooks, Peter, 289–290, 292
Brown, Laura, 95
Brown, Murphy, 179
Bubba, 227
Bule, 23–25
Bulesca, 23
Bunthorne, Reginald, 120
Burlador de Sevilla, 308
Burlesque, 46
Burn Marks, 232, 234
Busie Body, 10, 83, 88–97
Butler, Brett, 329
Butler, Judith, 278
Butterbeans and Susie, 175

C

Cabaret culture, 29
Calandria, 17–19
Camillo, 38, 39, 41
Camp (See Feminist camp)
Camper, Jennifer, 336

Candela, 299–300, 302, 310
Cant of Action, Time and Place, 87
Capra, Frank, 258, 261
Captain Cummings, 287
Carey, Rosa Nouchette, 166
Carlingford society, 150
Carlos, 300, 302
Carlson, Susan, 10, 85, 86
Carnival humor, 6, 338
Carte, D'Oyly, 120
Cartoonists, women, 6, 335–345
Casa de la Mujer, 309
Castle, Terry, 105–106, 107
Cathy, 339–341
Cavell, Stanley, 263
Celadon, 63–64
Celia, 57–58, 60
Centlivre, Susanna 10, 82–87
Chan Lo, 285
Characterization of women, 91
Charles II, 84
Childress, Alice, 8–9, 222–229
Cho, Margaret, 318, 324–326, 327–328
Chocolate Blondes, 180
Chodorow, Nancy, 193
Chus, 310
Circular Staircase, 237, 250
Cixous, Hélène, 9, 130–131, 241
Clarissa, 211–213
Class structure in women's humor, 9
Clayton, 287, 290–291
Cleghorne, Ellen, 329
Clinton, Kate, 318, 319
Clown, 43
Cocteau, Jean, 306
Code, Lorraine, 193–194
Colbert, Claudette, 258, 259
Collected Telegrams of Oscar Wilde, 127
Collins, 55
Colloquialisms, 104

Comedy
    and academic feminism, 313–330
    and gender, 1, 162–163, 189–201
    and racial differences, 173–184
    and social class, 139–140
    during World War II, 205–216
Comedy and the Woman Writer: Woolf, Spark, and Feminism, 1
Comedy team, male and female, 260
Comedy theory, 140–141
Comic distance 11, 192–196
Comic Spirit, 192, 195
Comic strip artists, 9, 335–345
Commedia erudita, 19
Commodification of women in literature, 94–95
Common sense, 193–194
Communism, 212–213
Compagnie delle Calze, 23
Completeness of comedy, 197
Condemnation of lust, 37
Congreve, 68, 72
Connollies, 207–209
Connor, Roseanne 327
Constant Sinner, 284
Consummation, sexual 8, 42, 43, 45, 47
Control by women, 92–93
Conversational tone, 224
Coquette, 71, 103
Council of Ten, 20–22
Couplism, 178, 260–271
Courtall, 106, 113
Courtly-genteel language, 108–110
Courtship routines, 9
    of African-Americans, 173–184
Cowley, Hannah, 10, 99–101
Crawford, Joan, 308
Creole Show, 180
Criterion, 127
Cross-dressing, 17–20, 23, 28, 281
Crumb, Robert, 338

Cukor, George, 261
Curry, Ramona, 276, 280, 285
Cuthbert J. Twillie (See Twillie)

D

Daiches, David, 197
Dan Flynn, 287
Dancing as a form of comedy,
    267–268
Danvers, 153
Darcy, 55, 72–77
Daston, Sandy, 341
Death, false, 113
Debutante, 210–213
Decadence in parody, 125–126
DeGeneres, Ellen, 317, 319,
    321–324, 326
Dehumanization, 214–215
Dekker, Thomas, 36–37
Delmar, Vina 262
Delusions, 307
De Man, Paul, 144
Depression, Great, 260–261
Desexed characters, 95
Designing Women, 178
Desire
    and laughter, 140–157
    expression of, 36
Detective fiction, 8, 231–251
Detective Jamieson, 241, 247, 250
Devil Girl, 338
Dialogic Imagination, 7
Dialogic tension, 7
Dialogues, dual, 235
Dialogues, multiple, 243–244
Diamond, Elin, 93, 94, 95, 96
Diamond Lil, 276, 283, 284, 286
Diana, 153–157
    as goddess of virginity, 44–45, 46
Diana of the Crossways, 196
Disguise (See Masquerade)
Disorder in society, 20
D'Lugo, Marvin, 300–301, 305

Doane, Mary Ann 279, 288–289
Dobbin, 146
Dollimore, Jonathan, 131
Domestic humor, 3–4, 8–9, 221–229
Domestic violence (See Violence,
    domestic)
Domination, 55, 57, 174–177, 183
Dona Ana, 305
Dona Ines, 304
Donahue Show, 326
Don Juan, 301
    parody of, 304–309
Don Juan Tenorio, 304–307
Don Pedro, 88
Doonesbury, 336
Doralice, 56, 64–66
Doricourt, 99, 101–103, 107–115
Doris Connolly, 207, 210
Doris Day, 178
Double-Barrelled Detective Story, 237
Doubled writing, 120
Double-voiced discourse, 7–8
Douglas, Alfred, 133
Drag, 284
Dragon Lady, 336
Dresner, Zita, 2, 8–9
Dr. Marjoribanks, 151
Dr. Walker, 246–248
Dryden, John, 62
Dumb Dora, 335
Dumont, Margaret, 179
Duncombe, John, 83
DuPlessis, Rachel Blau, 85
Dust Tracks on the Road, 181
Dutch Lover, 82
Dykes to Watch Out For, 336

E

Eat Your Way to a Better Relationship,
    342
Ecce Homo laundry soap, 310
Egoist, 196
Eisenberg, Nora, 199

Elena, 234
Elizabeth, 72–77
Ella Wall, 181
Emma Dunstane, 153, 155
End-man, 179–180
English Dramatic Form, 95
Enlightenment rationalism, 150
Epigram, 132–133
Equalization of the sexes, 259–261
Equipollence, 125–134
Erickson, Peter, 57
Eros, god of erotic love, 45
Erotic rhetoric in comedies, 35–47
Erotic sites, plural, 143–144
Essay on Comedy, 191, 194–195, 261
Eustace, 211
Evacuation in England, 207
Evacuees, 207–209

F

Face the Facts of Love, 343
Fainalls, 67, 69
Family likeness, 131
Faults of characters, 73
Female empowerment, 100
Female impersonation, 276
Feminiad, 83
Femininity as a mask, 245–246
Feminism in Eighteenth-Century England, 87
Feminist camp, 276, 281–282
Feminist comedy, 11, 140–141, 162–163, 189–201, 315–330
Feminist criticism, 163, 183
Feminist movement (See Women's movements)
Feminist theory, 191–201
Ferguson, Moira, 87
Fertility rituals, 190
Fessenio, 17
First Feminists, 87
Fishbein, Dr. Morris, 278
Flamingo, 336

Flavia, 63
Florimell, 56, 62–64
Florinda, 88–89, 92
Flower Belle, 279–280, 290
Flutter, 106
Flying Down to Rio, 264
Fontinelle 38, 39–42
Forc'd Marriage; or, the Jealous Bridegroom, 85
Fortune, 57–58
Foxx, Redd, 180
Fracao, 25
Fragmention in humor, 325–326, 327
Fraiberg, Allison, 9
Freedom, 222
Freud, Sigmund, 10, 140, 141–142, 144–145, 182
Friday Foster, 336
Friendship, female, 90
Frisco Kate, 284
From Mammies to Militants, 228
Fulvia, 18
Funny Ladies, 340
Further Fattening Adventures of PUDGE Girl Blimp, 344
Fuss, Diana, 144

G

Gable, Clark, 259
Gagnier, Regenia, 141
Gallagher, Catherine, 86
Ganymede, 57, 60
Gates, Henry Louis, 183
Gay Couple in Restoration Comedy, 62, 97
Gay Divorcee, 258
Gender
    and comedy, 162–163, 189–201, 310–313
    and sexual parody, 276–292
    conflicts, 210–213
    in Venetian literature, 17–29

Gender crossing, 7–8, 20, 28, 131, 153, 326–327
Gender stereotypes, 8, 95, 223–224, 301–313
Generalissimo Franco, 301
Genre
  in comedy, 189–201
  in detective fiction, 232–251
  of Mae West, 276–292
Gentlemen v. Players: A Critic Match, 132
Germany and theatrical culture, 29
Gertrude, 239, 241
Gestic characters, 95–96
Gestus, 93–94
Gilbert and Gubar, 7
Gilded Six-Bits, 182
Giles Oliver, 198
Giletta of Narbonne, 42
Gilligan, Carol, 194
Gindele, Karen, 5
Giovanni, 37
Girls of Apartment 3-G, 336
Gloeckner, Phoebe, 336
Gloria, 283, 303
Gnua, 25–26
Gomez, Marga, 329
Government, satire of, 207–210
Gracie, 260
Grafton, Sue, 233
Great Bore War, 207
Green, Anna Katharine, 235
Green Carnation, 128
Gripe, Sir Francis, 89
Grotesque realism in cartoonism, 336, 341–344
Group solidarity
  (See Solidarity, group)
Guisewite, Anne, 340–341
Guisewite, Cathy, 336, 339–341
Gus Jordan, 288

H

Halsey, 239–240, 241, 246–248
Hamilton, Linda, 336
Hands, 228
Hannoosh, Michele, 133
Hansome, Rhonda, 318
Harris, Trudier, 225, 228
Haskell, Molly, 259, 279
Hawks, Howard, 258, 261
Hays Code, 283
Health Card, 225
Heavy Flow, 344
Helena, 36, 37, 43–47
Hellena, 88, 90–92
Hepburn, Katharine, 260, 264
Hera, 124
Heroines, witty, 53–77
Hesiod, 124
High Heels, 300
Hilter, Adolf, 214–216
Hippolytus, 39, 41
Hirschberg, Hildy, 329
Hitchens, Robert, 128
Hogan, Ernest, 180
Hollander, Nicole, 336, 341
Hollywood comedies, parody of, 307–310
Holocaust, 215
Homoeroticism, 28
Homo Ludens, 270
Homophobia, 198
Homosexuality, 209–210, 284
Honeymooners, 176
Hopewell, John, 306
Horrible Prettiness, 277
Horus, 124
Hostile jokes (See Jokes, hostile)
Housewife humor (See Domestic humor)
How to Get Rich, Fall in Love, Lose Weight, and Solve All Your Problems by Saying "No", 342

Hughes, Diane Owen, 20
Human Voice, 306
Humiliation and laughter, 145
Humor, incongruity of, 141–142
*Humor in California Underground
Women's Comix*, 343–344
Hunter, G.K., 46
Hurston, Zora Neale, 9, 173–184
Hussy, 283
Hutcheon, Linda, 120, 290
Huxtable, Claire, 179

I

Ideal Husband, 123
If You Want to Get Along with Me, 225
I Go to Church, 227
Illicit sexuality, 21–22
I Liked Workin' at that Place, 227
I Love Lucy, 176
Imaginative flexibility, 247
*I'm in Training to be Tall and
Blond*, 342
Imitation
of an imitation, 122
of writing styles, 121
Immortali, 22
I'm No Angel, 283, 287, 290
Imperia, 36, 37, 40–42, 45, 46
Imperialist activity, 234
Importance of Being Earnest, 124
Inarticulateness, 178
Independence of the heroine, 54, 111
Individuation, 54
Instituto de la Mujer, 309
Intentions, 129
Intercourse (See Sexual intercourse)
In the Laundry Room, 229
Intrigue comedy, 95
Irene, 343
Irigaray, Luce, 141, 143, 287
Irony, 167
Isa Oliver, 198
Isabella, 37

Isabinda, 89–90, 91, 92
Isikoff, Erin, 10
Isn't it a Lovely Day, 268
It Ain't the Meat, It's the Motion, 181
It Happened One Night, 258–259
Iulio, 28
Ivan, 299–300, 304, 305–310
Ivanov, Andrea, 7–8
Ivy Anderson, 175
I Wish I Was a Poet, 228

J

Jack Bailey, 241
Jakobson, Roman, 144
James, Caryn, 300
James, Henry, 121–122
Janie, 176–178
Jazz Singer, 263
Jealousy, 66
Jessup, Florence Redding, 9
Jim Allen, 174–175
Jim Crow laws, 222
Jody, 177
Joe Willard, 174
Johnny Guitar, 308
Johnson, James Weldon, 180
Johnston, Claire, 280–281
Jokes, 141–142, 264–265, 267
hostile, 10, 182
in public, 178–179
naive, 142
obscene, 10, 288
*Jokes and Their Relation to the
Unconscious*, 10, 141, 338
Jong, Erica, 3
Jos, 146–147
Joyce, James, 162–163
Judgements by characters, 73
Juliet, 39

K

Kael, Pauline, 308

Kathy and Mo, 318
Keller, Evelyn Fox, 193, 194
Kendall, Elizabeth, 258
Kerr, Jean, 222, 223, 224, 226, 227
Kightlinger, Laura, 319, 329, 330
Killen, John O., 223, 226
King Wesley, 258
Kinney, Suz-Anne, 10
Kinsey Milhone, 233
Klages, Mary, 315
Klondike Annie, 285
Kofman, Sarah, 286
Kolinsky, Sue, 329
Kristeva, Julia, 142
Kroll, Richard, 68

L

La Cava, Gregory, 261
Ladman, Cathy, 329
Lady Brilliant, 101
Lady Frances Touchwood, 105,
    106, 113
Ladylikeness, 2
Lady Lou, 287, 288
Lamont, Margie, 283–284
Langdell, Cheri Davis, 84
Lascivious scenes, 36–37
Laski, Marghanita, 206, 210–213
Lassner, Phyllis, 6
*Last Laughs: Perspectives on Women
    and Comedy*, 311, 313
Laughter, 161–168, 338
    analysis of, 142–143
    in Victorian literature, 139–157
Law of Desire, 301
Lay, Carol, 336, 343
Learned comedy (See Commedia
    erudita)
Leggatt, Alexander, 57
Legislation, sumptuary, 22
Lehman, Gladys, 262

Leifer, Carol, 329
Lekesha, 339
Leonidas, 62
Leopold Bloom, 162
Letitia Hardy, 99–116
Letters of Silvia and Aurelia, 132
Letters of Wit, 82
Leverson, Ada, 8, 123–129, 131–132
Licensing Act, 97
Liddy, 238–239, 241, 248, 250
Lidio, 17–18
Lies, 307
*Like One of The Family: Conver-
    sations from a Domestic's Life*,
    8, 222–229
Lillums Lovewell, 335
Linguistic disguise, 100, 103–104,
    108–109
Lipscombe, Mance, 181
Listen for the Music, 228
Literary forms, 195
Literature of exhaustion, 126
Little, Judy, 1, 11, 191, 210, 236–237
Little Ottleys, 128
Logan, 177
Lombard, Carole, 259, 260
Lone comic, 263
Louise Armstrong, 246
Love, 54–55, 57–77
    in Renaissance comedies, 35–52
Love on the Supertax, 206, 210–213
Lover, characteristics of, 59, 63
Love's Contrivance, 86
Love's Shadow, 128
Lower body (See Body, lower)
Loy, Myrna, 264–267
Lucas, Sir William, 74
Lucetta, 91–92
Lucia, 299–300, 306, 308–312
Lucilla, 149–153
Lucille Ball, 179

Lurie, Alison, 280
Lust experienced by women, 35, 36, 37, 45–47, 115
Lust's Dominion, 36
Lyons, Richard, 199

M

Mabley, Moms, 180
Machismo, liberation from, 299–313
Mademoiselle, 1
Madonna, 336
Madwoman in the Attic, 73
Male impersonator, 287
Malveaux, Julianne, 340
Man and wife acts, 180
Marcolina, 23–25
Marge, 222, 224
Marisa, 300, 302–303
Marlo Thomas, 178
Marplot, 88, 94–95
Marriage
 arranged, 62, 88–89, 102, 113
 cynicism, 62–66, 68
 in romantic comedies, 263–264, 271
 of women, 10, 90, 91
Marriage, (a play), 62
Marriage a la Mode, 64
Mars, 24
Mary Tyler Moore, 178
Masculine and comedy, 193
Masquerade, 289
 and propriety, 101
 as feminine behavior, 10
 in a play, 99–116
Masquerade ball and social liberties, 105–107
Mayfair, 211
McCarey, Leo, 261
McEvoy, J.P., 277–278
McIntosh, Carey, 104
McWhirter, David, 11
Medusa-like character, 147, 149
Mein Kampf, 214

Melantha, 66
Melodrama, comedic, 289–292
Melodramatic imagination, 289–290
Men, and humor, 1–2, 5
Menato, 25–26
Meredith, George, 140, 145, 154–155, 261
 and objectivity, 190–192, 194–197
Metonymy, 144–145
Metz, Christian, 289
Mildred, 222–229
Miles Gloriosus, 23
Military bravado, 23
Millamant, 55, 67–72
Minstrelsy, 179–180
Minx, 123, 124
Mirabell, 55, 67–72
Miranda, 88, 90–93, 96
Miriam Henderson, 161–168
Miss Bingley, 75–76
Miss Butterworth, 235
Miss Lace, 336
Miss La Trobe, 197, 199–200
Miss Marjoribanks, 149
Miss Marple, 235
Miss Whatshername, 199
Mitchell, Dolores, 343–344
Modesty
 as feminine behavior, 10
 in a play, 99–116
Molly Brown, 162–168
Momentary release, 141
Monroe, Barbara, 9
Montresor, Jaye Berman, 6, 9
Moon and elusiveness of heroine, 155
Moore, George, 133
Moral drama, 97
Moral occult, 290
More's Better, 343
Mr. and Mrs. Smith, 270
Mr. Bingley, 74
Mr. Bones, 179
Mr. Hardy, 101, 102, 111–112

Mr. Harton, 249
Mr. Natural, 338–339
Mrs. Newlywed, 335
Mrs. Rackett, 101, 102
Mrs. Turner, 176–177
Mrs. Watson, 241, 248
Mrs. Woodburn, 151–152
Mr. Villers, 111–113
Mules and Men, 9, 173–175
Multiple lovers, 282–292
My Little Chickadee, 278–280, 289, 290
My Man Godfrey, 260, 262
My Weight Is Always Perfect for My Height — Which Varies, 342

N

Naive jokes (See Jokes, naive)
Naked Ladies, Naked Ladies, Naked Ladies, 337
Nancy Cleghorn, 233
Nanny, 177, 178
Narcissism, 285–286
Narrating consciousness, 168
Narrow Bridge of Art, 197
Nativity scene, 303–304, 312
Nena, 28
Nevo, Ruth, 57
New Kind of Prayer, 222
Newman Haye, 132
New Perspectives on Women and Comedy, 313
Nicholson, Eric, 7
Night Bus, 261
Noami, Diane 336, 343
Nom de plum Astraea, 82
Nora Ramsey, 283
Northeners Can Be So Smug, 223
Nuclear family, 322–324

O

Objectification, 287–288

Objectivity, conceptualization of, 193–194
Obscene jokes (See Jokes, obscene)
Obscurity of heroine, 155
Observational comedy, 321–324
O'Connor, Mary 337
Oedipus, 124
Okay, Thinner Thighs for Everyone, 342
Olinda, 63
Oliphant, Margaret, 145, 149, 150, 152–153
Olsen, Lance, 206–207, 215
One-liner jokes, 287
Opposition to authority, 141
Oppression of women, 90
Orlando, 55–61, 72
Ornstein, Robert, 57
Ortolani, 19–20, 22

P

Pablo, 301
Paglia, Camille, 130
Palamede, 64, 66
Palm Beach Story, 257, 258
Palmyra, 62
Paravisini, Lizabeth, 233
Paretsky, Sara, 233
Park, Clara Claiborne, 57
Parker, Dorothy, 3, 262
Parlamento de Ruzante che iera vegnu de campo, 25
Parodist, 119
Parody, 7–8, 119–134, 165–168, 233
   of detective fiction, 244–251
   of Hollywood comedies, 307–310
   sexual, 275–292
Parolles, 43–44
Passage of time, 40–41
Patch, 91
Patience, 120, 121
Patriarchal authority, 88

*Patriarchal Structures in
    Shakespeare's Drama*, 57
Patriarchy, 111, 115–116, 131
Patriciate and leveling tendency, 23
Paul Armstrong, 248
Paula Poundstone Show, 320
Paulina, 306, 311
Pearson, Jacqueline, 89
Peckham, Morse, 264
Penelope, 162, 165–166
Pepa, 299–300, 302–303, 304–313
Percy Dacier, 156
Perjur'd Husband, 82, 84
Perseus, 345
Pershing, Linda, 319
Persona
    of housewife, 224–227
    of Mae West, 276–282
Perspective, destabilized, 322–324
Peter Wimsey, 233
Petrarchan rhetoric, 36, 37, 38, 40,
    45–46
Petulant, 55, 70
Phallic woman, 280–282
Phantom body size, 341
Philocles, 62
Picture of Dorian Gray, 123, 132
Pilgrimage, 161–168
Pimp, 89
Pink Flamingos, 280
Plagiarism, 83, 129
Platonik Lady, 82, 84
Playwriting, countertradition, 85–86
Pleasure Man, 284
Pocketbook Game, 225
Pointed Roofs, 162, 163
Poirier, Richard, 130
Polhemus, Robert, 190
Politics and comedy, 320–321
Politicks and Morality, 82
Porch, and its role in literature,
    173–174
Positive Polly, 335

Postcourtship routine, 174
Poundstone, Paula, 317, 319–321, 326
Powell, William, 264–267
*Power and Allure: The Mediation of
    Sexual Difference in the Star
    Image of Mae West*, 276
Power of women in literature, 54,
    81–97, 131, 151, 236, 287
Power struggle, 89
Prejudice, 75
Pretty Sights and Good Feelin's, 228
Pretty Woman, 320, 326
Pride, 76
Pride and Prejudice, 72–77
Priuli, Girolamo, 22
Production Code, 259–260
Prostituted Muse, 89
Prostitutes and social attitude, 24
Prostitution
    and Mae West characters, 283–286
    in Italian works, 19, 21, 24, 26–27
Puns, sexual, 39, 266–267
Pursuits of Happiness, 263
Put Out More Flags, 206–210

R

Rabelais and His World, 344–345
Race in women's humor, 9, 177–178,
    222–223
Rachel Innes, 238–251
Racial stereotypes, 8–9, 223–229
Racism in stand-up comedy, 324–326
Rainey, Gertrude "Ma," 181
Rawdon, 147–149
Ray, Nicholas, 308
Rear Window, 308
Rebelliousness and housewives,
    221–223
Redressing the Balance, 2, 317
Release theory of laughter, 151–152
Remarriage, 263–264
Renaissance comedies of love, 35–52
Renaissance tragedies, 36

Renegade comedy, 236
Repetition of routine, 268, 271
Revenge, 207–208
Reverend Streatfield, 199–200
Rhodophil, 64–66
Richardson, Dorothy, 161–168
Right to vote by women, 3
Rinehart, Mary Roberts, 237–238,
    243–244, 248, 250
Rivals of women writers, 90
Rivers, Joan, 224
Robbery, 241–242
Robertson, Pamela, 276
Robeson, Paul, 227
Rodney, Terrill, 284
Rogers, Ginger, 259, 264, 267–269
Rogers, Katharine M., 87
Rohse, Corinna S., 8
Role reversal, 8, 225–226
Romance and the heroine, 54–77, 99
Romantic comedy, 257–271
Romantic couples, 258–271
Romeo, 38–39
Romeo and Juliet, 39
Room of One's Own, 81, 83, 197
Rosalind as a witty heroine, 55–62, 72
Rose Carleton, 285
Rosen, Marjorie, 277
Ross, Andrew, 279
Rover, 10, 81, 83, 88–97
Rover, Part II, 88
Ruby Ring, 283
Rudner, Rita, 320
Ruling class, self-interest, 208–209
Runaway Bride, 258
Russo, Mary 245, 337, 344
Ruzante, 25–26

S

Sabina, 63
Salome, 123, 126
San Francisco doll, 285, 286

Sandrich, Mark, 258, 264
Santilla, 18
Sanudo, Marin, 17, 20–21
Saville, 106, 113
Sbricho, 23–25
Scentwell, 90
Screwball comedy, 262–271
Sears, Sallie, 198
Second Capitalist International, 213
Secret chamber, 248–250
Secret Love, 62
Seducing, 55–56
Self-criticism and laughter, 146
Self-esteem, 66
Self-parody, 126–134, 165, 168,
    276–292
Sex, 276, 283–284
Sexism, 311–313
Sexual attractiveness, redefined,
    277–279
Sexual aversion, 154
Sexual bravado, 23–25, 181
Sexual conquest, 86
Sexual desire (See Lust)
Sexual double standard, 26–27
Sexual intercourse, 42, 45, 47
Sexual politics, 84, 93
Sexual practices in Italy, 19–27
Sexual puns (See Puns, sexual)
Sexual refusal, 43–44
Sexual role reversals, 56, 92
    in Venetian comedys, 19–22
Shakespeare, William 36,, 56, 57, 72
Shandy, Tristram, 130
Shaw, George Bernard, 126
She Done Him Wrong, 276, 284,
    287–290
Sheena, 336
Sheppard, Alice, 301
Sherlock Holmes, 233
Show People, 289
Shyness, 73
Sid Barker, 212–213

Signifying monkey, 182–183
Silence as method of manipulation, 93, 183
Silvia, 132
Sir Francis, 89, 90, 92–93
Sir George, 90
Sir George Touchwood, 106
Sir Hubert Porkington, 211–213
Sir Jealous, 89, 90, 92
Sir Patient Fancy, 85
Siruana, Elvira, 300
Sir Wilful, 55
Sissieretta Jones, 180
Sisters, 329
Sitwell, Osbert, 123, 133
Slapstick violence, 176–179
Slick Wiley, 290–291
Smith, Bessie, 181
Smith, John Harrington, 62, 97
Smith, Margaret, 329
Smut, 288
Snider, Alvin 68
Sochen, June 2, 213, 316
Sociability of humor, 6–7
Social class conflicts, 210–213
Socialism, 212–213
Social tensions, 206
Society's ills and masquerades, 106–107
Sodomy, 20–21
Solecisms, 104
Solidarity, group, 224
Somehow I'd Like to Thank Them, 227
Sommers, Martin, 283
Sonny Greer, 175
Sop-de-Bottom, 176
South Sea Girl, 336
Space, emotional, 242–247
Spectator, 289
Speech
    and social status, 103–104
    freedom of, 107
Spewack, Bella, 262

Sphinx, 124
Sphinx (a play), 123, 124
Stand-up comedy, 315–330
Stand-up comics, 9, 315–330
Status quo, 9, 88
Stereotypes (See Specific types of stereotypes such as Gender stereotypes)
Stevens, George, 261
Story Tellin' Time, 227
Stowe, William, 236
Stream of consciousness, 162, 165
Stringbeans and Sweetie May, 175
Sturges, Preston, 257, 261
Subject, Voice & Women, 337
Subjectivity of humor, 6–7
Subversive status
    of women, 113–115
    of women's humor, 9–10, 189–190, 319–328
Suffrage movement, 3
Sunnyside mysteries, 238, 241
Surinam, 84
Sylvia, 336, 339, 341–343
Symons, Arthur, 121

T

Talanta, 26–27
Tambo, 179
Tanguay, Eva, 277
Tap dancing as romantic comedy, 268–269
Taylor, Elizabeth, 336
Tea Cake, 176, 177
Tears and laughter, 146
Telos, 96
Thackeray, William Makepeace, 145, 148
That Woman Must Be on Drugs, 343
Thebes, 124
Their Eyes Were Watching God, 9, 173, 175–178
Thin Man, 258, 264–265, 270

This Sex Which Is Not One, 143
Thomas, 246
Thomas Redworth, 153, 154, 155–157
Those Perfectly Permeable Peters Sisters, 344
Tie Me Up! Tie Me Down! 300
Tira, 283, 287, 290–291
Tom, 152–153
Tonight Show, 320
Tony, 153, 177
Top Hat, 264, 267–268, 279
Toth, Emily, 235–236
Touch and desire, 144–145
Tracey, Spencer, 264
Traffick, Sir Jealous, 89
Tragicomedy, 36
Transgressive sexual behavior, 27–28, 277, 285
Transvestism, 17–19, 278–281, 326–327
Travesty of sexual laws, 17–19
Trial scene, 290
Triflers, 126
Tucker, Sophie, 277
Twain, Mark, 237
Twentieth Century, 258
Twillie, 279–280, 290
Twisted Sisters: A Collection of Bad Girl Art, 343
Tyler, Carole-Anne, 280

U

Ulysses, 162–168
Universal humor, 326

V

Valeria, 27–28
Vamp, 259
Van Upp, Virginia, 262
Vanity, 76
Vanity Fair, and laughter, 145–149
Vaudeville routines, 175, 180, 260

Venetian comic plays, 7
Venice, and comedy of sex, 17–22
Veniexiana, 27–28
Verbal duels, 173
Verbatim quotation, 132–133
Very Serious Thing: Women's Humor and American Culture, 312, 315
Victorian period, 200
Violence
    and laughter, 143, 145
    domestic, 173–177
Violetta, 36, 37, 38–47
Virginity, 36, 47
V.I. Warshawski, 231–251
Von Dyke, Woody, 258
Vulgarity, 102–104, 208–209

W

Walker, Alice, 174, 316, 319–320
Walker, Nancy, 2, 11, 235–236, 312
War and sexual relations, 25
Warner, 247, 248
Washington, Mary Helen, 174
Waugh, Evelyn, 206
Way of the World, 67
W.C. Fields, 278–280
Weekly Journal, 105, 107
Weldon, Fay, 317
We Need a Union Too, 227
West, Mae, 7–8
    and sexual parody, 275–292
Westenhoeffer, Suzanne, 329
What Does Africa Want? 222
What Have I Done to Deserve This? 303
Where I'm Coming From, 338–339
Whisper, 90
Whistler, James, 129
White, Allon, 155
Wickham, 55, 73, 77
Wilde, Oscar, 119–134
William Dodge, 198
Williams, Karen, 329

Williams and Walker, 180
Willmore, 91, 95
Wilt, Judith, 154, 190
Winfrey, Ophrah, 336
Wit, 140, 178–179
  and the heroine, 53–77, 105,
    232–234
Witwoud, 55, 69, 70
Wolf, Naomi, 328
Woman Hater, 37
Womanizer, 63
Women
  and stereotypes in movies,
    307–308, 312
  and their image, 222
  as investigators, 8, 231–251
  as writers, 2–3, 81–97
Women and Comedy, 85
*Women on the Verge of a Nervous
  Breakdown*, 9, 299–313
Women's Comic Vision, 316
Women's freedom, 243
Women's movements, 3–4
Wonder Woman, 336
Wooing, 55–56

Woolf, Virginia, 3, 11, 81, 83, 97,
  129, 196–200
Working class, 210–213
World War II, and comic novels,
  205–216
Writing Beyond the Ending, 85

X

Xenophobia, 206

Y

Yellow Book, 127
*Yes I Love Myself Enough to Stay
  on This Stupid Diet!!* 342
Yorio, Carlos, 233
Young Hitler, 206, 214–216
Young, Kay, 8

Z

Zardinieri, Compagnia degli,
  21, 22, 23
Zoccoli, 22
Zorn, Marilyn, 199
Zwerdling, Alex, 199

Lightning Source UK Ltd.
Milton Keynes UK
15 September 2010

159918UK00001B/19/A